To Eric,
With thanks for
all your help over
many years.
Paul
23.3.02

Cambridge Imperial and Post-Colonial Studies Series

General Editor: **A. G. Hopkins**, Pembroke College, Cambridge

This informative series covers the broad span of modern imperial history while also exploring the recent developments in former colonial states where residues of empire can still be found. The books provide in-depth examinations of empires as competing and complementary power structures encouraging the reader to reconsider their understanding of international and world history during recent centuries.

Titles include:

Anthony J. Barker
SLAVERY AND ANTI-SLAVERY IN MAURITIUS, 1810–33
The Conflict between Economic Expansion and Humanitarian Reform
under British Rule

Roy Bridges (*editor*)
IMPERIALISM, DECOLONIZATION AND AFRICA
Studies Presented to John Hargreaves

T. J. Cribb (*editor*)
IMAGINED COMMONWEALTH
Cambridge Essays on Commonwealth and International Literature in English

Robin Jeffrey
POLITICS, WOMEN AND WELL-BEING
How Kerala became a 'Model'

Gerold Krozewski
MONEY AND THE END OF EMPIRE
British International Economic Policy and the Colonies, 1947–58

Ged Martin
BRITAIN AND THE ORIGINS OF CANADIAN CONFEDERATION, 1837–67

W. David McIntyre
BACKGROUND TO THE ANZUS PACT
Policy-Makers, Strategy and Diplomacy, 1945–55

John Singleton and Paul Robertson
ECONOMIC RELATIONS BETWEEN BRITAIN AND AUSTRALASIA 1945–1970

Tony Ballantyne
ORIENTALISM AND RACE
Aryanism in the British Empire

Cambridge Imperial and Post-Colonial Studies Series
Series Standing Order ISBN 0–333–91908–4
(*outside North America only*)

You can receive future titles in this series as they are published by placing a standing order. Please contact your bookseller or, in case of difficulty, write to us at the address below with your name and address, the title of the series and the ISBN quoted above.

Customer Services Department, Macmillan Distribution Ltd, Houndmills, Basingstoke, Hampshire RG21 6XS, England

Economic Relations Between Britain and Australasia 1945–1970

John Singleton

and

Paul L. Robertson

palgrave

First published 2002 by
PALGRAVE
Houndmills, Basingstoke, Hampshire RG21 6XS and
175 Fifth Avenue, New York, N. Y. 10010
Companies and representatives throughout the world

PALGRAVE is the new global academic imprint of
St. Martin's Press LLC Scholarly and Reference Division and
Palgrave Publishers Ltd (formerly Macmillan Press Ltd).

ISBN 0–333–91941–6

This book is printed on paper suitable for recycling and made from fully managed and sustained forest sources.

Cataloguing-in-publication data

A catalogue record for this book is available from the British Library.

A catalogue record for this book is available from the Library of Congress.

10	9	8	7	6	5	4	3	2	1
11	10	09	08	07	06	05	04	03	02

Printed and bound in Great Britain by
Antony Rowe Ltd, Chippenham, Wiltshire

For Kathy, Mark, Joshua, Lewis, Elliott, and Lydia
And for Elaine

Contents

Tables

About the Authors

John Singleton is Senior Lecturer in Economic History at Victoria University of Wellington, New Zealand. His previous books are *Lancashire on the Scrapheap: the Cotton Industry, 1945–70* (1991), *The World Textile Industry* (1997), and jointly edited with R.M. Millward, *The Political Economy of Nationalisation in Britain, 1920–1950* (1995).

Paul L. Robertson is Professor of Management at the University of Wollongong in Australia. Among his previous publications are *The British Shipbuilding Industry, 1870–1914* (with Sidney Pollard; 1979) and *Firms, Markets and Economic Change: a Dynamic Theory of Business Institutions* (with R.N. Langlois; 1995). He is the editor of *Authority and Control in Modern Industry: Theoretical and Empirical Perspectives* (1999) and co-editor (with Nicolai J. Foss) of *Resources, Strategy and Technology* (2000).

Acknowledgements

This has been a lengthy project, which builds upon work on Australia that Paul Robertson began in 1983 as research into the role of the Australian government in the nation's industrialization following the Second World War. Ultimately, he collected well over 10,000 pages of photocopied documents from the Australian Archives in Canberra. As it turned out, the timing of this research was excellent, as the Commonwealth of Australia subsequently destroyed many of the original documents as part of a process of 'culling' that was designed to save public money but has also guaranteed that future studies will be written largely from the point of view of others with whom Australia had dealings. When he first met John Singleton in Manchester in 1992, Robertson suggested that they should do some joint work on economic relations between Britain and Australia. The scope was broadened when Singleton moved from the University of Manchester to the Victoria University of Wellington the following year, and in the years since 1993 the study has grown into a wider consideration of economic relations between Britain, Australia, and New Zealand. We both collected documents in Britain, Canada, and the United States and wrote several collaborative manuscripts over the next few years, but during the late 1990s Paul Robertson became increasingly involved in research on management, leaving him with less time than he would have liked for economic history. At the end of 1998, we decided that the final preparation of the book should rest with Singleton, to whom Robertson sent over 20,000 pages of photocopied documents from the Australian and other official archives. During 1999 and 2000, Singleton wrote the bulk (though by no means all) of the text that appears in this volume. Nevertheless, we wish to stress that this book remains in every sense a collaborative effort.

We wish to thank a number of people who helped us at various stages. Gary Hawke generously read most of the chapters, at least in draft form, and invariably provided us with incisive and constructive comment. Tony Hopkins, the editor of the Cambridge Commonwealth Series, was receptive to our initial approach, and greatly assisted us to arrange for publication. Among the others to whom we should like to express our gratitude are Tony Andres, Theo Balderston, the late Alan Beever, Gordon Boyce, Peter Cain, Forrest Capie, Peter Cozens, Kent Deng, Brian

Easton, Douglas Farnie, Grant Fleming, Morris Guest, Mike Hughes, John King, Rob McLuskie, Andy Marrison, John Martin, Bruce Muirhead, Tim Mulcare, the late Bryan Philpott, Tim Rooth, Boris Schedvin, Catherine Schenk, Simon Ville, Immanuel Wexler, John Wilson, and conference and seminar participants at the Australian National University, Massey University, University of Manchester, University of New England, University of New South Wales, University of Oxford, Victoria University of Wellington, and the University of Warwick. We apologize to anyone inadvertently missed out of this list.

We wish to thank the University of Melbourne, the University of New South Wales, and Victoria University of Wellington for financial assistance with research expenses. We also gratefully acknowledge the help of archivists at the Australian Archives in Canberra, Sydney, and Melbourne, the National Archives of New Zealand at Wellington, the Public Record Office, London, the Bank of England Archive, the Bank of Canada Archive, the National Archives of Canada in Ottawa, the Dwight D. Eisenhower Presidential Library, Abilene, Kansas, the Harry S. Truman Presidential Library, Independence, Missouri, and the National Archives in College Park, Maryland. The archivists at the Bank of England Archive, the Australian Archives, the Bank of Canada, and the Eisenhower and Truman Libraries were especially accommodating.

Parts of this book have been adapted from other publications. We thank the relevant editors and publishers for permission to reuse material from:

P.L. Robertson, 'Official Policy on American Direct Investment in Australia, 1945–1952', *Australian Economic History Review*, 26(2) (1986): 159–81.

P.L. Robertson, 'The Decline of Economic Complementarity? Australia and Britain 1945–1952', *Australian Economic History Review*, 37(2) (1997): 91–117.

J. Singleton, 'New Zealand's Trade Policy and Japan in the 1950s', *Australian Economic History Review*, 37(1) (1997): 1–16.

J. Singleton, 'New Zealand, Britain, and the Survival of the Ottawa Agreement, 1945–77', *Australian Journal of Politics and History*, 43(2) (1997): 168–82.

J. Singleton and P. L. Robertson, 'Britain, Butter, and European Integration, 1957–64', *Economic History Review*, 50(2) (1997): 327–47.

J. Singleton, 'Anglo-New Zealand Financial Relations, 1945–61', *Financial History Review*, 5(2) (1998): 139–57.

M. Guest and J. Singleton, 'The Murupara Project and Industrial Development in New Zealand, 1945–63', *Australian Economic History Review*, 39(1) (1999): 52–71.

P.L. Robertson and J. Singleton, 'The Old Commonwealth and Britain's First Application to Join the EEC', *Australian Economic History Review*, 40(2) (2000): 153–77.

J. Singleton, 'After the Veto: Australasian Commercial Policy in the Mid-Sixties', *Australian Economic History Review*, forthcoming 2001.

Abbreviations

AJBCC	Australia–Japan Business Cooperation Committee
APEC	Asia Pacific Economic Cooperation
BCSA	British Commonwealth Sugar Agreement
BoEA	Bank of England Archive
BP	British Preference
CAP	Common Agricultural Policy
CAPD	Commonwealth of Australia Parliamentary Debates
CCEFP	Cabinet Committee on Economic and Financial Policy, New Zealand
CDC	Commonwealth Development Corporation
CDFC	Commonwealth Development Finance Corporation
CEC	Commonwealth Economic Conference
CET	Common External Tariff
CRO	Commonwealth Relations Office
CTEC	Commonwealth Trade and Economic Conference, Montreal 1958
cwt	hundredweight
d.	(old) pence
DDEL	Dwight D. Eisenhower Presidential Library, Abilene, Kansas
ECA	Economic Cooperation Administration
ECGD	Export Credit Guarantee Department
ECSC	European Coal and Steel Community
ECU	European Customs Union
EEC	European Economic Community
EFTA	European Free Trade Area
EPU	European Payments Union
ERP	European Recovery Program (Marshall Plan)
FBI	Federation of British Industries
FDI	Foreign Direct Investment
FRUS	Foreign Relations of the United States
FTA	the proposed European industrial Free Trade Area (Plan G)
GATT	General Agreement on Tariffs and Trade
GDP	Gross Domestic Product
HSTL	Harry S. Truman Presidential Library, Independence, Missouri

IBRD	International Bank for Reconstruction and Development (World Bank)
IMF	International Monetary Fund
ITO	International Trade Organization
IWA	International Wheat Agreement
MFN	most favoured nation
MINFAT	Ministry of Foreign Affairs and Trade, Wellington
NAA	National Archives of Australia, Canberra
NAFTA	New Zealand Australia Free Trade Agreement
NNP	no new preference rule in GATT
NZA	National Archives of New Zealand, Wellington
NZIER	New Zealand Institute of Economic Research
NZOYB	New Zealand Official Year Book
NZPD	New Zealand Parliamentary Debates
OEEC	Organization for European Economic Cooperation
PAFTAD	Pacific Association for Trade and Development
PRO	Public Record Office, Kew, London
RBNZ	Reserve Bank of New Zealand
RSA	Rest of the Sterling Area
s.	shilling
SCAP	Supreme Commander for the Allied Powers
UKATA	United Kingdom–Australia Trade Agreement
UN	United Nations

1
Australasia in Context

[I]t had been the aim of . . . [British] commercial policy to secure the advantages of liberal trade practices in the world at large while retaining the benefit of the preferences [sic] system within the Commonwealth. This policy was now under pressure and we could no longer expect to continue to enjoy the best of both worlds. Australia had taken the initiative in seeking a review of the preferences system and New Zealand would follow her lead . . . We might soon be confronted in Europe by a powerful discriminatory economic bloc, dominated by Germany and developing into a formidable base for German competition in our markets overseas. There was no prospect of our being able to pursue our traditional policies undisturbed . . .

Peter Thorneycroft, President of British Board of Trade, 1956[1]

Writing in 1956, a Swedish economist, Gunnar Myrdal, described the Commonwealth as the world's most successful international economic and political community. By contrast, the nations of continental western Europe did not possess the Commonwealth's 'sense of solidarity'.[2] Sterling was one of the two leading reserve currencies and means of payment, and Commonwealth members accounted for one-quarter of world exports in the 1950s. Nevertheless, as Peter Thorneycroft indicated, the Commonwealth economic network was vulnerable to centrifugal forces.[3]

Australia and New Zealand were core members of the global web of financial, economic, political, and military ties characterized by US officials as the 'British complex'.[4] This relationship was very strong in the 1940s and 1950s. However, there was also a rising current of tension in relations with Britain over issues such as the payment of subsidies to

UK farmers, industrial protection in Australia and New Zealand, the inability of Britain to satisfy the dominions' thirst for capital, and Britain's growing interest in European integration. As the Commonwealth economic network started to unravel in the mid-1950s, the Australian and New Zealand governments faced a number of dilemmas. To what extent could they still rely on Britain for markets and for capital inflows? How easily could alternative markets be developed, and would the international food trade continue to be blighted by protectionism? Were the imperatives of full employment and national economic development compatible with multilateralism? What role should the dominions play in international organizations such as the International Monetary Fund (IMF) and the General Agreement on Tariffs and Trade (GATT)? How should they react to Britain's involvement in Europe?

This volume focuses on the efforts of Australia and New Zealand to manage their economic relationships with Britain and other countries between the 1940s and the 1960s. It also casts light on the workings of the wider Commonwealth economic community. Australia adapted more readily than New Zealand did to changes in the international environment, though even Australia showed considerable inertia. Japan overtook Britain as Australia's main trading partner in the mid-1960s, but New Zealand continued to depend on Britain until after the latter's entry into the European Economic Community (EEC) in 1973. While mineral discoveries assisted Australia to develop an increasingly diverse export base, New Zealand persisted in the supply of a narrow range of export commodities, including sheepmeat and dairy products, for which there were few outlets except Britain. Global agricultural protectionism damaged New Zealand's interests even more than it damaged Australia's. Both dominions were victims of the 'tyranny of distance', or isolation from the centres of world economic power, which imposed high transaction costs and hindered technology transfer. Economic policy errors account for some of the relative decline of Australia and New Zealand *vis-à-vis* other OECD countries, but do not adequately explain why New Zealand's economic performance was worse than Australia's, as their economic strategies were similar until the 1980s. Perhaps there was no margin for error in New Zealand, which was relatively poorly endowed with mineral wealth.

Most of our research was conducted in the Australian, New Zealand, and British national archives, and in the Truman and Eisenhower presidential libraries in the USA. We find that the policies of Australia, New Zealand, and Britain were strongly interdependent. All three countries, moreover, operated in a global economy dominated by the USA. Until the coming into force of the New Zealand Australia Free Trade Agreement (NAFTA) in 1966, the bilateral economic relationship between Australia and New Zealand was much weaker than either country's economic relationship with Britain. Although the British wielded superior bargaining power to either Australia or New Zealand, they could not prevent the dominions from pursuing independent lines over import substitution industrialization and commercial détente with Japan.[5] By the 1960s, the Commonwealth economic community was becoming increasingly irrelevant to Britain and Australia, but not to New Zealand.

This book concentrates on the formulation of economic policy, and does not provide a complete analysis of the determinants of economic performance in Australia and New Zealand after 1945. Nevertheless, it is worth reflecting on how policy may have influenced performance. The options of policy-makers in the 1940s were constrained by the inherited positions of Australia and New Zealand in the world economy. Crucial decisions were made in the light of assumptions about the world economy that were based on interwar experience. Unfortunately, the policies selected in the 1940s did not help Australia and New Zealand to exploit their potential for growth in later decades. Governments in both countries feared competition, especially from imported manufactures, and implemented policies that led to high cost structures in all sectors.

The next section establishes that Australia and New Zealand, contrary to the received interpretation, were crucial components of a Commonwealth economic network after the Second World War. The following section describes the origins and workings of the Commonwealth economic system.[6] After setting the postwar economic performance of Britain, Australia and New Zealand in an international context, this chapter concludes with a discussion of the constraints on economic growth in Australasia. Chapter 2 investigates the responses of Australia and New Zealand to the multilateral commercial and monetary proposals floated by the Americans in the mid-1940s. Chapters 3 and 4 consider the economic development strategies of Australia and New Zealand. Chapter 5 deals with the growth of trade conflict between Australia and New Zealand and Britain in the 1950s, culminating in the renegotiation of the Ottawa Agreements. Chapter 6 discusses the efforts of Australia and New Zealand to gain access to the American and Japanese markets in the 1950s, and to overcome agricultural protectionism in GATT. Chapters 7 and 8 consider Britain's economic relations with Europe, and its application to join the EEC in 1961–3, emphasizing the responses of Australia and New Zealand. Chapter 9 examines the aftermath of Britain's rejection by the EEC, and discusses the triangular economic relationship between Australia, New Zealand, and Britain in the mid-1960s.

The significance of the dominions

The Commonwealth economic community functioned on several planes. At the micro level, enterprises across the Commonwealth were linked in networks of some complexity.[7] Commonwealth governments also cooperated at the macro level, especially between the 1930s and the 1960s, over monetary and commercial policy. We challenge the preponderant assumption of British, Australian, and New Zealand economic historians that the postwar Commonwealth economic community is barely worth investigating. On the contrary, the Commonwealth economy was a central concern of policy-makers.

Pollard's standard text on twentieth-century British economic history largely ignores the role of the Commonwealth as an economic community in the 1950s and 1960s. Cairncross, formerly a leading figure in the British economic policy establishment, dismisses Commonwealth economic relations with a few vague allusions. Alford asserts that the Commonwealth rapidly lost its economic *'raison d'être'* after the Second World War, and concludes that Britain should have turned to Europe sooner than it did. Broadberry suggests in passing that Britain's industrial progress may have been hindered after 1950 by an over-emphasis on relatively stagnant and unsophisticated Commonwealth markets, but declines to pursue this issue.[8]

Australian and New Zealand economic historians, who tend to write within a nationalist framework, also discount the Commonwealth as an economic network. Economic relations with Britain after 1945 are given short shrift in Hawke's authoritative economic history of New Zealand. Easton's more recent study of the postwar New Zealand economy is equally sketchy on Commonwealth economic interaction. At the start of Pinkstone's history of Australian exports, Anglo-Australian commercial relations after 1945 are described as of no real significance. Meredith and Dyster also play down the postwar role of the British Commonwealth in their textbook, *Australia and the Global Economy*, despite the fact that Meredith has written extensively on other aspects of twentieth-century imperial economic history.[9] Moreover, there is no Anglo-Australian equivalent of Rix's volume on economic relations between Australia and Japan in the late 1940s and 1950s.[10]

Economists and economic historians concerned with international issues are somewhat less inclined to dismiss the postwar Commonwealth out of hand, though several of them are sceptical about the Commonwealth's economic impact. Pomfret argues that regional trading arrangements, including the Commonwealth Preference Area, had little power to affect either the direction of trade or the level of welfare. He acknowledges that preferential mechanisms may be important to some interest groups, but concludes that Commonwealth Preference should be regarded as an expression of Commonwealth unity rather than a potent economic weapon.[11] The authors of the economic chapters in the twentieth-century volume of the *Oxford History of the British Empire* are cagey about the contribution of the Empire/Commonwealth economic system. Fieldhouse hesitantly concludes that the Empire/ Commonwealth exerted a 'significant, if ambiguous' impact on the British economy.[12]

Schenk's book on the Sterling Area in the 1950s is the most detailed recent account of the economic history of the postwar Commonwealth. She refutes the thesis that the modernization of British industry was frustrated by capital outflows to the Commonwealth, and shows that Sterling Area markets were not safe havens for British manufacturers. Yet Schenk does not regard the Sterling Area as irrelevant. Though its 'effect . . . on the British economy and on British policy has been exaggerated', it proved a useful interim arrangement while the international monetary system was recovering from the war.[13]

Cain and Hopkins do not dwell at length on the postwar period in their major study of British economic imperialism. They contend, however, that the British government and the City of London continued to attach great economic value to the Commonwealth until at least the late 1950s. Their goal was to manage the Sterling Area in such a way that returns to the City were maximized and the pound was restored to convertibility with the US dollar. Towards the end of the 1950s the gentlemanly elite in London reached the conclusion that Europe offered better opportunities for further gain, and in due course the Commonwealth was demoted to a supporting role in British external economic policy.[14]

At the broadest level we reinforce Cain and Hopkins' conclusion that the Empire/Commonwealth economic nexus continued to be taken seriously by British, not to mention Australian and New Zealand, policymakers after the Second World War. We maintain that Commonwealth economic relations were, with ample justification, at the heart of the policy debate in Britain, Australia, and New Zealand between the 1940s and the 1960s. In this respect we extend and amplify the brief analysis of the postwar period in Cain and Hopkins' two-volume *British Imperi-*

alism. We also strongly endorse their view that the white dominions, or countries of British settlement, played a key role in the imperial economy in the twentieth century. Cain and Hopkins emphasize the importance of economic relations between Britain and the white dominions in the interwar period.[15] We go further in showing that bilateral economic ties between London and Canberra and London and Wellington retained much of their strength in the 1950s. Economic nationalism did not preclude a high level of imperial and Common-wealth economic cooperation. Britain's structural power in the Com-monwealth system encouraged, but did not compel, the dominions to accommodate British economic interests.[16]

Nevertheless, we differ from Cain and Hopkins on the important question of the priority to be accorded financial compared with com-mercial relationships. They suggest that financial considerations were usually of paramount importance to the British, and that they were pre-pared to make sacrifices in the area of trade in order to meet their objec-tives in this central sphere. The results of our archival research, however, suggest that the British took a more balanced approach. At some times they stressed the role of Australia and New Zealand in the defence of sterling. But at other times they attached greatest importance to the resolution of problems affecting agricultural and industrial trade.

For much of the postwar period, Australia and New Zealand were almost as anxious to cooperate with Britain as to confirm their eco-nomic independence. The Anglo-Australian economic nexus continued to be of real significance until the late 1960s. As for the Anglo-New Zealand nexus, it was finally, and brutally, snapped in 1973.

Development of the Commonwealth economic network

Despite certain defects, the Commonwealth was the most successful international economic community in the mid-1950s. Britain acted as banker to those countries that held the bulk of their overseas reserves in sterling. Inflows of British capital assisted the economic development of these mainly Empire/Commonwealth nations, and generated sub-stantial return flows of interest and dividends. Large quantities of British manufactures, not least of machinery, were shipped to Commonwealth markets, while Commonwealth primary produce was exported, often in British vessels, to Britain, the USA, continental western Europe and Japan.

Cooperation was underpinned by regular conferences of Prime Min-isters, Finance Ministers, and officials, and by the constant exchange of information and opinion. At the 1924 Imperial Conference, the British statesman Stanley Baldwin described the Commonwealth as a 'network of contacts'. In 1940, Keith Hancock explained that 'this network was intricate and intimate . . . [but that] neither the Dominions, nor Great Britain herself, intended that it should be a steel mesh' barring intercourse with other nations.[17]

Little formal intergovernmental economic cooperation had been necessary among the self-governing members of the British Empire before the First World War. The Bank of England was the only central bank in the British Empire, and sterling was on the Gold Standard. Exchange rates between sterling and the local currencies circulating in the dominions were fixed by the decisions of private sector banks. The dominions granted tariff preferences to Britain, but the latter did not reciprocate in view of its commitment to free trade.[18] Intergovernmental economic cooperation grew in the 1930s in response to the global depression. The slump of 1929–33 disrupted the international monetary system, reduced world trade, and stimulated protectionism. In 1931, the British government abandoned the Gold Standard and allowed sterling to float against other major currencies. Since Britain was the main commercial and financial partner of Australia, New Zealand, South Africa, and India, these countries resolved to peg their currencies to sterling instead of gold, thereby establishing the Sterling Bloc. If these countries had elected to follow gold, their revenue from exporting primary products to Britain would have fallen, and their economic distress would have intensified.[19] Canada, which had closer links to the American than to the British economy, did not join the Sterling Bloc. More generally, the potential for imperial monetary cooperation was enhanced between the wars by the creation of central banks in Australia, Canada, India, New Zealand, and South Africa. The collective float of the Sterling Bloc, while not decisive, did contribute to recovery.[20]

Britain gave up free trade in 1932 in response to the economic and political pressures generated by the depression. At the 1932 Imperial Economic Conference at Ottawa, Britain exempted imports from the Empire from the new tariff. Australia and New Zealand benefited from the tariff on foreign butter and associated restrictions on imports of foreign meat. The dominions reciprocated by raising tariffs on non-British manufactures. However, Britain continued to import some commodities, including wool, wheat, lamb, and mutton, duty-free from all sources. Cain and Hopkins argue that the main purpose of the Ottawa settlement was to improve the dominions' trade balances with Britain, and thus to reduce the risk of default on sterling debt. The Ottawa

Agreements, which took the form of bilateral treaties between Britain and each dominion, including Canada, were also designed to encourage Empire countries to trade with one another rather than with foreign countries. Although the resulting diversion of trade was modest, the USA reacted angrily to the extension of Imperial Preference, which it condemned as an unconscionable form of discrimination, setting the stage for later conflict.[21]

The Second World War transformed the loose Sterling Bloc into the much tighter Sterling Area.[22] Sterling Area countries reacted to the wartime shortage of dollars by introducing restrictions, including exchange controls, on dollar expenditure. They deposited dollar earnings into a central pool in London, and were credited with sterling. These sterling balances could be reconverted into dollars for the purchase of essential imports from the USA and Canada. The USA hoped to procure the abolition of Commonwealth Preference[23] and the Sterling Area, and to introduce a multilateral commercial and monetary regime after the war. In the event, it proved impossible to secure a fully multilateral economic settlement. The dollar shortage persisted until the late 1950s, and governments in the Sterling Area and western Europe retained import and exchange controls on transactions with the dollar area. Australia and New Zealand were trusted by Britain to exercise self-discipline in the expenditure of dollars.[24] Sterling Area countries held regular meetings on the balance-of-payments situation, and, with varying degrees of zeal, adjusted imports in line with recommendations from London. Sufficient joint action was forthcoming to permit the Sterling Area to weather a succession of financial crises in 1947, 1949, 1951–2, and 1956. Australia abolished all quantitative import restrictions in 1960. New Zealand continued to operate import controls, but ceased to discriminate against the dollar area.

As a mechanism for controlling trade, Commonwealth Preference was overshadowed by dollar discrimination during the 1940s and 1950s. However, the Ottawa system was more enduring, and persisted until Britain entered the EEC. Proposals to alter preferential margins caused intense debate within the Commonwealth until the late 1960s. In the early 1960s, about 60 per cent of UK imports from the Commonwealth and 55 per cent of UK exports to the Commonwealth received a tariff preference. Average margins on items subject to preference were 12 per cent on British goods in the Commonwealth as a whole, 11 per cent in Australia, and 17–19 per cent in New Zealand. Preference margins on British food imports also averaged 12 per cent.[25] Britain's structural

Table 1.1   Britain's main export markets, 1938–70

Destination (percentage of total exports)

	Australia	New Zealand	Canada	South Africa	United States	EEC (Six)	EFTA
1938	7.3	3.7	4.6	7.5	5.4	..	..
1946	5.8	2.9	3.6	7.8	4.1	14.6	11.8
1950	11.4	3.8	5.7	5.4	5.6	12.3	11.4
1955	9.6	4.7	4.8	5.6	6.6	14.1	10.4
1960	7.1	3.3	6.0	4.2	9.3	15.3	10.7
1965	5.8	2.6	4.2	5.4	10.5	20.0	12.5
1970	4.3	1.6	3.6	4.1	11.6	21.7	15.9

Note: EEC (Six) comprises Belgium, France, Germany, Italy, Luxemburg, and the Netherlands.
East Germany is excluded after 1950; EFTA comprises Austria, Denmark (including the Faroes and Greenland), Liechenstein, Norway (including Spitzbergen), Portugal (including Azores and Madeira), Sweden, and Switzerland.
Source: B.R. Mitchell, *British Historical Statistics* (Cambridge: Cambridge University Press, 1988), pp. 453–4, 507–15.

Table 1.2   Australia's main export markets, 1938–70

Destination (percentage of total exports)

	UK	USA	New Zealand	Japan	EEC (Six)
1938	55.5	2.4	5.0	4.2	16.8
1946	27.3	19.0	4.1	0.9	9.9
1950	38.7	8.1	3.5	3.9	18.4
1955	36.9	6.8	4.9	7.6	22.0
1960	26.4	8.1	5.8	14.4	18.7
1965	19.5	10.0	6.0	16.6	13.6
1970	11.8	14.5	4.8	24.7	10.9

Source: *Commonwealth Year Books.*

power in the postwar Commonwealth stemmed from its role as the architect of the Sterling Area and of the Ottawa system.

Tables 1.1 to 1.3 establish the importance to Britain, Australia, and New Zealand of Commonwealth trade. The value to Britain of the main Commonwealth markets during the 1940s and 1950s is shown in Table 1.1. Australia was Britain's single most important export outlet during the 1950s. New Zealand was also an excellent market. On a per capita

Table 1.3 New Zealand's main export markets, 1938–70

| Destination (percentage of total exports) | | | | |
UK	USA	Australia	Japan	EEC (Six)
1938	84.2	2.5	3.8	1.0	3.9
1946	70.1	9.6	3.6	–	6.3
1950	66.5	10.1	2.6	0.5	12.2
1955	65.6	5.9	2.5	0.8	16.2
1960	53.1	12.8	4.4	3.0	16.7
1965	50.9	12.3	4.7	4.3	16.2
1970	35.5	15.3	8.0	9.7	11.0

Source: *New Zealand Official Year Books*.

basis both were far better customers than the USA. Fieldhouse describes sterling markets as Britain's 'lifeline' between the 1930s and early 1950s.[26] By 1960, however, the share of the Commonwealth in British exports was falling, and the shares of western Europe and the USA were rising. The relative decline of Commonwealth trade preceded Britain's membership of the EEC. Australia and New Zealand depended on the UK market to a greater extent than the UK depended on their markets. But Australia's reliance on Britain was weaker than New Zealand's. By 1965, Australia had diversified to such an extent that Japan had overtaken Britain as its principal export market. Although Britain's share of New Zealand's exports was falling, it remained this dominion's key outlet into the 1970s. In the 1980s, Australia and New Zealand were finally drawn into the east Asian trading network.[27]

Independent Commonwealth nations had several reasons for cooperating with Britain in the management of the Sterling Area and the Commonwealth Preference system.[28] As the Commonwealth Relations Office (CRO) stated in 1956, 'Commonwealth countries . . . are accustomed to trade with us, as we are with them. That is why it is in their interest that their currencies are tied to sterling, and the fact that their currencies are tied to sterling increases the tendency for us to trade with each other.'[29] The Sterling Area dollar pool enabled Australia, New Zealand, India, and other dollar deficit countries to draw on the net dollar earnings of other parts of the Sterling Area, including the colonies. The Rest of the Sterling Area (RSA)[30] also had access to dollar loans and aid obtained by Britain. It would have been difficult for some RSA members to earn dollars directly in view of the subsidization and protection of US agriculture. Moreover, since RSA countries already possessed sterling balances, it was in their interests to maintain sterling's value. Tariff preferences survived because they mattered to important business groups, and were a possible source of leverage in negotiations with other countries. The commercial and financial aspects of the Commonwealth economic network were interrelated. Collapse of the Ottawa Agreements would have brought into question the right of Commonwealth producers to unrestricted entry into the British market, as well as Britain's willingness to permit RSA governments to borrow in London. Commonwealth and Sterling Area countries would have been worse off in the short run if they had broken ranks.

But short-term self-interest was not the only reason for solidarity. Commonwealth members hoped to derive lasting benefits from collaboration. By supplying the UK with food and raw materials, and buying British rather than perhaps cheaper or better quality American manufactures, they believed that they were helping to revitalize the British economy. With varying degrees of conviction, they expected to reap substantial future rewards in the form of augmented flows of British capital, larger orders for primary produce, and increased supplies of good quality British products. British men, money, and markets had been responsible for the economic development of Australia, New Zealand, South Africa, and Canada in the nineteenth century.[31] Asian Commonwealth countries may well have had a more jaundiced view of imperial economic history, but they too were interested in British markets and capital. The British planned to make profitable new investments in the Commonwealth after the completion of domestic reconstruction.[32] In 1944, Keynes predicted that Commonwealth demand for British capital goods and other manufactures would be buoyant for many years.[33] The fact that many of these aspirations were unrealized does not detract from their importance at the time.

Finally, the Commonwealth economic network at intergovernmental level was lubricated by trust. Casson suggests that cooperation among nations is harder to sustain than cooperation among firms. Most political leaders have short electoral time horizons, and therefore no incentive to invest in a good reputation abroad.[34] Within the Commonwealth, however, the temptation to act opportunistically was partially offset by a common purpose derived from a shared language, history, and culture. Furthermore, the civil servants involved in formulating and implementing Commonwealth economic policy had long time horizons, and expected to meet their counterparts from other Commonwealth nations regularly over a number of years. Officials often had close ties with several Commonwealth nations. For instance,

Robert Hall, Director of the British Cabinet's Economic Section (1947–53) and Economic Adviser to the British Government (1953–61), had been brought up in Australia and educated at the Universities of Queensland and Oxford. In wartime meat negotiations, a New Zealander sometimes represented the British government, while a Briton represented New Zealand. The price of meat was determined in 1944 by a snooker match between British and New Zealand officials at the Carlton Club.[35] An American commentator, Judd Polk, suggested that solidarity, reinforced by habit and informality, was a real, if intangible, characteristic of the Sterling Area as an international organization.[36] According to Mansergh, the leaders of India, Pakistan, and Ceylon were easily incorporated into the highest councils of the Commonwealth, which did not cease to be a 'fraternal association', to use Churchill's phrase, until after Suez.[37] For instance, Jawaharlal Nehru, the first prime minister of independent India, was a Cambridge man who moved with ease in British society. But trust was greatest between the leaders of Britain, Australia, and New Zealand. Further grounds for cooperation were provided by the fact that all three were governed by socialists in the early postwar period and by conservatives in the 1950s.

The Commonwealth economic network of the 1930s to the 1960s was a defensive mechanism against the actual and perceived vagaries of international economic conditions.[38] Organizational flexibility was a key feature of the Commonwealth and of the Sterling Area. The Ottawa Agreements established contractual obligations with respect to preferences, but the Sterling Area had no constitution. The Commonwealth was not conceived as a permanent or self-sufficient economic community insulated from the rest of the world by a 'steel mesh'. Indeed most Commonwealth members looked forward to the day when it would be possible to abolish controls on current transactions with the dollar area, and to return to the 'one world' monetary regime that had disintegrated in the 1930s.[39] Following the achievement of convertibility in 1958, the Sterling Area lost much of its rationale as an economic community, although bilateral ties between Britain and certain members remained strong.

Growth and stability

Many economists and policy-makers feared another global depression and the return of mass unemployment after the war. While there is considerable doubt about the extent to which Keynesian theory won formal acceptance in government circles, policy-makers came to emphasize the

Table 1.4   Economic growth in selected countries, 1950–73

	Compound annual growth rate of real per capita GDP (%)	Real per capita GDP in 1950 as % of US level		Compound annual growth rate of real per capita GDP (%)	Real per capita GDP in 1950 as % of US level
Japan	8.0	20	Ireland	3.1	37
W. Germany	5.0	45	Canada	2.9	74
Italy	5.0	36	UK	2.5	72
Finland	4.3	43	Australia	2.4	76
France	4.0	55	USA	2.4	100
Netherlands	3.4	61	New Zealand	1.7	89
Denmark	3.1	70	India	1.6	6

Source: Based on A. Maddison, *Monitoring the World Economy 1820–1992* (Paris: OECD, 1995), table 3-2, pp. 62–3; tables D-1a, D-1b, D-1e, pp. 195, 197, 199, 205.

instability of the world economy and the importance of being prepared for remedial action to boost demand. At international conferences on postwar reconstruction, Australia, New Zealand, and Britain urged other countries to maintain full employment, not least as a means of preventing an international economic crisis. To everyone's relief the world did not lapse into another depression. Despite the dollar shortage North America, western Europe, and Japan entered an unparalleled era of growth in trade, productivity and real incomes in the 1950s. Several factors contributed to world growth, including high rates of innovation and diffusion, investment in human capital, the liberalization of industrial trade, and improved macroeconomic management. However, policy-makers in the 1940s had no idea that they were about to enter a golden age.[40]

The fastest rates of growth were experienced in Japan and continental western Europe (Table 1.4). While growth rates in Commonwealth countries, including Britain, Australia, and New Zealand, were better than in the first half of the twentieth century, they were still comparatively low. Also worth noting is New Zealand's poor economic performance relative to Australia. In 1946/7, per capita GDP was higher in New Zealand than in any of the Australian states. By 1969/70 New South Wales had caught up with, and Victoria had overtaken, New Zealand. The most dynamic area in Australasia in the 1960s and 1970s was mineral-rich Western Australia.[41]

Individual Commonwealth countries would have done better if the Commonwealth as a whole had grown faster, but it does not follow that membership of the Commonwealth economic network actually hindered growth. Other factors may account for the slow growth of Australia, New Zealand, and Britain relative to Japan, Germany, and Italy. Catch-up growth, which was an important phenomenon during the golden age, occurred through the diffusion of technologies and organizational principles perfected in the USA. American multinationals played an important role in this process. Growth was fastest in industrial economies that were a long way behind the USA in 1950, such as Italy and Japan. In the USA itself, which was the pioneer of new technologies, as well as in countries such as Britain, Canada, Australia, and New Zealand, which boasted quite high incomes in 1950, growth was considerably weaker. The closer a country was to the US income level in 1950, the more restricted was its scope for catch-up growth.[42] Australia and New Zealand already outshone the USA in the production and marketing of temperate agricultural commodities. Furthermore, due to their limited domestic markets, they were in a poor position to adopt American mass-production techniques. After 1950, Britain gained marginally on the USA in the growth race, Australia just kept pace, and New Zealand slipped further behind. The reasons for the failure of Australia and New Zealand to achieve *any* catch-up are discussed in more detail later.

The theory of institutional sclerosis provides a complementary explanation of the relatively slow growth of the USA, Britain, Australia, and New Zealand during the golden age. According to Mancur Olson, nations that escaped revolution, occupation, or military devastation in the 1940s, experienced weak growth after 1950, whereas war-ravaged countries, including France, West Germany, Italy, and Japan, enjoyed rapid growth.[43] Olson observed a tendency for rent-seeking coalitions, consisting of business leaders, workers, or farmers, to gather strength over long periods of time. If undisturbed, these coalitions stifled growth by restricting competition, erecting barriers to the entry of new firms, and reducing incentives for existing firms to make cost-reducing innovations. Rent-seeking coalitions extended their tentacles into government, where they lobbied for subsidies and protection. Olson concluded that Australia and New Zealand suffered greatly from the depredations of rent-seekers after the Second World War.[44] Rent-seeking coalitions in defeated countries were eliminated, ushering in a new era of competition and innovation, but anti-competitive business and labour groups consolidated their power in countries that were on the winning side in the war.

The catch-up and institutional sclerosis theories explain much of the poor economic performance of the Anglo-Saxon economies, including the USA, relative to continental Europe and Japan between 1950 and 1973. Growth rates in western Europe and Japan were also boosted during the early part of the golden age by the final stages of postwar reconstruction. Thus slow growth was not the result of any particular failing of the Commonwealth as an economic community. Rather the Commonwealth included a number of countries, both advanced and underdeveloped, which were growing at a leisurely pace.

It is important to point out that by the sorry standards of the 1930s the economies of Britain and the dominions enjoyed a remarkable run of prosperity between 1945 and the 1960s. Failure to match German and Japanese growth rates was not a sign of complete stagnation. Incomes in Britain and Australia grew roughly as fast incomes in the USA. Before writing off the Commonwealth as an economic system, it is worth reconsidering its rationale, and discussing how the more vulnerable members, such as New Zealand, might have fared without it.

In the mid-1940s, the principal economic goals of most states were reconstruction, stability, and full employment, though these were not their only objectives. Australia, for example, also desired to encourage population growth, and India wished to reduce poverty. No government, however, thought in terms of maximizing the long-term growth rate. Consequently, the economic policies of this era should not be judged solely on the basis of their implications for growth.

As we have seen, the Ottawa Agreements and the Sterling Area were *ad hoc* responses to the depression and the Second World War. Their purpose was to reduce instability in prices, incomes, and employment within the Commonwealth. They acted as buffers against the transmission of shocks from the rest of the world.[45] The crises of the 1920s and 1930s seriously weakened trust in unfettered market forces. An economist and British Treasury adviser, Hubert Henderson, argued in 1943 that the 'idea of greater economic security is fundamentally incompatible with that of an unregulated external economy.'[46] Trade controls and preferences were required to underpin Britain's external stability in uncertain times. Edward Bernstein, a leading US Treasury adviser, empathized with British officials who maintained that a dash to multilateral trade and payments would be too risky. Bernstein, however, hoped that their fears could be allayed by the provision of US aid.[47] Australia and New Zealand also placed a heavy emphasis on economic security. Though the Ottawa Agreements appeared to be redundant in the 1950s, it was argued that British food preferences would prove invaluable again in another slump.[48] Even if the depression was, in Sachs' words, 'a once-in-two-hundred-year phenomenon . . . a one-time fluke of grotesque proportions', this could not have been known in 1945.[49] That there was no recurrence of depression proves neither that one was impossible nor that a multilateral system would have run smoothly in the conditions of the late 1940s. In the light of the Asian financial crisis of the 1990s, the intrinsic stability of global capitalism cannot be taken for granted.[50] The possibility that the stabilizing features of the Sterling Area, combined with demand management policies, helped to stave off another depression cannot be ruled out. It made sense not to take risks.

A defensive Commonwealth system became less attractive after about 1955, as politicians and economists became increasingly obsessed with growth. Nevertheless, J.O.N. Perkins of Melbourne University argued in the 1960s that the Commonwealth could still become a dynamic, open economic community. He contended that the hesitant growth of Commonwealth nations, including Australia and New Zealand, in the late 1950s and early 1960s, reflected a cyclical fall in the terms of trade of primary exporting relative to industrial nations. Australia and New Zealand would enjoy faster growth, and offer stronger markets for British manufactures, when the relative price of primary products re-covered. Perkins concluded that it was not certain that the fostering of closer ties with Europe, at the expense of the Commonwealth, would benefit Britain.[51] Numerous economists believed that the terms of trade of primary producers would continue to decline, but the evidence was capable of either interpretation.[52]

In assessing the Commonwealth economic network, it is useful to consider what might have happened in its absence. Anderson and Norheim argue that Commonwealth preferences did have a significant effect on trade patterns. In 1958 the intensity of trade between Britain and the south-west Pacific (Australia, New Zealand, Fiji, and Papua New Guinea) was much greater than would be expected on the basis of their weight in world trade. Tariff preferences, cultural affinity, and the fact that Commonwealth producers catered specially for British tastes, com-bined to raise the intensity of trade.[53] When Britain joined the EEC, and adopted the rigidly protectionist Common Agricultural Policy (CAP), the impact on New Zealand's exports was 'devastating' according to one statistical study. Exports from New Zealand to Britain fell by 50 per cent in real terms between 1970 and 1984.[54] The effect on Australia was less pronounced, although the producers of certain commodities, including butter, cheese, meat, sugar, and fruit, did suffer appreciably.[55] Earlier British entry into the EEC would have imposed a larger burden on both countries. The membership terms offered in the early 1960s were no better than those finally accepted in the 1970s. Abolition of the Commonwealth economic system, and the introduction of controls on imports of Commonwealth foodstuffs, would have resulted in substantial adjustment costs for Australia, and economic turmoil in New Zealand. During the 1960s, the alternative to the Commonwealth system was not multilateralism, but British participation in an exclusive European trading bloc, together with continued American and Japanese agricultural protectionism. The British, however, were naively confident of achieving a strong increase in industrial exports to Europe, and believed that they had little to lose from winding up the Commonwealth.[56]

The Commonwealth economic relationship should be assessed as a package rather than as a collection of distinct arrangements. There were strong links between Commonwealth Preference and other areas of policy. Preferences conferred financial benefits on politically influential British industries, including engineering and motor vehicles, enabling them to raise prices and profit margins on exports to the Commonwealth. If Australia and New Zealand had abolished British preference, the UK might have retaliated by imposing tariffs or quotas on Commonwealth food, restricting capital flows, or seeking EEC membership without safeguards for primary producers. Commonwealth Preference was one aspect of the wider economic settlement between Britain, Australia, and New Zealand.

Although Commonwealth countries were not in the vanguard of world economic growth, the Commonwealth economic network was of substantial importance. During the 1940s and early 1950s, the Sterling Area and Commonwealth Preference acted as insurance policies against economic instability and renewed depression. The Commonwealth network remained essential to some participants throughout the 1950s and 1960s. New Zealand relied on Britain for capital and for markets in a world permeated by agricultural protectionism. Australia did not depend on Britain to the same extent, as its exports were more diverse, but its food producers still needed an open UK market. Terminating the Commonwealth relationship would have imposed severe adjustment costs on New Zealand and Australia without helping either to find alternative outlets.

Table 1.5   Australia's principal merchandise exports, 1938–70

Percentage of total merchandise exports (excluding gold)						
	Wool	*Cereals*	*Meat*	*Dairy produce*	*Coal and ores*	*Manufactures**
1938	33.6	19.9	8.8	9.5	1.9	5.5
1946	36.0	9.3	7.3	8.8	1.0	16.3
1950	51.5	16.2	5.8	6.3	0.9	6.2
1955	46.9	10.1	7.3	5.0	2.0	10.7
1960	42.5	11.1	9.4	4.9	3.0	12.4
1965	31.4	15.4	11.0	4.3	4.9	17.1
1970	19.4	11.0	10.6	2.6	16.5	26.0

* Includes processed mineral ores, such as iron and steel, copper, etc.
Source: *Commonwealth Year Books*.

Table 1.6   New Zealand's principal merchandise exports, 1938–70

Percentage of total merchandise exports (excluding gold)				
	Wool	*Dairy produce*	*Meat*	*Manufactures*
1938	21.6	40.5	27.0	0.1
1946	26.6	30.1	24.9	1.7
1950	40.1	29.9	17.7	0.2
1955	36.2	27.2	26.3	1.7
1960	33.9	26.1	26.9	3.7
1965	28.7	24.9	29.2	5.2
1970	19.2	20.1	34.6	10.2

Source: *New Zealand Official Year Book*.

Constraints on growth

The reasons for the failure of Australia and New Zealand to record any catch-up growth deserve further consideration. Growth was constrained by the weakness of overseas markets for temperate agricultural commodities, domestic policies that suppressed competition and encouraged rent-seeking, and sheer isolation. (See Tables 1.5 and 1.6.)

Australia and New Zealand traditionally relied on exports of primary produce, especially of wool and temperate foodstuffs. The economic efficiency of the bulk of the rural sector in Australia and New Zealand was never seriously in question.[57] During the 1960s Australia also developed

Table 1.7 Terms of trade of Australia and New Zealand, 1950–75

Index of export prices divided by import prices (1960 = 100)					
Year ending 30 June	*Australia*	*New Zealand*	*Year ending 30 June*	*Australia*	*New Zealand*
1950	122	124	1963	99	103
1951	178	124	1964	109	115
1952	112	92	1965	104	113
1953	121	108	1966	104	110
1954	126	113	1967	103	105
1955	115	116	1968	99	94
1956	104	109	1969	101	92
1957	111	104	1970	102	91
1958	104	89	1971	96	88
1959	93	104	1972	95	97
1960	100	100	1973	114	117
1961	96	94	1974	123	117
1962	97	98	1975	116	81

Sources: Adapted from B. Pinkstone, *Global Connections: a History of Exports and the Australian Economy* (Canberra: AGPS, 1992), p. 368; R.S. Deane, P.W.E. Nicholl, and M.J. Walsh (eds), *External Economic Structure and Policy: an Analysis of New Zealand's Balance of Payments* (Wellington: Reserve Bank of New Zealand, 1981), p. 566.

a large export trade in mineral ores and processed minerals. New Zealand, however, lacked major reserves of minerals, and continued to focus on wool, meat, butter and cheese, supplemented by forestry products. In the developed world only Iceland's range of exports was narrower than New Zealand's in the 1960s. The commodity concentration of Australian exports also exceeded the OECD average. Lack of breadth in the export sector was a source of risk. After the boom in commodity prices at the start of the Korean War in 1950–1, Australia and New Zealand, along with other primary producers, experienced weak terms of trade until the next commodity boom in the early 1970s (see Table 1.7). Commodity prices tended to be more volatile than industrial prices, putting further strain on the balance of payments.[58]

The softness of international agricultural prices had several causes. Unlike producers of sophisticated manufactures, such as aircraft and industrial machinery, suppliers of undifferentiated primary commodities are price takers. The income elasticity of demand was relatively low for Australian and New Zealand exports in their main markets. Synthetic substitutes like margarine and man-made fibres posed a growing challenge to butter and wool producers. Agricultural mechanization across the developed world generated an outward shift in the supply schedule of temperate foodstuffs. But much of the responsibility for low agricultural prices must be laid at the door of governments in the major industrial economies. Food production in the USA, continental western Europe, and Japan was stimulated by lavish price support programmes and import restrictions. Even Britain subsidized its farmers, and allowed foreign countries to use it as a dumping ground for surpluses, depressing the prices received by Australian and New Zealand exporters. As a result of intervention, vast stockpiles of food were generated in the USA and western Europe. These surpluses were liquidated at subsidized prices in third markets or given away to poor countries. Farmers in the USA, western Europe, and Japan could not have withstood Australian and New Zealand competition in the absence of subsidies and protection. As is shown in Chapter 6, the efforts of Canberra and Wellington to persuade the industrial powers to adopt liberal agricultural regimes were ignored. Australia and New Zealand were too small to counter the influence of the American, European, and Japanese farm lobbies.[59] But the persistence of industrial protection in Australasia did not lead to retaliation by the USA and Europe, since negligible importance was attached to these small and distant markets. Agreement on strong agricultural protection was a cornerstone of the EEC, while the Americans and the western Europeans joined forces to stop GATT from reforming trade in foodstuffs. In the early 1990s, the elimination of world agricultural protection might have raised the prices of New Zealand dairy and meat exports by 40 per cent and 20 per cent respectively.[60] Hawke's assessment of the challenge facing New Zealand is difficult to dispute: 'World trends were not favourable to a country most efficient at producing primary products.'[61] The golden age did not extend to trade in foodstuffs.

If Australia and New Zealand were to achieve respectable growth rates despite the lamentable agricultural situation, they needed to choose growth-enhancing rather than growth-retarding policy frameworks. However, after the harsh experiences of the 1920s and 1930s policymakers in Canberra and Wellington anticipated a further period of instability. Instead of devising policies to promote intensive economic growth and the development of new exports, postwar governments concentrated on insulating employment levels from external shocks. Expansion of the manufacturing sector was viewed as necessary for job creation, but no thought was given to whether new establishments were capable of attaining international standards of competitiveness. Other countries emphasized stability and full employment after the Second World War, but not to the same degree as either Australia or New Zealand.

Economic security was secured by a mélange of demand management techniques and balance of payments restrictions. Import controls were tightened whenever export revenues fell, in order to minimize the impact of external disequilibrium on domestic demand and employment. Tariffs and import controls stimulated growth in the industrial workforce. During the Second World War new factories had been established producing substitutes for temporarily unobtainable imports, and after 1945 ministers were reluctant to see many of these facilities close.[62] Consequently, postwar Australia and New Zealand boasted the most heavily protected economies in the developed Western world. When Australia abolished import restrictions in 1960, tariffs were increased to ensure that domestic manufacturers suffered no adverse effects. In 1970, the average tariff on manufactures was 23 per cent in both Australia and New Zealand, compared with 9 per cent in the USA, 12 per cent in Japan, and 8 per cent in the EEC. Furthermore, 42 per cent of imports into New Zealand remained subject to quantitative control.[63] Bollard, Lattimore and Silverstone contend that New Zealand's trade policy had more in common with Latin American than with OECD practice.[64]

Protection lowered the incentive for firms to strive for efficiency. Wage and price controls that had been introduced to achieve stability and fairness encouraged further erosion of the competitive spirit. Even so, the Australian and New Zealand governments generally did not intervene at the microeconomic level to shape the industrial structure. There was no coherent view on whether labour-intensive or capital-intensive industries should receive priority, and protection was extended on a relatively undiscriminating basis. Bell describes Australian industrial policy as 'simultaneously interventionist and non-interventionist', a description that applies equally well to New Zealand.[65] When microeconomic intervention did take place, it was often in association with regional political interests. The eagerness with which the Australian states sought to attract motor vehicle manufacturers contributed to the dispersal of this industry in small plants incapable of obtaining scale economies.[66]

In the mid-1980s, Gruen adopted Olson's theory of institutional sclerosis to explain Australia's uninspiring growth rate, pointing out that local business leaders were addicted to restrictive practices and constantly lobbying for more protection.[67] Australian and New Zealand trade policy was sometimes described as 'protection on demand'. Business lobbying, however, was not the only influence over the breadth and depth of industrial protection. The state possessed considerable autonomy with respect to overall policy on imports, as is shown by Capling and Galligan for Australia, and Mabbett for New Zealand. Mabbett argues that stringent protection was the corollary of postwar governments' absolute commitment to full employment. Loose macroeconomic policies, coupled with unstable commodity export prices, rendered the balance of payments chronically weak. Since devaluation was ruled out, due to elasticity pessimism and concern about inflation, there was no alternative to quantitative controls. Another fundamental objective of tariff policy was to create work for the growing urban population.[68] Australian and New Zealand governments were not the creatures of the business lobby. Determined at all costs to preserve full employment, they almost inadvertently constructed a sclerotic environment. Protection generated opportunities for inefficient enterprises. Some firms extracted large rents under this regime, but many were content just to survive. Sclerosis also led to rising costs for the agricultural export sector. Duncan, Lattimore, and Bollard point out that the introduction of farm subsidies in the 1960s amounted to 'tacit acknowledgement' by the New Zealand government of the damage done to exporters by the high cost structure elsewhere in the economy.[69]

Although the comparative advantage of Australasia lay in primary production, this need not have prevented the emergence of at least some efficient manufacturing industries. Rising incomes and the weakness of overseas primary produce markets would have drawn some factors of production out of farming and into other sectors even without industrial protection. In any case, there is a difference between selective infant industry protection and a regime of blanket protection that stimulates industries that have no hope of attaining international standards of efficiency. Labour and other input costs were bid up to the detriment of the few industries that did have a chance of becoming competitive. Certain Asian countries, including Japan, South Korea and Taiwan, enjoyed far greater success than either Australia or New Zealand did in the development of export-oriented industries after the Second World War. Although infant industries enjoyed protection in these Asian countries, official policy stressed the encouragement of exports. Competitive exchange rates, subsidies, and tax concessions were used to propel firms into export markets.[70] Policy-makers in Canberra and Wellington paid lip service to the desirability of industrial exports, but rarely gave firms any material encouragement to transcend the home market.[71] Currency overvaluation also detracted from the export potential of Australasian firms.

It was not a matter of copying the Asians, as in the 1950s it was by no means clear that they were embarking upon a period of miraculous growth. Similarly, differences in factor endowments precluded Australia and New Zealand from taking the labour-intensive path to export-oriented industrialization. In the early 1960s, a Japanese economist, Professor Kojima, pointed out that, due to high labour costs, there was no future in Australia and New Zealand for labour-intensive consumer goods production. However, Kojima was optimistic that Australia could develop investment goods industries capable of exporting to Asia. Kojima argued that Australia's prospects were good in steel, aluminium, motor vehicles, heavy engineering products, ships, and chemicals, as were New Zealand's in pulp and paper manufacturing.[72] An advance along these lines would not have been easy, but it would have been more promising than the alternatives. Although there was a growing recognition in Australia and New Zealand that industrial performance was unsatisfactory, potential export industries continued to be hindered by competition for inputs from the import substitution sector.[73]

Geographical isolation also contributed to the relative economic decline of Australia and New Zealand. It is noteworthy that the economic performance of Canada, another primary producing dominion, was superior to that of either Australia or New Zealand during the twentieth century. Schedvin argues that Canada's proximity to the USA gave it a crucial advantage over Australia and New Zealand. Many American firms established branch plants in Canada in order to surmount the Canadian tariff. A brisk intra-industry trade developed cross the border in modern sectors like motor vehicles. American technological advances were rapidly introduced into Canadian industry, while large US orders helped Canadian factories to secure economies of scale. The Canadian industrial economy became increasingly integrated with its southern neighbour. By comparison, Australia and New Zealand could not have been more distant from their advanced industrial partner, Britain, and in consequence did not enjoy the same benefits of integration. Although branch plants were set up in Australasia by British and US firms, they catered for domestic rather than overseas customers, and often became neglected outposts.[74] Isolation increased transaction costs, and made it difficult for Australasian businesses to establish alliances with North American or European firms possessing better technology and distribution networks.

Greasley and Oxley add that Canada's closeness to the USA led to the adoption of American institutions in education, labour relations, and management that were in many respects superior to their British equivalents. Australia and New Zealand, however, were unable to transcend the institutional framework inherited from Britain.[75] The importance of proximity to large, sophisticated economies is confirmed by the postwar experience of several countries in northern Europe, including Denmark, Ireland, and Finland, which used to depend almost exclusively on exports of primary produce. These small nations turned to the major economies of western Europe for technology, markets, and, in the case of Ireland, EEC subsidies. In Denmark, manufactured exports had overtaken net agricultural exports by 1960.[76]

Global economic conditions after 1950 were less propitious for Australia and New Zealand than they were for Japan and continental western Europe. Agricultural protectionism was a serious obstacle to traditional exporters, as was isolation to potential industrial exporters. This unsatisfactory state of affairs was aggravated by domestic economic policies that were designed to avert depression rather than to hasten growth. Australia and New Zealand were slow to revise their policies in the light of changes in the international economic environment during the 1950s and 1960s, and in consequence did not fulfil their potential for growth. Institutional sclerosis and Australasia's comparatively limited scope for catch-up also constrained growth. Australia's burden was reduced by the discovery of minerals, but New Zealand was denied a similar windfall.

Conclusion

Australia and New Zealand emerged from the Second World War embedded in a defensive economic network centred on Britain. This network served them well until the mid-1950s. Britain offered the only secure export market in a climate of agricultural protectionism. The British supplied Australia and New Zealand with manufactures, sterling capital, and dollars. Australia, New Zealand, and Britain all regarded full employment as the central objective of domestic economic policy. The imperial economic system of the 1930s and earlier was transformed into the Commonwealth economic system. Australia and New Zealand continued to play vital parts in these arrangements. Whether this still constituted informal empire is hard to say. Australia and New Zealand would have refuted such an idea, though they were clearly the junior partners.

Commonwealth economic arrangements came under growing stress during the 1950s and 1960s, and Commonwealth countries looked beyond Britain for additional supplies of capital and expanding markets. Britain was gradually drawn away from the Commonwealth and into a wealthier and more sophisticated European economic network. Australia and New Zealand sought to improve their economic relations with the USA and Japan, but international economic conditions for exporters of temperate agricultural foodstuffs were harsh, and they were too small to wield much bargaining power in trade negotiations. Isolation hindered technology transfer and the growth of industrial exports, while economic policy focused on reducing rather than increasing competition. Policies that seemed rational in the 1940s and early 1950s were anachronistic by the late 1950s and 1960s. Australia and New Zealand were dealt poor hands and played them very badly.

2
Australia, New Zealand, and International Reconstruction

> The Commonwealth [of Australia] is so dependent upon world
> dynamics originating in the USA and UK, that it must become
> in the main a consenting party to world co-operation pro-
> grammes rather than a powerful influence upon those pro-
> grammes. Viewing the massive economic pressures in the world
> as a whole, the Commonwealth can do little more than to
> respond intelligently to international planning.
>
> *G.L. Wood, Professor of Commerce,*
> *University of Melbourne, 1947*[1]

During the Second World War, the Anglo-Saxon Allies differed over
certain aspects of the future management of the international economy.
Australia, New Zealand, and Britain argued that full employment should
be the key postwar economic objective.[2] By comparison, the USA, supported by Canada, gave priority to building a multilateral regime of free
trade and unrestricted payments.

As a recipient of US military and economic largesse, Britain could
not afford to dismiss any serious proposals emanating from Washington.
However, while many British economists and officials accepted that
multilateralism would contribute to long-term prosperity, they questioned whether it would deliver full employment in the short term.
American policy was viewed even more sceptically in Australia and New
Zealand, where the interwar depression was attributed to the contra-
dictions of the previous multilateral system. Australia and New Zealand
were cynical about Washington's commitment to free trade in agricultural produce. They regarded Commonwealth Preference and the Sterling Area as stabilizers, and had no intention of abandoning infant
industry protection. In the absence of a strong multilateral agreement

on full employment, Australia and New Zealand suspected that free trade and payments would render their economies even more vulnerable to external shocks.

This chapter examines the responses of Australia and New Zealand to Anglo-American proposals for a new international economic order. In brief, the Americans had to dilute their multilateral schemes in order to placate domestic protectionists, and avoid a breach with the sterling Commonwealth. For their part, Britain, Australia and New Zealand surrendered the right to increase preference margins. Britain and Australia but not New Zealand also undertook to abide by the rules of the IMF. In other respects, change was limited. Import controls, infant industry protection, Commonwealth Preference, and the Sterling Area all survived into the 1950s. Australia and New Zealand obtained some tariff concessions from the USA, but Britain remained the premier market for both countries.

Australia played a prominent role in world economic conferences during the mid-1940s. According to the US negotiator, Clair Wilcox, while the Australians 'generally opposed the U.S. position and assumed leadership of the opposition', they were 'intelligent' critics who were willing to 'compromise'.[3] New Zealand, however, was considered far less amenable, especially over import controls. Wilcox condemned states that sought 'an absolute free hand to impose quantitative restrictions', noting that 'leading the fight [were] New Zealand, Cuba, China, Chile, India and Czechoslovakia'.[4] Public opinion, which was wary of international economic organizations, imposed tighter constraints on the New Zealand than on the Australian negotiators.

Global economic cooperation in the 1940s

American and British politicians and economists believed that the failure of international cooperation had destabilized the world economy during the 1920s and 1930s. These decades saw the growth of protectionism, the formation of powerful trade blocs, and the replacement of the Gold Standard by a regime of floating exchange rates.[5] Followers of John Maynard Keynes also charged that the failure of governments to use fiscal and monetary policy to combat unemployment had exacerbated international economic chaos.

As a further slump was expected after the Second World War, in the early 1940s the USA and Britain set about designing a regime that would promote global economic stability.[6] Both parties supported freer trade, fixed exchange rates, and full employment, while differing over their relative priority. The future of Imperial Preference was a major source of discord. Washington expected Britain to dismantle the Ottawa Agreements in full or partial recompense for wartime aid.

Article VII of the Mutual Aid Agreement of 1942 called for action on three fronts by the USA, the UK, and their associates. Firstly, they would promote 'the expansion, by appropriate international and domestic measures, of production, employment, and the exchange and consumption of goods'. Secondly, they would work for 'the elimination of all forms of discriminatory treatment in international commerce'. And thirdly, they would seek the 'reduction of tariffs and other trade barriers'.[7] Article VII soon became a bone of contention. The British contended that the wholesale removal of trade barriers would be destabilizing unless the Americans were serious about maintaining full employment. But the Americans argued that Keynesian policies would lead to socialism and inflation, and declined to give any assurance that full employment would be preserved at all costs. While the British were prepared to swap cuts in preferences for cuts in American tariffs, they sought to avoid any prior obligation to abolish the Ottawa Agreements. Led by the Secretary of State, Cordell Hull, Washington ranked free trade and non-discrimination above full employment. But the liberal economic philosophy of the US administration was compromised by the protectionism of Congress and the nation.

With respect to international monetary policy, British and American officials advocated a fixed exchange rate system, supported by a fund that would make loans to countries undergoing balance of payments difficulties. Members' currencies would be made freely convertible into US dollars for current transactions. During the wartime dollar shortage, most currencies including sterling had become inconvertible, and the Americans were anxious to end this form of discrimination against their goods. Britain hoped that the international fund would be generously endowed, but the Americans, who would provide the lion's share of hard currency, had other ideas. At the Bretton Woods conference in 1944, a draft agreement emerged on a fixed exchange rate system, a frugal version of the IMF, and an International Bank for Reconstruction and Development (the IBRD or World Bank) to make reconstruction loans. After heated debate, Britain and the USA endorsed this settlement.

Unfortunately, the Bretton Woods system was designed to operate in normal conditions, and not in the aftermath of a world war. Many countries, including Britain, expected to incur large current account deficits with the USA in the early postwar years. They argued that the IMF would be swamped with cries for help, and stated that there ought to be a transitional period, with special arrangements, prior to Bretton Woods coming into force. In the event, the principal special arrangements were a US$3.75 billion loan from the USA, and a C$1.25 billion loan from Canada, to Britain. The accompanying Anglo-American Financial Agreement specified that sterling convertibility must be restored in July 1947, when Bretton Woods rules would be introduced. Washington assumed that the discriminatory framework of the Sterling Area would be dismantled at this date.[8] Predictably, convertibility had to be suspended after just six weeks, in August 1947, due to the rapid loss of dollars.

Following this debacle, the Sterling Area was restored to prominence. Britain obtained further American financial assistance in the late 1940s in the form of Marshall Aid, which enabled the Sterling Area to maintain a reasonable level of trade with North America. The Americans had good reason to be patient with Britain. Denied further aid, Britain, Australia, New Zealand, and certain other countries might have retreated into a rigid anti-dollar bloc, weakening the Western alliance against the Soviet Union. Postwar monetary cooperation was rooted in a compromise between the key currency states, the USA and Britain, which was accepted by other prominent countries including France, Canada, and later West Germany. Although Bretton Woods went into limbo, the IMF continued to provide loans to members, and to act as a forum.

The Americans used the 1945 loan negotiations as leverage to force the British into promising major concessions on Imperial Preference. Multilateral trade negotiations were held in 1946–7 on the basis of American proposals for an International Trade Organization. Acceptance of the initial draft ITO charter would have committed Britain and other countries to making large tariff reductions and eliminating preferences and non-tariff barriers. But such terms had little appeal. Developing countries wished to protect their infant industries, industrialized countries feared unfettered US competition, and Commonwealth nations fought to preserve important tariff preferences. Numerous escape clauses crept into the charter. Even the Americans required an escape clause covering agricultural policy. An interim General Agreement on Tariffs and Trade was signed in 1947 to facilitate tariff negotiations while national legislatures debated the charter. The GATT talks resulted in modest cuts in tariffs and preferential margins, but the bulk of the preference system, as it affected Australia and New Zealand, was left intact. The Commonwealth's main concession was to accept the 'no new preference' (NNP) rule. Most participants, including Britain, Australia, and New Zealand, were unwilling to sign the ITO charter before it had been ratified by the USA. However, the charter was torpedoed in Congress by an alliance of free traders and protectionists, the former objecting to the escape clauses, the latter claiming that it would destroy American jobs. GATT became a substitute for the ITO, and succeeded in reducing industrial tariffs but not barriers to agricultural trade.

Three main conclusions emerge so far. Firstly, the Americans' ambitious plans for multilateral economic cooperation were whittled down in debate. Secondly, the Americans failed to induce Britain and its clients to dismantle either Commonwealth Preference or the Sterling Area. Thirdly, despite these setbacks, there was far more international economic cooperation after 1945 than there had been before 1939.

The full employment imperative

Full employment was the overriding priority of Labour governments in Australia and New Zealand in the 1940s.[9] Their unswerving commitment to this goal stemmed from the harsh experiences of the 1930s. Even conservative opposition parties accepted full employment as a key objective. External economic policy was viewed through the prism of employment policy. Australia and New Zealand sought to persuade other countries, particularly the USA, that all-round full employment was the best guarantee of world prosperity.

'Full employment is a fundamental aim of the Commonwealth Government', stated the 1945 White Paper, *Full Employment in Australia*, and 'the people of Australia will demand and are entitled to expect full employment'.[10] The White Paper argued that fluctuations in employment were caused by swings in export revenue due to instability in overseas markets. Both countries were determined in future to preserve full employment, regardless of external shocks, by using counter-cyclical expenditure programmes. During balance of payments crises, the Australian government would restrict imports instead of deflating demand. New Zealand's position was almost identical. The 1945 Employment Act created a National Employment Service. The new Director of National Service, H.L. Bockett, announced that the 'policy of the New Zealand Government is based on recognition of the fact that the State is fundamentally responsible for the maintenance of full employment.'[11] Bockett added that the success of the peace settlement would depend on whether the world shared New Zealand's attitude.

Australia and New Zealand recognized that high internal demand would spill over into imports, rendering the external accounts even more vulnerable to any fall in export revenue. New Zealand went further than Australia in advocating the restriction of imports on a permanent basis. This policy, known as 'insulationism', was highly controversial. Critics warned that insulationism would stimulate inefficient domestic industries and reduce consumer welfare.[12] In practice, though, there was little to choose between the policies of Australia and New Zealand. Given the continuous dollar shortage, both countries had to restrict imports for many years, but rigid adherence to the principle of permanent controls proved a serious obstacle to New Zealand's full participation in the postwar economic settlement.

Australia and New Zealand judged Anglo-American economic proposals in terms of their compatibility with full employment. Canberra and Wellington were prepared to make large concessions over Commonwealth Preference and import controls if the Americans took the pledge on full employment.[13] Peter Fraser, the New Zealand Prime Minister, called in vain for an international employment conference that would have precedence over other meetings on the postwar settlement. Australia and New Zealand, with British support, proposed strong full employment amendments to the IMF, UN, and ITO charters, but the USA would not countenance any formula that interfered with domestic economic policy. Speaking at the San Francisco conference on the UN, an American official, John Foster Dulles, angrily repudiated the right of Australians and other foreign socialists to dictate economic policy to Washington. The Americans passed a mild Employment Act in 1946, having rejected a more radical measure in 1945.[14] Canada shared the USA's misgivings, while Britain drew back from confrontation on this issue. Australia and New Zealand had to be satisfied with vague sections in the IMF and UN charters urging members to promote full employment. The full employment provision in the ITO charter would have been more satisfactory had not this document been a dead letter.

In view of the frustrating US position on employment, Australia and New Zealand proceeded with caution in the commercial and monetary negotiations. They differed from the USA over the extent to which market forces could be trusted to produce economically desirable outcomes in the aftermath of war. Whereas the Americans were optimistic, policy-makers in the Sterling Area were pessimistic about the stability of the postwar international economy and the competitiveness of their industries.

The reaction to Article VII

In 1942, as Japanese forces advanced, Australia and New Zealand pressed Britain to sign the Mutual Aid Agreement on virtually any terms. However, when the Japanese retreated, the dominions soon developed qualms about Article VII's implications for the Ottawa Agreements.

Commonwealth officials met in London in June 1943 to consider Article VII and decide on a preliminary response to the USA's call for a multilateral trade settlement. The British were eager to forestall a reversion to economic isolationism in the USA. They also feared that in the absence of multilateral discussions the USA would conclude bilateral agreements with the dominions. Britain was determined to give nothing away. Reductions in preferences would have to be bought with tariff cuts. The British also contended that cuts in trade barriers should be part of a package dealing with the stabilization of commodity markets and the promotion of employment and growth.[15] They floated a scheme for a moderately liberal commercial regime and invited comments from the dominions.

While Australia and New Zealand were open to multilateral negotiations, they also wished to continue bilateral talks with the Americans in case important tariff cuts were forthcoming. H.C. Coombs, Director General of Post-war Reconstruction, stated that Australia 'attached great importance to the positive parts of Article 7', on the stimulation of production and employment, and felt that these 'should not be overshadowed by the negative undertakings', on reductions in trade barriers and discrimination.[16] Australia would hesitate to cut trade barriers until Washington was committed to full employment. Coombs indicated that preferences could be used as bargaining counters in an attempt to procure lower American tariffs. He made it clear that Australia would not reduce any tariffs needed to protect infant industries.[17] R.M. Campbell, speaking for New Zealand, echoed Coombs's comments on the importance of full employment. His government was interested in the establishment of international commodity buffer stocks, and the extension of intergovernmental bulk contracts with Britain. He added that New Zealand would be flexible about Imperial Preference if satisfaction could be obtained in other areas. Campbell was ready to contemplate, if not actually recommend, abolition of the Ottawa system as a gesture of goodwill to Washington. But he saw no reason why New Zealand should be banned from protecting local manufacturers in any way it pleased. The New Zealanders were gratified that the British appeared to see the need for a comprehensive settlement covering employment as well as trade.[18]

Pressnell suggests that the dominions became increasingly wary of American intentions in the later stages of the war,[19] not least because they doubted Washington's freedom to make substantial reductions in agricultural tariffs. The dominions had strong grounds for caution. As New Zealand officials pointed out in 1946, the 'possibility of finding an alternative market to the United Kingdom for our meat seems so remote that every effort appears necessary to retain a preferential position for our products in the United Kingdom.'[20] New Zealand dairy farmers, and Australian producers of meat, butter, cheese, fruit, and sugar, all depended on the British market. One New Zealand economist, Horace Belshaw, predicted that, unless US agricultural tariffs fell, the sterling and dollar areas would descend into a 'vicious circle' of protection and discrimination.[21]

The US commercial policy proposals

In November 1945, the British endorsed an American proposal for a multilateral trade conference. Australia and New Zealand noted with alarm that the British, under extreme pressure in the loan negotiations, had conceded that this conference would aim for sweeping reductions in preferences. Canberra and Wellington felt that Britain had no right to make unilateral commitments about agreements to which they were parties.[22]

Australian officials wondered whether it might not be better for Britain to manage without a dollar loan than to consent to commercial talks on disadvantageous terms. Ben Chifley, the Australian Prime Minister, had previously sidestepped an American attempt to link settlement of Australia's outstanding Lend-Lease obligations to a commitment on trade policy.[23] The British Prime Minister, Clement Attlee, assured Peter Fraser that there would be no 'unilateral or uncompensated sweeping away of preferences'.[24] But Canberra and Wellington remained lukewarm about the American proposals. It was not that they expected Britain to surrender over Commonwealth Preference. Indeed, they were confident that food preferences in Britain, except on fruit, would survive.[25] They simply resented negotiating with Washington from a position of moral weakness.

Leslie Melville, the economic adviser to the Australian central bank (the Commonwealth Bank), warned that the USA and Britain might combine against Australia and New Zealand over a range of commercial topics.[26] Canberra noted that the British would press for lower BP tariffs in the dominions in compensation for any reductions in most favoured nation (MFN) tariffs. The British Board of Trade feared that any cuts in BP margins would lead to a significant loss of orders, especially in engineering goods, to American firms. According to the Australians, however, it was BP, not MFN, tariffs that safeguarded local industry.[27] New Zealand too expected to incur British wrath if BP margins were reduced on sensitive products. Wellington also expected to come under intense American and British pressure to abandon permanent import controls. Even Australia regarded New Zealand's position on import controls as unreasonable.[28] Finally, both Canberra and Wellington were concerned lest any multilateral settlement ban further bulk purchase agreements with Britain.[29]

Rejection of the US invitation to the ITO conference would have cost Australia and New Zealand their MFN status, together with any American concessions on agricultural trade. Moreover, Washington indicated that employment as well as trade issues would receive consideration. The only alternative to the ITO approach was a strengthened Ottawa system, but Britain had already dismissed this option. Canberra agreed to participate, hoping that the US proposals could be rendered compatible with the 'Australian way of life', including full employment and infant industry development. The dangers of isolation, and a fall in prestige, were not lost on Chifley.[30] New Zealand also agreed to attend the conference, conceding that all countries would gain from a general increase in international trade. Nevertheless, the New Zealanders contended that the US proposals took insufficient account of the needs of small and developing countries: 'In this light . . . some of the proposals appear rather rigid, especially those referring to the elimination of quantitative [trade] restrictions.'[31]

The British were anxious to deter New Zealand from adopting an intransigent position in the ITO negotiations. Sir Percivale Liesching of the Dominions Office exhorted the New Zealand Minister of Finance, Walter Nash, not to make an issue of permanent quantitative restrictions, and remarked that if other countries took the same line, 'all our hopes of expansion of trade would be defeated'.[32] At a Commonwealth meeting in October 1946, Australia's suggestion that the ITO charter require members to pursue full employment policies met with general approval. However, the British, who feared for their exporters, were averse to legitimizing the use of quantitative restrictions for infant industry protection.[33]

Instead of one multilateral conference on commercial policy, several proved necessary. A preparatory committee met in London in October and November 1946 to recommend changes to the draft charter. In March 1947 a drafting committee was convened in New York to make further adjustments, and to prepare the text of the GATT. In April the GATT tariff negotiations began in Geneva, while the ITO preparatory committee resumed its discussions. The grand finale, at Havana, between November 1947 and March 1948, composed the final version of the ITO charter.[34]

The ITO charter

The ITO negotiations were difficult, especially for the Americans, who had to make extensive concessions in order to secure provisional agreement. Australia played an important role in the ITO talks, acting as spokesman for developing and primary producing countries.[35]

Australia and New Zealand were pleased with the full employment provisions in the final version of the charter. 'At Australia's insistence, supported by others, the chapter [on employment and economic activity] has not only been incorporated in the main body of the Charter but failure to satisfy its conditions has been made a cause of complaint to the Organisation', possibly leading to the suspension of the offending state.[36] The Americans, however, argued that this would mean nothing in practice. As usual, the text was capable of several interpretations.[37] Australia, New Zealand, and other Commonwealth and developing countries arranged for the inclusion of a chapter on economic development, which allowed 'developing' nations to use quantitative restrictions for infant industry protection, subject to ITO approval. Australia and New Zealand regarded themselves as developing countries for such purposes. They also overcame American opposition to making the ITO responsible for international commodity agreements. Most agricultural prices were strong in the mid-1940s, but dominion farmers expected to benefit in the long run from commodity agreements. Article XVI of the charter provided for the continuation of the Ottawa Agreements, while banning the introduction of new tariff preferences, a point tentatively conceded by Britain during the Washington talks of 1945.[38] Finally, developing countries, including Australia and New Zealand, thwarted an American attempt to prohibit ITO members from discriminating against inward investment from any particular country. According to Nash, this proposal threatened the sovereignty of small nations, and had 'the appearance of serving the expansionist aims of economic imperialism'.[39]

New Zealand's most persistent interventions in the charter negotiations were on the theme of permanent quantitative restrictions. The draft charter, to which New Zealand demanded an amendment, ruled out the imposition of quantitative restrictions in the absence of a balance of payments crisis.[40] The British and Australian delegations evinced little sympathy for New Zealand. The President of the Board of Trade, Sir Stafford Cripps, told Nash that 'success would only be achieved if all countries were prepared to make some sacrifices.'[41] Chifley warned that New Zealand's proposed amendment would open the door to 'disastrous abuses of the system'.[42] The New Zealanders confessed that their problem was in some degree presentational. The draft charter contained adequate loopholes, but the public would expect some explicit recognition of New Zealand's 'unique' situation. Australia tried to mediate, while Britain concluded that it would be better to accommodate Wellington than risk a breach. A clause was at length inserted granting a special waiver to a country in perpetual balance of payments crisis.[43]

To American dismay, the Havana charter became riddled with escape clauses. Legislative approval for the charter was now sought in each country. In the Australian House of Representatives, John Dedman, the Minister for Post-war Reconstruction, described the ITO as a 'beacon for the future.'[44] Without it he feared a return to the 'cut-throat' tactics that had damaged Australia in the 1930s:

> Our interests lie especially along the lines of flexible multi-lateral trade. We need new markets to pay for the imports which our development requires. Our old markets are located primarily in the United Kingdom and Europe, the relative world importance of which is declining. The population of western Europe will begin to decline sharply within a few years and this will limit its need for our foodstuffs. Our main avenues for development, particularly for the export of manufactured goods, point in new directions.[45]

Advocates of the ITO contended that the search for new trading relationships in Asia and the Americas would be facilitated under the new framework.[46] But powerful voices in the Australian parliament, industry and the unions claimed that ratification of the ITO charter and GATT would lead to unemployment, rupture with Britain, and loss of economic sovereignty. Melville considered it possible that, from Australia's perspective, a discriminatory alliance between the Commonwealth and western Europe might produce a superior outcome than multilaterlism. The path ahead was unclear and a mistake would be costly.[47] Even so, parliament endorsed the ITO charter subject to its approval by the USA and Britain.

A similar debate occurred in New Zealand. Despite Nash's trumpeting of the 'New Zealand clause' on import controls, the opposition portrayed the charter as a threat to full employment and imperial unity.[48] The National spokesman, F.W. Doidge, dismissed the ITO and GATT as 'cruelly one-sided' agreements that jeopardized 150,000 New Zealand jobs. Doidge objected to the attempts 'to sign away our right to govern ourselves in respect of our economic and fiscal policies . . . We do not want our destiny to be decided by an international organization.'[49] Fear of American domination was a powerful strand in New Zealand politics.[50] It is uncertain whether New Zealand would have ratified the ITO charter even if the USA had done so.

The GATT round

Zeiler argues that the 1947 GATT conference was a resounding defeat for US economic liberalism due to the intransigence of Britain, Australia and New Zealand.[51] Admittedly, Britain and the Commonwealth were determined not to sell their preferences for less than they were worth, however the US position was equally compromised. The protectionists were in full flow in Congress, and President Truman lacked the legal authority to reduce tariffs by more than 50 per cent. GATT delivered a modest compromise that was tolerable to both sides.

Britain had no intention of reducing preference margins on important primary commodities like meat, butter, and cheese. For their part, Canberra and Wellington hoped to persuade the USA and other foreign countries to reduce tariffs on primary produce. With this in mind, the dominions were prepared to offer cuts in MFN rates on industrial goods, thereby squeezing BP margins. Britain planned to protect BP margins in Australia and New Zealand by demanding cuts in BP tariffs. Before the GATT conference, Britain persuaded Australia and New Zealand to trim their offers to foreign countries. The British did not object to the abolition of preferences on some secondary items such as toilet preparations, as the Americans could not be sent home empty-handed, but the dominions were urged to refuse substantive concessions on important items like motor vehicle kits.[52]

As anticipated, the American wool tariff was the sticking point between Australia and the USA. Other industrial countries imported wool free of duty, but the USA exacted a tariff of 34 cents per pound on wool of the type supplied by Australia and New Zealand. Canberra and Wellington asked for this tariff to be halved to 17 cents. The Americans were in a difficult position, as Congress had recently passed a bill to raise the wool tariff. Truman had vetoed this bill, apprehending that it might provoke Australia and New Zealand into rejecting GATT and the ITO, but he felt unable to offer any reduction in the wool tariff. Australia reacted angrily, stating that negotiations would be pointless without some prospect of a major US concession on wool. New Zealand sympathized, but argued that it would be better to persevere with the talks.[53] The Australians curtly suspended negotiations with the USA, calling into question the success of the entire conference. The Secretary of State, George Marshall, persuaded Truman to offer an 8.5 cent cut in the tariff, pointing out that failure to accommodate Canberra might unhinge GATT, and lead to serious complications in the ITO talks. Marshall believed that the USA could achieve a 'substantial elimination of British Empire preferences' by appeasing Australia over wool.[54] Australia eventually accepted the improved US offer on wool, which was sweetened by further concessions on meat and dairy produce.[55]

Australian ministers expressed satisfaction with the results of the GATT conference. The cut in the wool tariff was 'valuable and important', and US concessions on meat and butter were of 'real importance in relation to the future development of primary production in Australia.'[56] Moreover, the reductions in US industrial tariffs would enable British exporters to replenish the Sterling Area dollar pool for the benefit of Australia. Some Australian tariffs had been reduced, but 'in every case' it had been ascertained that 'the concession would not adversely affect the competitive position of efficient Australian industries.'[57] Wellington echoed these sentiments, noting that British concessions to the USA, for instance on dried fruits, did 'not affect New Zealand materially.'[58]

Marshall's expectation that the wool offer would break the wider impasse over Commonwealth Preference proved groundless. Australia and New Zealand eliminated BP margins on goods accounting for just 1 per cent and 2 per cent respectively of the value of their imports from Britain. BP margins were unaltered on items responsible for 79 per cent of Australia's and 63 per cent of New Zealand's imports from Britain. By contrast, Canada abolished BP margins on 18 per cent of its imports from Britain, and left them unchanged on just 44 per cent. Canada and Britain also put their bilateral tariff preferences on to a non-contractual footing. The British estimated that up to £4.3 million sterling of their exports to Australia and £2.5 million of their exports to New Zealand were now at risk.[59] However, as imports from the dollar area were subject to quantitative control, the practical effects were negligible. Washington concluded that conference had been worthwhile mainly because of the Anglo-Canadian concessions.[60]

Most of the ITO charter, including the NNP rule, but excluding the clauses on full employment and commodity agreements, was reproduced in the GATT charter.[61] Before the agreed tariff cuts could be enacted, their proponents had to run the gauntlet of parliament. Debate was boisterous, particularly over the threat seemingly posed by GATT to the Ottawa system. In the New Zealand House of Representatives, J.R. Hanan (National, Invercargill) alleged that GATT was 'inspired entirely' by Washington, and that the USA was bent upon 'complete domination of the markets of the world'.[62] The Australian Associated Chambers of Manufacturers expressed 'unyielding opposition' to GATT.[63] However, both countries ultimately endorsed the GATT settlement.

In 1948, the USA offered treaties of commerce, friendship, and navigation to Australia and New Zealand. These treaties would have given US firms the same rights as British firms in relation to the repatriation of capital and the award of public sector contracts. Moreover, they would have compelled Australia and New Zealand to retain the NNP rule irrespective of whether they remained members of GATT. The Reserve Bank of New Zealand (RBNZ) argued that the proposed treaty would undermine the government's right to discriminate against the dollar area, while the Department of Industries and Commerce raised the spectre of US economic domination. The Australian reaction was similar.[64] Neither country accepted the US offer.

Several years of frantic commercial diplomacy had produced a modest compromise, which bore little relation to the ambitious American trade proposals of 1945. This reflected the differing objectives and outlooks of participants, and, in some measure, a lack of trust.

Bretton Woods

Australia and New Zealand approached the issue of global monetary cooperation with circumspection. Canberra and Wellington were jealous guardians of their economic sovereignty and their special relationship with Britain. New Zealand, which adopted a more uncompromising stance than Australia, declined to join the IMF.

The Australians took a broadly positive view of Keynes's plan for a postwar Clearing Union or world monetary fund, an expansionary scheme that appeared to be consistent with the government's emphasis on full employment. But Canberra deprecated the clause restricting the right of members to adjust their exchange rates in response to changes in international conditions. Australia also considered the provisions for disciplining persistent creditor nations to be too weak. A deflationary bias would pervade the international system unless creditors were compelled to reflate. The rival American plan, produced by

Harry White, failed to impress at all, as it involved even greater exchange rate rigidity, and a monetary fund with much lower reserves. Under the White Plan, but not the Keynes Plan, deficit countries would be under strong pressure to deflate. Australia was disappointed that the sterling dominions had been given little say in drafting the monetary proposals.[65]

White's plan formed the core of the Anglo-American monetary proposals to the 1944 Bretton Woods conference. The Americans rejected an Anglo-Australian request to consider the links between international monetary policy and full employment at this gathering. According to H.V. Evatt, the Australian Minister of External Affairs, the Americans were constantly brushing aside Australian concerns. Evatt could summon up 'no enthusiasm' for Bretton Woods, but accepted that Australia should participate.[66] Chifley, then Treasurer, argued that stable exchange rates were conducive to the expansion of trade and employment, and that in view of the importance attached to Bretton Woods by the UK and the USA, 'Australia would need to have very strong grounds in principle' for staying aloof.[67] Cabinet resolved that Australia would be represented by a team of officials, led by Melville, instead of a minister. The delegation was instructed to press for larger drawing rights, an emphasis on full employment, and greater exchange rate flexibility.[68] No objection would be made to the World Bank scheme.

Wellington's initial response to the Anglo-American monetary schemes was cautious.[69] Officials concluded that New Zealand would benefit from exchange rate stability and the resumption of multilateral payments, but questioned whether the proposals on phasing out quantitative import and exchange controls could be reconciled with insulationism. Consequently, New Zealand might have to apply for IMF membership on special terms, including a waiver on exchange controls. As overseas exchange reserves were rising, New Zealand did not anticipate having to borrow from the IMF, so that joining would be a gesture of goodwill. Nash argued that the government 'need have no difficulty in regarding the International Monetary Fund advantages as outweighing [the] disadvantages', although several of his Labour colleagues thought otherwise.[70] The World Bank proposal was unobjectionable: 'As . . . a young and developing country, we would be on the receiving end of . . . [its] investments.'[71]

At Bretton Woods, limited concessions were made to accommodate Australia and New Zealand. White assured Nash that New Zealand would not have to forsake insulationism, although it would be expected to make some changes in the exchange and import control regime.[72] States with weak currencies would be permitted to discriminate against hard currencies like the US and Canadian dollars. However, as the IMF would decide when a currency was scarce, this fell short of the comprehensive dispensation sought by New Zealand. Some concession was made to the Australians' position on exchange rates, but not enough to satisfy them. However, Australia did succeed in obtaining an increase in drawing rights.[73] All attempts to incorporate a firm full employment clause in the charter met with implacable American opposition. Melville pointed out that the US government was constrained by suspicion in Congress and the banking system about the orthodoxy of the Bretton Woods scheme. The Australians feared that the IMF, the USA, and other creditors would compel the dominions to deflate during the next world economic crisis, regardless of the implications for employment. It was with reservations that Melville and Nash recommended acceptance of the Bretton Woods agreements.[74]

Bretton Woods attracted vociferous opposition in Australia and New Zealand. C.M. Williams, a New Zealand Labour MP, was 'very apprehensive' about the IMF, because Bretton Woods had been 'dominated by the Federal Reserve Bank, [and] the United States Treasury'. Williams warned that if New Zealand fell into the IMF's clutches, it would 'dictate . . . our external policy', and concluded that the purpose of Bretton Woods was to assist American big business to capture Britain's export markets.[75] During the debate on Australian membership, the prominent socialist, Jack Lang, predicted that the IMF would force Australia to 'reduce, wages, pensions, [and] social services'.[76] Bretton Woods was attacked by socialists as a Wall Street conspiracy, and by conservatives as an American takeover bid for the British Empire. Hostility to the IMF also reflected the popularity of the Social Credit monetary heresy in Australasia.[77]

Canberra and Wellington waited for Britain to make the first move. The British parliament voted to join the IMF and the IBRD in late 1945. However, Australia and New Zealand continued to delay, due to cabinet and Labour Party divisions. After Chifley's election victory in 1946, and further bitter struggles in the Labor Party, Australia ratified Bretton Woods in 1947. But Nash failed to convince the doubters in Wellington, and New Zealand did not join the IMF until 1961.[78] IMF membership was not crucial to Australia in the 1940s and 1950s, although a US$20 million loan proved useful in 1949. Membership of the World Bank, though, conferred substantial benefits since it became a major source of development capital.

Ineligibility to join the World Bank was the main cost to New Zealand of remaining outside the IMF. Britain was incensed by New Zealand's apparently eccentric position, which reduced the Sterling Area's voting rights in the IMF, and made it easier for the USA to dominate proceedings.[79] New Zealand's rejection of Bretton Woods placed it in an awkward position in GATT. The IMF worked closely with GATT, and 'consulted' with the GATT Contracting Parties about their import restrictions. Wellington repeatedly dismissed GATT's request that New Zealand sign a Special Exchange Agreement committing it to abide by IMF regulations. The Americans criticized New Zealand's 'delinquency', but hesitated to do anything that might provoke it into quitting GATT in case others followed.[80]

The suspicious reaction of Australia and New Zealand to Bretton Woods was understandable. Both countries welcomed international economic cooperation, but not at any price. In Australian and New Zealand eyes there was a deflationary bias in the Bretton Woods system, which might come into conflict with full employment policy. Australia was prepared to take this risk, but New Zealand was not. However, New Zealand's position was tenable while it could still rely upon Britain for dollars.

Sterling Area relationships

Writing in the 1950s, Sir Douglas Copland expressed surprise that Australia had not given serious thought to the alternatives to membership of the Sterling Area in 1945. Copland accepted that participation in the Sterling Area had insulated Australia and New Zealand from the worst effects of the dollar shortage, and insured them against the possibility of a new depression emanating from the USA. But Copland feared that the long-term price of these benefits would be slower growth. Quantitative restrictions bred inefficiency, while Britain could not provide Australia with sufficient capital to support rapid economic development.[81]

On the other hand, Australia and New Zealand had no realistic alternative to participating in the Sterling Area during the mid-1940s. Leaving this group would not have helped either of them to overcome US agricultural protectionism. The Sterling Area's saving grace was that it provided Australia and New Zealand with access to the central gold and dollar pool to pay for essential imports from non-sterling, and especially dollar, suppliers. Each year some members of the Sterling Area were in deficit, and some were in surplus, with the dollar area. Fewer dollars in total were required under a pooling system than if each country had held separate reserves. Between 1946 and 1949, Australia and New Zealand made net withdrawals from the central pool of US$338 million and US$204 million respectively.[82] In its absence they would have had to earn these dollars directly in the protected US market. The Australian Minister of Customs elaborated on this situation in 1945. Before the war, Australia and New Zealand had run current account deficits with the USA. If denied the security and 'elasticity' afforded by the dollar pool, Australia 'would be compelled to [seek a] unilateral balance of exchange with any currencies which are not within the sterling group. This would mean, in effect, bilateral trade arrangements with a variety of countries and a return to the "bad old days" of trade restriction.' It was too early to tell whether the multilateral proposals would produce a workable postwar settlement between the dollar and sterling countries, but 'the chances of success will be lessened if sterling cannot meet the initial phase with freedom.'[83]

The role of Australia and New Zealand in the Sterling Area was to provide British workers with food and British mills with wool. British industrial exports to North America would earn the dollars required by Australia and New Zealand to sustain essential imports from the dollar area. The colonies also generated a surplus of dollars that could be used by Australia and New Zealand.[84] Britain promised to supply the RSA with ample quantities of industrial goods and capital once it had recovered from the war. In the meantime, it urged the RSA to restrain dollar expenditure. Australia and New Zealand were tempted to divert some food to North America, but Britain discouraged this practice on the grounds that it would provide no net benefit to the dollar pool, as reductions in Commonwealth supplies would have to be balanced by higher dollar imports. Furthermore, the Americans might react by intensifying the barriers to agricultural imports.[85]

Until the mid-1950s, Australia and New Zealand consigned meat, dairy produce, sugar, eggs, wheat, and flour to Britain under bulk purchase agreements based on wartime schemes. Bulk purchase offered Britain security of supply, and reduced the uncertainty faced by dominion farmers.[86] In 1950, Britain obtained 75 per cent of its wheat, 98 per cent of its beef, 98 per cent of its lamb, 96 per cent of its butter, and 63 per cent of its cheese imports under long-term contracts with Commonwealth members. Although wool was not covered by bulk purchase agreements, Britain and the dominions ran a joint sales organization to liquidate wartime stockpiles, sharing the proceeds.[87]

A large bureaucracy in each country administered the web of import and exchange controls that bound the Sterling Area together. Much effort went into distinguishing between necessary and unnecessary dollar imports. For instance, while high priority was generally given to imports of machinery from the dollar area, certain exceptions were made. When Flight Lieutenant Leslie of the Royal Australian Air Force applied in 1945 for permission to purchase a Canadian doughnut machine, he was told that this equipment was not essential and could not be imported from the dollar area. Leslie was advised to contact an English manufacturer of doughnut machinery, but it transpired that the UN was purchasing the entire output of this firm for use in relief work. Due to the lack of a sterling supplier, though, permission was finally granted to Australians to import doughnut machines from the dollar area.[88]

After some initial complaints, Australia and New Zealand attempted to comply with Britain's requests for greater economies in dollar expenditure during the sterling crises of 1947 and 1949. The will to cooperate was reinforced by the fact that all three countries genuinely needed to restrain overseas expenditure. In 1947, the New Zealand Treasury noted that:

> Just as [we] were endeavouring to limit imports so as to reduce expenditure and prevent any inroads into our accumulated balances, a request was received from the United Kingdom Government to live within our current income. This request provided a fortunate excuse for pursuing a policy which we were forced to adopt in any case.[89]

Britain, Australia, and New Zealand had a common interest in preserving the Sterling Area. As Schenk explains, this mechanism offered 'many of the Bretton Woods ideals of multilateral payments and free trade' on a regional basis.[90]

Sterling Area relationships were not frictionless. Import and exchange control systems were both cumbersome and inflexible. In September 1947 the Australian Cabinet approved import cuts of around US$35 million for the remainder of 1947 and 1948. But, due to the loose way in which previous quotas had been specified, and the large volume of dollar imports already authorized, dollar imports were actually higher in 1947–8 than in 1946–7.[91] Moreover, the British were critical of some types of dollar expenditure by Australia and New Zealand, which they regarded as opportunistic. The purchase of American machinery for secondary industries that competed with British exporters fell into this category, as did expenditure on luxuries. In 1947, the Commonwealth Secretary, Lord Addison, berated the Australians for the 'gross size' of their newspapers, which consumed large amounts of North American newsprint. In fairness, the meaning of 'essential' was debatable, and the British continued to import large quantities of US tobacco.[92] But snags of this sort were not serious enough to destroy the spirit of cooperation.

Lee argues that the dollar shortage, and the fear of renewed depression, encouraged the Chifley government to cooperate closely with its Sterling Area partners between 1945 and 1949.[93] Fraser's government was equally committed to the Sterling Area. For all its imperfections, the Sterling Area was a force for international economic stability, without which there would have been a greater risk of violent fluctuations in trade, exchange rates, prices, wages, and employment. International monetary relations continued to be dominated by the nations possessing reserve or key currencies. Small countries like Australia and New Zealand clung to a key currency for security in the period before general convertibility was restored.[94]

The American loan and the sterling balances

The more dollars Britain could extract in loans and aid from the USA, the larger the pool into which Australia and New Zealand could dip. Australia and New Zealand were in principle delighted with the 1945 US loan to Britain. Chifley informed cabinet that the loan would 'help [the] UK more immediately to play a greater part in world trade and will make our sterling balances more freely convertible into dollars. Australia will benefit accordingly.'[95] Wellington argued that the loan would facilitate a retreat from austerity, and increase New Zealand's capacity to buy imports from the dollar area.[96]

Nevertheless, there was disquiet in Canberra and Wellington about the terms of this loan, including the stipulation that Britain must reduce the overhang of sterling balances before moving to convertibility. RSA countries had replenished their sterling balances by selling Britain large quantities of primary produce and military supplies during the war, when imports of British manufactures were unobtainable. Washington and London suspected that RSA members would rush to convert accumulated balances into dollars as soon as sterling became convertible. Between 1938 and 1945 Australia's sterling balances had grown from £54 million to £129 million, while New Zealand's had grown from £8 million to £78 million. By comparison, British wholesale prices had risen by 74 per cent. To some extent, the spectacular increase in New Zealand's sterling balances reflected the low level to which they had fallen in 1938–9. Keynes, however, accused Australia and New Zealand of profiteering because they had not joined Canada in offering Lend-Lease aid to Britain.[97] The USA and Britain desired Australia and New Zealand to cancel some of their sterling balances, in order to strengthen Britain's hand in talks with India and Egypt whose balances presented the most danger.

Scaling down the sterling balances would have eroded the benefit to Australia and New Zealand of the American loan. The Australian Treasury argued that there was no scope for writing down Australia's balances, which were insufficient to meet postwar requirements. 'We have expressed the view to UK Government that [American] assistance can be bought at too great a price.'[98] Australia was not a signatory to the loan agreement, and maintained that Britain had no right to interfere with its sterling balances. However, Australia conceded that it might be prudent to make a friendly gesture to Britain.[99] In Wellington, Leicester Webb, the Director of Stabilization, argued that it would be 'illogical' for Britain to expect New Zealand to cancel any of its balances, as this would necessitate cuts in imports from Britain.[100] In 1946, Keynes and Hugh Dalton, the Chancellor of the Exchequer, asked Fraser to cancel half of New Zealand's sterling balances, and accept the release of the remainder by installment.[101] Fraser procrastinated, as did the Australians when presented with the same request. Finally, in 1947, New Zealand made a donation of NZ£12 million, or 15 per cent of its sterling balances, in recognition of Britain's war effort. Australia gave Britain A£25 million, amounting to 15 per cent of its balances.[102] Neither country accepted formal spending restrictions on the remainder.

Britain continued to regard Australia and New Zealand as core members of the Sterling Area. Their drawings on the dollar pool were tolerable while they supplied Britain with essential commodities at low prices. If the Sterling Area had collapsed in 1947, there were plans to create a new currency bloc comprising the UK, the Crown Colonies, Australia, New Zealand, and possibly Denmark.[103]

The Marshall Plan and Australia

Following the convertibility debacle, Britain needed additional US aid. It was fortunate that this crisis coincided with the launch of Secretary of State Marshall's scheme for the distribution of large grants to accelerate the economic recovery of western Europe and ward off communism. The European Recovery Programme (ERP), or Marshall Plan, served as a cover for further aid to Britain.

Australia, supported by Britain, wanted Marshall Aid to be extended to the entire Sterling Area. In particular, Marshall Aid could be used to fund the RSA's dollar deficit. Although New Zealand also stood to gain from the provision of ERP aid to the RSA, it took no active part in this campaign, much to the annoyance of Leicester Webb, who criticized the passivity of ministers. The Americans initially resisted the Anglo-Australian proposal, stating that the RSA would benefit indirectly from dollars given to Britain and continental countries, and pointing out that Congress had made no provision for including non-European countries in the ERP. Washington still regarded the Sterling Area as an anachronism, and maintained that Britain's primary responsibility was to help the recovery of Europe.[104]

By 1948, the Americans were ready to acknowledge the stabilizing function of the Sterling Area. As the Cold War intensified, Washington grew keener to accommodate its Commonwealth allies. The Americans also recognized that RSA members, especially Australia, bought large amounts of exports from continental Europe. Sterling receipts from this trade helped the continentals to pay for essential imports from Britain. Upon the decommissioning of the Sterling Area, Australia and New Zealand might invoice Organisation for European Economic Cooperation (OEEC) countries in dollars, 'creating a fresh and even more unmanageable set of difficulties' for the Economic Cooperation Administration (ECA), which administered Marshall Aid.[105] On 20 July 1948, Sir Oliver Franks, the British Ambassador to Washington, reported that the American attitude towards including the dollar deficit of the RSA in Britain's aid from the ERP 'is less intransigent than we at one time feared it might be'. Franks thought that it might be possible to convince Congress of the legitimacy of such a course, if 'we can demonstrate . . . that the rest of the sterling area contributes to [western European] recovery by giving credits to western Europe.'[106] The British gave Thomas Finletter of the ECA a memorandum showing that the Sterling Area as a whole had a surplus with the OEEC, excluding the UK, of US$387 million. Of this, US$359 million was accounted for by the 'other sterling area' (i.e. the Sterling Area excluding the UK, Eire, and the British colonies). This net surplus of US$359 million, which the OEEC nations would have to finance in some other way if the RSA were excluded from the Marshall Plan, was more than double the current US$169 million dollar deficit of the RSA. Thus, the ECA would be getting a bargain in terms of dollar usage if it allowed current trade patterns to continue by covering the dollar deficit of the entire Sterling Area.[107]

The US Treasury contemplated other ways of assisting the RSA, including making it easier for the dominions to borrow from the IMF and World Bank, allowing recipients of ECA funds to spend them in the RSA, or simply giving more money to the UK. In the event, the Americans agreed to meet the projected RSA deficit of US$169 million during 1948–9 only, in return for a contribution from the dominions to aid European reconstruction.[108] The ECA had 'Australia particularly in mind'. An ECA official in Washington called publicly for Australia to increase its contribution to European recovery or even to devise its own ERP. The British responded that Australia and New Zealand had already made gifts from their sterling balances, that they were selling produce to Britain at less than world prices, and that they needed their remaining balances as a cushion against a substantial fall in commodity prices.[109]

In practice the demands of the ECA meant a donation from Australia. Britain felt that New Zealand's position was too precarious to justify a contribution since its sterling balances were being rapidly depleted. British officials referred the American request to the Australian government in August 1948. Treasury prepared a memorandum for Chifley which rebutted American criticism of Australia, and explained that since the war Australia had made a number of grants and low interest loans to facilitate the recoveries of Britain and continental Europe. On 28 August 1948, Chifley was ready to propose a grant of A£10 million (£8 million sterling), which was accepted despite American complaints that it was too little. The following year, Australia made a further grant of A£10 million, this time apparently without being requested to do so.[110]

Canberra was under no illusion about Marshall Aid. It gave Australia and New Zealand more dollars during 1948–9, and enabled Australia's development plans to proceed, but it was not a long-term solution to the dollar gap. When the Americans agreed to extend Marshall Aid to the RSA, they urged sterling countries to apply for supplementary loans from the IMF. The sterling crisis of 1949, which resulted in devaluation of the British, Australian, and New Zealand currencies against the dollar, increased the appeal of IMF borrowing. Chifley reluctantly decided to borrow US$20 million from the IMF to assist Australia until further cuts in dollar imports could be made.[111] Although recourse to the IMF was not possible for New Zealand, the British encouraged Wellington to seek a short-term loan from the official US Export–Import Bank. Nash discussed the prospects for short-term assistance with the Americans and the Canadians, but nothing came of this initiative.[112]

Provision of Marshall Aid to the RSA demonstrated that the UK was still adept at extracting dollars at the margin from Washington for the use of the sterling dominions. Furthermore, the Americans were still prepared to use the British as intermediaries in their dealings with the sterling dominions, at least in the financial area. During the 1950s, this situation would change as the Australians made independent approaches to the Americans for financial help.

Conclusion

Progress towards multilateral trade and payments was slow, notwithstanding the aspirations of economists, civil servants, and politicians in many countries. Australia and New Zealand welcomed those elements of the Anglo-American postwar schemes that promised better opportunities for commodity exporters, and a more stable framework of international economic relations. Canberra and Wellington would not have remained so firmly committed to the British economic complex had the USA adopted full employment as its central economic objective, and opened its markets to imported primary produce.

But the obstacles to a comprehensive multilateral settlement proved insurmountable. Governments differed in their perceived economic interests, and were constrained by domestic public opinion. Consequently, each country demanded escape clauses to permit the continuation of policies that contradicted multilateralism. The USA persisted in protecting its agricultural markets, and declined to make full employment an overriding priority. Australia and New Zealand refused to abandon their secondary industries, and New Zealand recoiled from abolishing insulationism. In the area of international monetary policy, it soon became clear that the Bretton Woods system would not work until the British and western European economies had fully recovered from the war. Under these circumstances, Australia and New Zealand fell back on Commonwealth Preference and the Sterling Area as the best guarantees of external stability.

3
Development Policy in Australia

> Australians do not like other people, and especially the UK Government, telling them how they should run their country. . . . Whenever we argue that Australia should get back to the cowshed, she suspects that we are trying to featherbed our own manufacturers. Some Australians are extremely sensitive on this point.
>
> *A.W. Snelling, Commonwealth Relations Office, May 1952*[1]

The Japanese forces' advance through south-east Asia in early 1942 confirmed Australia's strategic vulnerability. The lesson drawn was that Australia needed more troops, and thus a higher population, in order to resist future aggression. More secondary industries would be required because there was insufficient agricultural work for a growing workforce. The development of modern industry would provide Australia with skills and technologies that would be needed in a future war. Agriculture's poor record between the wars was another reason for favouring the industrial sector. However, farming could not be ignored, since a growing population would require feeding, while Britain was pressing Australia to expand primary exports.

Population growth and development could not be sustained without high levels of capital formation in housing, agriculture, transport, power, plant, and equipment. Although most investment could be financed from domestic savings, Australia would also require some overseas capital. Britain was Australia's main source of external capital both before 1939 and after 1945. As Britain's ability to export capital was limited, however, Australia would also have to seek capital in the dollar area. The British were not totally unsupportive of the Australian desire for economic development, but they often resented the priority given to import substitution industrialization at the expense of their exports. From time to time, Britain also deprecated Australia's purchase of equipment in the dollar area. The Australians placed more emphasis on agricultural development from 1952 onwards, acknowledging that this sector was their leading earner of foreign exchange. But even this strategy was designed to assist manufacturing, since rising agricultural exports would pay for higher imports of capital goods. Development policy was both a focus of cooperation and a source of tension in the Sterling Area.

Our approach differs markedly from that of Gianni Zappalà, who argues that Australia's drift from a strategy of complementary development with Britain was gradual, and only gathered pace under the government of Robert Menzies. As one of us has explained elsewhere, and as we reiterate here, Australia never intended to follow a policy of complementarity after 1945. Furthermore, the strategy of industrialization was not designed as a challenge to the British, but as an affirmation of Australia's own needs. At least initially, Australia was willing to pursue its development aims within the constraints imposed by Commonwealth Preference and membership in the Sterling Area.[2] The subsequent increase in assertiveness by the Menzies Coalition did not reflect a change in strategy, but rather a change in tactics as doubts grew about the capacity of the Sterling Area to promote the interests of Australia. British attitudes towards the industrial development of Australia were not constant, but fluctuated during the postwar period depending on the depth of Britain's balance of payments and convertibility difficulties. While the British tried to curtail Australian development in 1947, 1949, and 1951–52, they were more sympathetic to Australian aspirations during the buoyant period at the beginning of the Korean Conflict in 1950. By the late 1950s, as the dollar shortage diminished, lingering British concerns over Australian development receded.

Development objectives in the 1940s

Australia's postwar development programme was based on the three pillars of improved national defence, population growth stimulated by European immigration, and rapid industrialization.[3] All three aspects were seen as closely related since improved defence capability was regarded as a function of an enlarged population and a broad-based manufacturing sector. Moreover, manufacturing could provide jobs that would both ease the unemployment problem of the interwar years and service the requirements of new migrants. By implication, less attention would be given to agricultural development.

Australians understood that they were vulnerable to attack from the north long before December 1941. The seminal report on tariff policy by the Brigden Committee, in 1929, argued that protection was necessary to generate industrial jobs for a growing population. British and Australian ministers agreed in 1938 that a substantial increase in Australia's population was in the 'interests of both countries and of the British Empire as a whole', and must be accompanied by an increase in secondary industry since primary industry alone would not provide adequate employment.[4] The Pacific war intensified these concerns. During 1942, the British government concluded that a substantial increase in the population of the dominions would be needed after the war to safeguard the prestige and power of the empire. The Australian government was also coming round to the view that the postwar development and defence of the nation would not be feasible without mass immigration.[5] By urging the Australians to increase their population, the British were in effect encouraging them to develop more secondary industries. The British, who were torn between the wish to populate the dominions and the need to protect British export markets, rejected the suggestion that they should draw up a joint industrial strategy with Australia.[6] Privately, Sir Percivale Liesching, of the Board of Trade, was scathing about pleas 'that on defence grounds Australia must promote uneconomic industry and that we should help her in doing so.'[7] British exporters and the British balance of payments were certain to suffer.

While the British had accepted Australia's need to raise industrial output during the war, they were concerned about the lengths to which the Australians seemed determined to go to expand manufacturing after the war. Australian policy was driven in the short term by a desire to avoid unemployment during demobilization.[8] Shortly afterwards, the Prime Minister, John Curtin, informed members of the Associated Chambers of Manufactures that, in the long run, rapid industrial growth was essential for the maintenance of full employment, and the generation of sufficient export earnings to pay for key imports. Australia would need higher imports to support its development plans, and it would 'not be sufficient merely to rely . . . on the sources of export income which had existed before the war.'[9] There was pessimism in government circles about the postwar terms of trade. In June 1945, the Minister of Trade and Customs indicated that the British were anticipating that their export prices would be 80 per cent above the prewar level. Shipping costs, which also accrued to the British, had also risen rapidly during the war. It seemed unlikely, however, that the prices of Australia's agricultural exports would increase by more than 40 to 50 per cent above the prewar level.[10] Thus the manufacturing sector would be expected to contribute to export earnings. The 'quick and satisfactory equipping of our factories is essential if the high level of factory employment is to be sustained and a permanent export trade in secondary products developed.'[11] As will become clear in the next chapter, there was a sharp contrast between the objectives of industrial policy in Australia and New Zealand. Wellington was planning to displace industrial imports, but not to stimulate exports of manufactures.

Curtin also told the manufacturers that it was 'important both for economic and defence reasons that the potential resources of our less developed areas be given special attention'.[12] Too large a proportion of the population lived in the cities of the south east. The establishment of secondary industries in smaller centres would encourage their growth by providing well paid work. Furthermore, decentralization would make industry less vulnerable to disruption in wartime.[13]

Australia intended to industrialize in depth. Chifley anticipated that the postwar development programme would force Australia to diversify into the production of civilian capital goods. 'It is probable that the world will be seriously short of goods in the first postwar years. Australia must rely to an increased extent on local manufacture if we are to obtain the plant and equipment necessary to carry out the investment projects on which a high postwar level of employment is dependent.'[14] Aided by discriminatory import controls, a wide range of industries including tractor production, ball bearings and machine tools was developed to displace US imports and save dollars.[15]

Agriculture suffered from comparative neglect in the 1940s. The farming sector had become run down during the war, due to shortages of skilled labour and fertilizers, low investment, and the poor performance of the agricultural machinery industry. After 1945, investment in agriculture continued to be constrained by severe shortages of plant, fencing, and other materials. Material deficiencies were exacerbated by the priority given by the government to public works schemes associated with immigration, regional development, and the expansion of secondary industry. This is not to suggest that the government ignored the needs of agriculture. Labor's rural policy statement of 1946 looked forward to the growth of farm production and exports. Rather than encouraging greater investment in this sector, however, the government focused on lobbying for the liberalization of agricultural trade at the ITO and GATT conferences.[16]

Some economists, including Colin Clark, were highly critical of the federal government's industrialization policy. Clark predicted that overseas demand for Australia's primary products would increase rapidly after the war, in response to rising population and incomes in the northern hemisphere, and contended that there could be no economic justification for the artificial fostering of industries behind protective barriers. Clark was active in popularizing his views, which were approvingly reported to the Dominions Office.[17]

Australia's development objectives in the 1940s were perfectly clear. Population growth, assisted by mass immigration, was required to underpin national security. The development of modern manufacturing industries would enhance Australia's war potential, provide work, and contribute to balance of payments stability. Farming would remain the main export earner, although the prospects for further expansion in this sector were thought to be more limited.

Development and the sterling area under Labor

Membership in the Sterling Area was believed to be an important buttress for Australian development. Through the use of import and exchange controls, Australia could build on close trading relations with Britain, which offered secure markets for staple exports. Moreover, as Copland pointed out, Sterling Area membership offered 'an implied guarantee that industry would be able to develop unhindered by a challenge from the dollar area and, in general . . . was [a] shelter from the cold blasts of the post-war world economy.'[18] Throughout the early postwar years, Australian policy reflected the tension between ambitious development goals and the scarcity of essential inputs in the disrupted world economy. Only the USA was a reliable source of manufactures, including capital equipment, for several years after 1945. Other nations, including Australia, could offer little that Americans wanted in return, and the result was an international dollar shortage. Participation in the Sterling Area was one way of dealing with this problem.

Down to the middle of 1947, Australia's development programme appeared to be compatible with the resources available. Although imports from the USA were relatively large, the balance of payments situation did not at first raise any alarms. A rapid switch in attitude and behaviour was called for by the crisis in mid-1947 when a brief interlude of convertibility concentrated attention on the weakness of sterling. The Australian government had already been shaken when, just prior to the onset of convertibility, the British urged that Australia not draw on its accumulated sterling balances, but live within its own export income from 1947–8 onwards. To accomplish this, the British indicated that Australia should further tighten its dollar area import restrictions and cover any future dollar shortages by borrowing from the IMF.[19] In August, it became obvious that Britain would have to suspend convertibility again, and Sterling Area countries were asked to make immediate cuts in dollar imports. This was the start of a long campaign that was much slower to take effect than had been anticipated. It was not until mid-1948 that Australia was at last in a position to reduce dollar imports to a meaningful degree. Nevertheless, throughout the period of austerity, the government continually reaffirmed its development plans and regretted the need for postponement.

When convertibility was withdrawn, Australia was at first slow in assessing the dimensions of the crisis and the steps that were needed. On 25 August, four days after suspension was announced in London, the Department of Trade and Customs in Canberra reiterated its relatively liberal rules on import controls for capital plant and equipment. These regulations stated that the government should not bar imports of machinery from hard currency areas if similar items from the Sterling Area were inferior in performance, substantially more expensive, or likely to be delivered more slowly.[20] Within days, the British made it clear that Australia would not get off so lightly. On 1 September, the Commonwealth Secretary, Lord Addison, who was in Canberra, delivered a 'strong request' that the Australian government 'may so conduct their external economy that they will need to make no net claims on the United Kingdom for dollars during the next six months.'[21] Two days later, Addison hinted in a discussion with senior Treasury and Commonwealth Bank officials that, if Australia could not manage its import policy itself, then someone else would do it for them. He concluded that, 'It is pretty clear that Australian Government have not yet brought themselves to face seriousness of implications of crisis and that implications as regards possibility of far-reaching effects on economic structure have not yet been fully appreciated.'[22] In a reply to Addison, Chifley noted that, 'On a literal interpretation . . . the United Kingdom request . . . [would involve] a revolutionary change in the conduct of our external economy.'[23] At first, Australian Treasury officials treated Addison's approach to Chifley as a gambit since they could see no way of complying on any other interpretation. Once they were convinced of the seriousness of the dollar shortage, however, the Government began to take meaningful action. On 2 September, Cabinet approved cuts in dollar imports, but it was many months before these and subsequent measures took effect, due to rigidities in the licensing system.[24]

Some Australian officials now began to waver in their commitment to industrialization at all costs. In directing import reductions, Cabinet had again stated that the procurement of equipment and raw materials for Australian industry were 'in the highest category of priority'. Cabinet conceded, however, that manufacturers would have to cooperate in finding non-dollar sources of supply. Trade and Customs also tightened its import licensing policy on capital plant and equipment to favour British and European sources.[25] However, when Australia proposed to divert orders from American to British firms, Sir Wilfrid Eady of the British Treasury said that it would be difficult for British firms to satisfy them because it was necessary to give priority to customers in countries such as Argentina.[26]

Australia's development programme in the late 1940s was, to some extent, constrained by the import cuts. As David Lee indicates, when given the option to adopt a more independent stance, Australia stood by Britain in the convertibility crisis and reaffirmed its attachment to the Sterling Area.[27] Although efforts were made to protect existing industrial facilities, few dollars were available for new investment. Reviewing the licensing of dollar imports in December 1947, officials concluded that 'the bulk of the amount should be reserved for the most essential materials for manufacture and replacement parts for equipment, and that there could be no provision for goods of a capital nature or purely consumer goods.'[28] But although dollar imports were scarce, other funds were available and substantial development did occur. Real GDP increased significantly in both 1947–8 and 1948–9. In the latter year, it was 32 per cent higher than in 1939–40. Even more impressive, perhaps, was the investment in human capital through the assisted migration program. Net immigration increased from 10,611 in 1947 to 55,115 in 1948 and more than 150,000 in both 1949 and 1950. Building on a population of barely 7 million in 1945, this represented a substantial continuing commitment to development.[29]

The consequences for welfare were less clear. Although Australia succeeded in exporting some industrial goods to New Zealand and Asia, where US dollars were particularly scarce, there was an overwhelming reliance on the protected home market. The direction of industrialization was far from satisfactory, according to some commentators. Writing in the *Economic Record*, Copland deplored Australia's 'milk bar economy' in which frivolous enterprises were allowed to expand, while more basic industries were stagnant.[30]

Labor and American direct investment

The Chifley government, like its New Zealand counterpart, was both averse to borrowing dollars and somewhat suspicious of large-scale American investment. Labor wished to ensure that the Australian economy did not fall under American control. Since it was felt that borrowing from the USA would increase Australia's exposure to global financial crises, the Chifley government preferred to draw dollars from the Sterling Area's central pool. However, as we saw in the last section, Australia's ability to take dollars from the pool was not unlimited. It depended on the size of the pool, and on understandings with the British government. Marshall Aid was, as mentioned in Chapter 2, also a substitute for dollar borrowing, and in 1949 Chifley did borrow from the IMF in an emergency. This section examines Australian policy towards American FDI in the 1940s.

Despite the superficial attractiveness of US direct investment at a time of dollar shortage, Canberra did not make it easy for Americans to invest in Australia. Restrictions were exceptionally severe under Labor down to 1949, but even the relative loosening of regulations during the early Menzies years left the government in firm control of US direct investment. In Australia, in the late 1940s, less than 2 per cent of private investment in fixed capital was American, whereas almost 10 per cent came from Britain.[31] Australian policies were based on the nationalistic desire to protect local firms, attachment to Britain, suspicion of the USA, and the fear that inflows of US investment could be reversed later, creating balance of payments difficulties for Australia and the Sterling Area. Finally, it was uncertain that large US investments were necessary when Australia was pressing against the limits of her other resources.

Australia's position on US foreign investment was strongly influenced by balance of payments considerations, and by Australia's responsibilities as a member of the Sterling Area. In the short run, the Australian government was concerned to keep out speculative funds. Between 1948 and 1951, currency speculation proceeded on two fronts. Before the devaluation of the British and Australian pounds in September 1949, there was a tendency for American importers of Australian goods to delay payment in the hope of reducing their dollar commitments. This was equivalent to a short-run outflow of dollars. Far more serious, however, was the enormous flow of capital, largely British pounds, which entered Australia in the expectation that the Australian pound would be revalued to parity with sterling. It was estimated that approximately A£450 million in private capital had come into Australia between July 1946 and June 1950. Two-thirds of this amount was regarded as speculative.[32]

The implications of a massive repatriation of this temporary capital led the Australian government to tighten its control over British short-term funds, and strengthened its resolve to maintain strict checks on US investment of all types. However, Australia consistently guaranteed that remittances of dividends and royalties, except in the case of motion pictures, would be permitted. The general view was that this was a sufficiently liberal regime to attract long-term investment since large American firms establishing subsidiaries in Australia would not anticipate divestment as long as profits flowed. Nevertheless, the long-term implications of guaranteeing remittances made the government reluctant to accept any more foreign investment than was absolutely necessary, and also bolstered the policy of discouraging American machinery as a contribution towards FDI. Long before Edith Penrose highlighted the problem, the Chifley government was aware of the cumulative effects of foreign investment on the balance of payments. Because of earlier Canadian experience, the government took active steps from the late 1940s to ensure that it would not accumulate commitments for servicing foreign investment that were in excess of current dollar investment inflows.[33] Furthermore, the right to repatriate capital was not guaranteed.

Regardless of potential drawbacks, however, American FDI was considered as a means of reducing the long-term dollar shortage. In May 1948, H.C. Coombs prepared a memorandum for Chifley on the dollar problem, which concluded that Sterling Area countries must reduce their dollar requirements in order to achieve a permanent solution. He contended that Australia should aim to meet its own dollar needs, and not to be a net drawer on the dollar pool. Independence would require higher exports and lower dollar imports. Action on imports could take the form of further controls, import substitution, or the diversion of imports towards soft currency suppliers. Coombs argued that restrictions could not be tightened much further. He listed the goods that were most suitable for import substitution, including tobacco leaf, chemicals, motor chassis and tractors, tinplate, newsprint, and cloth and yarn, and suggested that in some instances US investment could make a contribution. For instance, automotive products and tractors offered scope for US direct investment. Besides General Motors–Holden, Ford Australia was planning to increase the Australian content of its vehicles, and the Chrysler-Dodge group had similar plans.[34] However, Coombs pointed out in 1950 that Australia could absorb only limited amounts of US industrial capital without generating increased inflation, due to the chronic shortages in power, industrial buildings, basic raw materials, and social infrastructure brought on by the industrialization and immigration programmes. Unless US capital 'can be concentrated for some years at least on the development of our basic industries' and infrastructure, he feared that it could create more difficulties than it solved.[35]

Menzies turns to the World Bank

A conservative Coalition government was elected in 1949. R.G. Menzies, the new Prime Minister, was determined to press ahead with economic development, if anything at a faster pace than Labor. But a number of writers have commented on the realignment of economic policy under the Coalition.[36] One important aspect of this change was Australia's new-found willingness to borrow from international agencies to finance development. Britain's initial suspicion of and subsequent strong support for Australia's loan from the World Bank in mid-1950 illustrates the ambivalence of British policy towards Australian development.

The eventual direction taken by the Menzies government was signalled well before the election. The new policy was articulated forcefully by Country Party MPs who would soon occupy important places in the Coalition cabinet. In the House of Representatives in 1948, John McEwen drew an analogy with private enterprise to support borrowing. 'If a man encounters a financial crisis in his business affairs, he can, if his business is sound, overcome his difficulties by borrowing . . . there can be no reason why we should not seek relief from the present emergency by raising a dollar loan.'[37] Arthur Fadden, the Country Party leader and future Treasurer, was equally emphatic. In March 1949, he said that 'acute dollar restrictions' were retarding Australia's development. The solution, according to Fadden, was to borrow money for development purposes from the World Bank, the Export–Import Bank or on the New York market. Such borrowing would enable Australia to obtain goods from dollar sources without affecting the Sterling Area dollar pool.[38]

The new Menzies government was determined to force the pace of development. One British observer noted, rather extremely, that 'The present [Australian] Government seems to have no plan for remedying by internal measures [the] overloading of Australia's natural resources.'[39] In fact, the Coalition did have a set of priorities, if not a formal plan.

It wished to obtain funds to pay for purchases of equipment for use in mining, transport development, and agriculture, as well as in supporting manufacturing industries including textiles.[40] Menzies agreed with Labor that the government had an important role to play in the promotion and planning of economic development. Barely a month after taking power, the Coalition prepared a 'Survey of Development Requirements' for the Immigration Planning Council, and a few weeks later a paper on 'Population Increases and Investment Requirements' was presented for discussion by the Cabinet Committee on Industry and Development.[41] In March 1950, the government created a new Department of National Development, which was charged with the coordination and development of both primary and secondary industries. In October 1950, this became the Ministry of National Development, with 'overall coordinating authority for . . . any plan of national development'.[42]

The Coalition placed more faith than Labor had done in the ability of American investment to aid Australia's development. In the early years of the Coalition there was a noticeable softening in the rules on foreign investment, particularly with respect to the use that US firms could make of funds borrowed in Australia, and the large-scale importation of plant and equipment from the dollar area. By the end of March 1950 the government had already agreed that International Harvester could import heavy developmental machinery without a dollar exchange, a practice discouraged by the Chifley government.[43] Enthusiasm for US direct investment was tempered, however, by worries about inflation. In May 1950, the Cabinet Committee on Industry and Development turned down a request by General Motors–Holden for enough foreign exchange to support an increase annual production from 20,500 to 50,000 vehicles. The reasons were given were the 'present condition of strain on labour, materials and essential services, and of dollar shortage.'[44]

Both the Commonwealth Bank and the Treasury began to investigate loan possibilities before Labor left office.[45] After the election, the issue was canvassed again, but the Bank and the Treasury had opposing views. On 3 February 1950, H.C. Coombs, the Governor of the Commonwealth Bank, wrote to Treasurer Fadden:[46]

As you know, the Bank is very greatly concerned at the continued inflationary pressure. I am convinced that a major contribution to countering that pressure can be made by increased imports of those classes of goods of which particular shortages exist in Australia. This applies of course particularly to capital equipment. If a dollar loan could increase the supplies of this equipment and thereby help to break some of the bottlenecks in the Australian economy, it would, I believe, be making a major contribution to an anti-inflationary policy.

Despite Treasury objections, the government resolved to seek a dollar loan, and planned initially to approach the Export–Import Bank, since it feared that the New York market would not provide the funds, and that the World Bank was too slow and fastidious in approving loans. Trevor Swan of the Treasury was set to work to devise an approach that would be attractive to potential lenders but would not annoy the British too severely. Swan argued that,

> We should . . . not appear as supplicants, either in London or in Washington, but as colleagues ready to discuss the best means of dealing with problems in which the UK, the USA, and Australia have a common interest – problems already well-defined in public statements as an integral part of the world problems of economic equilibrium and military security.[47]

In order to gain 'enthusiastic British support' Australia should concentrate on the long-run benefits that the dollar loan would confer on the Sterling Area. Swan recommended that Australian negotiators attempt to persuade US officials to get the Export–Import Bank and/or the World Bank to offer generous terms. They should also try to persuade Congress to make a direct grant of funds in return for Australia agreeing to accept 75,000 to 100,000 continental European migrants annually over the next 5 to 10 years.

Australia's strategy and tactics followed Swan's suggestions quite closely. When Menzies visited London, in July 1950, to discuss raising a dollar loan, British Treasury opinion was by no means well disposed towards his economic policy. Following a meeting with Australian ministers and officials, R.W.B. Clarke of the British Treasury reported that Coalition development policies were generating inflationary pressures that the government would not try to control through fiscal measures. The Australian Treasury and the Commonwealth Bank were 'very conscious that Australia is sitting on a volcano – but they really cannot see what can be done about it.'[48]

The brief prepared by the British Treasury for the Menzies visit did show some sympathy for Australia's position, which involved trying to meet security requirements while providing enough capital for a rapidly growing population and making up for the shortfall in investment during the depression and the war. As the defence programme involved increasing the population through large-scale immigration, 'Fundamentally, Australia's problem is that, if she is to survive at all, she must follow a course which will involve her in very serious financial dangers.'[49] In analysing Australia's dollar needs, the report commented that while it was true that certain types of equipment could only be purchased from the dollar area, these items should require an increased commitment of under US$10 million per year. Australia, argued the British, should bear in mind that many goods could now be obtained in soft currency countries in western Europe. Finally, Australia needed to be reminded that any 'dollar borrowing must earn its dollar keep.' The brief concluded that, '<u>assuming that the principle of dollar borrowing by Australia is accepted</u>, we should try to persuade Mr. Menzies to approach the International Bank.' Not only would this course provide the best terms for Australia, but it would also be good for the World Bank to spend some of its money so that Congress would have to grant funds to Southeast Asian countries in the future when they asked for money.[50]

Sir Stafford Cripps, the Chancellor of the Exchequer, was supportive. Menzies wanted to raise money in a hurry, and planned to bypass the World Bank in favour of the Export–Import Bank, however he was persuaded that it would be best to approach the World Bank.[51] Although the British stressed that any dollar loan must be self-liquidating, they provided constructive advice on how to deal with the Americans.[52] Menzies then went to Washington, where his trip coincided with the decision to send Australian ground forces to Korea. After presenting Menzies with a decoration, President Truman and Secretary of State Acheson assured him that they would 'do all in their power' to get dollars for the Australian development programme.[53] The Americans agreed that Australia should contact the World Bank. Menzies' request for US$250 million over five years (later changed to accommodate an immediate loan of US$100 million) was regarded as reasonable by the US government.[54] Eugene Black, the President of the World Bank, was very cooperative, and Australia secured an immediate loan of US$100 million on unprecedented terms. Not only was the period of investigation drastically shortened, but Australia was also permitted to spend within specified categories rather than, as was usual, for narrowly defined uses. The designated categories included agriculture, public utilities, railways, the mining of coal and non-ferrous metals, the iron and steel industry, and other branches of manufacturing. Australia's migration program featured prominently in the Bank's announcement as a justification for the loan.[55]

A number of factors lay behind Australia's success in Washington, including the support provided by the British. The broad-based nature of the request, in which money for enlarging the manufacturing sector was balanced by funds for the development of the agricultural and extractive sectors, was attractive to the British. The Australian initiative had come at a time when both Britain and Australia were achieving some success in the management of their dollar requirements. British gold and dollar reserves had risen from US$1.4 billion at the end of September 1949 to US$2.4 billion nine months later, hence London could afford to humour the Australians. The boom in wool prices at the start of the Korean War gave a boost to Australia's overseas funds, and, according to Schedvin, rendered the World Bank loan unnecessary, though this windfall had not been foreseen.[56] By turning to the World Bank, Australia had shown that it was not prepared to allow the pace of its economic development to be constrained by the resources of the Sterling Area.

Australian development in the fifties and sixties

The improvement in the reserves of the Sterling Area continued throughout 1950, but a sharp deterioration occurred in 1951, reflecting the end of the commodity price bubble, the Iranian oil crisis, the start of the US and Canadian loan repayments, and the faltering of British exports in the world recession. Australia decided to gamble on the wool price staying at a record high level, and made provision for a further expansion in imports of development goods, including items from the dollar area. The collapse in the wool price in 1951 led to embarrassment.[57]

By early 1951, the World Bank loan had been spent, and further expenditure on dollar goods for development would have to come out of the general dollar budget. The Inter-Departmental Dollar Committee, meeting in March 1951, recommended a very substantial loosening in restrictions on dollar imports in 1951–2. Constructional timbers, iron and steel, crude asbestos, aluminium ingots and aluminium alloy ingots, sulphur and abrasive grains were also to be removed from the dollar import budget and allowed virtually unlimited import licences.[58] In July, the Inter-Departmental Committee raised the dollar ceiling still further, despite the fact that Fadden was becoming worried about falling wool prices and the deteriorating financial position.[59] By early 1952, the dollar situation had quite obviously become dangerous but, as in 1947, the government shrank from making meaningful cuts, largely because high imports were seen as anti-inflationary. At the preliminary meeting of officials that preceded the Commonwealth Finance Ministers' Conference in early 1952, Roland Wilson of the Australian Treasury gave a brief outline of postwar development policy. He admitted that several mistakes had been made, and indicated that the government had recently taken steps to restrict demand and curtail unnecessary investment. He added that if reductions in imports proved unavoidable they should be applied to the Sterling Area and other soft currency countries as well as the dollar area.[60]

In his opening statement to the conference, Sir Arthur Fadden lamented the lack of direction in Sterling Area policy. Sterling had lurched from crisis to crisis since the war, leading to regular bouts of emergency action to curtail dollar imports. However, drastic import cuts hindered the development programmes of member countries. Australia needed to attract American capital, but the US investor often doubted whether dollars would be available to 'pay his interest and redeem his loan'.[61] Fadden believed that the Sterling Area should set convertibility as its goal. This would make it easier to borrow capital for the development of the dollar-saving and dollar-earning capacity of member countries. Through development the Sterling Area would gain the strength needed for a successful convertibility operation. As Fadden reported to cabinet after the conference:

> Unless we and other countries in the sterling area can develop our resources and expand our earning power there can be no hope of breaking through the net-work [*sic*] that has enmeshed us since the war, and we must resign ourselves to living indefinitely within a largely closed system which appears to become more narrowly constricted with each successive crisis.[62]

These suggestions gained widespread support at the conference. A working party of officials drawn from the various Commonwealth countries was established to consider how to achieve progress on the development front. Each country agreed to draw up a development plan for consideration at the Commonwealth Economic Conference (CEC) later in the year.

In May 1952, in preparation for talks with Menzies, the British dissected Australia's development policy. Official British views pointed strongly, but not unambiguously, to the conclusion that Australia should place greater emphasis on primary production. According to the Board of Trade:[63]

> From the United Kingdom point of view, we wish to see Australian development concentrate considerably more than hitherto on expanding agricultural production, not merely to keep pace with, but to outpace the increasing domestic food consumption of the rapidly rising local population, in order to make more meat, wheat, butter and cheese available for the United Kingdom.

The Board of Trade criticized the Coalition's earlier 'populate or perish' mentality that had led to bottle-necks and the misallocation of resources. By 1952, however, the Board of Trade believed that Australian views had changed. Australia had not only, in the words of Richard Casey, 'bitten off more than she could chew'. 'She had also,' believed the Board of Trade, 'bitten off more than she could pay for.' Fortunately, Menzies now acknowledged the need to de-emphasize uneconomical secondary industry, and John McEwen, the Minister for Commerce and Agriculture, had announced a new emphasis on agricultural development. The British intended to encourage this trend.[64]

Cabinet endorsed the approach of the Board of Trade, but not everyone was enthusiastic. The Commonwealth Relations Office suspected that 'much more harm than good is likely to come from the UK saying to Australia that the right policy for her is to get back to the cowshed.' Furthermore, 'the proposition that Australia should now direct her energies away from secondary industries back to primary production is by no means self-evident.' Not only were defence considerations important, but the instability of the primary sector militated against concentrating too heavily on this sector.[65]

Whitehall feared that Australia would use the Menzies visit to ask for a loan, or credits, to the extent of £100 million sterling to spend on British goods. Menzies had written to the new Chancellor, R.A. Butler in April, enquiring about the possibility of an emergency sterling loan or credit, which could supplement a further application to the World Bank. It seems that the Australians had in mind the purchase of capital equipment, consumer goods, and armaments in Britain. Menzies also indicated that Australia and Britain should consider a joint approach to the USA to obtain dollar capital for investment. While the Board of Trade and the Ministry of Defence could see merit in an Australian credit, Treasury was frankly hostile. The Australians, it was suggested, had brought their problems on themselves through reckless expansion.

Britain's resources were limited, and the announcement of special treatment for Australia would cause resentment in other countries such as India and Pakistan.[66] The British were so discouraging that Menzies did not raise the issue of a sterling credit during his visit to London. Britain's attitude towards the provision of official loans and credits to Australia contrasted with its generous treatment of New Zealand which was not a member of the World Bank, and was almost totally reliant on the London market for official overseas loans.

Australia was already taking steps to obtain more dollar capital for its official development programme. A new US$50 million loan was approved by the World Bank in July 1952. Agriculture and land settlement would absorb US$17 million. Coal mining, iron and steel, electric power, railways, road transport, non-ferrous metals, and industrial minerals together would take up US$24 million, leaving just US$9 million for 'industrial development'. Commenting on the application for this loan, World Bank officials expressed satisfaction that the Australians now seemed to understand that a high rate of investment in the primary sector was essential to feed the growing population and to boost export earnings.[67]

The crisis of 1951–2 increased Australian anxiety to attract private investment from the USA, but relatively little was forthcoming. Treasury officials concluded that Australia's needs were simply not compatible with the interests of American investors. Very few small investors had ever placed their funds in Australia, and the scope for large corporations to establish operations was limited by the desire of Australian officials to channel all investment, foreign or domestic, into selected areas.[68] The Australians sought US investment in basic industries, but it is conceivable that the Americans were more interested in ice cream works. In addition, because of the healthy US economy, many American investors preferred to keep their money at home. In the early 1950s only 3 per cent of American new investment went abroad in contrast to 4 per cent in the 1920s. Australia was but one of many possible destinations for US foreign investment, and a small one at that.[69]

At the CEC, held in London in November–December 1952, the drive for convertibility received further impetus. The importance of complementary development in the British Commonwealth was reaffirmed, and it was explicitly recognised that investment from dollar sources would be required if development were to proceed. Although the British formally convened the CEC, the original suggestion came from Menzies, among whose concerns was the achievement of greater cooperation over economic development. British views on the purpose of economic development had changed little. 'Development to aid the balance of payments of the Sterling Area will involve an expansion both of the manufacturing capacity of the United Kingdom and of the production of primary products in the rest of the Sterling Area.' However, a broader approach was now taken to development finance. Capital should be sought from private sources in the USA as well as from the Export–Import Bank and the World Bank. As these were unlikely to be sufficient to meet the development needs of the Commonwealth, Britain would itself have to invest up to £250 million sterling a year, as well as deliver more capital goods.[70]

Concerning their own development, the Australians indicated that 'apart from the possibilities in food and other agricultural production, basic metals and iron and steel, no individual products are likely to make a substantial contribution to the sterling area balance of payments problem in the short-term.'[71] Additional manufacturing development would be conducted on a more selective basis than previously. For instance, plans for expansion in the production of earth-moving equipment, agricultural implements, drugs, and pulp and paper had been cut back or postponed. The Australians recognized that the 'most important single aspect of current development . . . is the emphasis on increased production of food and certain other farm products.'[72] Much would depend on the capacity of the British engineering industry to supply capital goods at a faster rate. Australian officials noted that investment from overseas was needed and called for further attempts to attract funds from the USA.[73] The Australians were not helped by the fumbling performance of Menzies. In one ministerial session at the CEC, the Prime Minister wondered aloud: 'Might not the need for capital from the United States have been exaggerated?'[74]

While the Australians had no intention of reverting to a prewar model of complementary imperial development, they were increasingly aware that it was not in their interests to neglect the agricultural sector which accounted for 85 per cent of export revenue. Australia could not avoid a serious balance of payments crisis in 1951–2 despite the rapid expansion of import substitution industries during the 1940s. As matters stood, it appeared to Coombs that the external accounts would remain weak, necessitating tight import controls, except during wool price booms. Industrialization could no longer be regarded as a panacea for the nation's economic difficulties. Higher exports were needed to safeguard the balance of payments, and these were most likely to come from the rural sector.[75] In view of the growth in population, the agricultural export surplus would decline unless further resources were devoted to farming. Australian officials announced at the preliminary meetings of the CEC that the Coalition had already taken steps to stimulate the expansion of agricultural production. Priority was being given to the immigration of people with agricultural skills, more equipment was being allocated to farmers, and the needs of agriculture were receiving greater emphasis in public works programmes. Moreover, farmers had been granted favourable treatment as regards depreciation allowances, and the controlled prices of certain foodstuffs for domestic consumption had been increased. As Secretary of the Department of Commerce and Agriculture, John Crawford played a key role in formulating the new policy and setting output targets for agricultural commodities. In October, J.F. Nimmo, a member of the Australian official delegation to the preliminary conference, stated that he thought that a reversal had already occurred in the sectoral distribution of investment.[76] This was pleasing news to British ears, although it did not fully compensate them for the imposition of import controls on Sterling Area products earlier in the year. Australia's short-term policy for managing the balance of payments, namely import controls, was at odds with its new long-term policy for strengthening the external accounts.

The combined development strategy agreed to at London had a far from revolutionary impact. Nevertheless, individual Commonwealth countries, including Australia, pressed on with their own development programmes. At the Commonwealth Finance Ministers' Conference at Sydney in 1954, Senator Spooner reiterated Australia's commitment to developing the primary sector. Spooner maintained that Australia could best contribute to the export earnings of the Sterling Area as a whole by supplying more meat, rice, tobacco, wheat, copper, zinc, and fertilizers to world markets.[77] Development had come to assume its more recent meaning by the time of the Commonwealth Trade and Economic Conference in 1958. Rather than worrying about overinvestment in secondary industry on the part of the older dominions, Britain was now more concerned with the performance of the economies of its former colonies in Asia and Africa.[78] Australia raised further development loans from the World Bank in 1954 (US$54 million), 1955 (US$54.5 million), 1957 (US$50 million), and 1962 (US$100 million) for the purchase of development equipment, and US$9.2 million in 1957 for airliners. In the period to 1965 Australia was the third largest borrower from the World Bank. Meanwhile, Australia actually paid off a portion of its official sterling debt, which fell from £385 million sterling in 1950 to £331 million sterling in 1958. New official borrowing on the London market was avoided until late 1958.[79] Even without borrowing in London, Australia could draw upon its sterling balances when dollars were needed.

In line with the spirit of Commonwealth declarations, Australian policy from the mid 1950s also strongly favoured FDI. For example, in 1955 the Minister for National Development announced the extension of the US Contact Clearing House Service to Australia. According to the Minister, 'By bringing opportunities for overseas investment in local private enterprises to the notice of American firms, this service will be a valuable aid in encouraging the investment of US overseas capital in this country. Australia needs these additional funds if we are to continue to maintain a high level of development of our industries.'[80] The Federal Treasurer, Harold Holt, strongly supported FDI in later years. He declared in 1959 that 'the Commonwealth Government welcomes overseas investment in this country . . . we suggest it would be in the longer term interests of all concerned for overseas capital to join Australian capital in partnership for the development of our resources and productive capacity.'[81]

Although Australia sought both official and private capital inflows during the 1950s, it must be stressed that the great bulk of investment was financed locally. Taxation funded about 75 per cent of expenditure on public works in Australia. Borrowing on the local market accounted for almost 25 per cent of public works expenditure. Overseas sources financed less than 1.5 per cent. The most dramatic public development scheme of this era was the Snowy Mountains project, which was designed to provide peak load hydro-electricity to Victoria and New South Wales, as well as to irrigate vast tracts of land. Work on the Snowy Mountains scheme began in the late 1940s. By the time that the first major (Upper Tumut) section was completed in 1962, almost A£200 million had been spent, and it was estimated that the entire project would cost more than A£400 million. These sums were very large indeed. During the 1950s the cost of construction work on the Snowy was in excess of Australia's cumulative borrowing from the World Bank. There was much public criticism of the slipshod way in which major investment decisions were taken in the public sector, not least in the case of the Snowy. The main justification used to steer this project through Parliament was defence, and according to Condliffe there was little consideration of its technical or economic aspects. But even if better methods of investment appraisal had been used it is doubtful whether they would have generated a reliable conclusion, since the relevant figures were certain to change over the lengthy gestation period. The Snowy project did produce cheap electricity.[82] And, as in the case of the Murupara pulp and paper scheme in New Zealand, the Snowy was probably of greater economic merit than an additional round of investment in sheltered manufacturing would have been.

Australia sought official development capital in the 1950s and 1960s because it was short of overseas exchange to purchase items, including many types of industrial machinery, that were not produced at home, rather than because it was unable to generate adequate savings domestically. The purpose of borrowing from the World Bank was to overcome strategic bottle-necks. The switch in the focus of Australia's development policies, which was announced in 1952, was genuine. Merrett has shown that the share of manufacturing industry in total private investment declined from about 65 per cent in the early 1950s to about 50 per cent by the end of the decade, and continued to fall during the 1960s. Investment in agriculture picked up: the capital stock in this sector grew at an annual rate of over 8 per cent between 1951–2 and 1957–8.[83] There were impressive increases in the numbers of tractors and other farm machines. The total area of farm holdings rose from 940 million acres in 1952–3 to 1,143 million acres in 1957–8. Due to adverse climatic conditions, export volumes of some commodities, such as wheat and lamb, did not rise as fast as had been expected in 1952.[84] The really disappointing feature of the primary production drive of the 1950s was that it occurred against a backdrop of falling terms of trade. Export returns were far from satisfactory, but this could not have been foreseen in 1952. Another, and ultimately more rewarding, sphere was minerals. After the government relaxed and then removed its embargo on iron ore exports, in 1960–2, ore mining developed rapidly, often in conjunction with overseas investors.[85]

The decision to apply more capital to infrastructure and the primary sector did not mean that industrial protection was to be phased out. It was rather a matter of adjusting the balance between the export-oriented and import-substitution sectors. Until the late 1950s a large majority of official and academic economists contended that it was necessary to protect secondary industry for employment and strategic reasons. They argued that the welfare losses from protection were minimal because protection underwrote high industrial wages and consumption standards. But agreement was never complete. One of the dissenters was the young Max Corden, who suggested in the mid-1950s that welfare would be compromised by the strategy of protectionism and rapid population growth.[86]

As it became apparent later in the decade that Australia's economic performance was lacklustre by international standards, faith in the local orthodoxy began to wane. Economic growth in Australia was debated by leading economists at a summer school in 1962. The most interesting paper, by Colin Clark, who was now at Oxford University, was by turns perceptive and eccentric. Clark indicated that protection had distorted the shape of the industrial sector. Australia had the potential to gain competitive advantage in capital- and skill-based industries such as metals, cement, chemicals, and engineering. However, due to the protection of labour-intensive trades such as textiles, the former industries had been denied adequate capital and other inputs. Reductions in tariffs, he concluded, would encourage greater specialization and improved performance. Clark regarded increased investment in education as a further prerequisite for long-term prosperity. He also attacked certain rent-seekers in the farming sector, especially the Queensland sugar producers, who benefited from generous subsidies and guaranteed prices in the British market, and condemned the waste of resources on what he alleged were unnecessary irrigation schemes. Nevertheless, Clark thought that agriculture still offered the best prospects for export growth, since in Australia value added per worker was higher in agriculture than in industry. There were great opportunities for meat exports, especially to the USA, while coal and mineral exports were also capable of expansion. John Crawford was sceptical about Clark's findings. He was understandably dubious about Clark's portrayal of meat as the saviour of the balance of payments. If the terms of trade continued to fall, argued Crawford, there would be a growing need for import replacement. As for eliminating inefficient industries, Crawford wondered how these were to be identified.[87] In other words, it would be too risky to implement a radical change in strategy. Crawford later stated that postwar external economic policies 'had not hampered' growth.[88] Of course, Crawford was not an arch-protectionist, but a representative of the Australian mainstream of the 1940s and 1950s.[89] To the credit of the industrializers, manufacturing exports grew rapidly during the 1960s, and this sector's share of total exports rose from 12 per cent in 1960 to 26 per cent in 1970 (see Table 1.5 above). Thus at least some Australian industries were internationally competitive.

The 1960s were years of growing dissension about economic policy in Australia. The official Vernon Report of 1965, over which Crawford had considerable influence, assumed that the existing balanced growth strategy, which was skewed in favour of manufacturing and against farming, would continue to prevail. This report was pessimistic about the balance of payments, principally because it underestimated the impact of minerals. It also suggested that long-term capital inflows should not be permitted to grow beyond the levels of recent years, lest servicing requirements become unreasonable and foreign ownership of Australian industry rise to an unpalatable extent.[90] John McEwen, the Deputy Prime Minister, shared the Committee's concerns:[91]

> [T]*here is just not enough development capital in Australia for the rate of growth we want so we have to import it.* But in the past we have imported it without regard to what it costs us as a nation. . . . we have somehow allowed it to command a degree of ownership and control of our industries which is unnecessary and I believe avoidable.

However, the Vernon Report was condemned by the Treasury and lambasted by the government. The Treasurer, Holt, complained that the Committee's recommendations, which allegedly went beyond its terms of reference, were based on faulty logic.[92] In the increasingly nationalistic climate of the late 1960s and early 1970s, regulations were brought in to ensure that potential foreign investors acted in the 'public interest', although this did not prevent the growth of FDI in Australia, of which Japanese interests provided an increasing amount.[93]

Whitwell suggests that in the 1960s the Treasury started to lessen the emphasis on growth as the ultimate economic objective, and to increase the emphasis on allocative efficiency. In a sense this neatly side-stepped the perennial debate about whether agricultural or industrial development was the ultimate source of national prosperity. The implication was that the government should concentrate on microeconomic reforms, such as reducing tariffs. Market forces would be left to determine the distribution of resources between the various sectors of the economy. It was not until later, though, that this philosophy was installed as the new orthodoxy.[94]

Conclusion

Australia's economic development policy remained substantially intact for at least a quarter of a century after the war. Far from endorsing economic complementarity, successive government were always concerned to reduce the dependence on trade in primary products that had proved so disruptive in the past, and to strengthen the manufacturing sector in order to improve the nation's defence capabilities and provide jobs for a greatly increased population.

To a large extent, the internal development policies of both the Chifley and Menzies Governments were intelligent responses to opportunities as they arose.

Chifley was certainly distrustful of the USA and its motives. In addition to passing up chances for American foreign investment and loans, he was bitter about the terms that the Americans imposed on the British in return for the postwar loan. A primary reason for Australia's support for the Sterling Area after 1945 was the pragmatic knowledge that access to the dollar pool allowed Australia to pursue its development objectives by spending more dollars than it earned. Although they viewed Australia's needs from a more cosmopolitan standpoint than Chifley did, Menzies, Fadden and McEwen were similarly pro-British in many of their policies, including their desire to participate in a concerted drive to develop the productive potential of the British Commonwealth. However, changes in the international political situation increased Australia's bargaining power in Washington shortly before the Coalition came to power at the end of 1949. The Communist victory in China in 1949 increased Australia's regional significance. Washington's blessing was then reinforced by the prompt commitment of Australian ground forces to Korea in mid-1950. This allowed Menzies and Fadden to take the intelligent course of drawing both on Britain, through the Sterling Area, and on the USA and international institutions for aid for Australia's development needs. Their subsequent attempts to reform the Sterling Area were intended to allow Australia to continue to draw on multiple sources of support. The emphasis placed on primary sector development, starting in 1952, was less a fundamental change of direction, than a response to the belief that the neglect of farming had gone too far under Labor.

The development programme was a constant in Australian policy from 1945 onwards. Although at times it was necessary to trim the programme severely because of balance-of-payments or other constraints, neither the Labor nor the Coalition Government wavered in its belief that large-scale migration and industrialization were desirable. Their policies varied according to the conditions of the moment, but both governments acted to support Australian interests, as they perceived them, rather than the interests of Britain, the wider Commonwealth or the USA. To critics who say that Australia's policies led to economic distortions and a lower level of welfare than would have been achieved under laissez-faire, it would be legitimate to reply that policy-makers were not unaware of this problem. They believed that Australia's strength as a nation depended on population growth, the development of a balanced range of industries, and full employment, and were prepared to accept a modest reduction in potential living standards to achieve this goal.

4
Development Policy in New Zealand

> It had formerly been assumed that the Southern Hemisphere countries were, and should remain, primary producing countries only. That idea was now obsolete. On a basis of primary production only, it would have been impossible for New Zealand to maintain her population. . . . In future, therefore, there must . . . be a parallel development in industry and agriculture, and in this respect her position was very similar to that of other Commonwealth countries.
>
> *Peter Fraser, Prime Minister of New Zealand,*
> *Commonwealth Prime Ministers' Conference, 1948*[1]

Rapid economic development was not accorded as high a priority in New Zealand as it was in Australia. Comparative isolation from predators limited the need for New Zealand to seek a large increase in population. Since most white New Zealanders already enjoyed an enviable standard of living, governments emphasized stability rather than further intensive growth. Both Labour and National were chary of resorting to overseas capital markets to fund development projects in the late 1940s. During the 1950s, however, New Zealand became a net capital importer for the first time since the 1880s.[2] The taboo on overseas borrowing was relaxed because governments showed even greater reluctance to squeeze domestic consumption in support of large-scale projects. At the same time, significant amounts of private FDI were drawn into New Zealand by the import licensing system.

Between 1955 and 1970 total investment as a ratio of GDP in New Zealand remained within the range of 22 to 28 per cent, which was respectable by international standards. Inflows of British capital averaged 4 per cent of gross domestic fixed capital formation between 1949 and 1957.[3] Essentially, overseas capital supplemented domestic savings. According to the Monetary and Economic Council, the problem for New Zealand in the early 1960s was poor investment allocation rather than an overall shortage of capital. Lavish investment in housing and other population-related infrastructure apparently crowded out investment in productive activities.[4] Industrial protection also hindered the efficient allocation of capital by encouraging the growth of uncompetitive firms.

This chapter examines New Zealand's rather ambivalent development policies. Having rejected Bretton Woods in the 1940s, the New Zealand government became heavily reliant on the London capital market in the 1950s. We consider the basis of economic development policy in the 1940s, the impact of the Murupara pulp and paper scheme, New Zealand's involvement in Commonwealth development planning, the rise of official overseas borrowing in the 1950s, Labour's industrial policies in the late 1950s, and attitudes towards private foreign investment.

Stability and development in the forties

After the experiences of the 1930s, New Zealand policy-makers of the 1940s believed that economic stability should be their principal objective. They recognized that a gradual increase in output would be required to support the rising population, but attached little importance to achieving intensive growth.[5]

In the 1980s, Colin Clark, perhaps in teasing, claimed to discern a powerful physiocratic strain in New Zealand economic thought. Between the wars the mainstream view, as advanced by Horace Belshaw of Auckland University College, was that in accordance with comparative advantage New Zealand's prosperity would continue to depend on the expansion of pastoral exports. In the 1940s, Colin Clark predicted a bright future for New Zealand and other primary exporters, anticipating that rapid industrialization and population growth in Europe and Asia would generate a strong demand for commodities. Keynes also believed that after the war the terms of trade would favour primary producers.[6]

However, the 1930s had spawned an alternative vision of New Zealand's destiny. Professor Allan Fisher of Otago argued that New Zealand was overcommitted to a few rural staples, and recommended a large dose of diversification. Foreseeing that world demand for primary products would grow more slowly than demand for industrial products and services, Fisher concluded that the state should prod capital into the production of sophisticated manufactures and services. Fisher was a friend of finance minister Walter Nash, and may have had some influence over government thinking from the late 1930s. Nash's economic adviser, W.B. Sutch, and several left-wing MPs hoped that the import controls introduced in 1938–9 would be used to encourage industrialization, although their immediate justification was the serious fall in overseas reserves.[7]

The Second World War and its aftermath created a congenial environment for manufacturers. Domestic firms made substitutes for imports that were temporarily unobtainable due shipping shortages.[8] Ministers were reluctant to see these businesses, which provided many jobs, collapse after the war. In 1946, New Zealand warned the US government that while new opportunities might eventually arise for agricultural exporters, as a result of trade liberalization and rising world incomes, the medium-term prospects for this sector were uncertain. Consequently, New Zealand would continue to protect its manufacturers in order to guarantee full employment and develop a more balanced economy.[9] As a Treasury memorandum of 1946 put it:

> Small in size, and mainly a food-producing country, exposed as no other nation on earth to the vagaries of international trade, [New Zealand] . . . has in recent years been nourishing her thinly scattered but growing population more and more by her manufacturing industries . . . Should her population continue to increase toward a size consonant with her expanse, her climate, and her resources, New Zealand will in time become the home of a great producing nation – compact, but endowed by nature with the essential elements of a highly productive economy. But should her present infant and small-scale manufacturing industries be devastated at this juncture by large-scale high-powered competition from abroad, New Zealand could look forward only to a servile and risky future, unsuited to population growth in spite of her open spaces, her bracing climate, and her untapped resources, and utterly dependent on a one-sided economy exposed nakedly to the periodic humiliation of every depression engendered elsewhere in the world.[10]

Extensive growth, driven by the need to provide jobs for the rising population, was a more urgent priority than intensive growth. It was anticipated that natural increase, coupled with agricultural mechanization, would lead to further urbanization. Since sprawling cities were deemed socially undesirable, a range of industrial jobs would have to be provided in smaller centres, even though this would preclude the attainment of economies of scale. New Zealand would still have to import some manufactures, but imports would not be allowed to destroy domestic jobs. Moreover, their level would be regulated in accordance with fluctuations in pastoral export earnings. A gradual retreat towards industrial self-sufficiency could not be ruled out if substitutes like margarine and synthetic fibres undermined the markets for traditional exports.[11] Agriculture would not be neglected, especially as Britain faced a serious food shortage, but it would attract fewer resources than before the war.

Britain had strong misgivings about the expansion of the manufacturing sector. James Meade, a future Nobel laureate, suggested that insulationism was an elaborate excuse for protecting New Zealand firms.[12] Under the Ottawa Agreement, New Zealand was supposed to protect only those industries that were likely to reach international standards of efficiency. In 1939, Nash had promised the British that import controls would not be used for protective purposes. But, in 1944, Bernard Ashwin, the Secretary to the New Zealand Treasury, informed a Bank of England representative that he favoured the use of selective import controls to encourage industrialization.[13] The British High Commission complained of New Zealand's delinquencies to London:

> By an order gazetted on January 30th [1947] the importation of undecorated cups and saucers, unless part of a complete dinner- or tea-set is prohibited. Object is protection of infant secondary industries. According to a press report, present wholesale cost of plain English cups and saucers is 14/1d a dozen; wholesale price of New Zealand-made cups and saucers will be approximately 21/- a dozen.[14]

In January 1945, London extracted an undertaking from Wellington that British firms would be invited to participate in any industrial developments. New Zealand also agreed to compensate Britain for any decline in consumer goods orders by placing large orders for capital goods. The British envisaged a new complementary relationship in which knowledge intensive and capital-intensive products were exchanged for primary commodities, while trade in consumer goods became less important.[15]

Martin stresses that neither Labour between 1945 and 1949, nor National between 1949 and 1957, had a coherent plan for the manufacturing sector. Manufacturing grew in a haphazard fashion behind a battery of import controls, the primary purpose of which was to insulate employment from external shocks.[16] This approach did not escape criticism. As early as 1939, J.B. Condliffe, a New Zealand economist at the League of Nations, warned that import controls would foster industrial inefficiency, saddle farmers with higher costs, and hinder improvements in living standards. In 1946, the Department of Agriculture indicated that the unrestrained expansion of manufacturing would deprive the pastoral sector of crucial inputs. This department anticipated a bright future for staple exports, and maintained that farming would provide sufficient work for the growing population for several decades. Condliffe returned to the attack in 1957, denouncing Labour for having cut against the grain of New Zealand's comparative advantage during the 1940s.[17] However, Labour's success in preserving full employment deflected most criticism.

Economic development policy was overseen by the Organization for National Development. Labour's plans were modest in 1945, and ministers hoped to finance them from savings, export receipts, and the sterling balances. New official overseas borrowing was considered out of the question. Service charges on official overseas debt had absorbed 25 per cent of national export earnings following the collapse in commodity prices in 1932, and ministers were determined to avoid any repetition of this crisis. New Zealand actually repaid some official sterling debt in the late 1940s, and Labour rebuffed a tentative offer of development capital from the British Overseas Food Corporation.[18]

Labour's lukewarm attitude to immigration was consistent with its overall stance on development. The issue in 1945 was whether to reintroduce assisted, or subsidized, immigration from Britain. (Self-financing, white British subjects were free to move to New Zealand.) Ministers wished to regulate assisted immigration in accordance with the state of the labour market. Once it became clear, in 1947, that there was no immediate threat of unemployment, assisted British immigration was resumed. New Zealand agreed to admit some displaced persons from Europe, but as yet there was no question of looking beyond the British Isles for large numbers of immigrants.[19] In 1949, Alister McIntosh, the Secretary of External Affairs, noted that the trade unions resented even British immigrants, and that as for 'foreigners or refugees, there is far too strong a prejudice'.[20]

In 1948, Britain urged its Commonwealth partners to submit development plans for inclusion in the Sterling Area's Long-term Programme for the expansion of dollar-saving and dollar-earning activities. The goal of this programme was to eliminate the dollar gap by 1952, the final year of US aid. New Zealand offered to expand the pastoral sector, develop the forest products industry, and increase hydro-electricity capacity, possibly in conjunction with an aluminium plant. But Wellington made it plain that little progress could be expected before 1952, due to shortages of labour and essential imports, including electricity generating equipment, tractors, steel and fencing wire. New Zealand complained that Britain sometimes gave priority to foreign buyers of these products in order to cement bilateral trade deals. Fraser protested to the Commonwealth Secretary, Lord Addison, about the preferential treatment given to Argentina in the allocation of producer goods. He warned that New Zealand would not be able to expand food production in line with expectations unless it could obtain adequate supplies of investment goods.[21] To be fair, however, some shortages reflected the hothouse development of manufacturing. Arnold Nordmeyer, the Minister of Industries and Commerce, admitted to a British official that excessive investment in the manufacturing sector was exacerbating shortages of labour and materials, and fuelling inflationary pressure.[22]

The British concluded that New Zealand's commitment to Sterling Area development was half-hearted. Leicester Webb, the Director of Stabilization, did nothing to dispel this suspicion, telling Eric Roll, of the British Central Economic Planning Staff, that the bulk of New Zealand's 'future development was going to be cultural rather than economic'.[23]

The Murupara pulp and paper scheme

During the late 1940s the New Zealand government stumbled into granting approval to the Murupara pulp and paper scheme. This large project could not have been funded without overseas borrowing. Murupara was in some respects a prestige development, though it did have the merit of being export-oriented. The authorities in London and Wellington argued that Murupara would augment the dollar-saving capacity of the Sterling Area by displacing Canadian imports from Australasia.[24]

Large tracts of radiata pine, which had been planted between the wars in the Kaingaroa forest, were ready for harvesting by the 1940s. The director of the State Forestry Service, Alex Entrican, was keen to enhance his department's role in national development. Walmsleys, a Lancashire paper machinery producer, was commissioned to report on the feasibility of building a pulp and paper mill in the vicinity. Walmsleys reported in favour of a mill, which it said would generate 700 jobs, but Treasury doubted Walmsleys' costings, and questioned the project's viability in view of North American competition and the poor quality of the wood. Nevertheless, in 1949, the Labour cabinet in principle endorsed the Murupara scheme.[25]

Entrican lobbied for Murupara on nationalistic grounds, and did not regard profitability as of paramount importance. He stated that Murupara would establish New Zealand's claim to the status of a modern industrial nation. 'Grave as the disadvantages appear under which such a plant must operate in New Zealand, they should be regarded not as insurmountable obstacles but as a challenge.'[26] Ministers did not accept this rhetoric at face value. However, the scheme did appear to offer significant benefits. Experts were predicting a world shortage of newsprint during the 1950s. As Murupara was expected to improve the balance of payments of New Zealand (and the Sterling Area) by up to C$20 million per annum, it was strongly supported by Britain. Prospects for exports to Australia were good, especially while dollar discrimination remained in force. On the other hand, Treasury wondered whether New Zealand could afford Murupara at a time of suppressed inflation. In August 1949, Ashwin told Nash that the 'present capital programme is much in excess of available capital resources and therefore inflationary, and it is clear that this large project in addition to . . . other large works cannot be financed from internal savings.'[27] The same message was given to the incoming National Prime Minister, Sid Holland, in December 1949. Large cuts were needed in public sector capital works in order to combat inflation; NZ£15.7 million, or one-third of the economies required, could be saved by either abandoning or delaying Murupara.[28] After lengthy deliberation, however, the National cabinet agreed in 1951 to proceed with Murupara. Cancellation of this prestigious development would have been embarrassing. The economic implications of Murupara remained murky, but at least it made more sense to allocate resources to an export-oriented project than to squander them on small-scale import substitution.

The issue of whether Murupara would be state-owned or a joint venture with the private sector was hotly debated. Entrican assumed that the forest products industry fell within the natural sphere of the public sector, whereas Ashwin argued that the private sector should subscribe half of the mill's capital. Even Ashwin acknowledged that the government would have to provide supporting infrastructure including railways, roads, power, and housing. In the event, National resolved to build and operate Murupara as a joint venture, in accordance with the 'colonial socialist' tradition, which stretched back to the railway boom of the 1870s, whereby large developments were mounted on a co-operative basis by the public and private sectors.[29]

Murupara dwarfed previous development projects. The total sum invested in this scheme was NZ£32.3 million, including NZ£13.8 million on infrastructure, which far exceeded initial projections. Tasman Pulp and Paper, the joint company established to run this complex, was granted a monopoly of newsprint production until 1960 under the 1936 Industrial Efficiency Act. Only one local business, Fletchers,[30] a building firm that had worked closely with the government in the state housing drive of the late 1930s, showed any interest in operating the mill. Fletchers offered to purchase NZ£700,000 of equity in Tasman, and suggested that credit for the purchase of American capital goods might be obtained through the US government's Export–Import (Ex–Im) Bank. Cabinet agreed to cooperate with Fletchers in December 1951. The associated construction contract was awarded to a consortium of Fletchers and the American firms, Raymond Pile, and Merritt Chapman Scott. However, officials doubted Fletchers' financial and technical ability to manage Tasman, and urged it to find an experienced overseas partner. The insistence of both Fletchers and the government that managerial control remain in local hands deterred some potential multinational collaborators, but a British paper manufacturer, Reeds, eventually agreed to provide capital and expertise on acceptable terms.[31]

The New Zealand government subscribed equity to Tasman, supplied it with advances, and accepted responsibility for associated public works. Treasury advised ministers to seek loan capital abroad in order to reduce the immediate burden on the domestic economy. Ashwin and other officials urged the government to join the IMF and apply for a World Bank loan, but public opinion was not ready for this step. E.C. Fussell, the Governor of the RBNZ, was sent to London to request permission to borrow £10 million sterling on the London capital market. Official sanction was required for such an operation because of the weakness of sterling. Fussell stated that New Zealand would prefer to borrow in London rather than in New York, and indicated that orders might be placed for British as well as American capital goods. Some British officials felt that Fussell was trying to jump the queue for loans, and recommended rejection, with a view to forcing New Zealand to ratify Bretton Woods.[32] But Cameron Cobbold, the Governor of the Bank of England, gave solid support to Murupara, which he viewed as 'an obvious dollar saver'.[33] In November 1952, New Zealand was granted permission to borrow £10 million sterling, and this bond issue was placed on the London market 1953. Britain and Walmsleys were rewarded with an order for newsprint machinery. Tasman also obtained debenture and equity capital from the Commonwealth Development Finance Corporation (CDFC), a semi-official organization set up to channel City money into worthy development schemes.[34]

The last element in the financial package was the Ex–Im Bank, which was regarded as a substitute for the World Bank. Although Ashwin approached the Ex–Im Bank in 1952, New Zealand was left in suspense for many months due to wrangling inside the new Eisenhower administration. George Humphrey, the Secretary of the US Treasury, opposed using public funds on Murupara, arguing that New Zealand should be made to join the World Bank. But other ministers feared that New Zealand would either disrupt or leave GATT unless its financial needs were met. Feelings were already running high in Australia and New Zealand over GATT's failure to restrain US agricultural policy. Washington eventually gave the New Zealand government permission to raise US$16 million in New York with the assistance of an Ex–Im Bank guarantee. This loan was spent in the USA and Canada on equipment for Tasman, and related public works. The Americans stressed that New Zealand could expect no further assistance from this source.[35]

Newsprint production commenced in 1955. The capital cost of the public and private works at Murupara was equivalent to 3.5 per cent of New Zealand's GDP in 1954–5. In 1965, Tasman contributed 0.4 per cent of GDP, 50 per cent of manufacturing exports, and 45 per cent of all exports to Australia. Although the company experienced severe financial difficulties in the 1950s, its performance improved during the 1960s. Gould draws a parallel between Murupara and the 'Think Big' projects of the Muldoon era of the late 1970s and early 1980s. Extravagant expenditure on plant and machinery was not unusual in pulp and paper schemes in developing countries. Tasman's monopoly status precluded the emergence of less capital-intensive, and possibly more economical, mills, but it was a better proposition than the vast majority of manufacturing establishments in New Zealand in the 1950s. Moreover, Tasman was a sunk cost by 1956–7, and future performance was the only relevant consideration. Tasman was genuinely competitive in Australia, which admitted newsprint duty-free from all sources, and from 1955 without dollar discrimination. While Tasman faced higher input costs than Canadian firms, and suffered due to overvaluation of the New Zealand pound, lower transport costs and the acceptance of lower margins enabled it to match the Canadians on price.[36] Finally, Tasman was central to efforts to build a closer economic relationship between New Zealand and Australia.

Sterling Area development in the early 1950s

During the sterling crisis of 1951–2, Commonwealth countries, including New Zealand, urged Britain to give a higher priority to developing the dollar-saving and dollar-earning resources of the Commonwealth. According to New Zealand officials, the Sterling Area would gradually fall under the sway of the USA unless Britain resumed its traditional role as a generous lender.[37] Commonwealth members also felt that the prospects for the resumption of convertibility would be enhanced by a drive to develop the Sterling Area's productive potential.

Sid Holland was more enthusiastic about economic development than his socialist predecessor, Fraser, had been. Murupara had convinced National that overseas capital could be of service. In 1952, New Zealand supported an abortive Southern Rhodesian proposal to establish a Commonwealth Development Corporation (CDC) to raise funds in Britain, the USA, and Europe for development projects. Cobbold thought that the CDC might cooperate with the World Bank, and Holland hinted that it could provide New Zealand with a 'bridge' to eventual membership of the IMF and World Bank. Although most Commonwealth governments opposed the CDC on the grounds that it would undermine their sovereignty, Holland was prepared to take this risk. At the 1952 Commonwealth Economic Conference (CEC), however, the less ambitious CDFC was established, and Britain promised to make a 'special effort' to release capital for development projects likely to improve the balance of payments of the Sterling Area.[38]

New Zealand reported to the rest of the Commonwealth in 1952 and 1953 on its postwar economic achievements. About 80,000 acres of unimproved land had been developed each year. Between 1945 and 1953, the population of breeding ewes and beef cattle had risen by 10 per cent, and the number of cows in milk had grown by 15 per cent. But the expansion of farm output was more sluggish than in previous generations because New Zealand was running out of good unused land. Land would have to be exploited more intensively in future.[39]

The development plans of Commonwealth members were discussed at the 1952 CEC. Each country outlined its prospective contribution to Commonwealth development, and specified its requirements of imported materials, equipment, and capital. Wellington cautioned that national resources were fully committed, and that it would not be possible to embark on major new initiatives. Although Murupara would make a substantial impact in the medium term, 'the major contribution which New Zealand can make in the present difficulties is to press on with the development of her farm production.'[40] Greater supplies of British capital, materials, and machinery were needed, but on the whole 'the New Zealand farmer, with his relatively lower cost of production [was] today in a favourable position.'[41] The British were assured that National would subject domestic industry to a 'chiller wind' of external competition.[42]

British officials commented that 'the emphasis in the New Zealand paper on farm production is the right one'. They acknowledged that the success of this plan depended on access to fertilizers and machinery, but held Wellington partly to blame for any apparent capital shortage: 'given a less restricted interest rate . . . policy there might be some increase in the local funds available for investment.'[43] Nevertheless, the British promised to do their best to provide New Zealand with more capital goods and fertilizers. Supply conditions improved in 1953, due to lower defence orders and slacker consumer demand in Britain, but certain items including heavy crawler tractors and electricity generating equipment remained scarce. The British submission on development mentioned plans to increase domestic production of beef, lamb, and milk, ostensibly to 'assist the sterling area as a whole to make itself less dependent on non-sterling sources for supplies of basic food and feed-ingstuffs.'[44] Curiously, New Zealand officials expressed no alarm at these proposals, and, in 1953, Professors Belshaw and Simkin still maintained that rising world incomes would ensure favourable conditions for staple exports.[45]

National introduced assisted migration for Dutch people in 1950. Even so, the new government continued to regulate assisted migration in response to economic fluctuations. Belshaw, with some support from Treasury and the Department of Labour, argued that immigration might actually exacerbate New Zealand's economic problems. Immigrants had to be fed, clothed, housed, and equipped with imported machinery before they could add to production. In 1953, the Working Party on Economic Policy admitted that immigration was a burden in the short run, but added that overseas borrowing could alleviate the strain. Officials were uncertain about the long-term effects of immigration, although they speculated that immigration from continental Europe might make New Zealand more civilized. Rather optimistically, it was suggested that the spending power of immigrants might enable local manufacturers to achieve economies of scale. After weighing the evidence, the Working Party recommended no change in the level of assisted immigration. Total net immigration was only 0.82 per cent of New Zealand's population in 1953; due to improved economic conditions in Britain and the Netherlands it fell to 0.37 per cent in 1954, and remained at a low level during the mid-1950s.[46]

The early 1950s saw several changes in New Zealand's development strategy. Murupara was an impressive, if isolated, attempt to establish a new export industry. By 1952, the government was pressing Britain to release more capital for agricultural and infrastructural development in the Commonwealth. Holland's government stressed the need for more agricultural development in discussions with Britain, but it did not seriously intend to abandon the protected manufacturing sector. Although development was accorded a higher priority in the early 1950s than in the late 1940s, it continued to be subordinated to full employment.

Overseas borrowing, the City, and the IMF

Whereas Labour tended to regard the City of London as a den of thieves, the Holland ministry viewed the gentlemanly capitalists as wealthy benefactors. Both parties had recourse to the London market on a number of occasions during the 1950s. At first, the government borrowed in order to fund development schemes, but, as the balance of payments deteriorated, it also began to borrow to maintain current consumption. This change in direction tarnished New Zealand's reputation, and aggravated both the City and the British government. However, official overseas debt remained low by the standards of the 1980s.[47]

From Murupara onwards, Wellington elected to finance development projects by floating loans in London rather than by squeezing domestic consumption and encouraging savings. In 1953, the British High Commission in Wellington reported that:

> They [i.e. the ministers] do not appreciate that much of the needed capital ought, in the present state of New Zealand's prosperity, to be created from domestic savings ... Nor does the Government as a whole feel that there is any necessity to join the International Bank and Fund in order to acquire dollar capital. They prefer to lean more heavily on the United Kingdom for the capital they need to improve their primary production and consequently the sterling area's balance of payments with the non-sterling world, but also for their more general capital needs for social development.[48]

The British were inclined to be accommodating because they still had great expectations of New Zealand as an export market and a development prospect. In 1954, New Zealand was granted permission to raise £10 million sterling for the development of agriculture, transport, hydro-electricity, and forestry. But approval was not automatic, and Britain rejected an application to borrow £4.5 million sterling to build a bridge across Auckland Harbour, deeming it of no economic significance.[49]

New Zealand's motive for overseas borrowing began to change in 1955, when E.L. Greensmith, Ashwin's successor at the Treasury, asked Britain for permission to raise a £15 million sterling loan in 1956. Greensmith indicated that this sum was needed because the balance of payments was being undermined by domestic inflationary pressure. The unpalatable alternatives to further borrowing were either stricter import controls or deflation. Britain reluctantly sanctioned an operation to borrow £10 million, but the market refused to subscribe more than half of this sum.[50] In 1956, Greensmith made enquiries about another £10 million sterling loan, stating that without further help New Zealand would have to tighten controls over British and foreign imports. The British duly authorized New Zealand to approach the market for £10 million sterling in 1957–58.[51]

London found it troublesome to meet the Commonwealth's heavy demand for capital. New Zealand absorbed 12 per cent of Britain's capital exports to the Commonwealth in 1954–6, compared with Australia's 16 per cent, and was vulnerable to the accusation that it had crowded out underdeveloped countries. The British concluded that New Zealand should be encouraged to borrow in New York, even though this would result in orders for American rather than British exports. They advised Greensmith, who was already contemplating an operation in New York, to proceed should the 1957–8 London flotation flop.[52]

Prominent British officials were now of the opinion that the modernization of the British economy was more important than Sterling Area development. Sir Frank Lee, the Permanent Secretary to the Board of Trade, grumbled that:

> I think that we are clearly over investing abroad (particularly in the Commonwealth) and under-investing at home ... But what troubles me particularly – it was borne in me [*sic*] constantly in my recent visit to Australia and New Zealand – is the ingrained belief in so many Commonwealth countries that the UK *must* finance somehow or another the great part of what are thought to be their essential investment needs (usually on the basis of a very rapid rate of economic growth).[53]

The 'special effort' was forgotten, and interest rates were raised as a deterrent to overseas borrowers. New Zealand soon felt the effects of this change in policy. In 1957, James Scrimgeour, the government's London broker, stated that disinterest in New Zealand's issues would not abate until they were priced more competitively.[54]

The potential benefits of joining Bretton Woods increased as the London market turned against New Zealand. In 1956, the New Zealand Royal Commission on the monetary system reported in favour of membership of the IMF and World Bank. Greensmith told ministers that, in view of falling export prices and budgetary problems, New Zealand might need to borrow abroad £10 million sterling per annum. He added that the IMF and World Bank offered very competitive interest rates.[55] But ministers, fearing a domestic backlash, equivocated. E.P. Haslam of the Bank of England concluded that 'political crankiness, funny-money and Cabinet nerves' were keeping New Zealand out of the IMF and the IBRD.[56]

New Zealand's balance of payments deteriorated rapidly in 1957, as a fall in export prices intensified the weakness caused by excess domestic demand. National was reluctant to deflate, but Labour, which was returned to power late in the year, acknowledged the need to reduce demand. Labour also moved to tighten import controls, arguing that macroeconomic measures worked slowly. The RBNZ deplored the intensification of import restrictions, and advised ministers to consider seeking a new overseas loan and membership of the IMF.[57] Nash eventually consented to request another London loan, but did not forgo tight import controls. In February 1958, the government obtained permission from Britain to raise £20 million sterling to meet emergency and developmental requirements. British export markets would have been put in jeopardy by a rebuff. As expected, this latest bond issue was unpopular, and two-thirds had to be taken up by the underwriters.[58]

In April 1958, Greensmith advised Britain that he would probably need an additional £25 million sterling – £10 million for 10 to 12 years, and a short-term revolving credit of £15 million.[59] Maurice Parsons of the Bank of England advocated a curt refusal followed by 'frank speaking to the New Zealanders' about their duty to join the IMF. But the Treasury's Sir Denis Rickett indicated that ministers were inclined to be generous, in the light of impending Anglo-New Zealand trade negotiations, although 'this might be rather like paying blackmail, with a number of other blackmailers waiting to take their turn'.[60] Britain offered New Zealand a gold swap, and an Export Credit Guarantee Department

(ECGD) loan to finance purchases of British goods. The Midland Bank also made available a £10 million sterling credit. British officials claimed that New Zealand was now in danger of becoming a candidate for direct exchequer aid, along with Third World countries.[61]

Wellington was forced into the New York market in 1958–9 by rising investor resistance to its issues in London. A government bond issue worth NZ£3.6 million was floated in New York, while American banks provided a three-year loan of US$34.5 million and a one-year credit of US$11.5 million.[62] National revelled in Labour's submission to 'the terrible international financiers', gloating that the Minister of Finance, Arnold Nordmeyer, had gone to them 'with his hat in his hand, in fear and trembling'.[63]

New Zealand could have borrowed more cheaply from the IMF and the World Bank than from the private markets. The government's denial of Bretton Woods also lowered its credit rating. Allan Fisher, who now worked for the IMF, pressed Nash to apply for membership in 1958, but the Prime Minister hesitated.[64] Business leaders and farmers favoured joining the IMF, but nationalists, populists, and left-wing socialists remained hostile. However, in 1960, senior figures in both the Labour and National parties assured the IMF that New Zealand would accede to Bretton Woods after the forthcoming general election.[65] In April 1961, the new National government indicated that it was ready to commence membership negotiations. Ministers argued that membership would help to insulate the economy from crises similar to that of 1957–8. Negotiations were complicated by New Zealand's demand for a larger 'quota', determining borrowing rights, than it was strictly entitled to. The British cautioned Wellington to be satisfied with a quota of US$100 million, but the Americans and the Australians were anxious to secure New Zealand's accession on political grounds, and obtained approval for a quota of US$125 million. They feared that too much quibbling would provide an opening for the anti-IMF lobby in Wellington. New Zealand finally joined the IMF and World Bank in 1961.[66]

The government made use of the facilities provided by the IMF and the World Bank in the 1960s, and continued to borrow in London and New York. What had New Zealand lost by declining to ratify Bretton Woods until 1961? IMF membership would have been useful during New Zealand's recurrent balance of payments crises. Australia drew US$20 million from the IMF in 1949, US$30 million in 1952, and US$175 million in 1961. The Australians also obtained nearly US$320 million from the World Bank to finance development projects during the 1950s. As New Zealand was a smaller country, it might have borrowed one quarter of this amount, say US$80 million. The net increase in borrowing would have been less than US$80 million, since the Ex–Im Bank and the British would not have been as forthcoming if New Zealand had been a World Bank member.[67]

It is doubtful, however, whether New Zealand would have put World Bank capital to good use during the 1950s. Access to an additional source of external finance would have rendered the government even less willing to encourage domestic savings. World Bank capital would have acted as a substitute for domestic capital that was being drawn by the lack of import competition into the production of expensive junk. As for accepting emergency assistance from the IMF, New Zealand would not have tolerated external interference in its economic policies in the 1950s. Membership of the Bretton Woods institutions would not have been a panacea for New Zealand. It could have been beneficial as part of a wider package of reforms to encourage savings, competition, and the efficient allocation of resources, but movement in this direction was precluded for political reasons.

Industrialization in depth

Macroeconomic policy was tightened in Nordmeyer's 'Black Budget' in 1958, but Labour denied that there was anything chronically amiss with the strategy of insulationism. On the contrary, the government argued that a further round of import substitution was needed to strengthen the balance of payments. Sutch, who became Secretary of Industries and Commerce in 1958, now exerted considerable influence. In January 1958, this department produced a memorandum calling for further import substitution industrialization, as 'all indications' showed that it would be difficult to obtain adequate export revenue in the coming years. Furthermore, Industries and Commerce was keen to encourage manufacturers to progress beyond the assembly of imported kits. It was considered desirable that importation occur 'at a more primary stage' than hitherto. Labour's emergency import cuts stimulated the development of a range of new product lines, including pop-up toasters, deep-frying pans, and vegetable turpentine, as Sutch revealed in 1960.[68]

Industries and Commerce drew up a list of criteria for the selection of industries worthy of assistance.[69] The import licensing system had long been manipulated to give certain industries privileged access to imports of machinery, and to protect struggling local firms from external competition. A government memorandum admitted in 1956 that 'import licensing may be the only satisfactory means of protecting some industries for a few years', including sanitary earthenware, tobacco pipes, fireworks, footwear, men's and boys' outerwear, and jams, regardless of the effects on British exports.[70]

Sutch and Nash outlined their vision at the Industrial Development Conference in June 1960. Sir Douglas Copland highlighted New Zealand's comparatively poor rate of economic growth during the 1950s. Nash then called for a new emphasis on growth, without which New Zealand would not be able to preserve its economic stability and high standard of living. Sutch explained that the outlook for agricultural exports was discouraging, and recommended the development of new export trades. For instance, cheap hydro-electric power could be used to process domestic and imported natural resources for overseas customers. Sutch admitted that New Zealand would not be able to develop internationally competitive mass production industries in the foreseeable future, due to the absence of a large domestic market. But he saw no reason why skilled New Zealand workers could not emulate the Swedes and the Swiss, who made capital goods such as machine tools in small batches for export.[71] The notion that New Zealand could export processed natural resources and skill-intensive manufactures was a step forward, but the attainment of this goal was hindered by Labour's perseverance with insulationism.

Labour's most controversial manufacturing initiative was in cotton textiles rather than machine tools. In 1960, the Labour government persuaded the British multinational, Smith & Nephew, to participate in a scheme to open a cotton mill at Nelson on the South Island. Assisted by the grant of monopoly status and infant industry protection, this mill would have supplied domestic clothing factories and provided work in an isolated region. Keith Holyoake, the National leader, assured Smith & Nephew that he had no objection to this scheme. Nevertheless, the mill's opponents, including textile importers, clothing manufacturers, retailers, and farmers, took heart from Labour's defeat in the 1960 general election. After a struggle inside the National government, the mill project was abandoned, Smith & Nephew was compensated, and the factory converted into a car assembly plant. In such a high-wage economy, a cotton mill could not have survived without permanent protection. Manufacturing for export may have been Labour's ideal, but the party could not resist the temptation to support the grossest form of import substitution. Hawke suggests that electoral considerations were germane to the original decision to proceed with the Nelson mill. At the Industrial Development Conference, A.P. O'Shea, the General Secretary of the Federated Farmers, lambasted the government's industrial

Table 4.1   Structure of the economically active population in New Zealand, 1936–71 (%)

	Economically active population	Agriculture, forestry & fisheries	Extractive industries	Manufacturing	Construction	Other
1936	645,000	27.3		24.3		48.4
1945	680,000	18.8	1.2	20.0	6.3	53.7
1956	817,000	16.2	0.9	25.0	9.9	48.0
1961	896,000	14.4	0.8	26.2	9.7	48.9
1971	1,111,000	12.3	0.5	26.0	7.9	53.5

Note: Manufacturing includes utilities; other includes the armed services. Maoris are not counted before 1956.
Source: Calculated from B.R. Mitchell, *International Historical Statistics: the Americas and Australasia* (London: Macmillan, 1983), p. 159.

policies, which he compared with those of the Nazis. O'Shea complained that farmers were unable to compete for labour with protected industries.[72]

National attempted to loosen import restrictions during the 1960s. Sutch, who was *persona non grata* with the new government, was dismissed. But National neither abandoned the essential features of insulationism nor totally rejected the policies of Industries and Commerce. For instance, the Development Finance Corporation was established to aid the expansion of small companies. Hawke points out that manufacturing grew faster under National in the 1960s than it had done under Labour in the late 1950s. NAFTA resulted in a rapid increase in industrial exports to Australia.[73] As Table 4.1 shows, the proportion of the working population in manufacturing grew relative to the proportion in agriculture, but declined relative to the proportion in services. New Zealand's manufacturing sector remained highly uncompetitive by international standards. The development of manufacturing exports was constrained by high transaction costs, reflecting New Zealand's poor location, and expensive inputs, due to competition from the import substitution sector. Such was the contradictory, even self-destructive, nature of industrialization in mid-twentieth century New Zealand.[74]

Foreign investment

Governments of both parties kept the door open to most types of inward foreign investment, but remained wary of the intentions of certain investors. Roderick Deane, author of the first detailed survey of FDI in

New Zealand, concluded that it had made a positive contribution to the manufacturing sector. But foreign investment continued to be viewed with suspicion by those who feared overseas domination.

Two-thirds of FDI cases in Deane's sample were postwar in origin. He identified a marked increase in the rate of establishment between 1958 and 1965. Overseas firms and their local affiliates accounted for one quarter of New Zealand factory production in the mid-1960s. They were more capital-intensive, profitable, and dynamic than purely local firms. British, American, and Australian companies provided New Zealand firms with access to additional capital, new products and technologies, and improved management techniques. However, Deane questioned whether New Zealand had made the best use of FDI. In two-fifths of cases, the principal reason for establishing production facilities in New Zealand had been to surmount import controls. High costs of labour and other inputs, and the smallness of the domestic market, prevented overseas firms and their affiliates from attaining international standards of efficiency.[75]

In January 1945, New Zealand undertook to give British firms an opportunity to take part in new industrial developments, and they did play a leading role in postwar economic expansion. For instance, British Petroleum and the New Zealand government formed a joint venture in oil distribution in 1949. Even so, the British sometimes felt excluded from promising developments. For example, in July 1945 the British Trade Commissioner complained that an Australian firm, International Radio, rather than British firms had been selected to produce wire and cable in New Zealand.[76]

In the 1940s, New Zealand granted British and Australian investors better terms than North American investors. Under the 1940 Finance Emergency Regulations, no overseas company could start a new business without the approval of the Minister of Finance. While British and Australian investors were allowed to repatriate capital, this facility was not normally offered to American or Canadian firms, due to worries about capital flight during the dollar shortage. New Zealand did not guarantee the right of North American subsidiaries to transfer profits to the dollar area, although in practice this was almost always permitted. Preference for British FDI was reinforced by fear of US economic domination. Industries and Commerce was particularly concerned lest American multinationals gain control of key industries.[77] Nevertheless, some American companies made successful investments in New Zealand. Wrigleys, the chewing gum manufacturer, opened a plant in Auckland in 1940, obtaining an official monopoly of the New Zealand market.

One of Wrigleys' executives, W.H. Stanley, a former school pal of Walter Nash, boasted in 1951 that the gum monopoly had 'not been an unprofitable undertaking'.[78]

New Zealand's attitude to North American FDI softened during the 1950s, as constraints on the supply of British capital became more obvious. In 1950, the government authorized the importation by General Motors (Canada) of 500 cars, the sale of which would finance expansion of local refrigerator manufacturing capacity by Frigidaire, the General Motors subsidiary. Officials encouraged International Harvester to extend its New Zealand operations to include the production of tractor implements.[79] The Sterling Area's need of more US investment was readily acknowledged at the 1952 Commonwealth conferences. In 1953, the US administration approached Wellington with a proposal for combined action to attract American private investment into New Zealand. They pointed out that New Zealand's ability to obtain FDI depended on its treatment of US firms. Most government departments, excepting Industries and Commerce, welcomed these American overtures. It was suggested that US capital and expertise could help New Zealand to add value to wool exports. In accordance with Commonwealth guidelines, New Zealand officials recommended that all overseas firms be given the right to repatriate profits, capital gains, and new investment. They argued that this concession would pose no threat to balance-of-payments stability. Ministers, however, had strong reservations, fearing that the underlying balance-of-payments situation might weaken, and that any assurances concerning repatriation of new dollar capital would be unfair to US firms that were already established in New Zealand. In the event, the Americans were informed that the government would endeavour to comply with all reasonable requests for repatriation of profits and capital. But the firms concerned would still need to seek RBNZ approval. This response did not fully satisfy the Americans. Not surprisingly, about 70 per cent of New Zealand's inflow of FDI came from Britain, while the dollar area provided 15 per cent.[80]

Strict import controls encouraged British, Australian, and American companies to establish subsidiaries or joint ventures in New Zealand in the late 1950s. However, New Zealand's stance towards FDI became increasingly ambivalent during this period. Every application from overseas to set up a new business or factory was closely scrutinized. Although the purchase by overseas parties of equity in New Zealand companies was not formally restricted until 1964, the government could discourage it by indicating that licenses to import machinery would be withheld. Sutch and the Department of Industries and Commerce were determined to ensure that each FDI proposal was consistent with their understanding of the national interest. In September 1959, Sutch drew up a list of principles to guide decisions. Firstly, foreign investment was welcome where its purpose was to establish a major new industry, such as steel, or introduce a new proprietary manufacturing process. Even so, it was desirable that a majority stake be reserved for New Zealand investors. Secondly, a case could be made for allowing overseas investors to purchase a small amount of equity in firms in need of assistance to obtain imported plant and foreign expertise. But foreign ownership of equity was discouraged where there was reason to believe that it would lead to the dumping of imported components, or the local manufacture of low-grade goods in competition with incumbent firms. Thirdly, all other sorts of foreign investment, especially takeovers of 'vital' industries, were undesirable. Fourthly, Japanese proposals for investment were to be treated with particular caution. Sutch pointed out that Japan still used unfair trading practices, and that investment from this source would be politically unpopular in New Zealand.[81] Nash elaborated on Labour's approach to foreign investment at the 1960 Industrial Development Conference. Although New Zealand could benefit from overseas investment, it must not be allowed a dominant position. Nash preferred overseas capital in the form of loans to the government, which could then be directed towards the most appropriate industrial projects.[82]

Many potential overseas investors were rebuffed. Superior Waxes of Australia was informed by Industries and Commerce that its investment was not needed, as 'the existing lines of supply for bee keepers' equipment are at present satisfactory'.[83] Another Australian firm, Victa, withdrew an application to manufacture small petrol motors because the government demanded local content of 60 per cent. Victa considered this proportion excessive in view of the high cost of local inputs.[84] Subsidiaries of overseas firms were not permitted to undermine the cosy domestic market environment. Indeed, few objected to this stipulation. The government also hoped that overseas investors would not confine themselves to final assembly work. It soon discovered, though, that overseas investors were more interested in taking advantage of the insulated conditions than in advancing the level of economic development. Insulationism reduced the efficiency with which overseas as well as domestic capital was allocated. A senior figure at Fisher & Paykel, New Zealand's leading electrical appliance manufacturer, was highly critical of this state of affairs, arguing that FDI should be used to increase competition in the local market, and to assist local firms to develop products for export. But most domestic manufacturers were happy with existing arrangements.[85]

The treatment of Japanese investment deserves special comment. On an official trip to Tokyo in 1959, Nash made it clear that Labour would not be rolling out the red carpet for Japanese investors. Visits by Japanese businessmen were restricted under the immigration laws. Sutch feared that Japanese firms would acquire control over New Zealand distributors and manufacturers, with a view to flooding the market with cheap imports and shoddy manufactures assembled from imported components. Genuine domestic firms, he pointed out, would lose business, and the public interest would suffer. The plans of Japanese firms to invest in Reslau, a textile importer, and Bell, a producer of radios, were regarded as anathema. Although Japanese firms and individuals could not be prevented from purchasing shares in New Zealand businesses, the government could decline to provide them with licenses to import machinery and materials. However, Sutch's department did not oppose all Japanese investment. In 1960, Industries and Commerce approved a proposal from Slidefast, which was 51 per cent New Zealand and 49 per cent Japanese owned, to establish a zip factory. Treasury and External Affairs were more open to Japanese investment, on balance of payments and diplomatic grounds respectively. These departments regretted the contradiction between the government's wish for good commercial relations with Japan and its distrust of Japanese investors.[86]

Wolfgang Rosenberg, an economist at Canterbury University, was the most trenchant academic critic of foreign investment and the IMF. He argued that if overseas investors were allowed too much economic power, then they would dictate policy to the government, resulting in the abandonment of full employment. Inflows of private capital would not improve the balance of payments in the long run, contended Rosenberg, as they generated large outflows of interest, profits, and dividends. Moreover, the balance of payments would be thrown into turmoil if overseas investors decided to repatriate their capital. Rosenberg pointed out that New Zealand would not require large inflows of capital from abroad if domestic savings could be increased. Although he did not advocate the exclusion of all private foreign investment, he recommended an even more rigorous scrutiny of proposals, and a ban on overseas takeovers of New Zealand firms. His preference was for the government to borrow abroad at a fixed interest rate when funds were needed for industrial development. The proceeds could be invested by a state Industrial Development Corporation in projects deemed in the national interest. Sutch also became more vocal in his criticism of foreign investment during the early 1960s. As well as reiterating many of Rosenberg's points, he claimed that the presence of too many overseas firms was stunting the growth of a domestic entrepreneurial class. Sutch concluded that the government should encourage suitable inward investment, while ensuring a gradual decline in the proportion of local industry owned by overseas interests.[87]

Although Rosenberg and Sutch were socialists, their analysis had a wide nationalist appeal. Under National, the political costs of Japanese investment were still perceived as exceeding the economic benefits. In 1962, the Japanese complained that high internal transport costs and inadequate port facilities were hindering the development of New Zealand's exports of timber and coal. The Japanese offered practical assistance, including labour, for urgent infrastructure projects, and enquired whether it would 'be possible to purchase whole forests'. Wellington was startled, and replied that the trade unions would not permit the employment of Japanese construction workers.[88] New Zealand did not allow the acquisition of forests by Japanese firms at this time. As late as 1995, Japan was responsible for just 3 per cent of New Zealand's stock of FDI.[89]

A crisis developed over foreign investment policy in 1964, when the British press tycoon, Lord Thomson, attempted to buy *The Dominion* newspaper of Wellington. Under pressure from Labour, the National government decided that it would be against the public interest to permit the takeover of *The Dominion*. The government issued a set of Overseas Takeover Regulations, empowering it to stop undesirable takeovers by overseas interests. A more specific News Media Ownership Act followed in 1965. These regulations did not prevent the growth of foreign investment, nor was this their purpose, but they did increase the uncertainty faced by potential investors.[90]

New Zealand governments were persistently ambivalent towards overseas investment. Wartime controls over the establishment of new businesses by foreigners were retained, and supplemented in the mid-1960s by restrictions on the foreign acquisition of existing businesses. The government also regulated inward foreign investment by informal means including the manipulation of import licensing. Governments hoped to capture overseas technology and know-how while keeping control of New Zealand industry in domestic hands. In the event, they attracted overseas firms keen to exploit the rent-seeking potential of an insulated economy. Overseas subsidiaries were more efficient than local firms were, but not efficient enough to compete in export markets. Basically, inward FDI made insulationism more tolerable by giving consumers a slightly wider range of choice.

Conclusion

New Zealand made slow progress in the field of economic development after 1945. An emphasis on stability rather than growth was part of the legacy of the 1930s. During the 1940s and early 1950s there was uncertainty about the optimal trajectory of the economy: the evidence for and against the proposition that further agricultural development offered the best hope of maintaining the growing population at a high standard of living was evenly balanced. In retrospect, it might have been wise to let market forces solve this conundrum. The government's inability to join the Bretton Woods institutions, the persistence of excess domestic demand, and the squandering of domestic capital on the protected sector, ensured that New Zealand remained a financial colony of Britain into the 1960s.

In New Zealand, neither systematic planning nor the market determined how resources were distributed between the primary and industrial sectors. New Zealand lacked a consistent development strategy, and government policy was driven by the short run imperatives of full employment and high consumption. Resources were drawn willy-nilly into small-scale manufacturing by a battery of import controls designed to safeguard the balance of payments and preserve full employment. Consequently, costs in both the primary and industrial sectors increased rapidly. Manufacturing would have developed at a more leisurely pace under a regime of freer markets and lower import barriers, but in all probability it would have attained higher levels of efficiency, especially in conjunction with FDI. Murupara demonstrated that there was at least some scope in New Zealand for export-oriented industrial development in the 1950s and 1960s, but this potential was not fully exploited.

5
Stresses in the Ottawa System

> Australia's changed attitude to the preference system reflected the fact that the United Kingdom was no longer able to fulfil her traditional role of providing the capital needed for the industrial [*sic*] development of the Commonwealth.... The preferences were still of great value to us and it was important that we should retain what preferences we could. It would now be necessary, however, to re-examine, in the light of the Australian attitude, the relative importance and future prospects of our trade with Australia and the Commonwealth, and with Europe and other overseas markets.
>
> *Harold Macmillan, Chancellor of the Exchequer, 1956*[1]

As Macmillan indicates, a turning point had been reached in Commonwealth economic affairs by 1956. Relations with Australia had cooled, and the future of Commonwealth Preference was in doubt. In subsequent years, Britain was increasingly drawn into the orbit of the EEC, which appeared to offer better opportunities for industrial exports. This chapter examines the reasons for the growing commercial estrangement of Britain and Australia and New Zealand. Chapters 7 and 8 consider Britain's attempts to reach a commercial settlement with western Europe.

Macmillan's personal evolution with respect to trade policy is of some importance. He began the 1950s as a staunch supporter of Commonwealth economic cooperation. When Minister of Housing and Local Government, in 1952, he argued that Britain and other Commonwealth countries 'should be free to extend the preferential system ... by new arrangements', irrespective of their obligations under GATT, until the central gold and dollar reserves reached a safe level.[2] In 1954, he assured colleagues that it might still be possible 'to build up the economic strength of the Commonwealth, by expanding trade among its members and between them and the rest of the world [including western Europe] as a counterpoise to the power of the United States.'[3] Western Europe's role in such an enterprise would have been subordinate to the Commonwealth's. By 1956, however, Macmillan had grown exasperated with Australian demands for revision of the Ottawa Agreement, and fearful of Germany's growing economic dominance in western Europe. In 1961, as Prime Minister, he launched Britain's first bid for EEC membership.

Britain's mounting disillusionment with the Commonwealth economic network was mirrored in Australia and, to some extent, New Zealand. Canberra and Wellington were dismayed by the generous subsidies paid to British farmers, and alarmed by Britain's reluctance to restrict imports of subsidized foreign food. Australia and New Zealand argued that the Ottawa Agreements were skewed in favour of Britain, and concluded that they hindered trade negotiations with foreign countries. Australia's demand in 1955–56 for sweeping reductions in contractual BP margins seemed to cut to the heart of the preferential system. This episode angered the British, who were already smarting over Australian import substitution policies, the tightening of import controls on British goods, and the stirrings of economic *détente* between Australia, New Zealand, and Japan. Britain realized that if concessions were made to Australia, New Zealand would demand equal treatment. Allegations of opportunism flew back and forth between London, Canberra, and Wellington. In reality, however, each government was simply endeavouring to maximize the perceived national interest in the light of changing circumstances.

This chapter examines the decision of Australia and New Zealand to cut imports from Britain during the 1952–3 balance-of-payments crisis; the failure of attempts to revive Commonwealth Preference by altering or eliminating the NNP rule in GATT; the evolution of British agricultural policy; and the revision of the Anglo-Australian and Anglo-New Zealand trade agreements in 1956–7 and 1958–9 respectively. Although the Ottawa Agreements lasted until the 1970s, it was becoming clear that the prosperity of all three countries would increasingly depend on access to markets outside the Commonwealth.

Cutting imports from Britain, 1952–3

Between 1950 and 1953, the Korean War disrupted the external accounts of many Commonwealth countries including Australia and

New Zealand. Exceptionally high commodity prices in 1950–1, due to strategic stockpiling by the USA, brought about a rapid improvement in the external financial position of Australia and New Zealand, as well as of the Sterling Area as a whole, which was a net exporter of commodities such as wool and rubber. As a net importer of strategic commodities, Britain did not contribute to this improvement, although it did benefit from the rise in the central reserves.[4]

In 1951–2, the position deteriorated as quickly as it had improved over the previous year. As US stockpiling abated, the price of a pound weight of wool, which had risen from 76 pence in May 1949 to 375 pence in March 1951, fell to 120 pence in December 1951, with predictable effects on the export earnings of Australia and New Zealand.[5] But David Lee's contention that the fall in wool prices was the sole cause of the financial turmoil in Australia, and by implication in New Zealand, is false.[6] In 1951, after discounting British pleas for caution, Canberra gambled on a further increase in the wool price, and authorized a large rise in dollar imports. The government wished to press ahead with the development programme, and dampen inflationary pressure by increasing the supply of goods.[7] The National government in Wellington, which had come to power on a free market platform, also decided to accelerate the liberalization of import controls, especially on goods from western Europe. It argued that faster liberalization would lead to a fall in input costs and an improvement in the export sector's competitiveness. In July 1951, as the wool price fell from its previous dizzy heights, Bernard Ashwin expressed confidence that it would soon rally. As late as December, Ashwin remained sanguine about the wool price, and advised against any hasty reversal of the import decontrol policy. He advocated the use of macroeconomic techniques to restrain demand and bolster the balance of payments.[8]

The gamble on wool proved costly for Australia and New Zealand. Aggregate demand could not be controlled quickly enough to prevent further deterioration in the external position. Moreover, the entire Sterling Area slid into financial crisis during the northern winter of 1951–2, prompting the British to call for tighter controls over dollar imports. In December 1951, the Australian Cabinet dismissed this option on the grounds that high imports were necessary to dampen inflation.[9] However, at a meeting of Commonwealth officials in January 1952, Roland Wilson of the Australian Treasury admitted that import cuts might be unavoidable. He ominously added that it would not be possible to obtain adequate savings without reducing imports from the Sterling Area as well as from foreign countries. 'What degree of importance,' asked Wilson, 'would the United Kingdom delegation attach to a reduction of imports from the sterling area by another member of the sterling area?'[10] From the British standpoint, Wilson's suggestion was outrageous. On behalf of the British Treasury, Otto Clarke reaffirmed the status quo: 'the United Kingdom delegation did not suggest there should be any directly imposed restriction of imports from the sterling area.'[11]

At the following Commonwealth Finance Ministers' Conference, most delegations, including those from Australia and New Zealand, criticized British policy. They claimed that ever since 1945 Britain had placed too much emphasis on cutting dollar imports as the solution to external financial crises, and suggested that instead of merely reacting to crises the Commonwealth should devise a strategy to prevent their recurrence. The Australian Treasurer, Sir Arthur Fadden, called for concerted action to restore convertibility and abolish dollar discrimination, thereby removing a major barrier to economic development. He acknowledged that this goal was unattainable without financial contributions from the USA and Canada, and recommended that the Sterling Area cultivate their good will. Steps should be taken to 'harmonis[e] the policies of the sterling area with, for instance, those of the United States. The sterling area could hardly fail in its endeavours if it proceeded in future by methods fully acceptable to the United States and other countries, and in the closest co-operation with them.'[12] New Zealand, Canada, and the Bank of England supported Fadden's call for a more imaginative and permanent solution to the sterling problem.[13] Fadden also appeared to signal Australian support for a less discriminatory trade policy. Given that he was speaking in a forum dedicated to the assertion of the Commonwealth's independence, this approach was provocative. Australia refused to guarantee compliance with the 1952 balance of payments target recommended by R.A. Butler, the Chancellor of the Exchequer. However, the New Zealand Prime Minister, Sid Holland, promised to 'stand by Britain through thick and thin'.[14]

Australia's stance in January 1952 foreshadowed the position that it adopted in March when it could no longer allow the import surplus to continue. Unlike the situation in either 1947 or 1949, when Australia's overall balance of payments had been sound despite a large dollar deficit, in 1952 Australia was in overall deficit, and even had a large deficit with the UK. On 8 March, Menzies announced that the import situation was worse than had been expected, and that he was now applying the same sort of controls over Sterling Area imports that were already exercised over dollar area and Japanese imports.[15] The reason for Menzies' decision to reduce imports from the Sterling Area was entirely practical. The total anticipated balance of payments deficit with the Sterling Area, including invisible items, was A£490 million for 1951–2, compared to an expected deficit of only A£77 million with the dollar area.[16] Accordingly, the greater part of the impact of the planned cuts in imports had to fall on Sterling Area goods. While dollar imports were to fall from A£141 million to A£132 million, imports from the Sterling Area were to be reduced by nearly 60 per cent, from A£680 million to A£265 million.

Sir John Crawford has noted that, 'anyone who cares to examine in detail the import figures for the fifties will not easily sustain a case that the United Kingdom was unfairly treated.' The cut in imports from the Sterling Area was well received by GATT: 'Australia gained a deserved reputation for the non-discriminatory administration of her controls.' Moreover, despite an adverse impact on some industries, Britain's share of Australia's imports remained above prewar levels.[17] Some British observers were sympathetic to Australia's actions. The economist, John Hicks, stated that 'the Australians have no alternative but to reduce their imports from sterling as well as from non-sterling sources.'[18] But most British comment was scathing, and Menzies was forced to defend his decision in parliament.[19]

New Zealand shared Australia's difficulties. In March 1952, Wellington complied with Britain's request for further economies in non-sterling imports by withdrawing all licences for imports from the USA, Canada, and Japan, and substituting new licences for smaller amounts. At the same time, all motor vehicle imports, including those from Britain, were brought under licensing control. The British High Commissioner urged New Zealand not to impose reductions on imports from the Sterling Area. But, as New Zealand's reserves plummeted, an emergency system of exchange allocation was introduced in April. Banks were 'requested' to ration each importer to 80 per cent of the overseas currency used in 1950. Imports from all countries, including Britain, were affected. New Zealand's imports from Britain fell by almost one half between the first quarters of 1952 and 1953.[20]

Once the British had recovered from their shock, they leaped into action. Firstly, they alleged that the speed and nature of the Australian and New Zealand development programmes had exacerbated the balance of payments crisis. Secondly, they argued that Australia should make exceptions to its import regulations so as to reduce their impact on vulnerable industries. As early as 31 March, a 'P.M. to P.M.' message was drafted to plead the case of textiles. Winston Churchill, the Prime Minister, was 'concerned about the rising unemployment in our great textile industries', and hoped for Australian cooperation 'in mitigating the effect of recent import restrictions upon them.' The Australians would be asked to 'temper the wind to these shorn lambs'.[21] But the Australians were immovable, and Wilson contended that 'the Australian market was hopelessly over-stocked with both cotton and rayon piecegoods.'[22]

Thirdly, the British tried to persuade Australia to accept that imports from the Sterling Area should be treated as a special case. Despite esoteric debates over the meaning of 'discrimination', the Australians insisted that adherence to GATT meant that the Sterling Area was not entitled to special treatment. A relaxation of the controls on Sterling Area goods might annoy the USA and endanger future attempts to borrow from the World Bank. If Australia were to increase imports from Britain, it would be necessary to make further cuts in imports from western Europe. Sometimes, the Australians were apologetic. In a letter explaining Australia's action to Butler, Menzies began one passage of his argument by writing, 'Much as I personally dislike GATT'. Wilson later argued that, once taken, the step to treat Sterling Area goods on a par with those from other nations was irreversible: 'The Australian view was that having ceased to discriminate against the non-sterling world, they had given up their right to do so.'[23] No matter how strongly they were urged to recant, the Australians would not drop their controversial action against British trade. However, Australia was able to relax controls over British imports in 1953, and to reverse the original cuts in 1954 as the balance of payments improved. New Zealand also moderated its import controls after the crisis. Facing renewed financial difficulties, however, Australia imposed a new round of import cuts in 1955, and ordered further reductions in 1956–57, before slackening them again.[24]

Australia and New Zealand were not the only Commonwealth countries to restrict imports from Britain in 1952. But the fact that Australia, in particular, slashed imports from Britain was taken as a bad omen in London. A fissure was opening in the economic relationship between Britain and Australia and New Zealand.

The No New Preference rule

The early 1950s witnessed a revolt against the NNP rule and GATT among Tory imperialists in Britain. Menzies also wished to loosen the NNP rule, but Britain and Australia were unable to present a common front on this issue because of divisions within the governments of both countries. The Australians were torn between their desire to change the NNP rule, and their need to obtain American goodwill for a concerted drive to convertibility. New Zealand's involvement in the NNP agitation was minimal. Wellington doubted that the Americans would concede the establishment of new preferences, and maintained that it would be counter-productive to badger them.

The British Conservative government, elected in 1951, included both free traders and protectionists. Although Churchill was inclined towards a liberal trade policy, an influential bloc of Tories, including Leo Amery, the former Secretary of State for India, and Lord Beaverbrook, propri-etor of the *Daily Express*, was critical of GATT and wished to intensify the Ottawa system. Protectionists could count on some support from the Board of Trade, which was dubious about the capacity of British industry to compete overseas in the absence of tariff preferences. Amery called for an exchange of preferences between the Commonwealth, western European countries, and their dependencies. On the Tory left, Macmillan agreed that greater economic cooperation between the Commonwealth and Europe would assist British industry to achieve economies of scale and meet the challenges of the USA and Russia. In 1952, the Council of Europe unveiled the Strasbourg Plan for a Commonwealth-European preferential area, although this did not meet with the approval of the Foreign Office.[25]

Motions were passed at the Conservative conference, in October 1952, demanding modification of GATT so as to render this agreement com-patible with the Ottawa system. Consequently, the government was obliged to place the question of the extension of preferences on the agenda of the impending Commonwealth Economic Conference. This conference had been called at the request of Menzies, who was inter-ested in a fundamental reconsideration of Commonwealth economic policy.[26] A range of issues, including the British proposal for a 'Collec-tive Approach' to convertibility, as well as development, trade, and com-modities would be considered. The 'Collective Approach' had emerged in response to a mixture of internal and external pressures, including the dissension at the Commonwealth Finance Ministers' Conference.[27] British ministers and officials regarded the NNP rule as an obstacle to the success of the 'Collective Approach'. Once convertibility had been achieved, the British would have no further warrant under the IMF and GATT charters to restrict imports. In order to maintain the protec-tion of domestic farmers and manufacturers it would be necessary to increase tariffs. However, the British would be obliged by the NNP rule to raise tariffs on Commonwealth as well as on foreign imports, breaching the Ottawa Agreements under which Commonwealth produce was imported duty-free. Although personally a supporter of a liberal regime, the President of the Board of Trade, Peter Thorneycroft, put his name to a ministerial memorandum calling for the replacement of the NNP rule.[28]

Britain's position on NNP was influenced by Japan's application for membership of GATT. The competitive menace of Japan was no longer confined to the least sophisticated branches of manufacturing. If Japan were to join GATT, and obtain MFN rights, British goods would face a growing challenge in Commonwealth and world markets. If Australia and New Zealand reacted to the Japanese threat to their manufacturers by increasing MFN tariffs, they would be compelled to increase tariffs on British goods as well.[29]

Although British ministers had no firm plans to revise preferences, they promised to canvass support at the CEC for abolition of the NNP rule. Even before the conference opened, however, it was plain that there was little support in the Commonwealth for making an issue of NNP. The Asian members were already losing interest in the Ottawa system, and the general mood of the conference was that the Americans, whose support was needed over the 'Collective Approach', would be alienated by any proposal to scrap the NNP rule. D.C. Abbott, the Canadian Minister of Finance, warned that a 'concerted approach' to Washington over NNP would be 'untimely and unwise'. Unusually, New Zealand declined to follow Britain's lead. Sid Holland remarked that, while his government 'supported in principle the idea of extended preference . . . they questioned the wisdom of raising the matter with the United States Government at the present time.'[30] Holland concluded that a decision on NNP should be deferred until another meeting. New Zealand officials argued that, in a world of bulk contracts and quantitative restrictions, Commonwealth Preference had 'more political and sentimental than economic value'. The key issue for New Zealand was the Americans' attitude: 'from the Commonwealth point of view the real reason for adherence to GATT is the presence in it of the United States.' If Britain were to procure the abolition of NNP, the Americans might leave GATT and withdraw tariff concessions on products such as wool.[31]

Menzies' comments were guarded. He acknowledged the contribution of the Ottawa system to the stability and prosperity of the Commonwealth, but he did not come out either for or against the British proposal on NNP.[32] The Australian government faced a dilemma. While Menzies was sympathetic towards Britain's position, he feared that any show of support for the possible intensification of Commonwealth Preference would aggravate relations with the USA, Canada, western Europe, and Japan, hinder the drive for new markets, and discourage international assistance for a convertibility operation. John Crawford, the Australian Secretary of Commerce and Agriculture, added that a 'super-Ottawa' bloc would experience high costs and capital shortages. As a net exporter of some important commodities, such a bloc could not be insulated from disturbances in the world economy.[33]

In the event, Commonwealth officials were instructed to consider the feasibility of amending the NNP rule to permit the revalorization of specific preferences. Commonwealth produce entering the UK attracted a specific margin of so many pence or shillings per pound or hundredweight, whereas BP margins were expressed in percentage *ad valorem* terms. Inflation had eroded the value of specific margins since the 1930s. Crawford accepted the desirability of revalorizing specific margins, but doubted its practicality, as foreigners would retaliate by revalorizing specific tariffs. He noted that the US wool tariff was a specific duty. New Zealand and Canadian officials agreed that the dangers were considerable, and that it would be unwise to proceed at this juncture, if at all.[34]

The Commonwealth resolved to put the 'Collective Approach', and the associated request for financial aid, to the USA. The post-conference communiqué acknowledged the lack of unity over the NNP rule.[35] Britain would confine itself to asking for a waiver of NNP in a couple of exceptional cases, affecting colonial commodities, while Australia would pursue the same course with respect to trade with New Guinea. In 1953, GATT granted these minor concessions. Despite the Americans' subsequent rejection of the 'Collective Approach', the British did not renew the attack on NNP. They realized that the chances of uniting the Commonwealth on this issue were negligible. At the Blackpool Conservative conference, in 1954, the champions of Imperial Preference were finally defeated.[36]

However, the Australians brought forward a new proposal to amend NNP in 1954. Under the rules of GATT, members were permitted to increase tariffs after negotiating with other Contracting Parties about compensation. The Australians maintained that this procedure should be applied to preference margins. Canberra was disgruntled with US agricultural protectionism, and intended to seek changes in GATT when this agreement came up for review in 1954–5. High on the Australian agenda were the revalorization of specific preferences, and the introduction of new preferential arrangements with neighbouring countries with a view to stimulating certain sectors such as forest products. New Zealand was intrigued by Australia's hints at cooperation, and foresaw that it would be advantageous to widen some preferential margins in any future renegotiation of the Ottawa Agreement with Britain. However, Wellington considered that it might be more advisable to request a waiver from NNP at the appropriate moment than to demand a change in the GATT charter. In Commonwealth discussions on the GATT review, Britain, Canada, and New Zealand questioned the wisdom of Australia's proposal for revising NNP. During the GATT review itself, Australia received only the most hesitant support from the rest of the Commonwealth. All hope of amending the NNP rule was now at an end.[37] It also appeared unlikely that GATT would grant New Zealand a waiver to increase preferences in the context of a revised Ottawa Agreement. Even so, GATT did permit the creation of new preferences when Australia and New Zealand signed a partial free trade agreement in 1965.

The events of 1952–5 indicated that, in the absence of a catastrophe of the magnitude of the 1930s, the Commonwealth would never agree on the intensification of the Ottawa system. Since inflation was eroding specific preferences, the Ottawa settlement was increasingly perceived as one-sided, and pressure mounted in Australia and New Zealand for cuts in BP margins.

British agricultural policy

When the postwar commodity shortage abated in the early 1950s, the British lost interest in providing safe markets for Commonwealth primary producers. In 1953–5, Britain abandoned managed agricultural trade, and introduced a comparatively liberal import regime, qualified by the Ottawa tariff preferences. Britain became a dumping ground for foreign food surpluses, leading to cries of betrayal from Australian and New Zealand farmers. In the late 1940s the British had pleaded for increased food supplies from the Commonwealth, but in the 1950s they seemed bent on forcing prices to uncomfortably low levels. Furthermore, Britain was now committed to a lavish agricultural subsidy programme, the counterpart of import substitution industrialization in Australasia.

British food output grew from 42 per cent of home consumption in 1938 to 52 per cent in 1946.[38] After 1945 the British were determined to maintain food production at a high level. The 1947 Agriculture Act established a system of guaranteed prices for eleven main products, including cattle, sheep, milk, wheat, sugar beet, and wool. Farmers received deficiency payments if market prices fell below the guaranteed levels. The government's aim was to raise net agricultural output to 60 per cent above the prewar level by 1956. Priority was given to livestock production, in direct competition with Australia and New Zealand. The rationale for these measures was multifaceted. Firstly, wartime experience seemed to demonstrate the value of a strong agricultural sector. Secondly, during the dollar crisis it was claimed that by increasing food production it would be possible to reduce the import bill and assist the balance of payments. Thirdly, farmers demanded to share in the prosperity of other sectors. Britain did achieve greater self-sufficiency in cereals, meat, and cheese, between the late 1930s and late 1950s, but continued to import over 90 per cent of its butter requirements.[39]

During the war, Australasian farmers had expressed concern about the future of British agricultural policy. In 1943, the British High Commissioner had noticed 'anxiety' in the South Island, 'about postwar prospects of New Zealand primary produce exports on account of development of United Kingdom agriculture.'[40] Long-term contracts soothed dominion farmers' nerves in the late 1940s. Moreover, in 1952, Britain undertook to admit unlimited quantities of Australian and New Zealand meat until 1967, while the British Minister of Agriculture called for the extension of the long-term dairy contracts with New Zealand.[41] But there was a sharp change in policy in 1953–4. Churchill was keen to end the unpopular system of rationing. Long-term contracts between the Ministry of Food and Commonwealth suppliers were brought to a premature end in 1953–4. Even dollar foodstuffs were admitted in larger quantities. It was argued that the conquest of postwar shortages eliminated the need for state intervention in the food trade. Britain also upset Australia and Canada by refusing to participate in the revised International Wheat Agreement (IWA) of 1953. The British contended that the price range for transactions under the IWA, which was designed to stabilize prices, was too high, and did not rejoin until 1959.[42] Australian and New Zealand producers were forced to compete in the British market for the first time since the 1930s.

Australia and New Zealand continued to derive some benefit from preferences on commodities such as beef, dairy produce, and fruit, as well as from the meat quotas established in the 1930s, the 1952 meat agreement, and the British Commonwealth Sugar Agreement (BCSA). However, whereas in the 1930s butter and beef preferences had been worth 15 per cent *ad valorem*, by the mid-1950s they were worth just 5 per cent, and offered no protection against dumping. Furthermore, foreign sheepmeat, wheat, and wool were not subject to tariffs. Although meat production had increased relative to demand in Britain and the Commonwealth between the 1930s and 1950s, the foreign meat quotas had not been tightened. Wholesale food prices fell between 1954 and 1957 as domestic and foreign supplies increased. Argentina strove to increase beef deliveries, while a number of butter producers, including Argentina, the Scandinavian nations, and some Soviet bloc countries, dumped surplus stock in Britain.[43]

The new environment produced growing anxiety among Australasian farmers. According to Geoffrey Scoones, the British High Commissioner in Wellington:

> Her Majesty's Government's frequent exhortations to New Zealand since the war to increase her exports of meat . . . are very much in New Zealand minds . . . it is felt here that such exhortations cannot now be unsaid, and that they, no less than the Ottawa Agreement, place an obligation on Her Majesty's Government to assure New Zealand producers a remunerative return in the United Kingdom market.[44]

Scoones noted, however, that New Zealand's case was weakened by its failure to expand the primary sector as rapidly as it could have done after 1945. The British made the same criticism of Australia.[45]

Dissatisfaction with British policy intensified during the mid-1950s. At the 1958 Commonwealth Trade and Economic Conference (CTEC), Australia and New Zealand condemned British agricultural policy. The New Zealanders pointed out that the deficiency payments scheme was a disguised form of protection. Arnold Nordmeyer argued that in the nuclear age there was no strategic justification for subsidizing agriculture, and stressed that all forms of agricultural protection undermined the credibility of GATT. The British sympathized but showed no inclination to recant. John McEwen, the Australian Minister of Trade, recommended that the Commonwealth take a more active role in the stabilization of commodity markets. Canada and New Zealand supported this proposal, but Britain, which gained from low food prices, was non-committal.[46]

The realignment of agricultural policy under the Conservatives contributed to the disenchantment of Australia and New Zealand with the Commonwealth economic network. It was in this context that Australia and New Zealand decided to seek the revision of the Ottawa Agreements.

The United Kingdom–Australia trade agreement 1957

In 1956, the Australians formally announced their intention of making deep cuts in contractual BP margins in order to facilitate trade negotiations with other countries. Canberra also demanded a guaranteed level of wheat sales in Britain. Crawford regarded this as a 'key' episode in the development of Australian trade policy.[47] While the Australian assault was eventually blunted, it caused the British acute embarrassment, and brought into question the Ottawa system.

McEwen produced a cabinet memorandum in April 1956 calling for revision of the Ottawa Agreement. He began by asserting that Australia faced 'two problems – balance of payments and internal inflation. To abate these we need wider opportunities for our trade and lower costs in Australia.' The Ottawa Agreement, 'constrains our scope and bargaining strength for promoting better opportunities for our exports.' In addition, British preferences 'raise the cost of certain imported products, and thereby raise Australian costs of production.'[48] McEwen contended that he would be in a stronger position to bargain with the USA over wool tariffs, Germany over access for wheat, and Japan over both wool and wheat, if he could offer to reduce contractual BP margins. The Australians noted that British industrial cartels, including suppliers of tractors, tinplate, and ammonium sulphate, were capitalizing on BP margins by jacking up prices. McEwen did not, however, plan to abolish Commonwealth Preference, and still believed in giving special encouragement to Anglo-Australian trade. He accepted that British firms were entitled to receive protection against foreign competition in the Australian market. As a *quid pro quo*, Australian farmers had the right to protection against dumping in the British market.[49] Australia was also worried about the impact on the wheat trade of British deficiency payments and foreign export subsidies. In 1956, British wheat growers were guaranteed the sterling equivalent of 20 shillings Australian per bushel (ex farm), while Australian growers received a mere 10/3d per bushel (ex farm). British wheat was displacing Commonwealth supplies. Moreover, the British were importing US grain and dairy surpluses.[50]

Australian officials estimated that Britain was enjoying a disproportionate share of the benefits of the Ottawa system. During 1954–5, preferences were granted on 86 per cent of the value of Australia's imports from Britain, at an average margin of 14 per cent. Britain accorded preferences on just 48 per cent of imports from Australia, at an average margin of 9 per cent.[51] McEwen wanted to take a tough line, claiming that it would be preferable to scrap the Ottawa Agreement than to negotiate a half-hearted compromise. However, he believed that the British would make substantial concessions because they would wish to preserve at least some preferences. A.S. Brown and Robert Durie, of the Prime Minister's Department, suspected that McEwen was exaggerating Australia's bargaining power. Even if the British were to give way, other countries, such as France, might demand cuts in BP margins as a condition for not reducing imports from Australia. Nevertheless, Cabinet endorsed McEwen's strategy. The Australian plan was to reduce contractual BP margins from 12.5, 15, or 17.5 per cent down to 5 or 10 per cent depending on the product. In addition, they would demand a guaranteed market for 40 million bushels of wheat annually.[52]

Britain wished to avoid full-scale trade negotiations with Australia in 1956, as France, West Germany, Italy, the Netherlands, Belgium, and Luxembourg were in the process of forming a Common Market. The British were uncertain how to respond to this development. In a paper for Anthony Eden, the Prime Minister, Sir Frank Lee explained that it would be inconvenient to enter into any new long-term commitment to Australia in view of the fluidity of the European situation. He hoped that 'it would be possible to discover the basis for a purely short-term understanding with Australia'.[53] Thorneycroft agreed that a holding operation was called for with respect to Australia. Officials predicted that Australia would demand cuts in BP margins on certain products, such as machine tools, tinplate, and textile yarns, currently imported duty-free from Britain, but at a tariff of 12.5 per cent from foreign countries. Britain had 70 per cent of the Australian import market in this category of trade, which was worth £100 million sterling per annum. The British were prepared to accept contractual margins of 10 per cent on these products, but if Australia attempted to cut margins to 7.5 per cent it would be necessary to consider either terminating the 1952 meat agreement or making no offer on wheat.[54]

The Anglo-Australian talks began in London in late June. Lee warned Crawford not to damage the Ottawa system for the sake of 'what might prove to be evanescent and illusory advantages in third country markets.'[55] Algernon Rumbold of the CRO assured the Commonwealth Secretary, Lord Home, that the Australian requests would be modest. Consequently, the British were horrified by Australia's opening proposal for the elimination of BP margins on capital goods, and reductions to unspecified levels on other manufactures. Thorneycroft reminded McEwen that British manufacturers were already suffering from the reimposition of sterling import cuts. Britain complained that the Australian tariff was being manipulated to exclude British goods, despite the fact they were guaranteed a fair chance of competing with local products under the Ottawa Agreement. The British were irked that McEwen wished to negotiate bilateral deals with other countries. Canberra had already agreed to exchange Australian motor vehicles for New Zealand primary products, an arrangement that discriminated against British vehicles. On 6 July Rumbold informed Home that the talks were approaching stalemate, adding that Britain would get nowhere until it threatened to abrogate all relevant agreements, including the meat guarantee and the BCSA.[56] On Sunday, Lee spent a quiet day 'in the country' with Crawford, 'swimming, playing croquet, and watching cricket'. Just 'before lunch', Crawford remarked that the Ottawa system was in irreversible decline, and stated that 'his advice would be unequivocally in favour of [Britain] joining the common market, in the belief that this would expand our markets without really jeopardising our position (in the longer term) in . . . Australia.' Lee 'was, fortunately perhaps, prevented from being able to continue this discussion by the arrival of a drink.'[57]

The British Cabinet was surprised, not just by the extent of Australia's demands, but by McEwen's insistence that the fundamentals of the Ottawa Agreement were negotiable. Thorneycroft apprehended that Australia was bent upon 'bringing virtually to an end the system of contractual preferences' enjoyed by British firms, especially those in the engineering industry.[58] Macmillan called for a complete reassessment of Britain's trade policy in relation to the Commonwealth and Europe. He chided Menzies and McEwen that:

> The Australian proposal opened up the whole question of future trade relationships within the Commonwealth. He did not regret this; this issue was already arising in Europe and in other parts of the Commonwealth and the United Kingdom would have to face it in any case before very long. But it might well lead to consideration of a much wider question – namely, the probable pattern of world trade in the next generation; and the United Kingdom Government needed time to look at some of these problems before they could propose a basis for a new Agreement with Australia. Above all it was important to avoid destroying what was left of the Ottawa system before they had anything ready to put in its place.[59]

Changing tactics, McEwen responded that Britain 'need not be unduly concerned about preferences', as Australia was prepared to compromise. But he stressed that he could not return home without some concession on wheat. The British, however, were reluctant to offer a wheat guarantee. British farmers were opposed to any special arrangements for marketing Australian wheat, and there was anxiety about the Canadian reaction. As Britain had justified its rejection of the IWA on free trade grounds, the announcement of special treatment for Australia would leave ministers open to the charge of bad faith.[60] Facing British resistance over wheat, McEwen threatened to denounce the Ottawa Agreement. Eden assured him that Britain would make a sincere effort to find a compromise. Temporarily placated, the Australians went home to prepare for the next round.[61]

In cabinet, Macmillan acknowledged the plight of Australian wheat farmers, whose market share had fallen since the 1930s. However, he suggested that agricultural concessions to Australia would encourage similar demands from New Zealand and other nations, making the reassessment of Britain's commercial strategy all the more desirable. Would it be worth enduring dearer bread and higher industrial costs, he asked, in order to safeguard manufacturing exports to Australia? Eden indicated that a wheat guarantee to Australia would disadvantage British farmers.[62] Macmillan acknowledged that it was difficult 'to reconcile a highly subsidised system of home agriculture with an export trade with countries overseas whose trade with us depended on our providing a market for their agricultural products.'[63]

Cabinet endorsed Macmillan's call for a thorough review of commercial policy. In fact, British commercial strategy was already under discussion in the light of the proposed Common Market. Britain floated a scheme for an industrial free trade area (FTA), encompassing the UK, the EEC, and the rest of the OEEC in September 1956. The struggle against Australia did not cause Britain to reject the Commonwealth in favour of Europe, but it did persuade ministers that the Commonwealth economic network was a wasting asset. Cabinet realized that New Zealand would follow Australia's lead on the Ottawa Agreement. In September 1956, Thorneycroft admitted that the economic interests of Britain and Australia were diverging, in view of the former's support for domestic agriculture, and the latter's emphasis on industrialization. Eden stated that, while an 'economic plan based on the Commonwealth connection would no doubt have been preferable . . . there was [now] little prospect of devising [such] a policy.'[64]

When negotiations resumed, in October, the British seized the initiative, and threatened to terminate the Ottawa Agreement unless Australia agreed to moderate its demands. McEwen was put on the defensive. The FTA proposal appeared to signal that Britain's commitment to the

Commonwealth was weakening, while the protectionism of the EEC countries was dampening Australian hopes of improved access to continental markets. The eventual British offer on wheat comprised a promise to exhort millers to purchase 28 million bushels (or 750,000 tons) of Australian wheat per annum over five years. Although this was hardly a firm guarantee, McEwen advised cabinet that it would be dangerous to assume that it was merely an opening position. He felt that, if the British insisted on 28 million bushels, then Australia should aim to cut BP margins to 5 per cent on capital goods and producer materials, and 10 per cent on other goods. If, however, the British could be pushed up to 37 million bushels (1,000,000 tons), Australia should settle for BP margins of 7.5 per cent on capital goods and producer materials, and 12.5 per cent on other goods. Cabinet authorized McEwen to negotiate on these lines.[65] But the British refused either to increase their cereal offer, or to countenance a 5 per cent margin on capital goods.[66] A final settlement was reached on 9 November, on the basis of 28 million bushels, and contractual BP margins of 7.5 per cent on capital goods and producer materials and 10 per cent on other goods. Australia also gave a confidential undertaking that it would eschew bilateral agreements that discriminated against British goods.[67]

The Economist commented that the cuts in contractual BP margins were justifiable, and would help Australia in negotiations with other countries.[68] But the Australian assault on the Ottawa system had been contained. Australia needed British markets more than Britain needed Australian markets. McEwen's blustering had unsettled the British, but they had rallied. His tactics boomeranged insofar as they made Britain more susceptible to the lure of Europe. Moreover, since most other countries had little interest in negotiating with Australia, there was no scramble to slash *actual* BP margins. In the mid-1960s, Crawford lamented that Australia was still 'awaiting the opportunity to negotiate with other countries'.[69]

The Anglo-New Zealand trade agreement 1959

As expected, revision of the Anglo-Australian trade agreement was followed by renegotiation of the Anglo-New Zealand agreement.[70] New Zealand shared Australia's concerns about British agricultural policy. In 1956, the government predicted that New Zealand's exportable surpluses of meat, butter, and cheese would rise by 38 per cent, 25 per cent, and 12 per cent respectively between 1952 and 1972. Officials doubted that these increased quantities would find remunerative outlets in

Britain. In July 1956, Wellington informed London that discontent with the Ottawa Agreement was rising, due to growing competition from Argentine meat, and that ministers might be compelled to seek renegotiation.[71]

Later in the year, after complaints from the British National Farmers' Union, the British government started to investigate the matter of Argentinian meat.[72] However, as the British were in no hurry to restrict foreign supplies, Wellington decided to initiate a full trade policy review. Submissions were received from every branch of the agricultural sector. The New Zealand Meat Producers' Board argued that, if 'we cannot be given effective protection [in Britain] then we would ask to be allowed . . . to use some of the preference enjoyed by the United Kingdom in New Zealand to bargain for other outlets.'[73] It was noted that Australia had secured an advantage over New Zealand through the revision of its Ottawa Agreement. W.B. Sutch advocated a radical policy, involving bilateral or barter deals with communist and Asian countries, regardless of the implications for GATT and Commonwealth Preference,[74] but this suggestion was treated with caution. In the event, the review found solid grounds for seeking cuts in BP margins in the light of Britain's failure to safeguard New Zealand's markets.[75] Britain would be given one last chance to reform, however, and a delegation would visit London to explain farmers' grievances.

Deputy Prime Minister Keith Holyoake, the leader of the 1957 mission to London, soon locked horns with Sir David Eccles, the President of the Board of Trade. Holyoake demanded action to restrict imports of foreign meat, and ensure that butter was imported only from 'consistent suppliers' such as Australia, New Zealand, and Denmark. He called for punitive measures against dumping, and requested annual bilateral agricultural consultations. The New Zealanders also asked for an assurance that all of their produce would continue to be exempt from tariffs and quantitative controls. Eccles declined to introduce stricter foreign meat quotas, citing Britain's responsibilities under GATT. The British stated that, in line with GATT policy, they intended to substitute tariff preferences for the meat quotas. Harsher meat quotas would also have damaged Britain's standing in Europe and the prospects for an industrial FTA. Holyoake responded by requesting immediate talks on the future of British preferences. The British threatened to suspend the agricultural talks if Holyoake insisted on discussing British preferences, and implied that New Zealand farmers would be punished if BP margins were cut. After hesitating, Holyoake agreed to postpone the reassessment of preferences until another year. In the meantime, he asked Eccles to give sympathetic consideration to any requests for cuts in individual BP margins, where these were needed to assist New Zealand in negotiations with other countries. No agreement was reached on this point, as New Zealand would not renounce barter trade.[76]

Deferral of the question of the Ottawa Agreement made it possible for Holyoake and Eccles to reach an interim agricultural settlement. The British agreed to hold annual consultations, and to consider legitimate requests for 'remedial measures' to counter 'serious injury' to New Zealand's meat trade. Britain also undertook to admit unlimited quantities of New Zealand dairy products and pork until 1967, provided that the Ottawa Agreement remained in force.[77] However, remedial measures would be activated only in an emergency. In view of New Zealand's demand for firm action against foreign suppliers, these results were disappointing, but Wellington had limited bargaining power. The *Financial Times* commiserated with New Zealand, but pointed out that Britain had little room for manoeuvre over agriculture, and suggested that the Ottawa system had entered 'a period of twilight'.[78]

The New Zealand Labour Party, which regained power in 1957, endorsed plans to revise the Ottawa Agreement. The 1957–8 balance-of-payments crisis, which was in part due to the low butter price, was taken as further evidence of unhealthy reliance on the British market.[79] New Zealand was also considering negotiating a trade treaty with Japan in order to secure parity with Australia in this growing market. Representatives of the British cotton industry advocated combining the Anglo-New Zealand and Japan–New Zealand talks, but British officials wished to delay the Anglo-New Zealand negotiations until after the Japan–New Zealand discussions, 'for we should then know where we stood.'[80] Any announcement of cuts in BP margins by New Zealand would be embarrassing in the approach to CTEC in September 1958, as this conference was designed to underline the Commonwealth's economic cohesion. In addition, the British were still waiting for the outcome of the industrial FTA talks in Europe. Acceptance of Britain's proposals would open up large new markets in Europe, in which case the value of BP margins in New Zealand would be diminished. However, in the event of stalemate in Europe, Britain would wish to maintain its grip on New Zealand. Warwick Smith of the Australian Department of Trade warned that Britain would use slippery tactics. Portraying the 1956 UKATA negotiations as an Australian triumph, he claimed that Menzies had finally mastered the British by threatening to scrap the Ottawa Agreement.[81]

Under the Anglo-New Zealand Ottawa Agreement, contractual BP margins were 20 per cent on most goods. Actual BP margins were even more generous. For instance, the margin on some wireless sets was 77 per cent. Ninety per cent of British exports to New Zealand were sheltered by tariff preferences. In 1957, the average BP margin in New Zealand was 24 per cent on consumer goods, 17.5 per cent on intermediate goods, and 18.1 per cent on capital goods. But Commonwealth produce did not enjoy margins above the contractual levels in Britain. At the start of formal negotiations, the New Zealanders outlined their intention to abolish contractual BP margins on basic chemicals, simple iron and steel products, tractors, aircraft and aircraft engines. They also wished to reduce contractual margins to 7.5 per cent or 10 per cent on other manufactures.[82]

Sir Frank Lee and A.E. Percival, of the Board of Trade, disputed that the Ottawa Agreement was biased, and argued that New Zealand's position was not identical to Australia's. New Zealand sent a larger share of its farm production to Britain than Australia did, and therefore reaped higher rewards from butter and meat preferences. The British were prepared to consider requests for cuts in contractual BP margins on individual items, but saw no need for wholesale reductions. British delegates also submitted a list of requests. They demanded that New Zealand renounce the use of import controls either for protective purposes or the promotion of barter agreements. New Zealand was asked to refrain from employing tariffs to protect inefficient producers from British competition, and also to guarantee that no other country would be accorded wider preferential margins than Britain.[83]

Sutch claimed that British preferences imposed a severe burden on New Zealand. As a developing country, New Zealand needed cheap, high quality steel and capital goods, but British firms often did not give value for money. British price rings took advantage of preferences by increasing prices and profit margins.[84] Iron and steel producers were among the prime culprits according to Sutch. M.R. Garner, of the UK Ministry of Power, admitted that steel producers operated a price agreement, but maintained that Commonwealth nations were offered a price discount in recognition of the fact that their markets were more stable than foreign markets. Britain, claimed Garner, had put up with shortages in order to satisfy New Zealand. He forecast that steel prices would fall, and concluded that there was no cause for discontent. Sutch replied that as British steel was dearer than foreign steel, British firms must be guilty either of inefficiency or of profiteering.[85] The British also had grounds for complaint against New Zealand. Although the official justification for import controls was the balance of payments problem, the British were convinced that New Zealand was rigging the system to protect local firms. Protests had been laid about restrictions on imports of woollen cloth, toys, fireworks, toilets, and footwear from Britain. Both sides had valid grievances, but it was commonly agreed that Sutch was responsible for the ill feeling that dogged negotiations.[86]

No progress was made until May 1958, when the New Zealanders gave a strong hint to Percival that they would not flinch from denouncing the Ottawa Agreement. Apparently chastened, 'Percival said that he would do his utmost to expedite completion of negotiations.'[87] A compromise over BP margins was soon in the offing, but the chasm between the British and New Zealand positions on non-discrimination brought negotiations to the verge of collapse. Eccles was adamant that New Zealand must refrain from discriminating against British goods in any way. He perceived 'disturbing signs that in future years there could be considerable pressures in New Zealand to use quota restrictions [and tariffs] discriminatorily in favour of other countries . . . I must stress that on these [points] we cannot give way.'[88] Britain had been annoyed by the deal under which newsprint, timber and fish from New Zealand were swapped for Australian motor vehicles, and looked askance at an impending agreement with Japan under which timber would be exchanged for textiles and sewing machines.[89] The British were anxious that such arrangements did not become an accepted feature of New Zealand trade policy.

Although New Zealand was willing to renounce tariff discrimination against Britain,[90] a commitment to non-discrimination as regards import licensing would have hindered trade with countries such as the USSR. Walter Nash, the Prime Minister, made a direct appeal to Macmillan, now the British Prime Minister:

> [T]he [British] request for an undertaking in regard to quota restrictions introduces a limitation which, in current world trading conditions, would make the initial development of new markets extremely difficult, if not impossible. Continued insistence by the United Kingdom on this kind of undertaking will leave us no choice but to consider the termination of the [Ottawa] Agreement.[91]

Macmillan was unresponsive until Nash threatened to abrogate the Ottawa Agreement at the conclusion of CTEC.[92] Macmillan now appreciated New Zealand's predicament: 'I sincerely hope that it will be possible . . . to find a flexible arrangement which would not prevent you entering into bilateral quota deals of the sort you contemplate but which would also give our exporters reasonable safeguards.'[93] A settlement was reached on the eve of CTEC. Under the Anglo-New Zealand trade agreement of 1959, which came into force in November 1958, Britain and New Zealand undertook in general terms to refrain from discriminating against each other's exports. But New Zealand would be permitted to 'resort to a limited measure of bilateral trading' with a view to opening new markets, provided no 'serious harm' was caused to British exporters. Eccles disliked this qualification, which was not part of the corresponding Australian letter of understanding. Nevertheless, he admitted that in practice Australia's commitment to non-discrimination had not amounted to much.[94]

The 1959 agreement obliged Britain to admit unrestricted quantities of all New Zealand primary produce, free of duty, until 1967. There was no change in preferences on commodities supplied by New Zealand. Contractual BP margins were reduced to 5 per cent on items where the original proposal had been to abolish them, and either 7.5 per cent or 10 per cent on other goods. Both sides promised to punish dumping by third parties.[95] Eccles did not know how to justify these cuts in contractual preferences to British manufactures, and told Sutch that, if 'New Zealand wanted to plan its economic affairs, he, too, would like to plan those of Great Britain and free entry of dairy produce could not be called planning'.[96]

The Anglo-New Zealand negotiations on the Ottawa Agreement could not be entirely divorced from the discussions on trade with Japan, butter dumping, and financial aid. During the middle of 1958, New Zealand and Japan entered into negotiations that resulted in a commercial agreement. As this agreement transferred Japan from the general tariff schedule to the lower MFN schedule, it effectively narrowed actual BP margins. Dumping attracted considerable attention as butter prices fell in the northern winter of 1957–8. In November 1957, New Zealand requested talks on the application of anti-dumping duties. C.F. Skinner, the Deputy Prime Minister, led a mission to London in April 1958 to put New Zealand's case. Britain was averse to introducing anti-dumping duties in case relations with other countries were damaged. However, in May, Eccles announced that Ireland, Sweden and Finland would be asked to accept voluntary export controls, while restrictions would be imposed on imports from the Soviet bloc. Voluntary controls proved reasonably effective, but New Zealand ministers regretted the grudging approach of the British towards their obligations under the 1957 agreement. Lee argued that it was unrealistic to expect Britain to impose countervailing duties when New Zealand was attacking British preferences. But New Zealand officials believed that the British would have ignored butter dumping in the absence of the threat to the Ottawa Agreement.[97] New Zealand's need for financial assistance was the other related issue. Britain's willingness to tide New Zealand over the 1958 external financial crisis owed much to the desire for an acceptable commercial settlement.

If Nash had carried out his threat to withdraw from the Ottawa Agreement, New Zealand's negotiating position *vis-à-vis* Britain would have been weakened rather than strengthened. Fortunately, the British were not prepared to risk a 'breach in the Imperial Preference system', as they anticipated that other countries including 'India and Pakistan might wish to follow New Zealand's example.'[98] Nash's biographer is mistaken in suggesting that 'New Zealand's preferential margins on British imports were . . . reduced very substantially or even abolished' after revision of the Ottawa agreement.[99] Most foreign countries had little interest in negotiating with New Zealand, and actual BP margins remained comparatively high during the 1960s. Revision of the Ottawa Agreement did not enhance New Zealand's economic independence.

Conclusion

During the 1950s the system of commercial treaties underpinning the Commonwealth economic network started to unravel. Although the early 1950s witnessed some stirrings of revolt against the NNP rule, it proved impossible for supporters of Commonwealth Preference to organize a coordinated attack on this aspect of the GATT charter. Commonwealth members were reluctant to confront the Americans over NNP, since their cooperation was required in a number of spheres including convertibility, agricultural trade, and the provision of development capital. While Australia and New Zealand were fairly cynical about GATT, they preferred it to a free for all in which there were no checks on large countries.

Once the NNP rule had been confirmed, the erosion by inflation of the protective value of specific Commonwealth preferences was irreversible. Pressure grew in Australia and New Zealand for the reduction of *ad valorem* BP margins. Deficiency payments, and Britain's reluctance to punish food dumping, added to the discord. For their part, the British resented the fact that Australia and New Zealand chose to cut sterling as well as foreign imports during balance of payments emergencies. Consequently, there was a gradual diminution in trust between the British and the Australian and New Zealand governments. Perceived interests were diverging, as Britain stimulated agricultural production, and Australia and New Zealand fostered infant industries and searched for supplementary markets. In the event, Australia and New Zealand failed to secure all of the desired reductions in contractual, let alone actual, BP margins. Canberra and Wellington could not afford to squeeze British manufacturers too far, because they relied on British goodwill in relation to dumping, capital flows, and European economic integration. Britain fought to protect its tariff preferences, and to obtain assurances that Australia and New Zealand would limit barter trade.

Before the CTEC meeting at Montreal in 1958, there had been speculation that the new Canadian government, which had assumed a strongly anti-American posture, would launch a crusade for the revitalization of the Ottawa system. However, after testing the waters, the Canadians decided not to proceed along these lines. Shortly after CTEC, the Canadian Prime Minister, John Diefenbaker, remarked to the French President, Charles de Gaulle, that the Ottawa Agreements were now mainly of 'sentimental' value.[100] Although this was an exaggeration, at least with respect to Australia and New Zealand, the Commonwealth Preference system was growing weaker. Australia and New Zealand were stepping up their efforts to find supplementary markets, and Britain was drawing closer to western Europe.

6
The Search for New Markets

Japan is inevitably a key element in US Far Eastern policy; accomplishment of US policy objectives in regard to Japan becomes in fact a fundamental to the security and economic welfare of the free world ... An expansion of her trade with sterling-area countries in south and southeast Asia, with Australia, and with other sterling-area countries is necessary. It is to such countries that Japan should be able to place an increasing reliance for exports. They also are potentially important sources of required food and raw materials.

US State Department memorandum, 1952[1]

We cannot have 86,000,000 Japanese locked up in that little island and refuse to trade with them ... [but that] does not mean that we should close down our clothing factories and bring in a lot of junk from a foreign country.

Sid Holland, Prime Minister of New Zealand, 1955[2]

Australia and New Zealand widened their commercial horizons in the 1950s, as it became obvious that the British market offered limited opportunities for growth. Japan, the USA, and continental Europe were the most attractive supplementary markets. Due to agricultural protection, however, it was difficult to gain entry for certain products to these markets. Australia and New Zealand had little bargaining power because their domestic markets for manufactures were small, while their actions were constrained by the Ottawa system and the need to safeguard local industries. The major industrial countries brushed aside their pleas in GATT for agricultural trade liberalization. The most that could be achieved in the 1950s and early 1960s was the establishment of footholds in the Japanese and American food markets.

Once Australia and New Zealand ventured outside the Common-wealth economic network they entered a global economic system dom-inated by the USA. The Americans were no less anxious than the British to mould the external economic policies of Australia and New Zealand, although their objective was different. Washington encouraged them to look to Asia, and especially Japan, for commercial opportunities. The USA hoped to sponsor a pro-Western economic grouping in the Far East. The alternatives for Australia and New Zealand were not encouraging, due to the power of the American and European farm lobbies to block agricultural trade reforms in GATT, and the reluctance of Washington to derail the Europeans' plans for greater economic integration.

After outlining early postwar thinking on the role of Australia, New Zealand, and Japan in the Far Eastern economy, this chapter examines the background to Japanese membership of GATT, the growth of trade contacts between Australasia and Japan in the 1950s, the attempts of Australia and New Zealand to reform GATT, and obtain greater access to the US market, and the reactions of these countries to changes in agricultural policy in western Europe.

America, Japan, and Australasia

In 1947 the Australian Minister for Post-War Reconstruction, John Dedman, called for the development of new commercial relationships with Asia.[3] He argued that Asian markets offered a greater potential for growth than either Britain or Europe. But words were not matched by deeds, as the British official M.E. Dening discovered on a visit to Aus-tralasia in 1949. John Burton of the Australian Department of External Affairs stated that Australia was unsure whether to take an active role in Asian economic and political affairs, or to abandon the region to communism. Alister McIntosh of External Affairs in Wellington said that New Zealanders regarded their country as an offshoot of Europe, and sought isolation from Asia. A minority in each country, of whom Burton was one, desired closer links with Asia, but their influence was not decisive. The British were disappointed by this attitude, since they had an understanding with the Americans that the Commonwealth would manage south and south-east Asia.[4]

The future of Japan, which was in the American sphere of influence, was an even more pressing economic question. Britain feared that the Commonwealth's position in the Far East would be weakened by Washington's promotion of Japanese economic recovery. The Americans regarded Australia and New Zealand as accessories of their economic strategy for Japan and the Far East. The US-controlled Supreme Commander for the Allied Powers (SCAP) governed Japan between 1945 and 1952. Initially, the Americans imposed tight restrictions on Japanese business in order to prevent the revival of the military-industrial complex and of low-wage competition for US consumer goods industries. But US attitudes soon changed, and in 1947 the doctrine of regional workshops was enunciated. Germany and Japan would become workshop economies, providing western Europe and Asia with capital goods, and thereby helping them both to resist communism and to become effective trading partners of the USA. Japan, it was hoped, would also be a strong market for the raw materials of India and southeast Asia.[5] During the 1950s, the Eisenhower administration viewed the Japanese economy as a locomotive for the rest of Asia. One American historian sees a parallel between this vision and the Greater East-Asian Co-Prosperity Sphere of the 1930s.[6] In practice, though, most Asian countries remained suspicious of Japan, while the Americans were increasingly distracted from Asia by the Soviet challenge, Latin America, and the emerging US balance-of-payments problem.

The Americans argued that Australia and New Zealand were ideal providers of food and raw materials to Asia, as well as convenient outlets for Japanese goods. The potential value of Australia and New Zealand as markets for Japanese industry was increased by Washington's imposition of draconian controls on trade with communist China. Since China had been Japan's main trading partner before the war, there was now an urgent need for alternative markets. From Washington's perspective, the solution lay in the eastern Sterling Area, ranging from Pakistan to New Zealand. If the West did not provide adequate outlets, Japan would require US aid on a permanent basis, and support for democracy would weaken.[7]

In 1954, senior ministers in the Eisenhower administration, including the Secretary of State, John Foster Dulles, and the Secretary of the Treasury, George Humphrey, argued that the USA could not import ever-increasing quantities of Japanese manufactures at the expense of domestic jobs. They contended that allied countries should share the burden of keeping Japan in the capitalist fold. Officials advised that Asia and Oceania had scope to raise their imports from Japan. Since Australia and New Zealand were importing less from Japan than they had done in the 1930s, they were well placed to double imports. In any case, Japanese capital goods would assist the Australian development programme.[8] However, the Commonwealth's opposition to Japanese membership of GATT presented a serious obstacle to Washington's plans.[9] The

Americans hoped that Japan would develop into a substitute for the protected US market, consuming rising quantities of primary produce from Australia and New Zealand. The National Security Council also believed that Australia, although not New Zealand, had the potential to export manufactures to Asia.[10] There appeared to be no role for Britain and the Sterling Area in this complex of relationships.

British and Commonwealth thinking on Japanese recovery was rather less expansive. Japan had purchased over 25 per cent of Australian wool exports in the mid-1930s, but very little merchandise from New Zealand. The Commonwealth was annoyed that its views on the Japanese economy were ignored by SCAP. Public opinion in Britain, Australia, and New Zealand was virulently anti-Japanese, reflecting wartime memories, and the perception that low-wage Japanese competition was 'unfair'. The Lancashire cotton industry had sustained large losses in Far Eastern markets at the hands of Japanese competitors during the 1930s.[11] Canberra and Wellington were conscious of Japan's potential as a market for primary produce, and anxious to restart trade in order to forestall an American monopoly of this market. Britain regarded the resumption of trade with Japan as necessary for sterling's reestablishment as a key currency in the Far East. But there was also a determination to safeguard industrial jobs in Australia, New Zealand, and Britain. While the British accepted that Japan must engage in trade, they resisted attempts to force large quantities of Japanese goods into the Sterling Area, and protested in vain against the embargo on Sino-Japanese commerce. Sterling Area wool exports to Japan recommenced in 1947, but the Australian public would not countenance the export of strategic raw materials to Japan until 1961. Government departments in Canberra were divided over trade with Japan. Officials responsible for foreign policy and exports, in External Affairs and Commerce and Agriculture, were more sympathetic to Japan than those responsible for protecting domestic industry, in Trade and Customs.[12]

Other parts of Asia had the potential to become important markets, but only in the long term. Australia, cautiously supported by New Zealand, played a leading role alongside Britain and Ceylon in designing the Colombo Plan, which was established in 1950 to channel aid into south and south-east Asia, but the immediate opportunities for trade were limited. New Zealand officials argued that only Japan was capable of becoming a major outlet in the foreseeable future. Trade with other Asian countries was constrained by low incomes, political unrest, and the absence of 'Westernized' tastes. Japan, however, could offer lucrative markets for various products, from racehorses and milk powder to timber and wool, provided Japanese manufactures were bought in return and quality was maintained. The Sterling Area as a whole would benefit if Japan switched from buying American to buying New Zealand produce.[13]

Until the early 1950s, trade between the Sterling Area and Japan was conducted under a series of trade and payments agreements, which were designed to facilitate recovery on a strictly reciprocal basis. It was intended that payments between Japan and the Sterling Area should balance, so that Tokyo could not accumulate sterling for conversion into dollars later. Washington initially welcomed these arrangements, hoping that they would encourage closer economic integration between Japan and the eastern Sterling Area. But the Americans later revised their view, concluding that the sterling payments agreements restricted the growth of Japanese trade. Australia and New Zealand did not permit Japanese goods to compete with domestic or British manufactures. However, when sterling's position became less precarious these controls were relaxed.[14] Canberra held that Australia should build up a large trade surplus with Japan on the basis of commodity exports, while other Sterling Area countries ran trade deficits with Japan in order to supply it with sterling.[15]

Pains were taken to identify vulnerable sectors. In 1952, Wellington drew up a list of industries that could be 'seriously affected' by Japan's accession to GATT and the achievement of MFN status. New Zealand's fancy goods, chinaware, clothing, and footwear producers, and British exporters of textiles, footwear, fancy goods, cameras, and bicycles would be in jeopardy. But the New Zealanders doubted the capacity of Japanese steel, cars, and heavy engineering goods to oust British exports. Australian officials concluded that the grant of full MFN status to Japan would lead to severe competition in textiles, iron and steel, some copper products, china, and toys. The British Board of Trade argued that the principal Japanese menace was still in textiles. However, in 1951 the British embassy in Tokyo reported that Japan was already a threat in markets for simple engineering products, such as sewing machines and bicycles, and would soon be able to supply low-quality capital goods including electricity generating equipment and diesel locomotives.[16]

In view of the overriding importance of full employment, the reluctance of Britain, Australia, and New Zealand to show Japan an open door is understandable. Trade with Japan seemed to involve as many risks as opportunities. Not until the mid-1960s did trade between Australia and Japan exceed trade between Australia and Britain, and it took even longer for New Zealand to reach this stage. Disharmony between the American and Commonwealth visions of the Far Eastern economic network came to the surface in the dispute over Japanese accession to GATT.

Japan's admission into GATT

Washington started to push for Japan to be allowed into GATT in 1948. Japan applied to become a Contracting Party to GATT in 1952, and was granted membership in 1955 subject to certain reservations. Tokyo wished to join for two reasons: firstly, to prevent discrimination against Japanese exports, and secondly, to achieve recognition as a member of the international economic community. As Japan was heavily reliant on imported food, fuel, and raw materials, it needed to remove all obstacles to export growth. Britain, Australia, and New Zealand were prominent in the struggle to deny Japan full membership of GATT.[17]

Under the 1951 Peace Treaty, Japan was obliged, for a period of four years, to offer MFN terms to any country that reciprocated. During this period it was anticipated that a permanent trade settlement would be reached. Britain, Australia, and New Zealand all declined to concede *de jure* MFN status to Tokyo in 1951, although Britain did offer Japan *de facto* MFN status as regards tariffs but not other trade barriers. Australia and New Zealand did not even go this far, and continued to apply a three-decker tariff, consisting of a low preferential rate, an intermediate MFN rate for GATT members, and a high general rate for other states including Japan. Goods from Japan also faced tight quantitative restrictions. Japan chose not to retaliate against these measures.

The British position was delicate. Outright rejection of Japanese membership would have offended the Americans and risked dividing the Commonwealth. Some Commonwealth countries, including India and Canada, were quite sympathetic towards Japan. But any surrender on this issue would have provided grist to the mill of GATT's critics in Britain. Sir John Hanbury Williams, chairman of Courtaulds, warned that the concession of MFN status to Japan would seriously damage the textile industry. Moreover, if Japan were to achieve full MFN status, Australia and New Zealand might have to increase tariffs on British and Japanese goods. The British feared that the Americans, who now guaranteed Australasian security, would force Canberra and Wellington to support Japan.[18]

Australia and New Zealand shared many of Britain's concerns about giving MFN treatment to Japan. By 1954, though, there was no longer any financial justification for discriminating against Japan.[19] Even so,

Canberra felt that it would be unwise to accord unqualified MFN terms to Japan, as 'Australia [must] retain the freedom necessary to ensure adequate protection for Australian industry against excessive Japanese competition.'[20] The Australians acknowledged that it might also be desirable to protect the markets of British firms. Wellington was equally determined to safeguard local industry.[21] Britain, Australia, New Zealand argued that the provisions in the GATT charter for controlling injurious imports were too weak to cope with the Japanese problem. They proposed that Japan's accession be made conditional on the negotiation of separate bilateral agreements between Tokyo and each Contracting Party, specifying penalties for unacceptable trading practices. Japan, backed up by the USA, dismissed this suggestion as insulting.[22]

Washington and Tokyo tried to persuade Commonwealth countries, including Australia and New Zealand, to give unqualified support to the Japanese application. The Americans would consider reducing tariffs on items of interest to the Commonwealth in return for their cooperation. For their part, the Japanese threatened retaliation against any Contracting Parties that, while voting for accession, also invoked Article XXXV of the charter, permitting discrimination against new members. The Japanese would consider taking 'penal action' against imports of wool and hides from such nations. Ignoring bribes and threats and threats, Britain, Australia, and New Zealand, together with India, France, and nine other nations, proceeded to vote for Japanese accession in August 1955, and to invoke Article XXXV.[23] In the event, the Japanese did not retaliate.

During the debate on Japan's accession to GATT, Britain, Australia, and New Zealand attached greater importance to the defence of existing jobs than to the extension of multilateralism. This was consistent with their approach during the commercial policy negotiations after the Second World War. Britain understood the risks that Commonwealth countries were taking. By invoking Article XXXV they were giving comfort to protectionists in the USA.[24] Nevertheless, they deemed it essential that trade with Japan be carefully managed rather than left to market forces.

Bilateral commercial treaties with Japan

As well as lobbying for entry into GATT, Japan approached Australia and New Zealand with requests for bilateral trade agreements. Initial contacts in 1952 bore fruit in the Australia–Japan Commercial Agreement of 1957 and the New Zealand–Japan Commercial Agreement of 1958.[25]

In May 1952, the Gaimusho (or Foreign Office) sent a *note verbale* to remind Australia that, in accordance with Article 12 of the Peace Treaty, Japan wished to negotiate trade agreements with individual allied powers.[26] Japan's goal was to obtain MFN status with respect to tariffs and non-tariff barriers. Australia and New Zealand acknowledged that bilateral agreements could provide greater security than the GATT charter did against 'unfair' competition, but were in no hurry to settle with Japan. They had to consider the reactions of the public, local manufacturers, and the British to the announcement of talks. But the 1954 Canada–Japan trade agreement encouraged Australia and New Zealand to act with greater urgency in defence of their Japanese markets.[27]

In 1953, New Zealand officials drew the attention of ministers to the advantages of a bilateral trade agreement with Japan. 'Such an arrangement could provide for the extension of certain existing MFN [tariff] rates to Japan in return for, perhaps, the binding against increase of rates on some of our exports.'[28] As Japan applied the same tariff to all comers, New Zealand would not need to request duty reductions. An agreement confined to selected products would shelter vulnerable New Zealand and British industries from Japanese competition. Officials also recommended that New Zealand discuss the mutual elimination of discriminatory import licensing and exchange controls on selected products. Import controls were the main form of trade regulation in Japan, which still had a weak balance of payments. It was argued that an agreement with Japan would boost the prospects for exports of wool, hides, and meat, although little progress was expected over dairy products. Cabinet agreed, in August 1953, to seek such an agreement.[29]

Gaining full admission to GATT was still Japan's main objective, and Tokyo indicated that any commercial agreement should terminate upon entry. New Zealand rejected this suggestion.[30] Formal trade talks were held in Wellington in June 1954. New Zealand offered a MFN tariff agreement covering a restricted list of items, and an exchange of letters abolishing non-tariff discrimination on the same products. The Japanese proposed to bind existing tariff rates on all New Zealand produce, and to provide a guaranteed market for a modest 10,000 bales of wool per annum. But Japan wished to retain the right to discriminate against New Zealand as regards non-tariff barriers, except relative to other Sterling Area countries, since it was constrained by other bilateral commitments and a shortage of sterling. When more sterling became available, the Japanese intended to import more from New Zealand.[31] More to the point, Japan's political stability depended on the alliance between farmers and the state, which was underpinned by stringent protection.[32]

The Japanese wanted New Zealand to make concessions on a wider range of products. However, their request for guaranteed quotas of certain goods was dismissed on the grounds that it would entail discrimination against Britain.[33] The Japanese demanded tariff concessions on sensitive products including hydro-electric equipment and woven textiles: 'cotton piece goods would be the first item the Diet would look for when the approval of the agreement was under consideration'.[34] New Zealand had already made an offer concessions on cotton yarn, and was reluctant to extend this to cloth. The Japanese were informed that 'the United Kingdom [cotton] manufacturers had strong agents in New Zealand who could cause political difficulties for the Government.'[35] The British Board of Trade was particularly worried about Japanese competition in cotton textiles.[36] New Zealand was in a quandary. Treasury questioned whether British weaving mills deserved special protection, and much was made of consumers' wish for more choice. But cautious counsels prevailed, and Wellington merely offered to apply existing import licensing rules in a 'liberal' spirit, leaving the tariff on Japanese woven cottons at the general level.[37]

The resulting draft settlement included reductions in tariffs, from the general to the MFN rate, on imports into New Zealand of certain Japanese goods, and the binding of Japanese tariffs on all New Zealand commodities. Wellington was disappointed that Japan had made no substantive concessions on non-tariff barriers. Nevertheless, officials argued that New Zealand should make the best of the situation. Consumers and capital goods purchasers would benefit from lower tariffs on Japanese goods, while Japan would obtain more foreign exchange to spend in New Zealand. But some politicians, including the Minister of Industries and Commerce, Jack Watts, feared an adverse public reaction to an apparently one-sided agreement. Watts recommended consulting Britain about the draft agreement.[38] The Labour opposition also cautioned the government to take care. Walter Nash reminded MPs of the case of a Japanese cardigan that had burst into flames in Christchurch. W.T. Anderton recalled that New Zealand had 'had plenty of cheap Japanese goods and seventy thousand unemployed' in the 1930s, spoke of the plight of workers in Lancashire, and urged ministers to seek guidance in London.[39]

In July 1954, the British at last expressed an opinion on the proposed New Zealand–Japan settlement. Britain was opposed to tariff concessions on cotton yarn and cloth, silks, rayon, scientific instruments, certain machinery and machine tools, and some iron and steel products. New Zealand was invited to provide a list of the items on which it proposed to reduce tariffs, so that London could 'examine the whole matter thoroughly'.[40] Having tentatively conceded MFN tariff rates on many sensitive products, Wellington was in a difficult position. Keith Holyoake, the Deputy Prime Minister, suggested modifying the draft agreement. Industries and Commerce complained that Japan's capacity to damage British trade had been underestimated, and warned that New Zealand's preferential position would be undermined by any failure to safeguard the market for British goods.[41] The British were under no illusion that they could prevent the growth of trade between Australia and New Zealand and Japan. As Peter Thorneycroft explained to Cabinet: 'we know that [the dominions] . . . are likely to reduce progressively their discrimination against Japan, to the disadvantage of our trade'.[42] The British government's tactic was to fight a series of delaying actions, as it could not afford to give the impression of acquiescing in the erosion of trading privileges.

After protracted reflection on British and domestic criticism, ministers decided to sign the draft treaty in April 1955. First, though, they made a final appeal to Tokyo over non-tariff discrimination. Tokyo responded by asking whether New Zealand would unreservedly support Japan's accession to GATT. As New Zealand did not give a satisfactory answer, the treaty remained unsigned.[43] British delaying tactics had succeeded, while the Japanese had shown that they would strike a hard bargain.

In November 1954, the Australian Department of Trade and Commerce accepted Japan's standing request for bilateral negotiations. Japan then stalled until after the GATT membership negotiations, and substantive bilateral discussions did not begin until 1956. John McEwen was the main advocate in cabinet of a deal with Japan. Although a protectionist in the industrial sphere, McEwen was also a pragmatist who understood the need for new export markets. His views on Japan were strongly influenced by John Crawford, the Secretary of Commerce and Agriculture. The merger, in 1956, of Trade and Customs with Commerce and Agriculture, to form the Department of Trade, gave McEwen, the new Minister of Trade, greater control over commercial policy. McEwen was particularly anxious to safeguard Australia's wool and wheat markets in Japan. Negotiations with Japan lasted from August 1956 until June 1957, the opening stages overlapping with the Anglo-Australian dispute over the Ottawa Agreement. Under the final settlement, Australia and Japan granted each another MFN treatment, with respect to tariffs and quantitative restrictions, across all trade categories. Japan also bound the duty-free status of wool until 1960. A safeguard clause gave

Australia the right to take emergency action to protect any domestic industries that incurred severe damage from Japanese competition. The Japanese promised to monitor and, if necessary, restrain manufacturing exports if Australian industries were in trouble. Australia undertook to give serious consideration to disinvoking Article XXXV within three years. The main sticking point had been Australia's demand for a larger share of Japan's wheat market, a request that went beyond non-discrimination. The Minister of Agriculture, Kono Ichiro, had recommended breaking off negotiations over this issue, on the grounds that a commitment to import specific amounts of Australian wheat would upset the Americans. But Kono was dismissed, and the Japanese government promised to facilitate imports of agreed volumes of Australian wheat.[44]

BP margins and public-sector contracting procedures were henceforth the only safeguards for British exporters against Japanese competition in Australia. Moreover, the Australia–Japan agreement eroded British preferences, as Japanese goods now moved from the general to the MFN tariff. Despite protests from Australian and British manufacturers, the treaty was signed in July 1957 for an initial term of three years. In view of Australia's deteriorating trade relations with Britain, Canberra was anxious to improve its standing in the Japanese market, while the Japanese were delighted to achieve a settlement with reputedly the most obstinate country in the Commonwealth.

Wellington became increasingly eager to reach agreement with Japan in 1958. New Zealand representatives in Tokyo warned that the Australia–Japan treaty would enable Australia to increase its share of the Japanese market at New Zealand's expense.[45] According to the *Otago Daily Times*: 'New Zealand can sign a trade treaty and consolidate [its] . . . market in Japan or continue without one and risk losing the lot to Australian competition.'[46] Even Industries and Commerce saw the need for a commercial treaty with Tokyo, as without one 'the Japanese might impose limitations on our exports'.[47] Visiting Wellington in 1957, Ushiba Nobuhiko, who had negotiated the agreement with Australia, expressed interest in an identical arrangement with New Zealand. The Prime Minister, Kishi Nobusuke, pointed out that Japan did not intend to undermine New Zealand's industries, but rather to supply 'some things that would be complementary to the New Zealand economy such as heavy machinery.'[48] Japan's objective was to supplant British exports.

Walter Nash's Labour government was initially suspicious of Japan. Nash stated that there would be no trade agreement with Tokyo, and condemned Japan's record of 'unfair' competition.[49] In view of New Zealand's poor trading outlook, this stance proved untenable, and Japan's offer of talks was taken up in 1958. Circumspection was urged on the government from several quarters. The British High Commissioner warned Nash not to make 'abrupt changes' in policy 'which might expose our trade to disruptive competition'.[50] The New Zealand Manufacturers' Federation called for 'extreme caution', and demanded the retention of licensing powers to manage disruptive Japanese competition, but some manufacturers looked forward to buying cheaper Japanese machinery and intermediate products. Farmers were curiously indifferent. Meat producers told the government that the US market was of greater consequence than the Japanese market. Dairy producers regarded trade with Japan as of secondary interest compared with the problem of butter dumping in Britain.[51]

When formal negotiations began in July 1958, Japan's requests were for MFN treatment for all its goods with respect to tariffs and import licensing, and for the disinvocation of Article XXXV.[52] Wellington asked Japan to confirm the MFN tariff status of all its exports, bind the duty-free entry of New Zealand wool, and refrain from discriminating against New Zealand in the application of non-tariff barriers. It was also suggested that Japan purchase 15,000 tons of New Zealand meat annually. The New Zealanders expected to make little progress on dairy produce.[53] Wellington hoped to avoid making concessions on sensitive textile products, engineering goods, and motor vehicles.[54] But Tokyo insisted on 'more reasonable treatment [of] Japanese textiles having regard to the United Kingdom supplies.'[55] New Zealand relented when it became clear that Japan would make no agricultural concessions unless all industrial exceptions were withdrawn. The resulting agreement, signed in September 1958, was almost identical to that between Australia and Japan, the main exception being that Japan would endeavour to import 10,000 tons of New Zealand meat per annum, confirming the dominion's status as principal supplier.[56] New Zealand had preserved parity with Australia. Nash told parliament that he had 'secured the best possible conditions for maintaining and expanding New Zealand's growing exports of meat and wool to Japan for the next three years.'[57]

It was anticipated that the extension beyond 1960 of Japan's commitment to import wool free of duty would depend on the disinvocation of Article XXXV. Indeed, it was feared that Japan would not renew either treaty unless satisfaction was forthcoming on this issue. Since the bilateral agreements with Japan made provision for safeguarding domestic industries, there was no further need to invoke Article XXXV.

Australian and New Zealand producers were adequately protected, and British firms bore the brunt of Japanese competition. For political reasons, however, Canberra and Wellington could not afford to appear soft on Japan. Fortunately, Tokyo was patient, and did not abolish the duty-free status of wool. New Zealand and Australia disinvoked Article XXXV in 1962 and 1964 respectively.[58]

As a result of their trade agreements with Japan, Australia and New Zealand obtained access to cheaper imports as well as a growing market for most primary commodities except dairy produce. British opposition thwarted New Zealand's first attempt to reach a commercial settlement with Japan in 1954, but the British did not actively interfere in the later negotiations between Australia, New Zealand, and Japan. There is some irony in the fact that the new economic relationship between Australasia and Japan was, like the old colonial relationship with Britain, based on the exchange of primary produce for manufactures.

GATT and the Americans

Economic relations between Australia and New Zealand and the USA had been far from smooth during the 1940s. In the 1950s, Australia and New Zealand continued to press the Americans to take the lead in liberalizing world agricultural trade. But US farmers enjoyed disproportionate influence, due to the over-representation of rural states in the Senate, and succeeded in repulsing all attacks. Anger over US policy and GATT's impotence boiled over from time to time. Australia and New Zealand often talked of withdrawing from GATT, but always drew back from this step.

Agricultural costs of production were higher in the USA than in Australasia. The US farming sector had been depressed between the wars, and a system of price supports, backed by tariffs and quotas, had been introduced to boost rural incomes. These measures stimulated production and led to the growth of stockpiles, which the government dumped abroad, undercutting Australia and New Zealand exporters. In 1954, GATT granted a comprehensive waiver to the USA, allowing it to continue to restrict imports under Section 22 of the Agricultural Adjustment Act. While the Randall Commission on foreign economic policy condemned agricultural protectionism, and the Secretary of Agriculture, Ezra Taft Benson, tried to extend the role of market forces, the farmers prevented substantive reform.[59] Washington lamented the effect of its own policies on small countries like Australia and New Zealand. One American official pointed out that offhand US actions in the agricultural arena could be 'of the greatest moment . . . to the entire population of a country such as New Zealand'. But the US government was reduced to offering sympathy to the victims of 'irresponsible' policies.[60]

During the early 1950s, the Americans clashed in GATT with Australia, New Zealand and other butter exporters over the virtual embargo on dairy imports. The Americans agreed to withdraw controls operated under Section 104 of the Defense Production Act, but still excluded all but token amounts of foreign butter under Section 22 of the Agricultural Adjustment Act.[61] In 1953, the Australian ambassador told Dulles that, due to US dairy policy, 'it [had] become increasingly difficult to find justification for the restrictions that the [GATT] Agreement imposes on the methods which Australia may adopt to foster its own developing industries.' New Zealand's ambassador remarked that his government had the right to retaliate against US dairy controls, and urged the Americans to abide by the 'letter and spirit' of GATT.[62]

In 1953–4, US protectionists stepped up the campaign for a higher wool duty. The State Department was alarmed by the possible implications for relations with the Commonwealth. Australia had threatened to reject GATT in 1947 because of the US wool tariff. It was noted that 'indications from Australia and New Zealand . . . point strongly to the conclusion that our concession on wool is what keeps these countries in the General Agreement and that they would withdraw if we increased our import charges on wool.'[63] Canberra's adherence to GATT was 'important because of Australia's key position as [an] industrialized country in south-east Asia and member of [the] British Commonwealth with contractual obligations to other Commonwealth countries under Ottawa Agreements'.[64] Other countries might follow Australia and New Zealand out of GATT, giving the detested Ottawa system a new lease of life. Eisenhower vetoed the proposed increase in the wool duty, offering the farmers subsidies instead.

Subsidized dumping of US dairy, wheat, and meat surpluses was stepped up in 1954 under the guise of the PL480 aid programme to developing countries. Washington's claim that surplus disposals did not interfere with regular trade was strongly disputed by Australia and New Zealand. Holyoake lectured the US ambassador on the iniquity of dumping milk powder. The New Zealanders added that the effect of dumping was to 'prejudice our ability to promote the development of our country and our own security, which is of mutual concern to both the United States and New Zealand under the ANZUS treaty.' American policies raised 'very serious doubts in New Zealand as to the value of the GATT.'[65] The chairman of the New Zealand Dairy Products Marketing Commission warned that he would have to send more produce to communist countries, where prices were stronger due to the absence of cheap US supplies. But Secretary Benson saw no alternative to large-scale dumping: he was keen to reduce support prices, but the farm lobby vetoed decisive action on this front. John Crawford requested that the Americans consult other interested parties before dumping surplus food, and called for the establishment of international authorities to monitor and control disposals. He was particularly galled by the recent sale of surplus wheat to Japan, over which there had been no consultation. US officials surmised that Australia would tolerate surplus disposals in return for proper consultation. While the Americans undertook to discuss disposals with other governments, they stressed that they were under strong domestic pressure to act unilaterally.[66]

Australia was prominent in the international campaign to secure a comprehensive review of GATT. Menzies claimed that GATT had fallen short of expectations, and stated that Australia, in combination with like-minded countries, would consider quitting if the review did not result in substantive reform. Washington observed that, while many countries were calling for a review, Australia was alone in openly disparaging GATT.[67] Wellington, however, was unenthusiastic about the proposed review 'because of the possibility that the preponderance of opinion among the Contracting Parties might be such as to enforce a balance of amendments contrary to New Zealand's interests', particularly as regards permanent import controls.[68]

Wellington's milder tone also reflected the fact that GATT was the only element of the postwar institutional settlement to which it was a signatory. Treasury felt that GATT membership gave New Zealand 'a voice in international economic matters . . . [that is] entirely disproportionate to our size and economic importance.'[69] Although New Zealand was far from satisfied with GATT's inability to tackle the Americans over agriculture, it accepted the need for a 'stabilising influence' in international trade.[70] It seemed likely that New Zealand would be even worse off outside GATT, as it would lose all recourse against the trade practices of other countries. New Zealand officials regarded themselves as allies of Washington in the struggle to curb the US farm lobby, and the Americans encouraged them to believe that their protests strengthened the hands of the administration.[71]

Addressing GATT, McEwen stated that the review must confront the central problems of agricultural trade, including quantitative restrictions, domestic subsidies, and export subsidies. He also foresaw a role for GATT in the promotion of commodity agreements to dampen price fluctuations.[72] New Zealand supported this approach. But nothing of consequence emerged from the 1954–5 review. The Americans were not prepared to recast their agricultural policies, although they did promise to show greater consideration to other countries over surplus disposals. Washington would not countenance any new commodity agreements, arguing that market forces should be given free rein. The Americans also emphasized that foreign interference in US agricultural policy would never be tolerated. Despite the review's disappointing outcome, Canberra decided that the alternatives to GATT, namely bilateralism and anarchy, were even less attractive. Australia even voted for the Section 22 waiver, as it was anxious not to precipitate a US walkout.[73]

Australia and New Zealand continued to urge the USA and other countries to liberalize agricultural trade. Canberra was instrumental in persuading GATT to commission a study group, chaired by Gottfried Haberler of Harvard University, on the effects of agricultural protection. Although the Haberler report was critical of protection, the committee was not allowed to pass judgement on individual countries. Australia and New Zealand hoped that this report would lead to reforms, but the vested interests would not agree to specific action.[74]

Surplus disposals, especially under PL480, continued to sour relations between Australia and New Zealand and the USA during the late 1950s and early 1960s. For practical reasons, the US Department of Agriculture was anxious to dispose of surpluses as quickly as possible. But the State Department was more sensitive about the impact of disposals on other exporters. After receiving another Australian remonstrance in 1957, the Acting Secretary of State, Christian Herter, acknowledged that surplus disposals had become 'a source of considerable friction in our international relations'.[75] State noted that the complaints of foreign leaders, who alleged that the USA was merely taking 'advantage of for-tuitous market opportunities to the exclusion of other suppliers', had 'considerable justification'.[76] As US policy remained unchanged, Australia and New Zealand continued to lose orders in developing countries, including parts of the Commonwealth, for wheat, cotton, and certain dairy products.[77] The introduction of tariffs on lead and zinc provoked a further round of Australian protests and an apologetic response from Eisenhower.[78] In 1959, the Americans launched the Food For Peace programme, which attempted to involve exporters such as Australia, New Zealand, Canada, and Argentina in decisions about surplus disposals. Food For Peace went some way towards meeting Australian and New Zealand concerns about lack of consultation, but did not prevent the generation of surpluses.[79]

Australia still had doubts about GATT. As Crawford remarked in 1958, Australia 'must continually examine where multilateral systems under the present real handicaps evident in the world to-day are getting us.' He 'would not hesitate to recommend leaving GATT and trying alternative policies if . . . this would enable us to do a better job'.[80] Sutch had no time for GATT, which he regarded as hopelessly biased against New Zealand. He advocated barter trade as a method of promoting exports to new markets in Asia and eastern Europe. The Dairy Products Marketing Commission and Wolfgang Rosenberg concurred that barter trade could open up large markets in the Soviet bloc. Rosenberg pointed out that Russia and Czechoslovakia were able to supply modern capital goods as return cargoes.[81] But New Zealand merely flirted with barter trade, as it was not prepared to break with either GATT or Britain.

Fortunately, the US market was not completely impenetrable. In 1954, Frank Holmes of Victoria University College in Wellington, remarked that 'meat seems to offer the best prospects for any significant expansion of New Zealand's dollar earnings.'[82] On a visit to New Zealand in 1957, J.B. Condliffe, then of Stanford University, advised New Zealand farmers to focus on the huge American market instead of wasting energy on smaller markets in Asia. Meat exports to the USA faced tariffs but not quantitative restrictions. In the 1950s, New Zealand overcame a number of obstacles to the development of meat exports to the USA, including poor hygiene standards, inadequate shipping services, overzealous customs inspections, and the reluctance of American distributors to push foreign meat. By 1960, the USA had outstripped Britain as an outlet for New Zealand beef and veal.[83]

Reporting on a tour of the Asia Pacific in 1960, Secretary Benson commented favourably on the opportunities for New Zealand lamb and low-grade Australian beef in the US market. Benson maintained that the expansion of meat imports from Australia and New Zealand would not cause undue distress to US livestock farmers, and hoped to encourage reciprocal purchases of American wheat, feeding stuffs, and tobacco. But American cattlemen and sheepfarmers called for increased protection on the grounds that they could not compete with Australasian producers. Rising quantities of imported mutton were finding their way into frankfurters and other sausages. As the US government wished to avoid any increase in protection, no action was taken until 1964, when the Johnson administration persuaded Australia and New Zealand to accept voluntary meat quotas.[84]

Australia made it clear in 1960 that one of its key objectives in the next GATT round would be to secure a reduction in the US wool tariff.

The USA was then buying only 1.5 per cent of Australian wool exports compared with 6 per cent in 1947–8. Crawford told the Americans that the economic development of Australia was vital to the strategic balance in south-east Asia. A rise of 30 per cent in total wool exports was needed in order to finance imports for the Australian development programme. If this target could not be met, Australia would have to reintroduce import licensing. Crawford also pointed out that the competitiveness of the US textile industry depended on access to wool at world prices. Australia regarded America as the 'natural' source of supply of many products, but the public was uneasy about the bilateral trade deficit with the USA. Crawford added that Australia might be prepared to enter into a trade agreement with the USA on terms consistent with both countries' responsibilities to GATT. Canberra had more discretion than formerly over BP margins.[85] However, the US administration was unresponsive. American farmers had already been promised that the wool tariff would not be reduced, and, as one official put it, 'Westerners feel very deeply indeed on this subject.'[86]

To some extent, Australia and New Zealand compromised their case on agriculture by their maintenance of high levels of industrial protection. Washington often complained about Australasian import restrictions. Some embarrassment was caused by the guaranteed prices and subsidies paid to Australian farmers. New Zealand's embargo on butter and cheese imports, which was part of the balance of payments crisis package in 1958, left it open to ridicule in GATT.[87] Nevertheless, agricultural policy in the USA and other industrial countries was driven by domestic considerations, not by any desire to punish Australia and New Zealand. As their domestic markets were so small, the threat of withdrawal from GATT was the only bargaining counter possessed by Australia and New Zealand. Washington occasionally responded to hints of withdrawal by making marginal adjustments to agricultural policy. But all three parties understood that the disruption of GATT, and the disappearance of even the semblance of order in international commerce, would damage Australia and New Zealand far more than it damaged the USA.

The Common Agricultural Policy

Continental western Europe was the other region into which Australia and New Zealand were keen to send more farm produce. Although the continental nations did not impose wool tariffs, they were unrelenting in the protection of domestic food producers, few of whom could have coped with Australasian competition. Western European governments assisted farmers with tariffs, quotas, subsidies, and price supports. Depressed farming areas had supported the extreme right between the wars, and postwar governments considered rural prosperity as a pre-condition for stable democracy.[88]

Agricultural policy was a central concern of the EEC. Its founders envisaged the staged introduction of free trade in agricultural products among member countries. The proposed Common Agricultural Policy would ensure decent living standards for farmers and fair prices for con-sumers. Details of this juggling act were not decided until the early 1960s, and the CAP did not come into force until the late 1960s. In the meantime, the key question for other countries was whether the EEC would follow liberal or protectionist principles. The system that emerged reflected the ingrained agricultural protectionism of EEC member states. Markets for foodstuffs covered by the CAP would be bolstered by price supports and variable import levies. Flexible tariffs would enable the authorities to regulate imports according to the state of the internal market. Food surpluses would be dumped abroad. Harry Johnson, a Canadian economist, justifiably described the CAP as a 'vastly expensive nonsense'.[89] Although Australia and New Zealand could not be certain how the CAP would develop, they had every reason to fear the worst.

The implications of Britain's growing involvement in the European project are discussed in the next two chapters. Irrespective of Britain's role in Europe, Canberra and Wellington had a strong interest in the structure of the new continental agricultural system. As soon as the Treaty of Rome became public, in 1957, the main exporters of temper-ate primary produce, including Australia and New Zealand, began to express concern as to whether it could be reconciled with GATT. Article XXIV of GATT made provision for the formation of a customs union with a common tariff against the rest of the world. But it was unclear whether Article XXIV permitted the trade controls contemplated by the EEC. Discussion of this issue was vitiated by high politics. The USA was anxious to avoid any action that might derail European integration.

Wellington sent the six prospective members of the EEC (the Six) a note in January 1957, asking them to respect the interests of food exporting nations. In November 1957, New Zealand sent a further note to all OEEC members about the impact of agricultural protectionism on extra-European states.[90] Australia and Canada tried to stimulate debate on the agricultural implications of the EEC at the Intersessional Committee meeting of GATT in September 1957. But there was a 'marked lack of interest among most countries' in discussing European agricultural policy. The American delegation claimed to be inadequately staffed to consider this issue, while the British warned against 'disclosing our hand to the Six before an opportunity had occurred to organise support for a common line against the Six.' The UK therefore favoured postponing discussion until the meeting of Commonwealth officials on the eve of the next session of GATT.[91]

The Australians, led by Crawford, played a significant part at the pre-GATT meeting of Commonwealth officials in October 1957. Australia recommended that the establishment of the EEC be used as a pretext for examining whether the rules of GATT, with respect to agriculture, should be entirely revised.[92] Crawford chided Sir Frank Lee for offering no more than 'sympathetic understanding' of the Australian position. At a time when Commonwealth unity was most needed, argued Crawford, Lee's lukewarm attitude could be interpreted as presaging a split between the UK, as a major importer of agricultural products, and the remainder of the Commonwealth, which relied heavily on agricultural exports.[93]

The British were not prepared to condemn the concept of the CAP, as they were involved in complex and sensitive talks with the Six and other European countries over the proposed industrial free trade area. Despite the efforts of Australia, New Zealand and Canada, the development of the CAP was not discussed at length in subsequent GATT meetings. Australia maintained that Contracting Parties would require regular information if they were to comment on the EEC's evolving agricultural policy. But the Six argued that progress reports were not desirable, and most other Contracting Parties were unwilling to press them on this point.[94]

The Six met at Stresa, in July 1958, to consider the broad outline of EEC agricultural policy. Australia and New Zealand pleaded with them to adopt a liberal stance. A note presented to the French Foreign Office emphasized New Zealand's dependence on earnings from agricultural exports. A protectionist regime would reduce New Zealand's capacity to import European manufactures: 'increased access [for Commonwealth produce] would be in the interests of a mutual expansion of trade between the European Economic Community and New Zealand.'[95] In a similar note, Canberra pointed out that the Six provided 25 per cent of Australia's export earnings, and stressed that the pace of Australian economic development depended on obtaining 'increased scope' for exports to continental Europe.[96] These pleas were politely disregarded.

At the GATT session in October–November 1958, New Zealand reiterated its views on European agricultural policy, and called for the establishment of procedures, under the auspices of GATT and the EEC, to safeguard the interests of third parties. The Six agreed to consult with third parties in cases of actual or imminent damage to exports, but New Zealand made a further complaint in GATT, in 1959, to the effect that agricultural tariff cuts were being nullified by the growth of non-tariff barriers.[97]

A preliminary draft of the CAP was issued in early 1960. New Zealand and Australia continued to lobby for the Six to acknowledge their responsibilities to exporters of agricultural produce. As well as working through GATT channels, Australia, Canada, New Zealand and the USA[98] proposed a separate joint approach to the EEC Commission and the Six on the CAP. Canada, which was responsible for this initiative, hoped that the Six would be more responsive to pressure from a group of agricultural exporters than from individual countries.[99] Since the intention was to maintain confidentiality, other nations, including the UK, were not officially informed. The British position was to 'leave New Zealand and the other interested countries to develop their views'. Britain would support an attempt to have the CAP thoroughly discussed in GATT, but would not take a prominent part in the debate in case attention was drawn to its own agricultural policies.[100] In the end, however, neither the collective meetings nor GATT were productive. Although the other EEC countries agreed to meet the exporters, the French refused to see all four nations together and demanded instead to meet first with the USA and Canada, and then with Australia and New Zealand. The New Zealanders then insisted on meeting the French alone and not in the company of Australians. The Six refused to bend on the protectionist nature of the nascent CAP, although several members including the Netherlands condoled with the exporting countries. Discussion of EEC policies in GATT petered out in a series of negotiations lasting several years over individual agricultural items including wheat and dairy products.[101]

The practical difficulties experienced by Australian and New Zealand exporters in continental markets, during the late 1950s and early 1960s, stemmed from the policies of individual EEC members. Australia and New Zealand succeeded in negotiating trade agreements with several European countries, including West Germany, but not France, during the 1950s. Nevertheless, Australian and New Zealand food encountered official resistance in every important European market except the

Netherlands. The Italians would not permit frozen or chilled meat to be sold in the same shops as fresh meat. Obstructive German bureaucrats made it difficult for New Zealand to fill the quotas agreed under the 1959 New Zealand–West Germany commercial treaty. France responded to complaints about rough handling of New Zealand exporters by criticizing New Zealand's import controls.[102]

In the early 1960s, there was a shifting, informal alliance between the main agricultural exporters: the USA, Australia, New Zealand, South Africa, Canada, and sometimes Denmark, Argentina, and Uruguay. These countries sought to pin down and confront the EEC over agricultural policy, but the Six refused to discuss the CAP in the Dillon Round of GATT. The ambivalence of the USA was a major frustration for other exporting nations. Although the Americans disapproved of the excesses of the proposed CAP, they regarded European unity as a crucial foreign policy goal. Furthermore, Washington had mixed feelings about supporting countries, such as Australia and New Zealand, which still discriminated against American products with British preferences.[103] In the absence of determined American intervention, the EEC could not be forced to moderate its agricultural policies. At times, even Australia and New Zealand were unable to present a united front. In 1959, lack of interest in Canberra and other Commonwealth capitals, resulted in the indefinite postponement of Wellington's plans for an offensive in the OEEC against discriminatory import controls in Europe. The New Zealand High Commission in Canberra concluded that the Australians were reluctant to cooperate because they had not suffered as badly as New Zealand had from such discrimination.[104]

The limited bargaining power of Australia and New Zealand over the CAP was further reduced by the need to avoid anything that could be construed as provocation, and which might render the Europeans hostile on other questions. As will be explained in the next chapter, during the late 1950s New Zealand and Australia contemplated the possibility of entering into an economic association with the EEC in the context of a wider Anglo-European settlement. When Britain applied for membership of the EEC in 1961–63, Australia and New Zealand sought the goodwill of the Six in arranging for special concessions to safeguard Commonwealth trade. The willingness of Australia and New Zealand to look beyond Britain and the Commonwealth, and to join with the USA and other countries in diplomatic action on the proposed CAP, was a modest but not insignificant departure from previous practice. But only an agreement between the USA and the EEC could have turned the tide of agricultural protectionism.

Conclusion

In 1962, Sir John Crawford explained the essence of Australian trade diplomacy to an audience at Sydney University 'We must sell our wool, minerals, wheat and other products wherever we can.'[105] Crawford anticipated that Asian markets would offer the best opportunities for growth. New Zealand's position was very similar. During the 1950s, Australia and New Zealand had conducted a sustained campaign for the liberalization of agricultural trade, both in GATT and in discussions with individual countries, including the USA and Japan, and groups such as the EEC. The results of this activity were rather modest. The European response to approaches from Australia and New Zealand was unsympathetic. Although the Japanese and the Americans were sympathetic, they declined to expose their farmers to unregulated Australasian competition.

In an international climate pervaded by agricultural protectionism, Canberra and Wellington faced daunting obstacles to the development of new markets. Moreover, they had to bear in mind the effect of any new trading arrangement on domestic and British manufacturers. The bargaining position of Australia and New Zealand was fatally weakened by their insignificance in the global economy. As their domestic markets were small, they could offer no credible enticements to potential trading partners. While Australia and New Zealand would have caused a stir by walking out of GATT, such a gesture would have been self-destructive.

The trade of Australia and New Zealand developed a strong Asian focus in the late twentieth century. This trend was foreseen by the Americans fifty years ago. Cold War restrictions on Sino-Japanese trade increased the likelihood that Japan and other countries along the Pacific Rim would come to terms over trade. Japan needed new markets for manufactures, as well as increased supplies of wool and minerals. Australia and New Zealand hoped to supply Japan with food surpluses that could not be sold at remunerative prices in Britain. The bilateral trade agreements of 1957 and 1958 laid the foundations for the development of commercial relations between Japan and Australia and New Zealand. As niche players in the global economy, Canberra and Wellington had to work within the framework constructed by the major powers.

7
Britain, the Commonwealth, and Europe, 1945–60

> Imperial Preference has had particular political significance since World War II as a hindrance to British participation in the movement towards European unification. The UK, fearing a fundamental incompatibility between the existing economic bonds with the Commonwealth and the adoption of similar close ties with Europe, chose to maintain the former and reject the latter. Recently, however, frightened by the prospect of exclusion from a unified European Common Market, Britain has attempted to find a means of reconciling the two relationships.
>
> *US State Department, 1957*[1]

The postwar movement for European integration was a reaction to the failure of the European state-system to guarantee peace and economic stability. Britain and the Commonwealth viewed this process with ambivalence. Having fought two world wars, the Commonwealth sought a democratic and prosperous western Europe. At the same time, however, there was concern lest British involvement in European integration weakened the Commonwealth economic nexus. Until the mid-1950s, the British viewed their economic ties with the Commonwealth as of greater value than their ties with Europe, but thereafter perceptions changed rapidly, and in 1961 the Macmillan government applied for membership of the EEC.

This chapter focuses on the evolution of Britain's policy on European economic integration in the 1940s and 1950s, giving special emphasis to the attempts of Canberra and Wellington to influence the debate. Due to New Zealand's extreme dependence on the UK market, it had more to lose than Australia did from close British involvement in Europe. By 1960, it was apparent that Britain would not be able to join

Europe without disrupting the Commonwealth economic network. After considering the proposal for a European Customs Union (ECU) in 1947, we examine Britain's reaction to the announcement of the Common Market, and the response of Australia and New Zealand to Britain's scheme for an industrial free trade area (FTA) in Europe. New Zealand in particular was interested in exploring the potential for associating the dominions with a free trade arrangement in Europe.

The European Customs Union

During the Second World War, British leaders indicated that they were prepared to take the lead in organizing some form of postwar European federation. In the House of Commons, in 1944, the Foreign Secretary, Anthony Eden, proposed a customs union between France, Belgium, the Netherlands, Luxembourg, Norway, and the entire British Commonwealth. However, this offer ought not to be taken at face value. Britain was anxious to encourage battered allies, and to stake a claim for leadership of a 'third force' capable of competing with the USA and USSR after the war.[2]

Apart from a few enthusiasts, including Churchill's son in law Duncan Sandys, the British viewed Europe at best as an accessory to the Commonwealth, and at worst as a liability due to its poverty and vulnerability to Soviet attack. The American attitude to European integration was rather different. Weary of European wars, the USA hoped to achieve a permanent end to European rivalries. Washington urged the British and the continentals to work towards greater economic integration, in order to hasten postwar recovery, provide a healthy market for US exports, and combat communism.[3]

Ernest Bevin, Foreign Secretary in the postwar Labour government, had been an advocate of economic cooperation between the British and other European empires in the 1920s. But in 1929–30 Britain and the dominions had rejected a French proposal for a European federation with a common external tariff, partly because it might have entailed discrimination against empire produce in the British market. In 1945, Bevin and the Foreign Office desired close political and military collaboration between Britain, France, and other continental countries, and to this end were open to proposals for economic cooperation. They also affirmed that the opportunities for greater commercial integration between western Europe and the Commonwealth were worth investigating in the event of the collapse of the ITO and GATT discussions. Announcement of the Marshall Plan in 1947 enabled the Americans to inject more urgency into the debate on European economic cooperation. Although Britain wanted the United Nations to manage the Marshall Plan, Washington asked the Europeans to establish a Committee on European Economic Cooperation (CEEC) to draw up proposals for the allocation of Marshall Aid. The USA intended the CEEC to be a catalyst for European integration, and welcomed France's proposal for a European Customs Union (ECU). Putting aside initial scepticism, Bevin and the Foreign Office argued that British involvement in the ECU would help to cement a military alliance in Europe. However, the Treasury, the Board of Trade, and the Commonwealth Relations Office contended that British participation in the ECU would undermine the Sterling Area and Commonwealth Preference. Sir Stafford Cripps, the Chancellor of the Exchequer, maintained that a Commonwealth customs union would be preferable, although the Commonwealth and Colonial Secretaries warned that empire free trade would be an unpopular policy. One interdepartmental study estimated that the long-term economic benefit to Britain of joining the ECU would outweigh the cost of any damage to the Ottawa system. Even so, it concluded that membership would involve an intolerable loss of sovereignty. Cabinet was perplexed.[4]

Britain apprised other Commonwealth governments of these developments. In a cablegram to Canberra, the Commonwealth Secretary, Lord Addison, was optimistic about Britain's ability to guide events in Europe:

> It has become increasingly clear that the Americans attach great importance to [European economic integration], and that the ability of the participating countries to produce specific and comprehensive plans of Economic co-operation may have a decisive effect upon the amount of [Marshall Plan] money that congress will be prepared to vote . . . The attitude taken by the United Kingdom will probably be decisive. . . . Sir Oliver Franks [the chief British negotiator] considers that we are likely to be able to rally the [missing word] to those projects which we recommend while, in the absence of our support and initiative it is unlikely that anything constructive will emerge.[5]

With respect to a European customs union, Addison explained that Britain was reluctant to take any decision that might jeopardize the Commonwealth economic nexus, as Anglo-Commonwealth trade was double the level of Anglo-European trade. Nevertheless, Britain welcomed the establishment of a study group on the ECU scheme, 'if only to forestall proposals which might present us with difficulties.'[6]

Australia and New Zealand accepted invitations to attend the ECU study group as observers. During the first meeting, the British discussed their position with Commonwealth representatives, and later refined their thoughts in a document circulated to Commonwealth delegates to the ITO conference in Havana. The British acknowledged that over the long run the UK economy might gain from participation in the proposed ECU. They pointed out that there were several ways in which the ECU could be reconciled with Commonwealth Preference. For instance, it might be feasible to establish a single customs union embracing Europe and the Commonwealth. Alternatively, Britain could participate in separate Commonwealth and European customs unions. Then again, it might be possible to adjust the Ottawa system to render it compatible with the ECU. Finally, Britain could join the ECU, dismantle Commonwealth Preference, and compensate Commonwealth countries with the award of long-term bulk contracts. The British concluded that none of these options was acceptable in view of the inevitable disruption of trade patterns.[7]

Australia and New Zealand did not question the desirability of European economic cooperation, since a prosperous Europe would provide a strong market for primary commodities. Dominion governments, however, feared that British membership of the planned ECU would result in the termination of Commonwealth food preferences or their extension to competitors such as Denmark. Britain might even be compelled to impose tariffs on Commonwealth produce. New Zealand wondered whether Commonwealth countries would be allowed to join the ECU as full or partial members in order to influence policy. Wellington suspected that France would do its utmost to undermine Commonwealth Preference in any talks on a customs union. But the French, who also had an empire to consider, accepted that some form of Imperial Preference would have to continue.[8] At the request of Commonwealth delegates at Havana, the British issued a statement promising that they would not enter a European customs union unless the terms were 'satisfactory to all (repeat all) countries concerned'. Nash, the leader of the New Zealand delegation, endeavoured to make sure 'that everyone realise[d] the serious position that would arise if British preferences were interfered with without concessions from the countries benefiting from the change'.[9] He was sceptical of British assurances. Moreover, Washington maintained that the Commonwealth would not

be entitled to compensation, in the form of a diluted preferential position in the European market, for any loss of Commonwealth preferences
arising from British entry into the ECU. The USA was vehemently
opposed to the extension of the preferential system into Europe. It was
possible that compensation would have been confined to long-term
bulk contracts between Britain and the dominions.[10]

While the attitudes of the Americans, the British, and the Europeans
gave cause for concern in Canberra and Wellington, there was never
much chance of the ECU coming to fruition. It is inconceivable that
Bevin, who was angling for a British-led Commonwealth–European bloc
as a counterbalance to Washington, would have sacrificed the Commonwealth for the sake of a customs union in Europe.[11] The impression
of the Australian delegate in Havana was that, 'the United Kingdom and
other Commonwealth Officials believe that the obstacles to be overcome are so great that the proposal is likely to come to nothing. At the
same time there is an anxiety not to be held directly responsible for
killing the proposal at this stage.'[12] The ECU talks fizzled out in 1948.
As the political situation in Europe deteriorated, Bevin concluded that
it would be imprudent to moor Britain too closely to the continent, and
turned his mind to the creation of a transatlantic rather than a western
European alliance.

As far as Australia and New Zealand were concerned, the ECU episode
had demonstrated that Britain possessed a plausible regional alternative
to the Commonwealth economic network. Britain was not ready to
pursue this option, but the preferential position of Commonwealth
foodstuffs was now under potential threat from the Europeans. To make
matters worse, Washington was unsympathetic to proposals for compensating the Commonwealth for the losses attending British entry into
a European trading bloc.

Common Market and Free Trade Area

The British adopted a cautious position towards European economic
cooperation during the 1950s, taking the lead in some areas but holding
back in other ones. As yet the British were under no circumstances prepared to pool economic sovereignty.

As a member of the CEEC and its successor, the Organization for
European Economic Cooperation (OEEC), Britain cooperated with its
neighbours with respect to the Marshall Plan and the relaxation of
quantitative controls on intra-European trade. In 1950 Britain joined
the European Payments Union (EPU), which put intra-European pay-

ments on a multilateral footing. The EPU originated in an American proposal for a regional monetary agreement to assist European recovery, and pave the way for the resumption of convertibility. London initially suspected that the Europeans would use the EPU to drain the Sterling Area's reserves of gold and dollars, but, after receiving satisfactory assurances, the British agreed to participate. The EPU incorporated the entire Sterling Area plus the overseas economic areas of France and other continental powers. Anglo-European monetary cooperation did not threaten Australian and New Zealand interests. As the EPU applied solely to current account transactions, it did not divert British capital exports towards Europe. Indeed, the EPU helped the dominions by encouraging European countries to import more Commonwealth primary produce. Finally, the EPU did not raise the spectre of European federation.[13] Britain declined, however, to join the European Coal and Steel Community (ECSC), the institutional precursor of the EEC, refusing to surrender control over these basic industries to a supranational authority.[14]

At Messina, in June 1955, the six members of the ECSC (France, West Germany, the Netherlands, Italy, Belgium, and Luxembourg) floated a scheme for a customs union or Common Market. Britain had no interest in a customs union at this stage, and assumed that this bold departure was beyond the capacity of the continentals. But the Messina Six were anxious not to exclude the British, and invited them to further talks on the Common Market in Brussels. Russell Bretherton, a Board of Trade official, went as an observer. The British hoped that squabbling between France and Germany would wreck the Common Market project. However, it soon became clear that the Six, fortified by US support, were determined to proceed.[15]

There was no question of Britain joining a European Common Market under the premiership of Anthony Eden, who was strongly committed to the Commonwealth. Even so, the British were obliged to study the implications of the Common Market, and make a considered response to the Six. In November 1955, an official report to the Cabinet Economic Policy Committee on the planned Common Market concluded that a definitive assessment was impossible in view of the number of imponderables and the complexity of the issues. On the assumption that the scheme would collapse without Britain, it was uncertain whether the benefits to Britain of Common Market membership would outweigh the costs. Although British industry would gain from free access to continental markets, it would have to face increased German competition. Furthermore, participation in the Common Market would undermine the Ottawa system, while confidence in sterling would be weakened if Sterling Area countries concluded that in future Europe would secure the bulk of British capital exports. If, however, the Six had the temerity to establish a Common Market without Britain, the Germans would enjoy an even greater competitive advantage in continental markets, and the outlook would be gloomy.[16] Treasury officials, including Sir Leslie Rowan, who had a close interest in the Sterling Area, were hostile to the Common Market. According to Rowan, the Common Market would have 'most grave consequences' for the Commonwealth and the Sterling Area, especially if Britain became a member.[17] But Sir Frank Lee, the Permanent Secretary to the Board of Trade, put the economic case for joining the Common Market. Lee reflected the views of Britain's largest manufacturers. The Federation of British Industries (FBI) urged the government to take a full part in the discussions of the Six.[18]

In December 1955, Britain informed the OEEC that it disapproved of the Common Market proposal; but this snub failed to deflect the Six.[19] A more imaginative response to the Common Market scheme was now required. After considering various alternatives, namely Plans A to H, the British opted for Plan G, a scheme for a European free trade area (FTA) in industrial products, which was unveiled to Commonwealth ministers in September 1956. In the intervening months, ministerial and official perceptions of Britain's options and interests had altered. Winthrop Brown, the US economic representative in London, explained the reasons for the softening in Britain's attitude towards Europe economic integration, in a message to the State Department. Firstly, Britain could not afford to give German industry a free run in western Europe. Secondly, the Anglo-Australian trade dispute had highlighted the underlying weakness of the Ottawa regime. Thirdly, membership of a European trading network would force British industry to modernize. Fourthly, Britain desired a leading political role in the construction of the new Europe. Furthermore, pressure was building in the OEEC for another round of European trade liberalization.[20]

Harold Macmillan's position on European integration was ambivalent. He was dismayed by the trade conflict with Australia, and painfully aware of the economic challenge posed by the Six.[21] Along with other ministers, he sought a compromise that would allow Britain to enjoy the remaining benefits of the Commonwealth economic relationship as well as any new opportunities in Europe. A free trade area in industrial products and raw materials would reassure British manufacturers who were anxious about their continental markets. By excluding agricultural trade from the scope of Plan G, it would also be possible to meet the concerns of other interest groups. In a free trade area inclusive of agriculture, however, Commonwealth farmers would lose their tariff preferences, and the British government would be pestered by the Europeans to reduce deficiency payments to farmers. Moreover, if a later government were to give in to European pressure to introduce a price support regime, consumer prices would rise.

Cabinet discussed Plan G in September 1956. Thorneycroft argued that it 'had been devised to turn the developments in Europe to the advantage of the United Kingdom and of the Commonwealth as a whole.'[22] Membership would be open to all European members of the OEEC, but the government was undecided whether the objective should be to promote the FTA as a substitute or a complement for the Common Market. Macmillan, who judged that the pros and cons of Plan G were nicely balanced, voted to proceed on condition that the government obtained the Commonwealth's approval before approaching the Europeans. He suggested presenting Plan G 'as a considered plan to preserve and strengthen sterling in the long term, to provide a more secure market for Commonwealth agricultural products and to make possible the creation of adequate investment capital from the resources of the old world for the needs and benefit of the new.'[23] Alan Lennox-Boyd, the Colonial Secretary, and Lord Home, the Commonwealth Secretary, were more critical. They worried about the effects of an industrial free trade area on the British market for Canadian and Asian manufacturers. Home also warned that 'as the United Kingdom turned to Europe, Canada, Australia, and New Zealand ... must be expected to turn increasingly towards the United States.' If Cabinet endorsed Plan G:

[E]very effort must be made to convince Commonwealth countries that the plan, by strengthening the United Kingdom, would strengthen them. But Commonwealth countries would not be convinced by this argument alone, for they would see how vulnerable under the plan our balance of payments would be [as a result of German competition] in the short term. . . . In adopting an expansionist policy towards Europe we must therefore be prepared to pursue a corresponding policy towards Commonwealth trade. This would entail a positive and far-reaching plan for trade in Commonwealth agricultural products without which the support of the Commonwealth could not be expected.[24]

Home suggested that an increase in the foreign meat tariff might sweeten Australia and New Zealand, but Cabinet rejected this idea.

Derick Heathcoat Amory, the Minister of Agriculture, could offer little comfort. He discounted the prospect of Britain absorbing larger amounts of Commonwealth primary produce. In view of the spread of import substitution in the Commonwealth, and recent Australian posturing, Thorneycroft questioned whether the Commonwealth would have cause for complaint about a change in British commercial strategy.[25]

For his part, Eden acknowledged with deep regret that it was no longer possible to base British commercial policy on the Commonwealth:

> The Australians appeared to be determined in pursuit of their present commercial objectives and both Australia and New Zealand were bound to be attracted, if only for reasons of defence, towards an increasingly close association with the United States. The attitude of the Asian members of the Commonwealth towards the British connection was uncertain and they diverged from us on many matters. Unless, therefore, we were capable, acting alone, of meeting formidable European competition in oversea [*sic*] markets, there seemed no alternative but to base our policy on the proposed plan for closer association with Europe, or some suitable variant or extension of it.[26]

The Prime Minister also spoke of the possibility of a close partnership with France, and wondered whether Belgium, Holland, the Scandinavian countries, Italy, and Germany might apply to join the Commonwealth. Incredibly, France enquired about membership of the Commonwealth in 1956, resurrecting Churchill's wartime offer of an Anglo-French union. Eden thought that only Australia and Pakistan would strenuously object to France entering the Commonwealth, but officials advised that France would be an economic liability. It was resolved that the French application would receive consideration once the FTA came into operation.[27]

The possibility, however unlikely, of French membership of the Commonwealth illustrates the fluidity of the European situation in the mid-1950s. It was by no means clear that the Common Market would triumph over rival conceptions of European cooperation. The British evidently had reasonable grounds for doubting France's commitment to the Common Market. While the notion that an enlarged Commonwealth could form the basis for European economic cooperation was far fetched, the British scheme for a partial free trade area merited the serious attention of European countries. Cabinet concluded that Macmillan should write to Commonwealth finance ministers, outlining the FTA proposals and seeking their support for an approach to Europe.

Commonwealth reaction to Plan G

In his message of 16 September 1956 to Commonwealth finance ministers, Macmillan explained that the markets of individual European nations were too small to support efficient modern industries. Britain sympathized with the aspirations of the Six, but 'could not in any circumstances join such a Customs Union [because] to do so would mean giving up our own tariff and our external trading arrangements' based on the Commonwealth. However, if Britain did nothing, either the Common Market would fail, setting back the cause of European cooperation, or it would proceed under German leadership, and British goods would be 'squeezed out' of continental markets. Macmillan depicted the FTA scheme as a means of satisfying all parties. Commonwealth food preferences would remain in place. A strong and prosperous Europe, and a revitalized Britain, would provide improved market opportunities for the Commonwealth. He took pains to emphasize that Britain's priority was still to preserve a close relationship with the Commonwealth.[28]

Macmillan was able to gauge the initial reactions of Commonwealth governments to Plan G at the meeting of Commonwealth finance ministers later in the month in Washington. For Australia, Sir Percy Spender said that he understood Britain's need for an arrangement with the Europeans. Although Spender was concerned about the impact of the proposed FTA on Australia's industrial exports to the UK, he did not condemn the plan. Jack Watts, New Zealand's Minister of Finance, accepted Macmillan's claim that both the UK economy and Commonwealth trade would falter if British exports were discriminated against in Europe. New Zealand officials had cautioned Watts that Britain would come under growing pressure from Denmark and other countries to incorporate agriculture in the FTA. He sought assurances from the British that 'certain foodstuffs' would be 'rigidly excluded from the provisions of the FTA and that the UK would continue to be in a position to exclude them.'[29] Thorneycroft replied that there was no cause for alarm, as continental countries were not interested in free trade in foodstuffs. Both Spender and Watts indicated that their governments would need to consider the scheme in detail. Macmillan informed cabinet that the FTA proposals had received a 'surprisingly friendly reception'. In particular, 'New Zealand had taken up a characteristically helpful attitude and had indicated her willingness to follow the lead and judgment of the United Kingdom.'[30]

In general, Canberra welcomed the involvement of the British in discussions on European economic integration, and hoped that they would succeed in persuading the continentals to establish a liberal rather than a protectionist regime. Australian overseas missions were advised that 'whatever might be the ultimate result for Australia, there was merit in encouraging the United Kingdom to participate in discussions about the promotion of the Customs Union and the Free Trade Area and to endeavour to influence them in the right direction and we have notified the United Kingdom in this sense'.[31] As regards the proposed industrial FTA, the Australian Ministry of Trade concluded that, 'with the position on wool and foodstuffs protected, the prospect for Australia of United Kingdom association with a European Free Trade Area is a possible but not a serious loss of trade.'[32] In October 1956, New Zealand reiterated its cautious support for Plan G, but requested clarification of the status of marginal animal products such as tallow and casein. Lord Home gave the less than satisfactory reply that the definition of agriculture was a matter for negotiation.[33] It remained to be seen whether Britain would succeed in reconciling the interests of the Commonwealth and Europe. France, the Netherlands, and Denmark were unlikely to be impressed with a scheme that increased British manufacturers' access to continental markets, but denied their farmers greater access to the British market.

Washington initially welcomed the industrial FTA proposal. The Americans hoped that Plan G would be a stepping stone to deeper British involvement in European integration. Despite the exemption of agricultural trade, the Americans predicted that Commonwealth Preference would be undermined by the withdrawal of preferences from Canadian and Asian manufactures and raw materials. Washington also foresaw that the question of colonial association with the FTA would pose great difficulties for the British. The overriding interest of the Americans was to prevent Britain from using the FTA proposals to delay or wreck the introduction of the Common Market.[34]

An OEEC committee, chaired by Reginald Maudling, the British Postmaster General, was set up to examine the industrial FTA scheme. Discussion revolved around the status of agriculture and the relationship between the FTA, the dominions, and present and former colonies of prospective member states. Since the colonies and dominions were important food exporters, it was necessary to consider the agricultural and territorial issues together. At an early stage, the Six had resolved to include French, Dutch, and Belgian overseas territories in the Common Market. The British, however, were keen to exclude all countries' colonies from participation in the FTA. They argued that incorporation of the colonies would make it harder to confine the scheme to non-agricultural products. Furthermore, it would be politically impossible to include the colonies in the FTA without also extending invitations to Australia, New Zealand, and other independent Commonwealth countries.[35] Britain doubted whether the continentals would wish to welcome efficient temperate food producers into the FTA. The Europeans might insist on the abolition of British tariff preferences in Australia and New Zealand in return for such a concession.

Australia and New Zealand at first agreed with Britain that the FTA should incorporate neither overseas territories nor foodstuffs. The Australian Ministry of Trade indicated that Australia 'should ask the United Kingdom for an assurance that she will not embrace her territories in the new preference area, and that she will not support a move to have dependent territories of the other European powers included.'[36] The Australian Department of Primary Industry warned that the 'association of territories with the scheme could have the effect of providing more severe competition for Australian primary products in Metropolitan Europe and for our secondary products in the territories themselves.'[37] New Zealand was particularly concerned about the possible association with the FTA of Ireland, a rival producer of meat and dairy products. Wellington felt that New Zealand's exports to French Oceania would be jeopardized by the association of overseas territories with the area. If the FTA proved damaging to New Zealand's interests, the government would have to reconsider its obligations to Britain and the Sterling Area, and might offer to cut BP margins as an inducement to new trading partners.[38]

As expected, the Europeans asked the British to drop their opposition to the inclusion of agriculture in the FTA. It appeared increasingly likely that, in the absence of any British flexibility on agriculture, Denmark and possibly Sweden and Norway would apply for membership of the Common Market. France was adamant that Britain must either offer agricultural and horticultural concessions, or relinquish some tariff preferences in Commonwealth markets. Maudling was in favour of minor concessions, such as including wine and horticulture in the FTA, reducing British farm subsidies, or eliminating food quotas. But cabinet refused to compromise, anticipating a hostile domestic and Commonwealth reaction to any show of weakness in the face of French pressure.[39] Nevertheless, there could be no guarantee that Britain would stick to its policy, and the Department of Trade in Canberra wondered whether the UK might relent over agriculture in order to reach a settlement.[40] Generally speaking, however, the Australian cabinet showed considerable stoicism, as well as sensitivity to the complications of the British position:[41]

> [Cabinet] noted that the most acute problem which the Economic Community proposals could present for Australia might very well come from their effect on the United Kingdom and the sterling area as a whole if the United Kingdom does not become satisfactorily associated with the Community.

Cabinet's general conclusions were:

> [T]hat the need for [the] United Kingdom's association with the Community should be kept in mind; . . . [and] that if the United Kingdom [*sic*] association with the Community should require widening of the UK Free Trade Area proposals to include some agricultural products, Australia should be willing to do what it can to co-operate, and should be giving thought to the issues in advance, but any first move on this aspect should be for the United Kingdom to take and not Australia.

Australia and New Zealand were more relaxed about the FTA proposal than they would be about Britain's first application to join the EEC in 1961–3. Australia and New Zealand stood to lose a few relatively unimportant preferences as a result of the industrial FTA, whereas British entry into the EEC would have involved the erection of reverse preferences against all imports of temperate foodstuffs from the dominions. In the late 1950s, the essential weakness of Britain's bargaining position was not fully apparent to ministers and officials in Canberra and Wellington.

Commonwealth association with Europe

Although Europe was not a key market for Australia and New Zealand, the dominions were anxious to increase exports to the continent in view of the growing saturation of the British market. Consequently, Canberra and Wellington were dismayed to learn that the Six were intent upon intensifying rather than relaxing controls over agricultural trade. As well as criticizing the emerging agricultural policies of the Six both in GATT and in bilateral discussions, Australia and New Zealand explored alternative solutions to the agricultural problem, including a possible agreement of association between the Commonwealth and the European bloc.

In 1958, an Australian economist, Max Corden, suggested the extension to Commonwealth countries of either full or partial membership in a European free trade area, covering agricultural as well as industrial trade, as a resolution to the impasse in Europe. He explained that, as part of such an arrangement, it would be necessary to abolish or substantially modify the Ottawa system. As far as Australia was concerned, he envisaged an increase in BP tariffs rather than a reduction in MFN rates. Under Corden's plan, Commonwealth members would preserve duty-free entry into the British market, and gain either duty-free or preferential terms of access to continental markets. Corden considered that it was pointless carping about EEC protectionism. In 'the final analysis it may be necessary to offer something in return if the adverse effects of the Community on Britain and other members of the Commonwealth are to be avoided.'[42]

Extending the scope of the FTA talks by including British preferences was unlikely to appeal to either London, Washington, or GATT, although it might interest the dominions and the Six. Wellington was already thinking along these lines. New Zealand's initial opposition to the inclusion of agriculture in the FTA had waned. In January 1957, Denmark had raised the possibility of associate or full membership in the FTA for Australia and New Zealand, apparently as a means of overcoming British objections to the incorporation of agriculture.[43] A group of New Zealand officials and economist circulated a paper arguing that the government's priority should be to persuade the Six to adopt a more liberal stance and admit more Commonwealth foodstuffs. To this end they recommended that New Zealand, in conjunction with Britain and Australia, seek membership of a European FTA incorporating foodstuffs. Moreover, they hoped for support from Denmark and the Netherlands, the most efficient farming nations on the continent. Significant benefits would be conferred on local consumers if British preferences in New Zealand were eliminated by cutting MFN duties on goods supplied by continental Europe.[44] Keith Holyoake acknowledged that some form of association with the FTA would merit serious consideration if Britain failed to secure the exclusion of foodstuffs.[45]

In July 1957, New Zealand, with tepid Australian support, asked Britain to leave the door open to the association of the dominions with the FTA. Sir Frank Lee responded testily, accusing the New Zealanders of wanting the benefits of being in 'the club' without accepting any of the obligations, which was exactly how the Six viewed Britain's motives for floating the FTA proposal.[46] The British reluctantly consented to consider New Zealand's request, although the cabinet had already set its face against the association of either the African colonies or the Commonwealth as a whole. Cabinet's position was that most colonies were averse to association, and that discussion of this issue would only slow down the negotiations with Europe. Furthermore, Commonwealth association would be incompatible with the exclusion of agriculture from the FTA, which Britain still desired on domestic grounds.[47]

Copenhagen raised the stakes in August 1957, indicating that Denmark would apply to join the Common Market if Britain refused to include agriculture in the FTA.[48] Wellington and Canberra had long feared that Denmark would attempt to secure a privileged position in continental dairy markets. John McEwen believed that the British were wavering over agriculture, and were likely to propose reductions in Commonwealth food preferences. He concluded that Australia would have to consider the pros and cons of seeking association, if Britain could not exclude agriculture from the FTA, and prevent the association of dependent territories.[49] New Zealand was understandably keen to involve Australia in any bid for association. Canberra was doubtful about the prospects for restraining European agricultural protectionism through action in GATT. Association with the FTA would give Australia direct access to the decision-making process in Europe. John Stone, an Australian Treasury representative in London, advocated throwing BP margins into the FTA negotiations. A.J. Bunting of the Prime Minister's Department considered it possible that Australia would derive greater benefits from participation in a European grouping than from membership of the Commonwealth.[50] Nevertheless, Australia allowed New Zealand to take the lead on association.

At the Commonwealth Finance Ministers' Conference, in September 1957, the New Zealanders returned to the issue of possible Commonwealth association with the FTA. They reminded the British of the Strasbourg Plan of 1952, which had envisaged a combined European–Commonwealth preference area.[51] Australia and New Zealand stressed that they wished to participate directly in the FTA discussions. While the Netherlands, Denmark, and Germany were amenable to this suggestion, the British argued that the continentals would exploit the presence of Australia and New Zealand at the bargaining table by attacking the British positions on agriculture and tariff preferences.[52] Consequently, the Australians and the New Zealanders were reduced to hovering on the sidelines of the main debate, setting a precedent that was followed during British applications to join the EEC.

In October 1957, the New Zealand ambassador in Paris relayed a rumour that the British and the Europeans were approaching a settlement over the FTA on detrimental terms to the Commonwealth. He thought that the Commonwealth as a whole should make a bid for association while there was still a chance of success.[53] In an attempt to break the deadlock, Maudling indicated that, although Britain could not accept free trade in foodstuffs, there was no reason why other members of the FTA should not lower or eliminate food tariffs amongst themselves. The British were also considering making offers on wine and horticulture. Alarmed officials in Wellington noted that Maudling's latest initiative would strengthen Denmark's position in continental markets at New Zealand's expense.[54] New Zealand representatives visiting the French Foreign Office were informed that Maudling's compromise might be acceptable if the British were willing to sacrifice some BP margins, for instance on motor cars. However, the New Zealanders suspected that the French were merely trying to stir up trouble between Britain and the dominions.[55] After considerable delay, the Six, marshalled by the French, formally replied to Maudling's offer. They stated that there could be no progress in the FTA talks until Britain was prepared to either abolish British Preference or partially extend BP margins to other European countries. Maudling told cabinet that the response of the Six posed considerable difficulties. Britain wished to retain its industrial preferences, at least for the time being. It was unclear what the Europeans would give the dominions for cooperating in the reduction of BP margins, but there was speculation about agricultural concessions.

> [W]e must recognise that the French proposals might have some attractions for some members of the Commonwealth, particularly Australia and New Zealand, who were increasingly concerned at the prospect of losing their Continental markets as a result of the Treaty of Rome and might be tempted to seek to secure an enlargement of those markets by reaching agreement with the Six Powers on preference margins at our expense.... [Britain] must... remain on... guard against the risk of being gradually subjected to a combination of pressure from the Six and from certain members of the Commonwealth.[56]

British ministers pointed out that the Six's latest proposal would be anathema to GATT. There was anger that the French appeared to be inciting the dominions to make reductions in BP margins in return for a settlement involving improved access to European agricultural markets. In order to instill discipline into the dominions, Britain might have to threaten the abolition of food preferences or the restriction of capital outflows to the Sterling Area. As the Europeans could not be trusted, Britain risked losing the remaining benefits of the Ottawa system without securing an industrial free trade area.

Maudling warned Walter Nash that the French would not be content with a general lowering of MFN rates in the Commonwealth, and would demand a share in BP margins. Any serious departure from GATT principles, Maudling added, would 'arouse international hostility including hostility from the USA.'[57] He stated that France had no intention of opening its markets to Commonwealth producers, whatever its representatives might say for tactical reasons. Maudling indicated that the British government would not negotiate with the continentals over BP margins in the Commonwealth. Hence, if Commonwealth countries wished to bargain with the Europeans, they would have to do so on their own account.[58] He stressed that any reductions in contractual BP margins would require British confirmation. New Zealand brushed aside this advice and hinted that 'direct approaches to Europe on the part of individual Commonwealth countries might be necessary', in view of Britain's reluctance to safeguard their interests.[59]

Instead of entering a more dramatic phase, however, the industrial FTA talks rapidly fizzled out. In November 1958, the French informed Macmillan that they had never been seriously interested in this scheme. Macmillan, enraged by this admission, spoke of a possible trade war and the political division of western Europe. Australia and New Zealand, though, still hoped to secure generous terms of access to continental markets, and the Europeans continued to angle for a share in British preferences. Professor Hallstein, President of the European Commission, told the *Financial Times* in 1959 that he would welcome a new approach incorporating British membership of the EEC, the preservation of Commonwealth duty-free entry, the creation of secure outlets for the Commonwealth on the continent, and the extension of British preferences to the Six.[60]

New Zealand anticipated that Denmark and other rivals would now attempt to forge bilateral commercial agreements with the Six. Officials argued that New Zealand was too weak to engage in bilateral negotiations with the Europeans, and suggested that the Commonwealth as a whole, or a subgroup including Australia and New Zealand, apply for associate membership of the European bloc. Full membership would not be feasible due to the commitment of Wellington and Canberra to industrial protection, but the abolition, or extension to continental suppliers, of BP margins was negotiable. Ministers in Wellington endorsed this plan, and took encouragement from a speech at Palmerston North by Peter Thorneycroft, which they interpreted as a hint that a Commonwealth initiative in Europe would not be unwelcome.[61] Pressure from New Zealand and Australia on the Commonwealth Liaison Committee resulted in the formation of a study group to devise a concerted trade strategy towards Europe. Britain reluctantly conceded the establishment of this group, hoping to avert or delay an independent approach to Europe by Australia and New Zealand. According to the Bank of England, Australia and New Zealand made no attempt to conceal the fact that 'the remains of Ottawa [would] be cut up freely as bait' in any Commonwealth encounter with the Six. This would have deprived Britain of the opportunity to extract a 'better price' in GATT, particularly from the USA, for ending the Commonwealth Preference system.[62] It was uncertain what inducements the dominions would offer the EEC. W.B. Sutch recommended the extension of British preferences to the European countries in order to create a larger preferential bloc. But other New Zealand officials, as well as the Australians and Canadians, strongly disagreed with Sutch, maintaining that the Commonwealth and the Europe should agree on MFN tariff cuts. Stone, however, concluded that it would be better to leave any MFN tariff negotiations until the next round of GATT, when the bargaining power of the USA could be brought to bear on the EEC. Britain was gratified by the study group's inability to reach agreement. The Canadians were lukewarm about a Commonwealth initiative, while the Asians and the Africans feared a new colonial system.[63] At a Commonwealth meeting in September 1959, the Australian minister, Harold Holt, indicated that, in view of the lack of consensus, Canberra would not insist on a concerted appeal to the EEC. The President of the Board of Trade, Sir David Eccles, was 'sent in to deliver the coup de grace' to New Zealand. He warned that the EEC would make short work of the Commonwealth, by which he meant New Zealand and Australia, if a reckless approach were made to the Six in defiance of Britain's wishes.[64] The disparity in bargaining power between the Six and Australia and New Zealand was enormous. Canberra and Wellington were also constrained by their commitments to the protection of domestic industry, and their obligations under GATT and the Ottawa Agreements.

Following the collapse of the industrial FTA scheme, the British scrambled to create a smaller, still largely industrial, European Free Trade

Association (EFTA) in conjunction with Sweden, Norway, Denmark, Portugal, Switzerland, and Austria.[65] As the ramifications of this move were unclear, the Australians declared that there was now a 'clean slate' as far as they were concerned, and once again reminded the British of the interests of third countries, and especially of agricultural exporters. Canberra and Wellington were annoyed that Britain had rushed into the EFTA negotiations while the Commonwealth was still discussing New Zealand's proposed concerted approach.[66] Although Macmillan hoped that EFTA would act as a bridge between Britain and the Six, in practice it was a source of further complications. Britain had to abolish Commonwealth preferences on blue veined cheese, canned cream, bacon, and tinned pork luncheon meat in order to persuade Denmark to join EFTA. As these preferences were of little intrinsic value, Australia and New Zealand grudgingly consented to their elimination. But Wellington regarded Britain's willingness to grant even minor agricultural concessions to Denmark as a bad omen.[67]

The industrial FTA episode had aroused concern in Canberra and Wellington that Britain would ultimately endorse a European commercial settlement that made no provision for Commonwealth food preferences. New Zealand, with hesitant Australian support, argued that membership of a European free trade area should be open to Commonwealth countries. Wellington's goal was to secure new continental markets in compensation for any loss of preferences in Britain. In the event, New Zealand and Australia failed to exert much influence over the Anglo-European trade negotiations. The British were delighted with the disintegration of the proposed joint Commonwealth approach to Europe.

Conclusion

Britain was a slow convert to the cause of European economic integration. Not until the Anglo-Australian trade dispute of 1955–6 was the wisdom of according the Commonwealth economic network priority over Britain's commercial relationship with Europe seriously called into question. The British government regarded the 1956 industrial free trade area plan as a means of enabling the UK economy to participate in European developments, without causing distress to dominion exporters, domestic farmers, and domestic consumers. But Wellington and Canberra were increasingly sceptical of Britain's capacity to retain a separate food market while engaging in the process of European economic integration. Australian and New Zealand food preferences were bound to come under threat, and the imposition of reverse preferences could not be ruled out. Under these circumstances, New Zealand, and to a lesser extent Australia, concluded that it might be advantageous to include foodstuffs in the free trade area, and to forge a link between the Commonwealth and Europe. Since this approach would have necessitated reductions in BP margins it found no favour in London. Furthermore, its incompatibility with non-discrimination and European agricultural protectionism rendered a successful outcome highly unlikely. However, the proposal for a Commonwealth initiative on Europe did at least confirm that New Zealand and Australia were troubled by the direction of British policy.

Tratt contends that in 1959 Macmillan resolved to allow neither the farmers nor the Commonwealth to stand in the way of whatever he deemed to be in the long-term interests of British industry.[68] Although Macmillan did not yet advocate a merger between Britain and the EEC, the implications of his train of thought were potentially enormous. The cracks in the economic relationship between Britain and Australia and New Zealand had widened during the 1950s in the light of bitter disputes over import controls, agricultural policy, and the Ottawa Agreements. Britain's attitude towards European economic integration was changing. By 1960, it was apparent to observers in the Commonwealth that Britain was in danger of becoming a supplicant in Brussels.

8
Britain's First EEC Application

> If it ever came to a choice between Europe and the Common-
> wealth, there could be no doubt about the answer, about the
> Government, the Conservative Party, and the British people.
> (*Cheers*) That was not the question, and Europe was now
> realizing that.
>
> *Edward Heath, Conservative Party Conference, 13 Oct. 1960*[1]

During the unsuccessful talks on Britain's first application to join the
EEC, it became evident that few safeguards would be available for Commonwealth trade. Temporary arrangements would have cushioned the
blow to Commonwealth producers, but the Six declined to offer any
permanent guarantee of access to either the British or the enlarged EEC
market, only a vague expression of goodwill and an undertaking to work
towards world commodity agreements. These austere terms were similar
to those imposed on Britain in the 1970s.

This chapter considers the evolution of British policy in the early
1960s. It covers the EEC entry negotiations, and the largely forlorn
attempts of Australia and New Zealand to influence the terms of
prospective British membership. The stakes were higher for New
Zealand, which consigned 53 per cent of its total exports to Britain in
1960, than for either Australia or Canada, which sent Britain 22 per cent
and 17 per cent respectively of their exports. Mindful of its dependence
on British goodwill, New Zealand adopted a less critical stance during
the EEC membership talks than Australia was prepared to sustain. The
British regarded Keith Holyoake, who became Prime Minister in 1960,
as more cooperative than Walter Nash had been in the late 1950s.[2] But
Menzies and McEwen, who still ruled the roost in Canberra, made no
attempt to conceal their dislike of British goals and tactics. While the

British genuinely attempted to obtain a reasonable settlement as regards Commonwealth trade, they were disinclined to let the EEC negotiations fail through inflexibility on this score.

A decision 'in principle'

Recent analyses of the Macmillan government assign Sir Frank Lee, who moved in 1960 from the Board of Trade to the Treasury as Joint Permanent Secretary, an important role in the British decision in July 1961 to seek membership of the EEC. Lee exerted considerable influence over Macmillan, who, unlike either Churchill or Eden, had a keen practical interest in economic issues.[3]

In April 1960, a group of officials, chaired by Lee, produced a report entitled 'The Six and the Seven'. This document advocated a close form of association or 'near identification' with the Six, amounting to membership in all but name. Lee's group stressed that, whereas the EEC was flourishing, the Commonwealth trading network was decaying. Lee accepted that large concessions would be required in order to woo the Six, and that it might even be necessary to restrict imports of Commonwealth foodstuffs. Optimistically, he suggested that Commonwealth members would be prepared to lose some trading privileges, as they would reap many benefits from the strengthening of the British economy inside the EEC. Large manufacturers in particular were anxious to enter the customs union.[4]

A period of introspection and discussion ensued. Macmillan was slowly convinced of the industrial advantages of EEC membership, but other cabinet members were sceptical. In July 1960, the Chancellor of the Exchequer, Amory, and the President of the Board of Trade, Maudling, expressed grave concern about the impact on the Commonwealth and EFTA of British entry into the EEC. The ministerial balance of power was tipped in favour of the EEC by the appointment of Edward Heath as Lord Privy Seal with responsibility for Europe, Duncan Sandys as Commonwealth Secretary, and Christopher Soames as Minister of Agriculture. At Heath's prompting, cabinet conceded, in September 1960, that the imposition of the common external tariff (CET) on certain products could not be ruled out in any settlement with the Six, which was tantamount to admitting that Commonwealth free entry might not survive.[5] Later that month, in a speech drafted by Lee, Heath warned Commonwealth ministers that, in any future talks on close association between Britain and the Six, 'the basic questions [would be]: How much derogation from the principle of free entry would be acceptable to the United Kingdom and the Commonwealth? and how much derogation from the full application of a common tariff would be acceptable to the Six?'[6] Thus Commonwealth food preferences might be abolished, and reverse preferences erected for the benefit of EEC suppliers. Heath's statement provoked a strong reaction among Commonwealth ministers, including the New Zealand Minister of Finance, Arnold Nordmeyer, but the extent of disquiet was played down in reports to cabinet.

Dominion unease was heightened by the knowledge that Britain's commitment to unrestricted duty-free entry was waning for separate reasons. The British Treasury deplored the escalating cost of deficiency payments. Treasury officials maintained that under a system of managed agricultural trade, involving import quotas and rising food prices, it would not be necessary to give large handouts to farmers. The 1960 Annual Review of Agriculture recommended that the government examine the merits of regulating the food trade by international agreement. It goes without saying that this suggestion was at odds with the British government's public advocacy of freer trade. As Whitehall became more interested in managed trade, its opposition to the CAP softened. Soames also sought the abolition of Commonwealth free entry, which he regarded as a hindrance to an accommodation with Brussels.[7]

In May 1961, Soames indicated that, in any settlement with the Six, it ought to be possible to preserve the market shares of Commonwealth farmers in Britain by squeezing imports from other extra-European suppliers. Although Soames was confident that Britain would be able to secure decent terms for the Commonwealth during the transitional phase of EEC membership, he acknowledged that the prospects would deteriorate during the permanent or Common Market phase. Nevertheless, he concluded that Britain should press for a quota regime that would maintain Commonwealth food imports at traditional levels during the Common Market phase.[8]

The British took soundings on the continent, early in 1961, about a possible EEC entry application. The French questioned whether the interests of the Commonwealth and the Six were reconcilable, but the British were not unduly discouraged by this response. Britain still intended to agitate for a liberal CAP, and hoped to secure American diplomatic support for this objective. France was determined to preclude British interference in the CAP, the terms of which were yet to be settled. As far as Macmillan was concerned, however, the key issue was not agriculture but British industrial competitiveness, which he believed would be enhanced by membership of the Common Market. Macmillan understood that other ministers would not be convinced by economic arguments alone, and in cabinet emphasized the strategic advantages of joining the EEC, deftly skirting around the controversial issue of Commonwealth trade. Even so, the Commonwealth would have to be consulted prior to a decision 'in principle' on an application for membership.[9]

Washington was relieved that, after many unfruitful detours, the British were approaching the correct line. But the Americans cautioned Macmillan not to demand any unrealistic derogations from the Treaty of Rome for the benefit of domestic and Commonwealth farmers. For political reasons, the Treaty and the CAP would have to be accepted in their entirety. George Ball, the US Under Secretary of State, blithely assured Walter Hallstein that the 'Commonwealth problem seems to be soluble if transitional measures can be found.'[10] During a *tête-à-tête* with General de Gaulle, President Kennedy suggested that the principal economic obstacles to British membership were domestic and New Zealand farmers, implying that Australian interests could be disregarded. De Gaulle was adamant that Britain must abandon the Commonwealth in order to enter the EEC.[11]

In June 1961, British ministers resolved in favour of joining the EEC provided that satisfactory terms could be negotiated for British farmers and Commonwealth exporters. Only Maudling dissented from this conclusion. Macmillan sent ministers to Commonwealth capitals to explain that Britain was 'inclined' to apply for EEC membership, and to enumerate the political and economic benefits that would accrue to all and sundry. Commonwealth governments would be apprised that, while Britain would strive to safeguard their trade, there was no real prospect of saving unrestricted duty-free entry. In addition, at the conclusion of negotiations with the Six, Britain alone would decide whether or not to sign the Treaty of Rome. According to Lamb, the real objective of these consultations was to silence critics in the Conservative Party who felt that the Commonwealth was being sold out. Over the coming months, Macmillan preferred to consult Commonwealth governments on a bilateral basis rather than through the potentially explosive medium of a Commonwealth conference.[12]

The Sandys mission

Duncan Sandys was delegated to visit New Zealand, Australia, and Canada, during July 1961. As exporters of temperate foodstuffs including wheat, dairy produce, and meat, these countries were direct competitors of the Six. It was no secret that continental farmers expected to take the place of Commonwealth suppliers in the event of British entry into the Common Market, hence Sandys' task in explaining Britain's position was rather delicate. The British intended to stress the advantages of joining the EEC before the CAP was set in stone. Sandys was warned not to provoke the dominions into open resistance, as they could count on solid support in Britain, especially on the right wing of the Conservative Party, and in the powerful organs of the press magnate, Lord Beaverbrook. Macmillan hoped to engineer a liberal economic settlement between a British-led EEC and the USA.[13] However, Sandys did not draw attention to this long-term goal in his meetings with dominion governments.

Sandys' first port of call was Wellington, where ministers and officials were already in a state of anxiety. As early as June 1960, New Zealand officials had observed that it was increasingly likely that Britain and Denmark would join a European customs union. In April 1961, the New Zealand High Commission in London warned that the question of agricultural safeguards for the Commonwealth might not be resolved until after Britain had reached overall agreement with the Six.[14] The French admonished Wellington to abandon any expectations of winning increased access to continental markets in compensation for British entry into the EEC. Sutch, however, hoped that the sympathies of the French public could be swayed by a display of 'good clean football' during the forthcoming rugby tour of New Zealand.[15]

Holyoake and John Marshall, the Deputy Prime Minister and Minister of Trade, told Sandys that the New Zealand economy would be permanently damaged by the imposition of the CAP on Britain. They called upon the British to present the Six with a demand for the extension, in perpetuity, of unrestricted duty-free entry for Commonwealth foodstuffs. Marshall indicated that for political reasons the New Zealand government could not ask for less. Nevertheless, he accepted that as negotiations progressed New Zealand might have to consider alternative approaches to the problem of safeguarding the future of pastoralists. The British and the New Zealanders agreed that prices under the CAP should be kept as low as possible, but Sandys and his officials were disinclined to confront the Six with provocative demands relating to market access. They reminded Marshall that, under current agreements, unrestricted duty-free access would lapse in 1967. In view of the rising cost of subsidies, the British government might not renew this privilege regardless of EEC membership. Sandys believed that an element of Commonwealth preference could be retained during the transitional phase.

With respect to the permanent phase, however, he suggested that it would be more realistic to request an arrangement based on comparable outlets; in other words, any fall in the major Commonwealth exports to Britain would be balanced by an increase in exports to the rest of the EEC. Marshall rejected this formula, and the communiqué issued at the end of Sandys' visit acknowledged the differences between Britain and New Zealand over safeguards to be sought from the Six. Sandys, who may have been flustered, exceeded his brief in promising that Britain would not sign the Treaty of Rome unless the terms were acceptable to New Zealand.[16] Much was later made of this veto, although its use would have exhausted New Zealand's political credit in London.

The New Zealanders did not exaggerate the danger. In 1962, a British economist, James Meade, wrote that 'New Zealand would face the risk of economic catastrophe' if Britain were to enter the EEC without obtaining safeguards for Commonwealth trade. Sales of dairy produce to Britain would fall dramatically, while the customs revenue collected on this trade would be 'used to subsidise surplus exports of . . . Dutch butter to undercut Australia and New Zealand in outside markets.'[17]

By contrast, Australia did not face a serious economic challenge as a result of Britain's efforts to enter the EEC. Although Canberra raised some economic issues with the British, it was predominantly concerned with political factors. In particular, Australia wished to demonstrate that Britain was not entitled to act unilaterally in matters affecting the entire Commonwealth. The Australians were unsure how hard the British would fight to protect Commonwealth interests. In February 1961, McEwen told Cabinet that, 'The United Kingdom will make her own decision regarding the extent to which she will be prepared to modify Commonwealth trading arrangements in order to secure an association with the EEC, and oppos[i]tion by Australia might be of doubtful effect as a deterrent.'[18] During preparations for the Sandys visit, both sides weighed up the practical consequences of Britain's accession to the Treaty of Rome. Australia was Britain's second largest customer, and Britain was Australia's largest supplier. The British were warned that their exports to Australia would be vulnerable to any cuts in preference margins. Sandys realized that Australia, inspired by McEwen, would be a tough negotiator. Canberra was expected to demand a seat alongside Britain in negotiations with the Six, and a pledge that Britain would not permit any deterioration in Australia's trading position.[19]

By May 1961, Australia had begun seriously to consider the difficulties that might arise if Britain joined the EEC. In a cabinet submission,

McEwen indicated that, if Britain were to embrace the Treaty of Rome, 'the consequences for our trade could be disastrous'. Australia's exports to the UK were already declining relative to imports. It was contended that 55 to 60 per cent of Australian exports to Britain could be adversely affected. While exports of wool and metallic ores would perhaps remain as before, exports of wheat, butter, cheese, dried and canned fruits, wine, meats and even sugar would suffer. McEwen also brought up the question of Australia's exports of manufactures. These currently amounted to only A£6 million annually, but he felt that they had the potential to grow substantially.[20]

Australia began to highlight the political implications of the loss of sovereignty that would result from British membership of the Common Market. Commonwealth political structures would be weakened and British development aid might be diverted away from the Commonwealth. But there could be compensating factors. The security of the 'Western system' would be improved if Britain, France, and Germany were bound more closely together.[21] External Affairs suggested that Britain's economic interest in the Commonwealth would diminish, and newer members would turn away from Britain and towards foreign powers. But then the author added, 'as Australia, for that matter, has already done'. Australia's military relationship with Britain had already lost much of its significance. The submission concluded by pointing out that:[22]

> United Kingdom entry into the Community would accelerate tendencies which are already established: towards the transformation of the United Kingdom into a European rather than a world power and towards a decline in its commitments beyond Suez; and towards the transformation of the Commonwealth. Likewise, it would make plainer than before the existing and accepted fact that Australia is essentially dependent for effective physical resistance to aggressive powers in Asia, and for national survival, not on the United Kingdom but on the goodwill, self-interest and strength of the United States.

Sandys met Australian ministers between 8 and 11 July. The Australians attempted to cast doubt upon the proposition that the EEC would prove a better trading partner than the Commonwealth. McEwen argued that it would be risky to swap the tried and tested Ottawa system for the uncertain benefits of EEC membership. He suggested that the prospects for Commonwealth trade, especially between Britain and the developing countries, were excellent. Membership of the EEC, added McEwen, might hinder rather than improve Britain's industrial competitiveness, if dearer food resulted in growing wage demands and higher labour costs. Menzies enquired whether, as a member of the EEC, Britain would expect to retain tariff preferences in Australia. The Prime Minister was troubled by the possibility that Britain might be forced to support than EEC rather than the Commonwealth in GATT meetings. Many of Australia's concerns related to exports. Wheat was a commodity of special sensitivity. Under the Anglo-Australian trade agreement, the British were obliged to encourage the purchase of 750,000 tons per annum of Australian wheat. McEwen was sceptical of British assurances that the French could be persuaded to find comparable outlets for Australian wheat on the continent. The Australians were also worried about meat, sugar, dairy produce, canned and dried fruits, and certain raw materials. For instance, it was claimed that the loss of Commonwealth preference on dried fruit would ruin Australian suppliers. Sandys and his team endeavoured to be reassuring, and argued that over 60 per cent of Australian exports to Britain would be unaffected by EEC membership. As in Wellington, however, the apparent optimism of the British was heavily discounted. Australia decided to take a hard line, and Menzies indicated that he would reserve judgement on any bid to join the EEC.[23]

The Australians briefly drew attention to the financial implications of British membership in the EEC, but it was agreed that this aspect should be considered separately because of its technical nature. Australian concern about the effects on sterling was initially mild, although it became more intense in the course of deliberations. In June 1961, Harold Holt, the Australian Treasurer, had advised cabinet that British membership in the EEC might have little effect on Australia's international financial condition, except insofar as a loss in trade with Britain might reduce Australia's growth and render it less attractive to other foreign investors.[24] But, two months later, Holt had changed his mind. At the request of the British, he sent Selwyn Lloyd, the Chancellor of the Exchequer, a summary of the likely impact of Britain joining the Common Market. More than 60 per cent of private overseas investment in Australia between 1947–8 and 1959–60 had come from Britain, while additional capital had been raised by official borrowing on the London market. Canberra was concerned lest British membership of the EEC should limit the capacity of Australia to obtain private and government funds.[25] Lloyd's emollient reply indicated that the British did not wish to disturb current Sterling Area relationships. But Holt, without doubting Lloyd's good faith, commented that 'we must view what [the UK] has said on these matters with some scepticism.'[26] Australian concern about investment flows was not fanciful. Meade drew attention to the possibility that EEC membership might weaken Britain's balance of payments. He added that if Britain responded to any external difficulties by restricting capital exports, the EEC might demand privileged treatment relative to the RSA.[27]

Reporting back to cabinet, Sandys remarked that his public reception in Canberra, and also in Ottawa, had been coloured by electioneering, but that the economic consequences of British entry into the EEC would not be critical to either Australia or Canada. However, he acknowledged that 'New Zealand would be utterly ruined if Britain joined the Common Market without far-reaching arrangements to maintain an outlet for New Zealand lamb and butter.'[28] The Commonwealth Secretary predicted that the dominions would probably accept a decision by the British government to seek entry into the EEC. By implication, the Commonwealth case on temperate agricultural products was reducible to a plea for special arrangements for New Zealand. In cabinet on 27 July 1961, British ministers, fortified by testimony from Sandys, decided to proceed to negotiations with the Six. Although parliament endorsed this approach, dissent could not be quelled in the Commonwealth, and, at a ministerial meeting in Ghana, in September, the Canadians launched a stinging attack on the British.[29] Macmillan dryly noted in his memoirs that 'the atmosphere' at Accra had been 'somewhat strained'.[30]

In economic terms, Macmillan's determination to seek membership of the EEC was an act of faith. The economic theory of regional trading arrangements was rudimentary in the early 1960s. Subsequent research suggests that policy-makers usually exaggerate the net benefits to their country of entering a geographical discriminatory arrangement.[31] As Britain was proposing to migrate from one preferential regime to another, or at least to engineer a compromise between the Commonwealth economic network and the EEC, the issues were even more complicated. Macmillan evidently believed that the benefits of EEC membership to British manufacturers would outweigh the costs to British food consumers. Sandys tried to assure the old dominions that they too would gain from British accession to the Treaty of Rome, but they were not convinced. For New Zealand in particular, the net welfare effect of British accession was likely to be both substantial and negative. Macmillan's critics could take heart from the low probability of British success in the forthcoming talks, due to the hostile attitude of the French in particular.

Comparable outlets and the first stage of negotiations

The Six were in no hurry to proceed, as they wished to thwart any attempt by Britain to influence the structure of the CAP. Heath, who led the British negotiating team, was invited to make an opening oration at a ministerial meeting of the Six in Paris on 10 October 1961. A further lengthy delay ensued while the Six thrashed out the fundamentals the CAP, and negotiations did not begin in earnest until 1962.[32]

Heath's Paris address failed to satisfy either the Commonwealth or the Six. The dominions acknowledged that the statement could have been worse, but bemoaned Britain's reluctance to fight for unrestricted duty-free entry. For their part, the Six were exasperated with Heath's request for a transition of between 10 and 12 years before Britain was subjected to the full rigour of the CAP.[33] Australia and New Zealand were not allowed to participate directly in the Brussels talks. In November 1961, Macmillan convinced Menzies that it would be counter-productive for Australia to approach the Six with a demand for a seat at the negotiating table.[34] But this did not prevent the representatives of Australia and New Zealand from putting their case, and being in close attendance while Britain and the Six conducted their business.

Britain's strategy on temperate foodstuffs was to seek 'special arrangements (not only for the transitional period, but for the common market period as well) which would safeguard the substance of the Commonwealth's present position.'[35] During the transition, the Six would expect Britain to phase out Commonwealth preferences, commence the erection of the CET, and begin to phase in the CAP. Heath argued that Commonwealth exporters of temperate foodstuffs deserved to receive comparable outlets, in the form of duty-free, levy-free, or preferential quotas, market sharing arrangements, or bulk contracts. Thus Commonwealth producers would have opportunities to maintain exports at traditional levels. As the agricultural regime in Britain gradually converged on the European model, comparable outlets would have to be found on the continent as well as in Britain. Heath hoped that comparable outlets would sooner or later be merged into global agreements on the management of international trade in foodstuffs.[36]

In the ominous words of one UK Board of Trade official, there would be plenty of 'horse-trading' between Britain and the Six over Commonwealth agriculture.[37] Australia regarded it as a tactical error by Britain to have proposed the nebulous principle of comparable outlets, when what really mattered were the concrete arrangements for each commodity. The French were able to delay talks on individual commodities by disputing the general principle. As W.A. Westerman, of the Australian trade ministry, explained, Britain and the Six 'argued like hell about the suitcase', but did not adequately discuss the contents.[38] Solutions for each commodity would have to be mundanely practical. For instance, the British recommended that comparable outlets for butter take the form of levy-free quotas. While the proposed quotas were lower than the quantities Australia and New Zealand were accustomed to delivering, Britain contended that export revenue would be protected by an increase in price. But any suggestion that volumes should be reduced was anathema to New Zealand and Australia, which had few alternative markets. If marginal dairy farmers were ruined, the Australian and New Zealand governments would face serious political backlashes in their rural heartlands. Under the British butter quota regime, introduced in 1961 in response to New Zealand's request for anti-dumping duties, the dominions were allocated generous shares of the UK market. Australia and New Zealand would not willingly exchange this system, despite its imperfections, for comparable outlets.[39]

It distressed Australia and New Zealand that Britain did not demand comparable outlets for all Commonwealth foodstuffs, only for those regarded as 'essential', including wheat, meat, dairy produce, fruit, and sugar.[40] Britain contended, with some justification, that a claim for comparable outlets across the board would test the Six's patience, and alienate the USA and GATT. The British felt that, in most cases, comparable outlets be expressed in terms of preferential quotas. However, for sheepmeat, and certain raw materials, including lead and zinc, of interest to Australia, the British would seek either a zero or a minimal CET. Australia and New Zealand were relieved that the EEC had no plans to impose a tariff on raw wool. Regarding manufactures, Britain would concentrate on securing concessions for the textile industries of India, Pakistan, and Hong Kong.[41]

The Australian cabinet was annoyed that the British seemed to treat some of Australia's exports as expendable.[42] Menzies cabled Macmillan, in October 1961, that, 'we want the whole of our trade interests in the United Kingdom to be protected'. Macmillan replied, somewhat disingenuously, that, 'As regards Ted Heath's statement on October 10th I can assure you that it will not suggest that any item of Australian Trade is expendable.'[43] In April 1962, in an address to senior officials of Britain and the Six, Westerman maintained that Australia expected comparable outlets for all agricultural exports, including rabbits and hares.[44] McEwen admonished the British to remember their 'contractual relationship' with Australia.[45]

Wellington also felt that the British were focussing their efforts too narrowly. In September 1961, New Zealand officials wryly observed that 'the United Kingdom evidently propose to enter the negotiations with a much more flexible position than New Zealand had considered desirable.'[46] While the British were devoting ample energy to the issue of comparable outlets for butter, they appeared to be neglecting other important commodities such as cheese and meat. Meat producers were incensed by the laxity of the British in advancing their case, which they suspected was motivated by the wish to protect domestic suppliers from Commonwealth competition. John Ormond, the chairman of the New Zealand Meat Producers' Board, publicly campaigned against Britain's bid to join the EEC. Despite sharing the producers' concerns, the government explained that it would be unwise to confront the British over comparable outlets, as New Zealand would receive no safeguards at all without their goodwill.[47]

Comparable outlets would have involved an opportunity to sell, and not a guaranteed level of sales.[48] The ability of Commonwealth producers to fill their quotas would depend on the state of the markets. But food markets in the EEC were extremely distorted. High support prices fostered uneconomic production and choked off demand, often leaving little room for imports. Britain and the dominions hoped that the EEC could be persuaded to choose relatively low target prices. It was in Britain's interest to secure low food prices in the Community, as consumers would resent a substantial increase in the cost of living. The Dutch government also advocated low prices, since its farmers were relatively efficient, while its export-oriented industries wished to avoid rising wage costs, but other members of the Six were not inclined to undermine the rationale of the CAP. In autumn 1960, for instance, the wholesale butter price was 286s. 8d. per cwt in Britain, whereas the weighted average price in the EEC was 515s. 4d. Britain and the Commonwealth sought for a butter price of no more than 350s. per cwt in the enlarged Community, since it was anticipated that many consumers would switch to margarine above this level. However, New Zealand officials did not expect to achieve this objective because the purpose of the CAP was to protect continental farmers. In view of the rising agricultural surpluses in Australia and New Zealand, Westerman argued that quotas should include provision for growth, but this suggestion was ignored. Under comparable outlets, deliveries in excess of quota would have encountered serious obstacles.[49]

British proposals for world commodity agreements were extremely sketchy. It was unclear how they would have procured a consensus in

GATT for the regulation of trade in sensitive products such as cereals, meat, and butter. If the major importing and exporting nations had been unable to agree on a suitable mechanism, Australia and New Zealand would have had to request the extension of comparable outlets in the enlarged EEC. While the British could be counted on to lobby in Brussels on the Commonwealth's behalf, continental resistance to special arrangements would have grown over time. Britain was not the only advocate of managed agricultural trade in the early 1960s. At a GATT meeting in November 1961, the French Minister of Finance, Wilfried Baumgartner, called for a new international regime, that would provide adequate export opportunities for states such as Australia and New Zealand, without compromising the agricultural policies of major importers. He proposed that interested countries agree on a world price for each commodity. Efficient producers would obtain higher profit margins at this price, although export volumes would drop. High cost producers, such as the EEC, would impose a levy in order to raise the import price from the world to the domestic level. Revenue from this levy would be used to subsidize the export of food surpluses to poor nations. Ludlow argues that the French regarded the EEC enlargement talks as an opportunity to increase support for their commodity proposals.[50]

New Zealand's response to the French initiative on commodities was cautiously positive. As hope was fading for a genuinely liberal world agricultural regime, it was necessary to explore alternatives. GATT established study groups to examine the possible application of the French plan to cereals and meat. Separate talks were held on the dairy trade. The EEC reiterated its opposition to global agreements couched in quantitative terms, and expressed a preference for arrangements based on price. But most other countries, including the USA and many Commonwealth members, demanded quantitative assurances with respect to the European market. Both GATT and the EEC accepted that no real progress on commodities could be expected until the result of Britain's application for entry into the EEC was known. Whether or not British membership would have facilitated a solution is uncertain. In the event, wrangling between the EEC and the USA ensured that nothing of substance emerged from the cereal talks, while the meat and dairy problems proved equally intractable. The first, and extremely limited, International Dairy Agreement did not come into force until 1980.[51]

Australia and New Zealand argued that, if world commodity agreements were to replace comparable outlets, they should be given con-

crete form as soon as possible. Although Canberra was genuinely interested in global arrangements to manage the food trade, Westerman
warned ministers not to accept ethereal assurances as a substitute for
firm and continuing safeguards for Australian trade in advance of a decision on British membership of the EEC.[52] He later stated that neither
the British nor the Six had 'the vaguest idea what a world agreement
was'.[53] The New Zealanders were dubious about the prospects for world
commodity agreements, especially for complex product groups like
meat. Representatives of the producer boards feared that larger countries would vote to reduce New Zealand's share of world markets once
international agreements were in operation. New Zealand officials asked
the British whether they had given any thought to the fate of Commonwealth countries in the event of the collapse of a commodity agreement. The British were confident that agreements would be robust, but
declined to offer any guarantee.[54]

Much would depend on Washington's attitude. In August 1961,
W.E.G. Salter, of the Australian Prime Minister's Department, suggested
that the USA might be Australia's most valuable ally in the struggle
to obtain satisfactory terms for the Commonwealth.[55] Unlike the
Eisenhower administration, the Kennedy administration was not dia-
metrically opposed to new international commodity agreements. However, Salter underestimated Washington's hostility to preferential
trading mechanisms, especially those involving the British Commonwealth. The scheme for comparable outlets was certain to meet with
American disapproval. George Ball explained to President Kennedy that,
'To permit the Commonwealth to have either free or preferential access
to the Common Market would be highly prejudicial to our own temperate agriculture as well as to both the tropical and temperate agriculture of Latin America.'[56] Ball expressed concern about the possible
extension to European suppliers of British preferences in the Commonwealth, although in fact neither the British nor the Six now
expected these preferences to survive. Ultimately, said Ball, the USA
might have to accept some form of 'cushioning arrangements' for individual Commonwealth countries, especially New Zealand and its butter
producers, but these ought to be strictly limited, and the British should
be given no encouragement at this stage. Ball reiterated the American
position on preferences in subsequent meetings with British, Australian,
and New Zealand representatives, and dismissed a request that the USA
compensate New Zealand for loss of trade arising from British entry into
the EEC by granting improved access to the American market. Nevertheless, Ball indicated that the Kennedy administration would not

oppose a solution for Commonwealth wheat and butter based on world commodity agreements.[57]

At the Anglo-American summit, in April 1962, Kennedy hectored Macmillan on the subject of safeguards for Commonwealth exports: 'Britain could not take care of everyone in its wake as it joined'. Kennedy accepted that preferential arrangements would be needed during the transitional phase, but stressed that these must terminate at a fixed date. In the long term, he added, the interests of the Commonwealth could be protected by world commodity agreements. Macmillan spoke wearily of the plight of those in the Commonwealth who would find it difficult to adjust, such as 'old soldiers settled in New Zealand and taught to grow pineapples.' But the Americans were unmoved.[58] Ball and the French Foreign Minister, Couve de Murville, assured each other in May 1962 that there could be no long-term derogations from the Treaty of Rome to cater for Commonwealth suppliers of temperate foodstuffs. The proper course would be to seek global commodity agreements.[59] During the same month, Dean Rusk, the Secretary of State, visited Canberra and Wellington, and elaborated on the US government's uncompromising stance on new preferential arrangements. McEwen, who was incensed by this intervention, launched a public attack on the Americans. While he was not seeking new preferences, claimed McEwen, he had every right to preserve existing trade privileges, in modified form, should Britain enter the EEC. In McEwen's opinion, arrangements for comparable outlets could not be confined to the transitional period. He added that Australia was willing to negotiate in GATT for the elimination of preferences, in return for substantial cuts in the level of protection on primary commodities.[60] American policy was in essence to encourage the Six, and especially France, to reject the British proposals for comparative outlets.

An association agreement between the enlarged EEC, New Zealand, and perhaps Australia was occasionally canvassed as an alternative to comparable outlets. In September 1961, the British Economic Steering Committee indicated that the government should not rule out 'the possibility of negotiating some form of special association between New Zealand and the Common Market despite the embarrassment this might cause *vis-à-vis* Australia', India, and other Commonwealth members.[61] Under the Morocco Protocol, former French colonies in North Africa enjoyed a special status in the French market. North African produce was allowed into France free of duty. Algeria, Morocco, and Tunisia granted tariff preferences on industrial imports from the EEC. Greece also became an associate of the EEC, and the founding father of the European movement, Jean Monnet, thought that a similar arrangement might suit New Zealand. Although Monnet was out of favour in France, he still had influence in Brussels. New Zealand asked Britain to make explorations on its behalf. However, the chances of agreement were slim, and the British warned that it would be unwise to regard association as an alternative to comparable outlets. The EEC did not wish to be linked to a dangerous competitor in the sensitive dairy trade. Moreover, it would have been difficult for Wellington to cut tariffs on European manufactures in the face of protests from domestic industrialists and Washington. Canberra rejected the concept of association with the EEC on the grounds that it was incompatible with the protection of domestic industry.[62] Association was not a realistic option in the 1960s, although it might have been in the 1950s when the European trading bloc was more malleable.

Under the circumstances, neither Australia nor New Zealand could muster any enthusiasm for comparable outlets. A memorandum by Salter encapsulates the prevailing pessimism:

> There are limits to the UK's ability to both join the EEC and, at the same time, protect our interests. Her own negotiating position is weak: She is seeking to disturb the balance of power and compromise; the Six are not likely to devalue their achievement by admitting of many derogations from the Rome Treaty . . . [Moreover, Australia's] own negotiating position is pitifully weak. Much has been made of our preferences. But on closer examination they are not proving to be a really strong card. The main reason is that the spirit of the Rome Treaty (and, on some interpretations, its text) do not allow one member to enjoy preferences in third markets not shared by others. Hence, the Europeans can argue that simply by sitting tight, B.P.T. preferences will be eliminated. Why should they then offer us anything to achieve this result?[63]

Salter's fears were well founded. In June 1962, after months of procrastination, the Six rejected comparable outlets as a solution to the problem of temperate Commonwealth foodstuffs. The British, to whom this came as no surprise, adjusted their expectations and revised their proposals accordingly.[64] By the end of July, Whitehall had completely given up the idea of comparable outlets.

The end game and special arrangements for New Zealand

The Six dismissed the scheme for comparable outlets because it involved serious discrimination against other countries, including the USA, and was at odds with the ethos of the CAP, which was to protect European, and not Commonwealth, farmers.[65] It was not just the French who were anxious to restrict the access of Commonwealth farmers to the European market. If, Chancellor Adenauer warned the German Cabinet, the Six were to meet the Commonwealth's demands, 'God help us, particularly agriculture'. Adenauer wished that the Commonwealth would 'just swim off'.[66] British negotiators, who evidently viewed comparable outlets as an interim negotiating position, concluded that the objections of the Six were 'not unreasonable'.[67]

Although neither Australia nor New Zealand had been satisfied with comparable outlets, they now had reason to fear the emergence of an even worse scheme, as the initiative passed from Britain to the Six, or in practice France. New Zealand officials predicted that the British position would continue to erode; 'In their determination to force negotiations to a conclusion, the British are likely to make further considerable concessions to the Six. . . . we may have to pay a high price for the speed with which the British' are inclined to move.[68] It soon became clear that there would be no definite safeguards for Commonwealth temperate foodstuffs during the permanent phase of British membership. In the transitional phase, Commonwealth foodstuffs would be permitted to share in the intra-Community preference on a degressive basis, thereby retaining some advantage over non-EEC suppliers.[69] But special quotas would not be available for temperate foodstuffs, with the possible exception of New Zealand dairy produce and lamb.

The Six asserted that all transitional arrangements would have to terminate in 1970. They hoped that long-term global agreements on temperate foodstuffs would emerge from a series of conferences, which they planned to convene in late 1962 or 1963. If, however, international agreement proved elusive, the EEC might consider entering into narrower arrangements with principal suppliers including the dominions. The Six undertook to follow reasonable pricing and production policies in order to provide scope for imports into the enlarged EEC.[70] In June 1962, a report to the European Parliament on agricultural aspects of British accession raised the prospect of an EEC dairy regime of low tariffs and direct subsidies to farmers, but nothing came of this suggestion.[71]

As the dominions resented the EEC's insistence on a sharply degressive transitional regime, the British were prepared for conflict with their partners. New Zealand, for instance, was arguing that its butter producers needed a transitional phase of 12 years.[72] The British were under intense pressure to accept the principles enunciated by the Six, which they endeavoured to show in the best possible light. The EEC's commitment to reasonable pricing was depicted as a significant concession, although it was operationally meaningless. Sandys informed Menzies, in late July, that Britain was fairly satisfied with the EEC's suggestions for commodity agreements as well as its price and production strategies. But it was difficult for the British to conceal their disappointment with the proposed transitional arrangements. The Commonwealth Secretary suggested that transitional quotas might not be necessary if the EEC kept its commitments on pricing and production. This hint was not well received in Canberra. Macmillan also suggested to Menzies that Australia should be pleased that the Six were now advocating international commodity agreements, since this had long been an Australian objective.[73] Such rhetoric made no impact in either Canberra or Wellington. Westerman continued to dismiss British thinking on commodity agreements as 'mumbo-jumbo', and pointed out that nothing definite had emerged with respect to the central issues of market access and pricing.[74] Menzies was adamant that any safeguards for Australian trade must extend into the permanent phase of British membership. Vague assurances about international agreements would not be acceptable. If, however, Britain and the Six were to endorse a clear set of principles on the operation of commodity agreements, these could be included in an overall settlement.[75]

Following the Six's rejection of comparable outlets, the Australians decided to open a second front in Washington. In July, Menzies, McEwen, and a group of Australian officials, led by Westerman, held talks with President Kennedy and US government representatives. Menzies argued that it would not be in America's interests to force Britain to choose between the Commonwealth and Europe. Australia, he hinted, would do its utmost to oppose the European option in such a situation. Menzies asked the Americans to use their bargaining power in GATT to secure a more liberal CAP, a lower CET, and sensible commodity agreements. Although the USA would have to make unrequited tariff concessions to the EEC in order to reach these goals, Menzies contended that it would derive significant commercial benefits from the modification of the CAP, and any associated reductions in BP margins and Commonwealth food preferences. A satisfactory outcome in GATT would eliminate the risk that Australia would obstruct British accession to the Treaty of Rome. The Americans responded sympathetically to

Menzies' rollicking performance, but did not commit themselves to any particular course of action.[76]

The Americans were increasingly anxious about the entry negotiations. Rusk told the British that Washington was ready to intercede in the event of an impasse. But London feared that 'an American démarche in Paris [at this stage] would probably be resented by the French as an unwarranted interference in a purely European matter'.[77] In the light of de Gaulle's obsessive suspicion of Anglo-Saxon machinations, this was a realistic assessment. Menzies saw Kennedy again in September 1962, and, on his return to Australia, expressed the hope that the US Trade Expansion Act would facilitate reductions in agricultural protection during the next GATT round.[78]

Over the northern summer of 1962, it became clear that the Six would deal less harshly with New Zealand than with the other dominions. New Zealand, as Macmillan reminded de Gaulle, was still 'an English farm in the Pacific' with few alternative outlets.[79] Public opinion would not allow the British government to join the EEC unless it could create the appearance that New Zealand's essential commercial interests were secure. The Six were familiar with the New Zealand problem. In 1960, the Italians had assured Macmillan that they would willingly forgo imports of Yugoslavian and Hungarian butter in order to aid New Zealand. Prior to the Sandys mission, French officials had hinted at a special arrangement for New Zealand butter, while Monnet had made a similar suggestion in November 1961.[80] Wellington realized that a special arrangement was lurking in the background. Camps argues that this issue would have come to the fore earlier if the British had not floated the scheme for comparable outlets, which was predicated on the equality of the dominions. New Zealand had been working on the assumption that any formal consideration of its special needs would follow the conclusion of a wider settlement on Commonwealth agriculture.[81]

Speculation about a special deal for New Zealand intensified after the demise of comparable outlets. Dr Mangold, a senior German representative in Brussels, warned the New Zealanders that any special arrangement for butter would have to exclude Australia in order to minimize disruption of the EEC's dairy regime. In August, at a confused ministerial meeting in Brussels, the Italian Minister of Agriculture, Emilio Colombo, announced that the Six would review New Zealand's case with sympathy. It would have been more accurate to say that five of the EEC's members were willing to show compassion to New Zealand, since France did not agree with Colombo's statement. No indication was given as to how any special arrangement might work or which products might be included. New Zealand was rapidly losing confidence in the fighting spirit of British negotiators, and looked forward to direct talks with the Six. The New Zealanders envisaged a permanent guarantee with respect to current levels of trade in all categories, plus some scope for growth. Wellington was prepared to put British industrial preferences on the bargaining table. In the event, New Zealand was not permitted to negotiate directly with the Six, and Britain continued to act on its behalf.[82]

Expectations were falling when Marshall addressed the Council of Europe in September. The Deputy Prime Minister pleaded for special arrangements to protect the volume and value of New Zealand's exports, especially dairy produce, until satisfactory world commodity agreements could be brought into force.[83] Marshall's stress on export volume was deliberate, as Britain and the Six had hinted at an arrangement for butter based on 'half the quantity, twice the price'.[84] Britain was dismayed by New Zealand's objection to this solution, since it would be easier to reconcile a revenue guarantee than a quantitative guarantee with the CAP. Allusion was even made to a settlement in the form of an overall revenue guarantee covering a basket of commodities, reducing New Zealanders to the status of 'pension[ers]' of the EEC.[85] Australia viewed these developments with anxiety. Westerman warned the British that Canberra 'would naturally be concerned if there were to be any discrimination in the arrangements for products like butter and lamb'.[86] Wellington was embarrassed by any suggestion that it was about to break ranks with the other dominions. The New Zealanders attempted to assure the Australians, the Canadians, and the British that their primary goal was a reasonable general settlement for the Commonwealth. Although Wellington denied having lobbied for special treatment, it had to admit that this topic had been mentioned in talks with the Six.[87] This was an accurate statement of the position in August 1962, but New Zealand would have to accept what was offered regardless of the implications for Australia.

Macmillan's diplomacy faced a stern test at the Commonwealth Prime Ministers' Conference in September 1962. The British sought the Commonwealth's blessing for their efforts to join the EEC. British speakers emphasized the political advantages of EEC membership. Britain's world influence, they claimed, would be increased by the assumption of a leading role in Europe, and the status of the Commonwealth would rise. But the British still had nothing of substance to offer in the area of temperate foodstuffs. Macmillan and Heath repeated the Six's vague assurances about commodity agreements, reasonable pricing policies, transitional arrangements, and special treatment for New Zealand. Holyoake told Macmillan that 'New Zealand would be ruined' unless the British could obtain fair terms for Commonwealth trade.[88] Menzies was sceptical about the political and economic advantages to Britain of EEC membership, and remained dissatisfied with the progress of negotiations with the Six on Commonwealth trade. Australia would continue to reserve judgement on the EEC application.[89] Although both New Zealand and Australia were careful to avoid a breach with Britain, the Canadian leader, John Diefenbaker, mounted an uncompromising attack on Macmillan's policy. Macmillan was disgusted by Diefenbaker's intervention, and indicated that his tactics would not be allowed to succeed.[90]

No new information about a special deal for New Zealand was revealed at the Commonwealth Conference. Shortly afterwards, Marshall and Holyoake visited Paris, where de Gaulle and his ministers warned them not to expect too much. Any special arrangement would be temporary and degressive. Although the British sympathized with the New Zealanders over de Gaulle's attitude, they stressed that the Six were in a strong bargaining position.[91] Wellington was growing impatient with the procrastination in London and Brussels. In September 1962, New Zealand tentatively advanced a plan for a pilot international dairy agreement, which would have come into force during the transitional phase. New Zealand and the enlarged EEC would have been the founder members, but other countries would have been invited to join later. An agreed share of the total butter market in the enlarged EEC, based on recent performance, would have been allocated to New Zealand. Import prices would have been regulated, and surpluses disposed of in the third world. The ultimate objective would have been to share international dairy markets among the major suppliers. British officials regarded this scheme as a distraction, and pointed out that it was at odds with the general stance of the Six, which was to push for international agreement on prices rather than market shares. Moreover, as Wellington's proposal involved discrimination, it was certain to arouse the ire of the USA and GATT. Jean Monnet strongly advised the New Zealanders to desist.[92] Earlier in the year the French officials, Kojeve and Wormser, had encouraged New Zealand to devise a commodity agreement for butter. Whether or not this was a deliberate trap is uncertain.[93] At any rate, this episode provided further confirmation that New Zealand would have little say in the arrangements determining its commercial future.

Lamb was the other commodity of major concern to New Zealand. Britain was the main competitor of Australia and New Zealand in the lamb trade. Continental Europe was not an important sheepmeat producer, but the Six were expected to demand a CET of 20 per cent in order to discourage consumers from switching to lamb from beef and pork. Although the British formally asked the Six to confirm the unrestricted duty-free status of Commonwealth lamb, they were actually angling for a compromise involving a 20 per cent CET and the continuation of domestic subsidies. In the absence of subsidies, British producers would not have been able to withstand New Zealand and Australian competition. New Zealand feared that the Six would agree to these terms, and later give the British *carte blanche* to write a restrictive CAP for sheepmeat. On the other hand, a special deal for New Zealand lamb producers could not be ruled out, possibly in the form of a market sharing agreement.[94]

As New Zealand became more desperate, its solidarity with Australia and Canada became less pronounced. By December 1962, there was strong support in cabinet for the view that 'Australia could not be allowed . . . to veto any special arrangements for New Zealand on the grounds that Australia was not being treated equitably'.[95] But the precise terms of any special arrangement remained murky. Officials listed the alternatives: an association agreement between New Zealand and the EEC in dairy products, a revenue guarantee covering one or more groups of commodities, a revenue-volume guarantee, a simple quantitative guarantee, a limited commodity agreement, or a system of tariff quotas. Whether the solution would have been couched in terms of an opportunity to sell or something more definite also remained unsettled. The British were still considering these options when de Gaulle issued his veto of British accession in January 1963.[96]

Realizing that they could expect little from either Britain or the Six, the Australians increasingly washed their hands of proceedings in Brussels. McEwen and the Department of Trade concluded that Australia's interests were not sufficiently threatened to warrant the amount of effort needed to rein in the British. On 19 December 1962, the British asked Australia to have a senior official available in London and Brussels 'to be on hand when decisive stages are reached on problems of particular concern to Australia'. The Department of Trade felt, however, that it did not want to spare anyone of sufficient rank and suggested that the British be told, 'the Australian Government feels that it had done everything possible to inform your government on the important problems of Australia's trade requiring special consideration'.

As the Australian Treasury pointed out, 'the rejection by the Trade Department of the British suggestion could only be read by the British ... as a marked change of attitude.... The Department of Trade are really giving the game away'.[97]

When de Gaulle's veto of British accession was announced in January 1963 most New Zealanders, and many Australians, breathed a sigh of relief. Toasts were drunk to General de Gaulle at annual conferences of the New Zealand Association of Economists during the 1960s.[98] However, the New Zealanders felt that the British had let them down: 'The most unsatisfactory feature of the present negotiations is that the United Kingdom have accepted the kind of approach adopted by the Six, namely "good intentions and reasonable policies".'[99] Britain and the Six had been moving towards a settlement including few safeguards for Commonwealth producers of temperate foodstuffs. New Zealand might have secured reasonable special arrangements for dairy produce, and possibly lamb, during the transitional phase, but it would have encountered the abyss in 1970. No special arrangements would have been available to alleviate the difficulties of Australian producers. Attempts to accommodate the Commonwealth by procuring world commodity agreements would have run into daunting political obstacles. Perhaps the EEC would have entered into narrower commodity agreements with the Commonwealth, but, in all likelihood, New Zealand would have had to petition Brussels for the extension of any special arrangements.

Conclusion

According to his official biographer, Harold Macmillan faced three particularly worrying problems when he decided that the United Kingdom should opt for full membership in the European Economic Community. In the event, two of the problems – convincing Cabinet and the Conservative Party of the need to join Europe – were dealt with easily. The third problem – convincing the Commonwealth – was to prove nearly intractable.[100] But the real lesson of 1961–3 was that Britain did not need to convince the Commonwealth that membership of the EEC was desirable. With the exception of the Diefenbaker government, which was heading for electoral defeat, it was obvious by September 1962 that Commonwealth members would accept whatever terms were put in front of them. The sullen acquiescence of New Zealand was a reflection of its weakness. While the Australians' bargaining position was also quite weak, the British market was not as crucial to Australia as it was to New Zealand. Having observed that the British, despite their good intentions, were unable to do much to protect the Commonwealth's economic interests, the Australians withdrew to the sidelines.

It was the French, and not the Australians or the New Zealanders, whom Macmillan had to persuade. Here he failed miserably. Whether there was any realistic chance of success while de Gaulle was President is another matter. De Gaulle repeatedly expressed the view that Britain must abandon the Commonwealth as well as the special relationship with the USA in order to join the EEC. In 1961, he told Donald Fleming, the Canadian Minister of Finance, that 'We are willing to have the United Kingdom in the Common Market, but not the Commonwealth.' On another occasion, he declared, 'I want her naked!', meaning that Britain must cast off her wider loyalties.[101] Britain's readiness, admittedly under pressure, to eliminate all Commonwealth preferences, and to erect reverse preferences by the deadline of 1970, was an indication that the first steps towards satisfying France had already been taken. Britain would soon be ready to cast off the Commonwealth economic network and embrace Brussels. Both Canberra and Wellington realized that the British would submit another application for membership of the EEC when there was a 'better atmosphere' in Europe.[102] Heath's cautious and dignified response to de Gaulle's intervention, and his promise that Britain would not turn its back on Europe, can have left few doubts on this score.

9
After the Veto: Trade Policy in the Mid-1960s

> *Australian TV interviewer:* Do you think there is any possibility that there may be complacency in Australia now that Britain is not going in [to the EEC]. We may feel that there is no need to seek further markets. Do you think there is any danger of that?
>
> *John McEwen, Australian Deputy Prime Minister and Minister of Trade:* No, I don't think there is danger that this development should produce complacency ... we go on discussing our trade relationship with the United Kingdom and go on searching the world ... [for] trading opportunities.[1]

Britain's failure to gain entry into the EEC gave some relief to worried farmers in Australasia. But the long-term commercial prospects for New Zealand and Australia continued to be shrouded in uncertainty. It was widely expected that Britain would renew its attempt to join the Common Market. In the meantime, it was possible that it would adopt a restrictive, European-style agricultural policy, offer agricultural concessions to EFTA, and exploit BP margins to the full. Consequently, New Zealand and Australia could not afford to relax the search for alternative outlets.

Although it seemed doubtful that the projected Kennedy Round in GATT would succeed in reducing the barriers to agricultural trade in Europe and North America, there were opportunities in the buoyant Japanese market, especially for Australian mineral exporters. Building on foundations laid in the 1950s, Canberra and Wellington strove to improve their economic relations with Tokyo. In New Zealand's case, the development of trans-Tasman trade was of even greater significance than the development of trade with Japan. In 1966, the New Zealand–

Australia Free Trade Area (NAFTA) came into operation, safeguarding New Zealand's pulp and paper exports, and providing export opportunities for manufacturers. As bilateral ties with Britain withered, the economic relationship between New Zealand and Australia intensified.

By the early 1970s, Australia had little to fear from British membership of the EEC. But access to the UK market remained vital to New Zealand, which had not been able to attain Australia's level of market diversification during the ten-year hiatus between the French veto and British accession. This chapter examines developments in commercial relations between Britain, Australia, and New Zealand after the rejection of Macmillan's application for EEC membership. It considers the role of Australia and New Zealand in the Kennedy Round, the Commonwealth trade policies of the Wilson government, the origins and development of NAFTA, and the course of economic relations between Australia and New Zealand and Japan. Finally, it touches upon, but does not cover in depth, the second and third British approaches to the EEC.

Regrouping after the veto

Wellington and Canberra were apprehensive about the future direction of British commercial policy following the collapse of the Brussels negotiations. Would the British attempt to revive the Commonwealth, either as an interim or a permanent solution to their difficulties, or would the process of disengagement continue?

New Zealand officials advised ministers that membership of the EEC would remain the ultimate goal of the British establishment. In the short-term, however, they felt that the British would attach even greater importance to the Kennedy Round, and that a new campaign for a European industrial free trade area, or even a transatlantic economic association, could not be ruled out. Any progress over agriculture in the Kennedy Round would be to New Zealand's advantage, even if Commonwealth preferences in Britain were reduced as part of the settlement. Since Macmillan's approach to Europe had been rooted in the assumption that the outlook for Commonwealth trade was poor, Britain was not expected to agitate for a tighter Ottawa system. Indeed, any steps in this direction would make it more difficult later on for Britain to enter the EEC. But London would have an incentive to strike hard bargains with Australia and New Zealand over the extension of their bilateral trade agreements with the UK. Britain might even abolish the unrestricted duty-free status of Commonwealth foodstuffs, with a view to reducing the financial burden of deficiency payments, and narrowing the gap between British agricultural policy and the CAP. New Zealand would have to fight to preserve its position in the British food market, while keeping up the pressure on the CAP in GATT.[2]

The Australians also had reason to be concerned about the British reaction to the breakdown in Brussels. It was possible, argued one Australian Treasury official, that the British would surrender over the terms of EEC entry, in a desperate effort in concert with the 'Five' to persuade the French to withdraw their veto. At any rate, cabinet anticipated that in order to smooth the way for a future membership application the British would steer away from policies likely to aggravate the Europeans. Menzies promised that Australia would not give up the quest for new markets. While the British were unlikely to press for a more inward-looking Commonwealth economic system, they might blame the dominions for the failure in Brussels, and demand compensation in the trade sphere. Further ahead, Australia envisaged a more critical British posture in relation to the Ottawa system and international commodity agreements. The British might throw Commonwealth food preferences into the Kennedy Round, make dairy concessions to Denmark in EFTA, or even impose quotas on imports from the dominions. Reconsideration of the Anglo-Australian trade agreement (UKATA) had been postponed by mutual consent during the EEC membership talks. Australia now hoped that this agreement would be extended for five years. However, British officials indicated that they intended to take a tougher line than previously in bilateral negotiations. They did not wish to tie their hands either in the Kennedy Round or in any future negotiations with the EEC. The collapse of the Brussels negotiations had generated a new set of uncertainties.[3]

In 1962, a team of British civil servants, led by Arnold France of the Treasury, had examined Britain's options in the event of stalemate in Brussels. They concluded that a retreat into the Ottawa system would be impracticable. It appeared that Commonwealth countries were strongly committed to import substitution policies, wished to purchase capital goods in the cheapest markets, and planned to use British preferences as counters in negotiations with other countries. Finally, unrestricted Commonwealth duty-free entry was deemed inconsistent with Britain's evolving agricultural policy. Christopher Soames, the Minister of Agriculture, recommended the introduction of variable levies or quantitative restrictions on cereal and meat imports from all sources regardless of the outcome of the Brussels talks. Britain, he stressed, had the right to terminate at six months' notice the agreements under which Commonwealth food was imported in unrestricted quantities.[4]

Macmillan told cabinet, in late January 1963, that Britain's immediate 'objectives should be to strengthen relations with the Commonwealth, the European Free Trade Area and the member countries of the EEC, other than France, and to work for greater freedom in international trade.'[5] Diefenbaker, the Canadian leader, was thought to be angling for another Commonwealth economic conference. Fearing that Diefenbaker would make an embarrassing plea for the strengthening of Commonwealth economic ties, the British decided against holding a conference, and instead resolved to seek bilateral negotiations with countries such as Australia and New Zealand. Cabinet argued that Britain should deal sternly with Australia:

> To commit ourselves . . . to importing large quantities of Australian wheat for a further period while accepting the continuance of Australian discrimination against some of our more important industries would be inconsistent with the realistic approach to economic problems which we must advocate if we were to succeed in promoting greater freedom in international trade.[6]

In May 1963, cabinet decided in principle to move towards a regime of minimum import prices for cereals, and the voluntary restriction of beef and lamb imports. These plans were discussed with Australia, New Zealand, and other countries in 1963–4. It proved impossible to reach agreement on controls over meat imports, except bacon, but an understanding was reached with Australia and other wheat suppliers on a regime of minimum import prices and market sharing.[7]

A working party was established to advise on the strategy to be adopted in economic discussions with individual Commonwealth states. Officials suggested that it would be advantageous to delay the reconsideration of trade agreements with Commonwealth nations until after the Kennedy Round. A successful outcome to the Kennedy Round in the agricultural sphere would have wide reaching implications for the Ottawa system. Commonwealth preferences would be eroded by cuts in British food tariffs, while BP margins would be squeezed as Australia and New Zealand responded to offers from other Contracting Parties. After the Kennedy Round the conclusion of new bilateral agreements with the dominions for up to five years would not damage Britain's chances of admission into the EEC. Britain still valued its industrial preferences in the Commonwealth, and expected them to become even more effective as foreign competition intensified. British exporters would lose confidence if BP margins were slashed in Australia and New

Zealand. However, as demand in Britain for Commonwealth foodstuffs was unlikely to grow rapidly, it would be difficult to persuade Commonwealth nations to retain industrial preferences. The best tactic, according to some officials, would be to threaten Australia and New Zealand with the imposition of tariffs and quotas on their commodities unless they agreed to preserve key industrial preferences. 'In order to bring pressure on Australia, for instance, we might need to put duties on their butter and fruit without applying duties to New Zealand butter or South African fruit.'[8] Pressure could also be applied to persuade Australia to buy British instead of American airliners. The British High Commissioner in Wellington advocated threatening the termination of the Anglo-New Zealand trade agreement in order to dissuade New Zealand from engaging in barter trade with Yugoslavia, Japan, and other rivals.[9] W. Hughes of the Board of Trade suggested that Britain purchase stated quantities of primary produce from Australia and New Zealand, in return for an agreement to maintain BP margins and protect Britain's market share.[10] But no immediate action was taken. While the British were keen to make the most of the Ottawa system, they realized that if they pushed Commonwealth governments too far they might precipitate its collapse.

British exporters still derived considerable advantage from tariff preferences in Australia and New Zealand. In 1961, Australia granted preferences on 85 per cent of imports by value from Britain at an average margin of 11 per cent. New Zealand granted preferences on about 85 per cent of imports from the UK at an average margin of 17 to 19 per cent. The average margin across the Commonwealth was 12 per cent. Harry Johnson estimated that, in 1961, Britain's tariff preferences in New Zealand were worth £21.3 to £23.3 million sterling, while those in Australia were worth £20.4 million sterling. Only the British preferences in Canada were worth anywhere near these amounts. Commonwealth preferences in Britain were of considerable value to Australia and New Zealand. In 1962, 59 per cent of Australian exports to Britain enjoyed a preference, at an average margin of 10 per cent, while 49 per cent of New Zealand exports to the UK enjoyed a tariff preference, at an average margin of 9 per cent. Johnson calculated that Commonwealth tariff preferences were worth £11.3 million sterling to Australia, and £7.1 million sterling to New Zealand. Britain had the better of the bargain with both Australia and New Zealand, but the worst of the bargain with most other Commonwealth members.[11]

In 1963, Menzies and McEwen were eager to ascertain Britain's intentions with respect to UKATA and the Kennedy Round. Menzies asked

Macmillan whether he would seek either an early resumption of talks with the Six, or closer economic ties with the Commonwealth. If Britain could not guarantee continued free access to its markets, he added, Australia would have to make a substantive offer on industrial tariffs in the Kennedy Round. But Menzies could not disguise the fact that Australia was on the defensive, and McEwen admitted to Frederick Erroll, the President of the Board of Trade, that any reduction in Australia's MFN tariffs would hurt domestic as well as British manufacturers. Australia still wished to retain a strong bilateral trade agreement with Britain. Since McEwen's priority was to promote economic development, he was not in a position to offer large reductions in MFN tariffs during the Kennedy Round. The British concluded that McEwen would have swallowed the modification of the UKATA wheat clause to Australia's disadvantage in order to gain a significant extension of this agreement. Nevertheless, the reconsideration of UKATA was postponed because of the Kennedy Round.[12]

Australia and New Zealand were unsure how to approach the Kennedy Round. McEwen told the Americans that Australia's main contribution would take the form of reductions in BP margins, effected by raising BP tariffs rather than by cutting MFN tariffs. The Americans gave McEwen the impression that this would be acceptable, although their goal was to halve all MFN tariff rates. McEwen also hinted that, if Britain did not squeeze Commonwealth preferences, Australia would hesitate to cut BP margins.[13] The New Zealand position was that the Kennedy Round would be worthless unless it led to substantive reductions in non-tariff barriers to agricultural trade. New Zealand would observe developments in the agricultural area before submitting its offer. The government argued that New Zealand was entitled under the GATT charter to expect open access to foreign markets, and was under no obligation to pay for the restoration of this right.[14]

In order to secure Danish agreement to speeding up the elimination of industrial tariffs in EFTA, Britain offered to suspend the foreign butter tariff. New Zealand and Australia reluctantly agreed to this concession, on condition that Britain promised to retain quantitative controls over imports of foreign and Irish butter. Under pressure from Denmark and Ireland, however, the British reneged on this understanding, abolishing rather than suspending the tariff, and marginally squeezing the dominions' share of the butter market. While these were not major blows to the New Zealand and Australian dairy industries, they were further indications that Britain was prepared to sacrifice the Commonwealth to further its European policy.[15]

Following the breakdown of negotiations with the Six, all parties needed breathing space in which to reassess their trade policy objectives and tactics. Britain, Australia, and New Zealand decided to wait until the dust had settled before deciding how to proceed in relation to the Kennedy Round and the Ottawa Agreements.

Wilson, the Ottawa System, and the Kennedy Round

Harold Wilson, who became Britain's third Labour Prime Minister in 1964, was at first inclined to emphasize the role of the Commonwealth as opposed to Europe in Britain's external economic policy. By 1966, however, Wilson had come to the conclusion that Europe offered better long-term opportunities for British trade, not least because the Commonwealth was increasingly riven by bitter political divisions, for instance over Rhodesia and Kashmir.

Wilson sought to link the pace of economic development in the Commonwealth to the expansion of Britain's capital goods industries. Before the 1964 general election, he had called for the underdeveloped members of the Commonwealth to coordinate their development plans. Upon coming to power, Wilson established the Ministry of Overseas Development with a view to strengthening Britain's ties with the developing world. Wilson was keen to bolster the ailing British balance of payments and to promote the growth of science-based industries. All Commonwealth countries were requested to give British firms preferential treatment in the allocation of public sector contracts. Although Wilson favoured the developing members of the Commonwealth, he did not ignore wealthier members such as Australia and New Zealand. Labour hinted that Britain was prepared to offer bulk contracts and support for commodity agreements in return for capital goods orders. One of Wilson's economic advisers was Thomas Balogh, a staunch supporter of the Commonwealth nexus since the 1940s.[16]

Commonwealth countries were encouraged by Wilson's interest in their affairs. New Zealand hoped that Britain would now pay less attention to the EEC,[17] but little support was forthcoming for Wilson's trade proposals at the 1965 Commonwealth conference. Neither the developing countries nor Australia desired the introduction of formal structures to guide Commonwealth economic cooperation. Disappointed by this response, and distracted by the sterling crisis, Wilson retraced his steps. By 1966, the British were preparing to make another bid to enter the Common Market. According to the Foreign Office, Britain outside the EEC faced political and economic isolation:

A satisfactory alternative [to EEC membership] had to be considered not only in terms of the . . . size of market for a major industrial complex but also in terms of the size of research and development potential for future expansion in a highly technological world. . . . The Commonwealth would not provide a satisfactory alternative; the new Commonwealth was in need of technical assistance and they were in no position to contribute to research and development resources. On the other hand, among the old Commonwealth countries Canada was linked to the United States in research and development, and Australia and New Zealand pursued their own policies.[18]

There seemed to be no real scope for reviving the Commonwealth economic relationship. A tentative analysis of the prospects for a free trade area comprising Britain, Australia, and New Zealand produced discouraging results. Supporters contended that such a grouping would enhance the leverage of Britain, Australia, and New Zealand over the terms of the UK's accession to the Treaty of Rome. But sceptics argued that an Anglo-Australasian free trade area would alienate the EEC, and that Australia and New Zealand would never expose their industries to unrestrained British competition. The chances appeared equally dim for securing more favourable bilateral agreements with Australia and New Zealand. British tenders for public sector contracts already received special treatment in both countries. Britain had nothing to offer in the agricultural sphere, while strong-arm tactics, such as threatening to exclude Australia from the Commonwealth Preference Area, would have back-fired politically.[19] Wellington was certain to retaliate against hostile British measures by imposing tighter import controls. 'About the worst we could do [to New Zealand] would be to hold over her the general threat of paying less regard to her interests in the future, e.g. in any renewal of negotiations with EEC'.[20] In the light of these considerations, any trade talks with Canberra and Wellington would have to concentrate on adjusting existing arrangements.

By 1965, it was becoming obvious that the Kennedy Round would make few inroads into agricultural protectionism. Britain had volunteered to reduce preferences on Commonwealth foodstuffs by 50 per cent across the board, but this offer had not been taken up because the USA and the EEC remained at loggerheads. The industrial offers of Australia and New Zealand in GATT were in practice confined to selected products. Only in a few instances did Australia and New Zealand propose to reduce contractual BP margins, although they did offer to cut many non-contractual margins.[21] Australia and New Zealand were in a difficult position. Although they wished to encourage the USA, EEC, and Japan to reduce agricultural trade barriers, they could not afford either to provoke Britain or to jeopardize domestic industries.

Given the stalemate in GATT, there was no further reason to postpone the bilateral trade talks between Britain and New Zealand and Australia. The British were reasonably satisfied with the framework governing Anglo-Australian and Anglo-New Zealand trade, and did not expect to obtain large new concessions, though they were anxious to discuss NAFTA's effect on the New Zealand market for manufactures.[22] Holyoake approached the British, in June 1965, with a request for commercial talks. New Zealand wished to put the Anglo-New Zealand trade agreement, which was subject to cancellation at six months' notice, on a five-year rolling basis. It also hoped to extend the agreement on unrestricted duty-free entry of its meat until 1977, confirm the butter quota system and the duty-free status of its butter, and persuade Britain to adopt of regime of minimum butter prices. Clear commitments on meat and dairy produce would strengthen New Zealand's case for special treatment when Britain embarked upon another attempt to join the EEC. The British acknowledged that they would have to grant identical terms to Australia once a settlement had been reached with New Zealand.[23]

Wilson had been working on the assumption that the rights of New Zealand meat producers under the 1952 agreement would be extended as a matter of course, and was surprised to learn that they were anxious on this score. However, British officials regarded Wilson's position as naïve, and presented the New Zealanders with counter proposals relating to tariff preferences, non-tariff barriers, and public sector contracts. As compensation for NAFTA, New Zealand was asked to bind the duty-free status of certain British products, and to bind some BP margins at levels above the contractual minima in the 1959 agreement.[24] These demands related to certain oils, textiles, chinaware, iron and steel products, machinery, lighting, vehicles, medicaments, toys, glass, and electrical equipment. Furthermore, Britain asked New Zealand to refrain from using non-tariff barriers to restrict imports of certain British products, including televisions, gin, and coffins. An undertaking was requested that British tenders for public sector contracts would receive even more favourable treatment than in the past. Douglas Jay, the President of the Board of Trade, tried to hustle New Zealand into buying British rather than American airliners. The New Zealanders replied that over two-thirds of government overseas purchases were already made in Britain, and that nothing more could be done since in many instances British equipment was uncompetitive. An order was subsequently placed for Boeing 737s instead of BAC-111s.[25]

The 1966 record of understanding between Britain and New Zealand adjusted the 1959 trade agreement. Britain undertook to admit unrestricted quantities of all New Zealand foodstuffs, except butter, until 1972, provided no satisfactory international commodity agreements came into operation before this date. Butter quotas were to remain in force until 1972, and New Zealand's quota was raised. Wellington reciprocated by binding the duty-free status of certain British goods, and raising some contractual (but not actual) BP margins. These concessions affected trade worth £8 million per annum to Britain. For instance, contractual BP margins on bolts, screws, and chains were increased to 20 per cent, while those on some cotton fabrics were increased to 15 per cent. Although New Zealand's dairy and meat outlets were now secure until 1972, the rise in sensitive contractual BP margins would hamper negotiations with third countries. The Australians were quick to complain about the increase in New Zealand's butter quota.[26]

Actual BP margins in New Zealand were at roughly the same level in 1967 as they had been in 1952. Generous margins were granted on many British goods, including cars. The BP tariff on unassembled cars was 6.25 per cent, but the MFN rate was 45 per cent; the BP tariff on assembled British cars was 20 per cent, whereas the MFN rate was 55 per cent. This testifies to the strength of Britain's bargaining power. British preference continued to distort the pattern of New Zealand's imports. Even though Britain's share of New Zealand's total imports was falling, it remained the principal supplier in 37 import categories in 1966–7, including ships, telecommunications equipment, motor vehicles, office machines, and textile machinery. By comparison, Australia led in 14 categories, the USA in 8, Japan in 3, and other countries in 11.[27]

Britain and Australia held negotiations on the future of UKATA in 1967. Australia pressed for the indefinite extension of the 1957 trade agreement, the 1952 meat agreement, and other understandings on specific commodities. The British demanded the binding of certain BP tariffs, which were under investigation by the Australian Tariff Board, in return for the extension of the meat agreement. Recent increases in some BP tariff rates had alarmed British manufacturers. The Australians replied that it would not be feasible to bind BP tariffs, and rejected the suggestion that they endorse the latest UK approach to the EEC, as the British did not intend to demand any safeguards for Australian agriculture. Australia refused to sign the memorandum of understanding offered by the British. The meat agreement lapsed, but UKATA remained in force, subject to cancellation at short notice. Australia was unhappy with the uncompromising attitude of the British.[28]

As far as Australia and New Zealand were concerned, little of consequence emerged from the Kennedy Round. Changes to tariff preferences in Britain and the Commonwealth were minimal. Australia's satisfaction with Japan's decision to permit greater imports of beef was negated by the collapse of trade talks with the EEC and the USA. Washington withdrew an offer to halve the US wool tariff because Canberra was not prepared to make an equivalent cut in the tariff on tobacco.[29] The New Zealand government described the Kennedy Round, in the *Economic Review* for 1967, as 'extremely disappointing'. It had 'merely served to emphasise how deeply entrenched have become the protectionist agricultural policies of most of the industrial countries.'[30]

The preference system stuttered on into the 1970s, as it provided Commonwealth members with a measure of security that they were reluctant to give up without adequate compensation. However, Britain would readily have abandoned the Commonwealth Preference system in return for EEC membership, while Australia and New Zealand would have discarded it had the industrial powers agreed to reduce the barriers to agricultural trade.

NAFTA

The New Zealand–Australia Free Trade Agreement was the product of a New Zealand initiative, the purpose of which was to safeguard the main export market for the pulp and paper industry. In return for concessions on pulp and paper, Australia demanded improved access to New Zealand for its industrial exports. The agreement that emerged was broader in scope than New Zealand's original conception, but narrower than Australia's.

Tasman Pulp and Paper was an early advocate of a new trade agreement between Australia and New Zealand. Although newsprint could be imported into Australia duty-free and in unlimited quantities from all sources during the early 1960s, Tasman feared the introduction of a tariff to encourage the Australian pulp and paper industry. As Tasman's giant Murupara plant was not yet competitive further afield, it could hardly afford to face a tariff in Australia. Visiting Australia for preliminary talks on a partial free trade agreement in 1961, John Marshall 'opened the bowling [against McEwen] by putting forward the case for better access to the Australian market for New Zealand forest products as our main objective'.[31] Murupara was an important consideration in trans-Tasman commercial relations.

New Zealand formally proposed a free trade area in forest products in 1963. Wellington was anxious about plans to establish a new paper mill in South Australia with the support of the state government. The other pressing issue was New Zealand's substantial bilateral trade deficit with Australia, which the government wished to reduce for political reasons. Australia responded with a plan for a more or less comprehensive free trade area, and demanded that New Zealand permanently renounce the use of import controls on Australian products. Partly for tactical reasons, Canberra argued that GATT would not endorse a free trade area confined to a handful of products. Australian industry was untroubled by the prospect of competition from New Zealand, but Wellington doubted the ability of local industry to withstand Australian competition. The senior New Zealand officials, Foss Shanahan and M.J. Moriarty, indicated that it would be impractical for New Zealand to embrace genuine free trade at this stage, and asked the Australians to be patient. An Australia–New Zealand joint standing committee was set up to consider the alternative proposals.[32]

The New Zealand government was divided over the free trade area plans. External Affairs felt that it was important to chain the vulnerable New Zealand economy to Australia, and hoped that the most efficient manufacturers would take advantage of new export opportunities in Australia. But Industries and Commerce and the New Zealand Manufacturers' Association were afraid that freer trade would undermine local industry and full employment. Industries and Commerce argued that even a partial free trade area would be undesirable, as GATT would press for its generalization. This department also questioned the ability of New Zealand to compete in certain secondary forest lines, including kraft products. The second largest firm in the forest products industry, New Zealand Forest Products, which manufactured these products, was opposed to the free trade area.[33] New Zealand politicians dreaded the electoral consequences of opening the domestic market to increased competition.

The Australian Department of External Affairs, which was in favour of closer trans-Tasman relations on political grounds, urged the Department of Trade to avoid 'frightening off' New Zealand by demanding too broad a commodity coverage.[34] But the Australian High Commissioner in Wellington, D.A. Cameron, offered a more cynical interpretation of New Zealand's intentions. Cameron believed that New Zealand viewed a trade agreement with Australia as a reserve position, which would be occupied if important agricultural talks with Britain, the USA, and other countries ended in failure. In Cameron's opinion, New Zealand's sole objective was to gain short-term commercial advantage.[35] Cameron's assessment was rather harsh. In fact, Marshall held that the free trade proposals were part of 'a desirable general trend towards closer co-operation with Australia on a broad front – political, defence, and economic – having regard to the common security threat faced by both countries in the Asian/Pacific region and their relative isolation.'[36]

New Zealand was persuaded to include more products in the proposed free trade area. Even so, consultations with worried manufacturers led to the exclusion of numerous lines, including dog biscuits, broomsticks, and aircraft engines, from New Zealand's free trade offer. The Australians attempted to sweeten their demand for industrial free trade by calling for greater cooperation between firms in the two countries. For instance, they suggested that in the motor vehicle industry New Zealand should concentrate on making certain components for Australian assemblers. Although the New Zealanders acknowledged the potential benefits of specialization, they pointed out that the Australian proposal would prevent the development of a balanced industrial structure in the smaller country. The question of import controls also created difficulty. Australia was willing to renounce the introduction of import restrictions on any New Zealand product,[37] regardless of whether it was part of the free trade area. But Wellington felt unable to reciprocate, since its balance of payments, industrialization, and full employment policies were all underpinned by import controls. New Zealand's goal was to substitute tariffs for import controls, but rapid progress towards this objective was not anticipated. All Marshall could offer was an informal undertaking to fiddle the import selection system in Australia's favour. New Zealand was concerned about the British reaction to any overt discrimination against its products. After considerable wrangling, McEwen decided to give way to New Zealand over import controls in order to obtain a settlement.[38]

Britain's response to NAFTA was ambivalent. London was inclined to 'welcome the closer relationship between Australia and New Zealand, and the strengthening of the two economies, which it is designed to promote.'[39] However, it noted that foreign countries might use the precedent of NAFTA, which was not a genuine free trade area, to justify other agreements flouting the MFN principle. Britain pointed out that any weakening of the MFN ideal would harm small nations like Australia and New Zealand. Jay admonished McEwen that Britain would expect compensation for the erection of reverse preferences against some of its products in Australia and New Zealand. Britain was concerned about the implications of NAFTA for import selection in New Zealand, and regarded it as the precursor of a more extensive trans-Tasman free trade agreement. The British, though, did not regard NAFTA as a major threat, and anticipated that local manufacturers would bear the brunt of increased Australian competition in the New Zealand market. Board of Trade officials estimated that £2 million sterling of British exports to Australia and £10 million sterling to New Zealand, in such categories as machinery, textiles, and iron and steel, could be affected by reverse preferences. Marshall dismissed British quibbling on the grounds that any trade diversion would be neither immediate nor large. He maintained that Britain had no right to complain about NAFTA since it was negotiating a free trade area with Ireland. McEwen added that Australia had never gained much advantage from GATT, and did not care what the Contracting Parties thought of NAFTA.[40]

NAFTA was signed in 1965 and implemented by stages beginning in 1966. Eighty-five per cent of New Zealand exports to Australia and 51 per cent of Australian exports to New Zealand were subject to this agreement. Among the trade categories excluded were butter, various manufactures, and certain less significant forest products, including several of concern to New Zealand Forest Products. Australia renounced the use of quantitative controls on imports from New Zealand, while New Zealand promised to grant access to Australian goods on the most liberal terms possible within the constraints of the import licensing system. The Contracting Parties expressed concern about some aspects of the agreement, but did not seek confrontation with Australia and New Zealand. NAFTA secured the future of Murupara, and stimulated trade in both directions in manufactures and non-manufactures. Between 1970 and 1984, the growth in New Zealand's exports to Australia outweighed the decline in exports to the enlarged EEC. Contrary to some gloomy forecasts, many New Zealand manufacturers were able to compete successfully on both sides of the Tasman. The Australian market provided New Zealand firms with a relatively soft introduction to exporting. Successive devaluations of the New Zealand dollar, which replaced the New Zealand pound in 1967, also boosted industrial competitiveness relative to Australia.[41]

Although the net economic benefits are difficult to quantify, it cannot be denied that NAFTA was a milestone in the development of trans-Tasman cooperation. Consequently, it is curious that Meredith and Dyster trace the origins of economic collaboration between Canberra and Wellington to the Closer Economic Relations agreement of 1983.[42]

Of course, trans-Tasman economic cooperation was a higher priority for New Zealand than it was for Australia. New Zealand's absence from the Australian common market, established at the time of federation in 1901, proved to be a drawback during the twentieth century. NAFTA constituted a first step towards the reintegration of the Australian and New Zealand economies.

Japan and Pacific economic cooperation

During the 1960s, Australia and New Zealand endeavoured to achieve further improvements in economic relations with Japan. Largely as a result of the mineral trade, Japan became Australia's most important export market in the mid-1960s. Trade between New Zealand and Japan, which started from a much lower base, expanded at an even faster rate. Despite increasing its exports of manufactures to Australia and New Zealand, Japan continued to run a trade deficit with both countries. The main focus of this section is the response of Canberra in particular, but also of Wellington, to Japanese proposals for greater regional economic cooperation in the Pacific.

British officials and industrialists resented the growth in Japanese exports to Australia and Zealand. Australia began to use Japanese as well as British heavy electrical equipment in the mid-1960s, on development projects such as the Snowy Mountains scheme.[43] The British were especially indignant about Japanese penetration of New Zealand. In 1963, the British High Commissioner, Sir Francis Cuming-Bruce, and the Senior Trade Commissioner, G.C. Dick, claimed that a group of civil servants in Wellington was encouraging firms and government departments to buy Japanese rather than British materials and equipment. New Zealand's proclivity for small-scale bilateral exchanges with Asian and east European states fuelled British suspicions. While the Board of Trade regarded the Cuming-Bruce allegations as exaggerated, Whitehall acknowledged that New Zealand would come under increasing pressure to participate in discriminatory bilateral agreements if the Kennedy Round failed to reform world agricultural trade.[44]

Japan took the lead in proposing closer economic ties among the countries of the Pacific Rim. Initially, the idea of a Pacific economic community was not taken seriously in Australasia. In 1960, the New Zealand Embassy in Tokyo commented that this concept was 'not new and always attractive to the Japanese (if less so to some others).' The New Zealanders described Japanese references to a Pacific community as 'kite-flying and distinctly non-official.'[45] But the Japanese returned to this theme with increasing frequency in the following years. Tokyo feared being marginalized either by the EEC or by an Atlantic economic community. The Japanese envisaged the formation of an economic community in the Pacific to act as a counterweight to the EEC, and provide a framework for the economic development of east Asia. But the structure of the proposed community was left in the air. Tokyo hoped that low-level cooperation between the developed economies of the Pacific Rim would evolve into a deeper arrangement with wider membership as mutual trust increased.[46]

Business cooperation was regarded as a suitable first step. The first approach was made to Australia, partly because of the close ties between Japanese economists and their Australian counterparts, especially Sir John Crawford, who had left the Ministry of Trade in 1960 to join the Australian National University. The Australia–Japan Business Coopera-tion Committee (AJBCC) was established in 1964. American, Canadian, and New Zealand businessmen were invited to subsequent sessions. At AJBCC conferences, the Japanese, with the backing of their government, canvassed support for a vague Pacific Basin Organization for Economic Cooperation. Nagano Shigeo, President of the Japan Iron and Steel Federation, denied that their objective was a Pacific Common Market. A Pacific version of the OEEC appears to have been one of the alterna-tives under consideration. However, Kojima Kiyoshi, an academic econ-omist and confidante of senior policy-makers, advanced a scheme for a free trade area incorporating Japan, the USA, Canada, Australia, and New Zealand. He argued that membership could be extended to devel-oping countries at a later date, and even hinted at associate member-ship for Britain. Kojima admitted that under his scheme the bilateral trade balances of both Australia and New Zealand would worsen with each of Japan, the USA, and Canada. But he added that the outlook would improve if Australia and New Zealand abandoned their insular industrialization policies, and instead encouraged the growth of resource-intensive industries with genuine export potential, such as steel, heavy engineering, and forest products. The Japanese trade min-ister, Miki Takeo, endorsed the principle of Pacific economic integra-tion, and called for the establishment of a free trade grouping in 1967.[47]

Whether the Japanese government really envisaged a formal free trade agreement, or merely a looser settlement rooted in voluntary MFN tariff cuts, similar to the open regionalism of Asia Pacific Economic Coopera-tion (APEC) in the 1990s, remains unclear. There was plenty of scope for misunderstanding. Reaction to Japan's tentative proposal for Pacific economic integration was mixed. One Australian official, who evidently feared a resurgent Japan, thought there were 'overtones to all this which bear watching'.[48] Australian business leaders were confused and embarrassed. Manufacturers pointed out that free trade with Japan would ruin many local industries. The Australians on the AJBCC had a rather different conception of economic cooperation, and advanced a scheme for a joint Australian-Japanese private–public sector fertilizer and chemical development, using natural gas, in Papua. Japanese delegates were bemused by this response.[49] The Australian economist, H.W. Arndt, concluded that a Pacific Common Market was an 'absurd' notion, as the member states would be at different stages of economic development. In the light of NAFTA, Australian officials suggested that it would be 'extremely complicated and time consuming to negotiate' a Pacific free trade area. More substantively, Australia's freedom to protect secondary industries and regulate foreign investment would be compromised by membership of a Pacific trade bloc. The Australians also questioned whether Japan truly intended to subject its farmers to free trade.[50]

Speaking to the AJBCC in 1966, McEwen outlined the Australian position without specifically mentioning the free trade plan:

> If we were economists and not representatives of business organisations or political governments, we might well be questioning [sic] the economic advantages of each country limiting its production to those items which it could produce more cheaply than the other. In theory, this is perfect. But in practice, of course, on that proposition Japanese agriculture could not survive against the competition of Australian agriculture, and Australian manufacturing industry would be very seriously damaged. All of us accept that in the real world of business and government this cannot be: indeed, it must not be.[51]

New Zealand's response was similar. Wellington had no objection to discussing Pacific economic cooperation. If and when Britain entered the EEC, New Zealand would have to develop closer economic ties with Japan and other Pacific states. In the short term, though, it would be risky to publicize the concept of a Pacific trade association, as this would provide the British with an excuse to conclude a quick deal with the EEC without insisting on safeguards for New Zealand trade. Kojima and his scheme took centre stage at the Pacific Association for Trade and Development (PAFTAD) conference, held at Tokyo in 1968. Consideration was also given to a pilot free trade scheme limited to Japan, Australia, and New Zealand. Professor L.V. Castle, representing New

Zealand, indicated that his country feared economic domination by Japan and Australia. He stated that any Pacific grouping should include the USA and Canada, and operate within the GATT charter.[52] The four Western countries, the USA, Canada, Australia, and New Zealand, would not entertain discrimination against third parties.[53]

The British realized that the Japanese would do everything possible to weaken the Commonwealth Preference system. In 1965, Miki had urged Australia to grant Japan a share in British preferences.[54] But Britain heavily discounted the prospects for a trading bloc encompassing Japan and Australasia. According to the Board of Trade, such an arrangement would be incompatible with the import substitution policies of Australia and New Zealand. Furthermore, it would be inexpedient for Canberra and Wellington to hazard the loss of preferences in the British market. Their 'trade in temperate agricultural products (and sugar) with us is more vulnerable to switches to new suppliers (either British farmers, EEC peasants or, on sugar, to l.d.c.'s) than their trade with Japan.'[55]

Any sort of Pacific economic community was a distant aspiration in the 1960s, and several more pressing matters needed consideration. The Japanese were disgruntled about their large bilateral trade deficits with Australia and New Zealand, the favouritism shown to British tenders for public sector business, the exclusion of Japanese banks from Australia, and the lack of a double taxation agreement. Japanese industrialists resented the fact that contracts for the export of iron ore still required approval from Canberra. Permission to export iron ore to Japan was sometimes refused if the price was considered too low.[56] For their part, the Australians were concerned that, except for Kojima, the Japanese did not envisage progressing beyond a vertical economic relationship in which Australian primary products were exchanged for Japanese manufactures. McEwen pleaded with the Japanese to buy more processed minerals, such as billets, pig iron, and aluminium. Australia also tried to drum up orders in Japan for motor cars.[57]

Japan could not be counted on to continue buying Australian raw materials while its exports to Australia were frustrated by high and discriminatory tariffs. By the mid-1960s, Japan was investing in the development of primary production in Asia, Africa, and Latin America. It was possible that China would emerge as a strong competitor in the iron ore trade if relations between Beijing and the West were to thaw. The potential for Australia's position in the Japanese market to be usurped raised the difficult question of whether Canberra should try to forge an even closer economic axis with Tokyo, even if this later rendered Australian foreign policy vulnerable to commercial pressure from Japan.[58]

New Zealand faced the even more daunting challenge of gaining greater access to the Japanese food market. Mutton, which was losing ground in the UK, found a new outlet in Japanese sausage factories. But Japanese agricultural policy continued to thwart New Zealand's main export ambitions. Tokyo's goal was to increase the Japanese dairy herd from 587,000 beasts in 1956 to 4,000,000 in 1975, regardless of cost. Nevertheless, demand for food was expected to rise faster than domestic supply, due to the projected growth in population and living standards.[59] The Japanese dairy lobby and its allies in government, however, rejected New Zealand's requests for trade liberalization. New Zealand's ambassador to Tokyo stated that the dairy industry had erected a 'brick wall' against imports.[60] Under pressure from GATT and the USA, Tokyo began to relax import controls during the 1960s, but almost half of New Zealand's exports to Japan remained subject to restriction in 1969. It was difficult for New Zealand to seize the moral high ground, though, due to its own import selection policies. The Japanese argued that British preferences contributed to the trade imbalance between New Zealand and Japan, and indicated that BP margins should be unilaterally reduced. New Zealand refused to cut BP margins without reciprocal concessions from Tokyo. Wellington was not as confident as Canberra about the prospects for trade with Japan: 'there is no thought in our mind that Japan would ever replace Britain in importance as either a market or a source of supply'.[61] The Secretary of Industries and Commerce, M.J. Moriarty, who visited Japan in 1969, discovered that his hosts were preoccupied with political and economic relations with the USA, and did not listen to requests for liberalization of the meat, dairy products, and forestry trades.[62]

The experiences of Australia and New Zealand diverged during the 1960s. Japan surpassed Britain as Australia's, but not as New Zealand's, main trading partner. This bifurcation reflected the changing commodity structure of Australian exports rather than any fundamental difference in policy between Canberra and Wellington. Since neither Australia nor New Zealand was particularly anxious to encourage a rapid expansion in imports, Japan's bilateral trade balance with both countries remained firmly in deficit. While Kojima's Pacific free trade area scheme attracted little support, it played a role in stimulating a debate on regional economic cooperation that led to the formation of APEC in 1989.[63]

Britain and Europe again

In 1967, Wilson's government began 'high level probings' in the capitals of the Six, in preparation for a further application to enter the EEC. By this stage, the British had no intention of asking the Six to provide safeguards for Commonwealth exporters in the permanent phase, except for tropical sugar producers and New Zealand farmers. Australia could expect to share in the intra-Community preference on a degressive basis during the transitional phase, but would have to shift for itself in the Common Market phase. There was no suggestion that New Zealand's veto would carry over into a new round of negotiations. Moreover, the scope for dairy concessions would be limited, since Ireland and Denmark were also expected to apply for EEC membership.

Holyoake told Wilson that he would not be satisfied with anything less than long-term special arrangements for butter, cheese, and lamb. As in 1962, New Zealand hoped that any guarantee would be specified in volume terms, with some provision for growth. The British questioned the need for a lamb guarantee, wished to defer consideration of cheese until after they had joined the EEC, and argued that it would be pointless to ask for anything other than a revenue guarantee for butter.[64] The Minister of Finance, Robert Muldoon, was urged by the Board of Trade to think positively: 'within a short space of time Japan would virtually replace Britain as New Zealand's main market for temperate food products.'[65] According to the CRO, revenue from a 'half quantity-double price' arrangement could be used to assist dairy farmers to find other livelihoods.[66] Officials at the European Commission could not understand why New Zealand wanted to 'send all that butter over here when it just has to be dumped in the sea'.[67] Nicholas Kaldor, another of Wilson's economic advisers, suggested buying New Zealand's butter exports and throwing them into the sea.[68] Despite British pressure, New Zealand continued to demand quantitative guarantees.

New Zealand diplomats were told that the Six had not ruled out a separate dairy market in Britain. A separate market would not have released Britain from the obligation to raise prices and impose the CET, but it would have allowed the government to conclude a special bilateral deal with New Zealand. Officials in Wellington devised a forlorn scheme for boosting European food consumption, whereby consumer prices would be subsidized with revenue from import levies. However, the duration of any special arrangement, and the likelihood of renewal, remained cloudy. Wilson and the Foreign Secretary, George Brown, resurrected the possibility of an association agreement between New Zealand and the

EEC for an initial period of ten years. But this would have restricted New Zealand's freedom to enter into closer trading relations with Japan, Australia, and other Pacific Rim nations.[69]

In May 1967, the British informed Canberra of their intention to reopen membership negotiations with the EEC. They intimated that Australia should follow New Zealand's example and confine any requests for safeguards to a couple of commodities. Canberra replied that this would not be possible, as Australia's exports were more diverse than New Zealand's. The Australians were left with the impression that further bilateral consultations would occur before the British presented their case to the Six. In June 1967, multilateral discussions were held on the implications of EEC entry for the British Commonwealth Sugar Agreement, under which Britain bought agreed volumes from Australia and developing countries at negotiated prices. The British said that they would attempt to secure the extension of the BCSA beyond the expiry date of 1974, but held out no hope that the EEC would permit Australia to remain in the agreement after this point. Canberra was taken aback by this admission, as the UK market contributed 47 per cent of the export revenue of Australian sugar producers. The Australians were equally dismayed by a statement from George Brown, on 4 July, to the effect that New Zealand and sugar from the developing countries were the only Commonwealth issues on which he was prepared to make a stand.[70]

Wilson's 1967–8 initiative soon broke down, but thereafter discussions between the British and the Europeans were virtually continuous. The possibility of an interim commercial arrangement between Britain and the Six, in preparation for full accession, was floated in 1968–9.[71] Paul Einzig, a British economist, stated that Britain would have to abandon New Zealand in order to join the EEC, a prospect he likened to 'handing over Cornwall to France'.[72] In March 1970, before the election that brought Edward Heath to power, the British were making plans for a third expedition into Europe. They warned New Zealand that they did not intend to make an issue of lamb, and hinted that the Six were likely to offer a degressive five-year quantitative guarantee for New Zealand butter. All except the French were prepared to make an offer on cheese, either by treating it as a separate item or specifying the dairy guarantee in milk equivalents. After the transition, the EEC would place New Zealand in the hands of a prospective world dairy authority. If such an authority could not be established, the 'Friendly Five', but not the French, would reconsider New Zealand's case.[73] The Belgian Trade

Minister, Hendrik Fayat, spoke in terms of a 'permanent arrangement subject to periodic review' for New Zealand.[74]

Soon after Heath became Prime Minister, Marshall met the Chancellor of the Duchy of Lancaster, Anthony Barber, for talks on Europe. Marshall admitted that New Zealand would have to make further concessions, but stressed that he could not say so in public. He understood that Britain would not be able to introduce lamb into the discussions with the EEC. Subsequently, in order to secure French acquiescence in special arrangements for less developed sugar exporters, the British agreed to give the EEC a tariff preference over Commonwealth countries on all products from the outset of UK membership. During the transitional phase, lasting until 1977, Commonwealth farmers would be allowed a small degressive preference over third countries, while British preferences in the Commonwealth would be phased out. No special arrangements would be offered to Australian farmers. Although the British market was no longer of vital importance to Australia, Canberra was bitter about the terms of British entry, and Malcolm Fraser's government conducted a running battle against the CAP between 1975 and 1983.[75]

Anglo-EEC negotiations ranged over familiar ground in relation to New Zealand: association with the Community, a revenue or a quantitative guarantee, mechanisms to ensure the sale of any special quotas, and the price to be received by New Zealand farmers after deducting import levies. Heath was informed that there would be a trade-off between safeguards for New Zealand and Britain's contribution to the EEC budget. Consequently, the British were reluctant to press New Zealand's demands too vigorously. Marshall was in close attendance when the final settlement was reached.[76] Under the 1971 Luxembourg Agreement, New Zealand's butter and cheese exports to Britain were to be reduced to 80 per cent and 20 per cent respectively of recent volumes over five years. The EEC would arrange for the agreed volumes to find buyers. Prices were to be based on 1967–72 levels, but Wellington mounted a successful campaign to have them increased. Some provision was made for substitution between butter and cheese, though the reexport of New Zealand produce from Britain to the continent was forbidden. If it proved impossible to negotiate an international dairy agreement, the EEC would consider extending the special arrangement for butter only after 1977. The butter quota continued in modified form into the 1990s. New Zealand officials described the terms for dairy products as 'broadly satisfactory'. No provision was made for sheepmeat, but New Zealand was granted a quota in the enlarged EEC in 1980.[77]

As far as Australia was concerned, the Commonwealth economic nexus had been terminated. In New Zealand's case, however, the arrangements set in place by the EEC, while less than generous, did not amount to complete rejection. It might be said that New Zealand had entered into an informal agreement of association with the EEC in relation to dairy produce. New Zealand's dependent economic relationship with Britain was preserved at a much lower intensity.

Conclusion

The trade strategies of Britain, Australia, and New Zealand followed increasingly divergent paths during the 1960s. Britain was only temporarily deflected from its course by the French veto in 1963. Despite the British Labour Party's flirtation with a Commonwealth economic strategy, in 1967 it embarked upon another attempt to join the EEC. From the British perspective, the Kennedy Round and EFTA appeared to offer more scope for the expansion of industrial exports than did a revamped Commonwealth. But the industrial preferences in Australia and New Zealand remained of value, and the British government was determined to make the most of them in the years that remained for the Ottawa system. Britain's policy on Commonwealth trade took on an increasingly short-term aspect.

Australia's interest in the British connection waned during the 1960s as opportunities for trade with Japan and other countries blossomed. Australian minerals, but not food, found ready markets in the industrial countries of the northern hemisphere. However, there were limits to the willingness of Canberra to enter into closer relations with Japan. Australia was even more determined to protect domestic industry from Japanese than from British competition, not least because in many areas the Japanese were more efficient. The failure of the Australians to reciprocate was a matter of concern in Tokyo. Since Canberra was reluctant to substitute a dependent economic relationship with Japan for a similar relationship with Britain, Tokyo's proposals for a Pacific economic community were viewed with suspicion. Australia's protectionist industrial policy also prevented it from playing a full part in the Kennedy Round. The Australians sought to safeguard their privileges in the British market for as long as possible. But, like the British, they grew to accept that the Commonwealth economic relationship would not survive in the long term.

New Zealand's position was more difficult. It had no minerals, except a little coal, to sell to Japan. The domestic industrial sector was believed to be even more vulnerable than Australian industry to external competition. New Zealand hoped in vain that the Kennedy Round would produce large agricultural benefits. The approach to Australia that led to NAFTA was defensive in conception. New Zealand wished to protect its pulp and paper exports against a possible Australian tariff. Britain remained the focus of New Zealand's external economic policy. The British had to be dissuaded from restricting imports from New Zealand, and persuaded to secure decent terms for the dominion in any future membership agreement with the EEC. New Zealand was a supplicant with little leverage. In fact it was lucky to enjoy 10 years of respite before Britain finally obtained entry into the Common Market in 1973.

10
Conclusion

The Second World War and the following period of dollar shortage were marked by close economic cooperation between the governments of Britain, Australia, and New Zealand. State involvement in the management of international economic relations was more intense during this era than ever before or since. Britain, Australia, and New Zealand had a common interest in conserving dollars and in maintaining secure export markets in times of great uncertainty.

The role of Australia and New Zealand within the Sterling Area, in the late 1940s and early 1950s, was to supply Britain with food and wool invoiced in sterling rather than dollars. Thus Australia and New Zealand made important indirect contributions to the central reserves, even though on their own accounts they were net drawers of dollars. Australia and New Zealand valued their membership of the Commonwealth Preference and Sterling Areas because they had few reliable outlets apart from Britain. The potentially lucrative US market was hemmed in by tariffs and import restrictions. There was also an expectation that large amounts of British capital would flow into the dominions after the postwar hiatus. As it was widely feared that another global depression would arise in the USA, officials and ministers in Australia, New Zealand, and Britain were reluctant to forgo the insulation afforded by Commonwealth Preference and the Sterling Area. In view of the emphasis given to safeguarding jobs and infant industries, there was little chance of significant reductions in protection in Australia and New Zealand. Under these circumstances, multilateral negotiations between the USA, the Commonwealth, and other countries over the liberalization of trade and payments were only partially successful.

The strength of Commonwealth economic cooperation in the postwar period should not be underestimated, although it tends to be ignored by economic historians of Britain, Australia and New Zealand. As Cain and Hopkins suggest, economic relations within the Commonwealth continued to be a prime concern of British governments in the 1950s. Furthermore, the dominions played a major role in the Commonwealth system, which they viewed not as a threat to national economic sovereignty, but rather as a bulwark against global economic stability and potential US domination. This book has shown that there was far more to the Sterling Area in the 1950s than Britain, Malaya, and an assortment of colonies in Africa and the West Indies.

Subsequently, the perceived economic interests of Britain and Australia and New Zealand started to diverge in a number of respects. Disagreement had been masked in the 1940s and early 1950s by the need for a cooperative solution to reconstruction and the dollar problem. During the mid-1950s, however, a feeling of disenchantment with the Commonwealth economic nexus emerged in Britain and Australasia. Over the years that followed, Britain and the two Australasian economies began to drift apart. This process of disengagement was not complete until Britain entered the EEC in 1973.

Separation occurred in response to a combination of developments at the centre and on the periphery, and it would be fruitless to search for the original impetus. However, the decisive factor was Britain's growing entanglement in European economic integration. Demands emanating from Australia and New Zealand for the revision of their commercial treaties with Britain *could* have been accommodated within an attenuated preferential relationship. Although Canberra and Wellington sought the power to reduce BP margins in order to facilitate trade negotiations with other countries, neither intended to abolish the Commonwealth Preference system, not least because Britain remained an essential food market. Britain, on the other hand, ultimately conceded that leadership of the Commonwealth economic community was incompatible with membership of a European customs union. While consideration was given to several schemes for linking the Commonwealth and Europe, none proved generally acceptable. Thus it was British rather than Australasian ambitions that were irreconcilable with the continuation, for better or worse, of the Commonwealth as an economic community. Indeed, as the British were drawn deeper into Europe, they came to view the Commonwealth as a nuisance rather than an economic asset. This conclusion summarizes the reasons why the British and Australasian economies drifted apart in the 1950s and 1960s.

Australia and New Zealand were strongly committed to import substitution industrialization. Preferential tariffs and dollar discrimination afforded British firms a competitive advantage over their American, European, and Japanese rivals in these markets. However, despite the Ottawa Agreements, British goods were not permitted to compete on equal terms with the products of Australian and New Zealand manufacturers. Canberra justified import substitution on grounds of national development, security, and employment generation. Wellington also stressed the need to keep the growing population fully employed. The pursuit of uncompromising full employment policies required checks on imports from all sources. Rather than cut domestic demand in periods of balance of payments crisis, the Australian and New Zealand governments preferred to intensify import restrictions. Although the Australian and New Zealand markets were among the most important in the world for British exports during the 1950s, they failed to live up to the expectations of British manufacturers. The British were particularly incensed by the Australian import cuts of 1952.

To be fair, Britain also practised a form of import substitution. Generous subsidies were given to the agricultural sector, nominally for reasons of national security, but actually in response to skilful lobbying by farmers. Domestic food production was stimulated, and the returns of Australian and New Zealand suppliers were squeezed. Furthermore, the British lost interest in safeguarding Commonwealth primary producers from foreign competition when the global food shortage abated in the early 1950s. British consumers clamoured for cheap food, and the Churchill government opened the doors to subsidized imports from non-Commonwealth countries. Australian and New Zealand farmers felt aggrieved by these changes of policy, since the British had formerly agitated for higher food deliveries from the dominions. Irrespective of these misfortunes, however, the British market was simply too small to absorb the growing surpluses of Australia and New Zealand at remunerative prices.

Australia and New Zealand were unable to raise sufficient capital in London to satisfy demands associated with a series of major state-sector and quasi state-sector development projects. The British regulated issues of loan capital by overseas borrowers on the London market. Although preference was given to public sector borrowers in the Commonwealth, it proved difficult for Australia and, to a lesser extent, New Zealand to raise the desired amounts of capital. Hence in 1950 Australia turned to the World Bank for a dollar loan, and in 1953 New Zealand was awarded an Export–Import Bank loan relating to the Murupara project. Australia subsequently made regular borrowings from the World Bank, but New Zealand, which was not a member of the Bretton Woods club until 1961, remained tied to the London market for some years.

Due to the manner in which preferences were specified in the Ottawa Agreements, inflation eroded the tariff margins on Australian and New Zealand foodstuffs in the British market between the 1930s and 1950s. The Ottawa Agreements came to be regarded as unfair, prompting Canberra and Wellington to call for their renegotiation. Widening the margins on Commonwealth foodstuffs was out of the question while Britain and the dominions were members of GATT, which did not permit the establishment of new preferences. Balance would have to be restored to the Ottawa Agreements by scaling down contractual BP margins. Overestimating their bargaining power, Australia and New Zealand hoped that other countries would respond to the offer of lower BP margins by opening their food markets. But the Americans, the Japanese, and the Europeans were unwilling to subject their farmers to rigorous Australasian competition. GATT repeatedly failed to tackle the question of agricultural protection because the major economic powers adopted an obstructive attitude. Canberra and Wellington won some trade concessions from Japan under bilateral agreements in 1957 and 1958, but pressure from Japanese farmers, Australasian manufacturers, and even from Australasian farmers, worried about British retaliation, imposed limits on economic détente with Japan.

Unfortunately, the Anglo-Australian dispute over the Ottawa Agreement coincided with the decision of the Six in Europe to form a Common Market. In the early postwar years, the British had been sceptical about the prospects for an integrated European economy, as the continent was thought to be politically unstable and vulnerable to Soviet attack. But the robustness of the West European economy, combined with the sluggishness of many Commonwealth economies, encouraged a change of heart in the 1950s. Faced with McEwen's demands for a guaranteed wheat market and large cuts in contractual BP margins, and the danger that German industry would secure preferential access to west European markets under the Common Market, the British had good reason to reassess their commercial interests. London's subsequent proposal for a European industrial free trade area was designed to put British firms on an equal footing with German firms in Europe, while preserving an open food market for the benefit of domestic interests and Commonwealth suppliers. New Zealand, with some support from Australia, attempted to involve the Commonwealth in negotiations over the industrial free trade area, with the intention of securing greater access to continental markets. The Europeans, however, were determined to protect their farmers from Australasian competition. Moreover, they had no interest in a commercial arrangement that denied their farmers a strong preferential position in the British food market. In 1961, the British, who were by now thoroughly chastened, requested negotiations with the Six with a view to obtaining full membership of the EEC. Heath pleaded with the Six to grant comparable outlets to Commonwealth food suppliers, but this initiative was never more than a forlorn hope. The Six wished to shut Commonwealth food out of the British market, and declined to offer permanent guarantees of market access. New Zealand was promised better transitional terms than Australia, but it too would have faced the abyss in 1970 if the British entry negotiations had not ended in fiasco. It was apparent in Canberra and Wellington that de Gaulle's veto of Britain was not the end of the matter. Britain would apply again (and again) until the French relented.

After the termination of the EEC entry negotiations in 1963, the British made dairy concessions to Denmark and Ireland, wavered over the continuation of unrestricted duty-free Commonwealth entry, and made it clear that they would fight to preserve their preferential rights in Commonwealth markets. For New Zealand, the sixties were years of reprieve from the almost inevitable loss of the British market once de Gaulle left the scene. For Australia, however, the 1960s witnessed the dramatic growth of mineral exports, especially to Japan, and a new phase of expansion and prosperity. By the mid-1960s, Japan had overtaken Britain as Australia's main export market. Although New Zealand attached itself to Australia through NAFTA, it lacked Australia's mineral wealth and faced an uncertain future. The development of both countries was constrained by the lack of an export-oriented manufacturing sector. Persistently high levels of protection had fostered the growth of large but ramshackle manufacturing industries. Torn between the competing imperatives of economic nationalism and comparative advantage, Australian and New Zealand governments had fudged.

Britain, Australia, and New Zealand were driven apart by changing perceptions of national self-interest, and by evolving commercial and financial incentives. Australia and New Zealand believed that import substitution industrialization would best serve their interests. The inability of Britain to provide rapidly growing markets and endless supplies of capital impelled the dominions to seek new economic partnerships in Asia and North America. Meanwhile, the pull of continental European markets persuaded the British government to devalue the Commonwealth economic relationship. Australia and New Zealand were, in Konrad Adenauer's telling phrase, invited to 'swim off'.

Notes

Chapter 1: Australasia in Context

1. CM (56) 65th mtg, 14 Sept. 1956: PRO: CAB 128/30.
2. G. Myrdal, *An International Economy* (London: Routledge and Kegan Paul, 1956), p. 7. In the 1940s, the British Empire became the British Commonwealth. Although Australia is also a 'Commonwealth', in this book, the Commonwealth is the British Commonwealth unless explicit mention is made of the Commonwealth of Australia.
3. Commonwealth Economic Committee, *Commonwealth Trade 1950 to 57* (London: HMSO, 1959). A schematic analysis of the effects of changing conditions on the British Commonwealth in the postwar period is given in P. Robertson and J. Singleton, 'The Commonwealth as an Economic Network', *Australian Economic History Review*, 2001 41(3).
4. J. Charmley, *Churchill's Grand Alliance* (London: Hodder & Stoughton, 1995), p. 237.
5. The dominions were the self-governing white members of the Commonwealth.
6. Emphasis is placed on the politically sovereign Commonwealth members.
7. On micro-level networks see, for instance, G. Jones and J. Wale, 'Merchants as Business Groups: British Trading Companies in Asia before 1945', *Business History Review*, 1998 72(3): 367–408; *idem*, 'Diversification Strategies of British Trading Companies: Harrisons & Crosfield, c.1900–c.1980', *Business History*, 1999 41(2): 69–101. On macro-level networks see Robertson and Singleton, 'Network'.
8. S. Pollard, *The Development of the British Economy, 1914–1990* (London: Edward Arnold, 1992), pp. 92–6, 193–9, 314–15; Sir A. Cairncross, 'Economic Policy and Performance, 1945–1964', in R. Floud and D.N. McCloskey (eds), *The Economic History of Britain* (Cambridge: Cambridge University Press, 1994), vol. 3, pp. 32–66; B.W.E. Alford, *Britain in the World Economy since 1880* (London: Longman, 1996), pp. 231–2, 241, 256, 300–2; S.N Broadberry, *The Productivity Race: British Manufacturing in International Perspective, 1850–1990* (Cambridge: Cambridge University Press, 1997), pp. 153–4, 292, 335.
9. G.R. Hawke, *The Making of New Zealand* (Cambridge: Cambridge University Press, 1985), chs 9–16; B. Easton, *In Stormy Seas: the Postwar New Zealand Economy* (Dunedin: University of Otago Press, 1997); B. Pinkstone, *Global Connections: a History of Exports and the Australian Economy* (Canberra: AGPS, 1992), p. 2; D. Meredith and B. Dyster, *Australia in the Global Economy* (Cambridge: Cambridge University Press, 1999), chs 7–9; M. Havinden and D. Meredith, *Colonialism and Development: Britain and its Tropical Colonies* (London: Routledge, 1993).
10. A. Rix, *Coming to Terms: the Politics of Australia's Trade with Japan 1945–1957*

(Sydney: Allen and Unwin, 1986). Lee's recent volume contains much of interest on Anglo-Australian economic relations, although this is not its primary focus. D. Lee, *Search for Security: the Political Economy of Australia's Postwar Foreign and Defence Policy* (St Leonard's, NSW: Allen & Unwin, 1995).

11. R. Pomfret, *The Economics of Regional Trading Arrangements* (Oxford: Clarendon Press, 1997), pp. 8–9, 73, 79–80.

12. D.K. Fieldhouse, 'The Metropolitan Economics of Empire', in J.M. Brown and W.R. Louis (eds), *Oxford History of the British Empire* (Oxford: Oxford University Press, 1999), vol. 4, p. 112.

13. C.R. Schenk, *Britain and the Sterling Area* (London: Routledge, 1994), p. 136; *idem*, 'The Sterling Area and British Policy Alternatives in the 1950s', *Contemporary Record*, 1992 6(2): 266–86.

14. P.J. Cain and A.G. Hopkins, *British Imperialism: Crisis and Deconstruction, 1914–1990* (London: Longman, 1993), ch. 11; T. Hopkins, 'Macmillan's Audit of Empire, 1957', in P. Clarke and C. Trebilcock (eds), *Understanding Decline: Perceptions and Realities of British Economic Performance* (Cambridge: Cambridge University Press, 1997).

15. Cain and Hopkins, *Crisis and Deconstruction*, ch. 6.

16. P.J. Cain and A.G. Hopkins, 'Afterword: the Theory and Practice of British Imperialism', in R.E. Dumett (ed.), *Gentlemanly Capitalism and British Imperialism* (London: Longman, 1999), pp. 204, 207.

17. W.K. Hancock, *Survey of British Commonwealth Affairs* (London: Oxford University Press, 1940), vol. II, pt 1, p. 104.

18. A preference is the margin between the tariffs on imports from the preferred country and from other countries.

19. Most primary products were traded on the London market in sterling. As sterling fell, exporters in countries still on gold received less in local currency for their produce.

20. I.M. Drummond, *The Floating Pound and the Sterling Area* (Cambridge: Cambridge University Press, 1981); Cain and Hopkins, *Crisis and Deconstruction*, esp. chs 5–6; B. Eichengreen and D.I. Irwin, 'Trade Blocs, Currency Blocs and the Reorientation of World Trade in the 1930s', *Journal of International Economics*, 1995 (38): 1–24.

21. The Ottawa Agreements established minimum contractual preference margins. In many cases the margins actually accorded to British goods were much higher. I.M. Drummond, *Imperial Economic Policy 1917–1939* (London: Allen & Unwin, 1974); Cain and Hopkins, *Crisis and Deconstruction*, pp. 83–93; T. Rooth, *British Protectionism and the International Economy* (Cambridge: Cambridge University Press, 1993), pp. 71–100; D. MacDougall and R. Hutt, 'Imperial Preference: a Quantitative Analysis', in D. MacDougall, *Essays in Political Economy* (London: Macmillan, 1970), vol. 1, pp. 244–68; B.M. Rowland, *Commercial Conflict and Foreign Policy: a Study in Anglo-American Relations 1932–1938* (New York: Garland, 1987).

22. P.W. Bell, *The Sterling Area in the Postwar World* (Oxford: Oxford University Press, 1956); Schenk, *Britain and the Sterling Area*.

23. After 1945 Imperial Preference was usually termed Commonwealth Preference.

24. Britain did, however, limit spending from accumulated sterling balances

by India, Pakistan, Burma, Ceylon, Iraq, and Egypt. J.O.N. Perkins, *Sterling and Regional Payments Systems* (Melbourne: Melbourne University Press, 1956), p. 12.

25. R.W. Green, 'Commonwealth Preference: Tariff Duties and Preferences on United Kingdom Exports to the Preference Area', *Board of Trade Journal*, 11 June 1965, pp. iv–xix; *idem*, 'Commonwealth Preference: United Kingdom Customs Duties and Tariff Preferences on Imports from the Preference Area', *Board of Trade Journal*, 31 Dec. 1965, pp. 1551–8.

26. Fieldhouse, 'Metropolitan Economics', p. 108.

27. P.A. Petri, 'The East Asian Trading Bloc: an Analytical History', in J.A. Frankel and M. Kahler (eds), *Regionalism and Rivalry: Japan and the United States in Pacific Asia* (Chicago: University of Chicago Press, 1993), p. 37.

28. Bell, *Sterling Area*, ch. 13.

29. EP (56) 72, The Probable Development of the Commonwealth over the Next Ten or Fifteen Years, 31 Aug. 1956, p. 3. PRO: CAB 134/1231.

30. The Sterling Area minus Britain.

31. P.J. Cain and A.G. Hopkins, *British Imperialism: Innovation and Expansion, 1688–1914* (London: Longman, 1993); Hawke, *Making of New Zealand*, chs 1–6; Meredith and Dyster, *Australia in the Global Economy*, chs 2–3.

32. Investment in the Sterling Area did generate a higher rate of return than investment in other countries in the 1950s. Schenk, *Britain and the Sterling Area*, pp. 104–6.

33. J.M. Keynes, 'The Problem of Our External Finance in the Transition', in D. Moggridge (ed.), *The Collected Writings of John Maynard Keynes* (London: Macmillan, 1979), vol. XXIV, p. 60; J. Singleton, 'The British Engineering Industry and Commonwealth Development', *Journal of European Economic History*, forthcoming.

34. M. Casson, *Enterprise and Competitiveness* (Oxford: Clarendon Press, 1990), pp. 16–17.

35. M. McKinnon, 'Equality of Sacrifice: Anglo-New Zealand Relations and the War Economy, 1939–45', *Journal of Imperial and Commonwealth History*, 1984 12(3): 68–72, 74.

36. J. Polk, *Sterling: Its Meaning in World Finance* (New York: Harper & Brothers, 1956), pp. 244–5.

37. N. Mansergh, 'The Commonwealth: a Retrospective Survey, 1955–64', in W.B. Hamilton, K. Robinson, and C.D.W. Goodwin, *A Decade of the Commonwealth, 1955–1964* (Durham, NC: Duke University Press, 1966), pp. 5–8.

38. B.R. Tomlinson, 'Imperialism and After: the Economy of the Empire on the Periphery', in *Oxford History of the British Empire*, vol. 4, p. 366.

39. Restoring the one world system was not the same as reverting to the Gold Standard.

40. H. van der Wee, *Prosperity and Upheaval: the World Economy 1945–1980* (Berkeley: University of California Press, 1986); A.G. Kenwood and A.L. Lougheed, *The Growth of the International Economy 1820–1990* (London: Routledge, 1992), chs 16–21; J. Foreman-Peck, *A History of the World Economy* (Hemel Hempstead: Harvester Wheatsheaf, 1995), chs 12–14.

41. P.A. Cashin, 'Real GDP in the Seven Colonies of Australasia: 1861–1991', *Review of Income and Wealth*, 1995 41(1): 19–39; D. Greasley and L. Oxley,

'Outside the Club: New Zealand's Economic Growth, 1870–1993', *International Review of Applied Economics*, 2000 14(2): 173–92.

42. M. Abramovitz, 'Catching Up, Forging Ahead, and Falling Behind', *Journal of Economic History*, 1986 46(2): 385–406; A. Maddison, *Dynamic Forces in Capitalist Development* (Oxford: Oxford University Press, 1991); N. Crafts, 'Economic Growth in the Twentieth Century', *Oxford Review of Economic Policy*, 1999 15(4): 18–34.

43. M. Olson, *The Rise and Decline of Nations* (New Haven: Yale University Press, 1982); *idem*, 'The Varieties of Eurosclerosis: the Rise and Decline of Nations since 1982', in N. Crafts and G. Toniolo (eds), *Economic Growth in Europe since 1945* (Cambridge: Cambridge University Press, 1996), pp. 73–94; E.F. Denison, *Why Growth Rate Differ* (Washington: Brookings Institution, 1967).

44. Olson, *Rise and Decline*, pp. 135–6.

45. D. Copland, 'Problems of the Sterling Area With Special Reference to Australia', *Essays in International Finance No. 17* (Princeton: Princeton University Press, 1953).

46. H.D. Henderson, *The Inter-War Years and Other Papers*, ed. H. Clay (Oxford: Clarendon Press, 1955), p. 294.

47. E.M. Bernstein, 'British Policy and a World Economy', *American Economic Review*, 1945 35(5): 891–908.

48. Preference margins on Commonwealth exports to the UK were set in shillings and pence, not percentage terms. W.R. Carney, 'The Ottawa Agreement Now', *Economic Record*, 1956 32(1): 102. See also F.V. Meyer, *Britain, the Sterling Area and Europe* (Cambridge: Bowes & Bowes, 1952), pp. 62–70.

49. J.D. Sachs, 'Twentieth-century Political Economy: a Brief History of Global Capitalism', *Oxford Review of Economic Policy*, 1999 15(4): 96, 100.

50. J.Y. Lim, 'The Macroeconomics of the east Asian Crisis and the Implications of the Crisis for Macroeconomic Theory', *The Manchester School*, 1999 67(5): 428–59.

51. J.O.N. Perkins, *The Sterling Area, the Commonwealth and World Economic Growth* (Cambridge: Cambridge University Press, 1967).

52. B. Pinkstone, 'The Terms of Trade Debate: a Critical Realist Approach', paper read to the Australasian Economic and Maritime History Conference, Wellington, Nov. 1998; D. Evans, 'The Long Run Determinants of North–South Terms of Trade and Some Recent Empirical Evidence', *World Development*, 1987 15(5): 657–71.

53. K. Anderson and H. Norheim, 'From Imperial to Regional Trade Preferences: Its Effect on Europe's Intra- and Extra-Regional Trade', *Weltwirtschaftliches Archiv*, 1993 129(1): 78–101.

54. S. Brownie and P. Dalziel, 'Shift-share Analyses of New Zealand Exports, 1970–1984', *New Zealand Economic Papers*, 1993 27(2): 247.

55. A. Benvenuti, 'Australia's Battle Against the Common Agricultural Policy: the Fraser Government's Trade Diplomacy and the European Community', *Australian Journal of Politics and History*, 1999 45(2): 181–96.

56. Moore, however, doubts that British industry gained from entry into the EEC, and laments Britain's loss of preferences in dynamic Asian Commonwealth countries such as Malaysia and Singapore. L. Moore, *Britain's Trade and Economic Structure* (London: Routledge, 1999), p. 3.

57. Admittedly, there was some doubt about the economic viability of one or two minor branches of Australian agriculture, such as fruit and sugar, but this did not extend to the main products such as wool, sheepmeat, and wheat. Pinkstone, *Global Connections*, p. 174.

58. D.A. Carey and A.A. Smith, 'The External Dependence of the New Zealand Economy', in R.S. Deane, P.W.E. Nicholl and M.J. Walsh (eds), *External Economic Structure and Policy: an Analysis of New Zealand's Balance of Payments* (Wellington: RBNZ, 1981), pp. 552–5.

59. F.O. Grogan, *International Trade in Temperate Zone Products* (Edinburgh: Oliver & Boyd, 1972); M. Tracy, *Agriculture in Western Europe: Challenge and Response 1880–1980* (London: Granada, 1982), chs 11–12.

60. Easton, *In Stormy Seas*, pp. 78–9.

61. Hawke, *Making of New Zealand*, p. 230.

62. S.R.H. Jones, 'Government Policy and Industry Structure in New Zealand, 1900–1970', *Australian Economic History Review*, 1999 39(3): 201–4.

63. K. Anderson and R. Garnaut, *Australian Protectionism* (Sydney: Allen & Unwin, 1987), pp. 6–7; A.C. Rayner and R. Lattimore, 'New Zealand', in D. Papageorgiou, M. Michaely, and A.M. Choksi (eds), *Liberalizing Foreign Trade* (Oxford: Blackwell, 1991), vol. 6, p. 47; R. Pomfret, 'Trade Policy in Canada and Australia in the Twentieth Century', *Australian Economic History Review*, 2000 40(2): 114–26.

64. A. Bollard, R. Lattimore and B. Silverstone, 'Introduction', in B. Silverstone, A. Bollard, and R. Lattimore (eds), *A Study of Economic Reform: the Case of New Zealand* (Amsterdam: North Holland, 1996), pp. 1–23.

65. S. Bell, *Australian Manufacturing and the State* (Cambridge: Cambridge University Press, 1993), p. 5.

66. Meredith and Dyster, *Australia in the Global Economy*, p. 190.

67. F.H. Gruen, 'How Bad is Australia's Economic Performance and Why?', *Economic Record*, 1986 62(2): 180–93.

68. D. Mabbett, *Trade, Employment and Welfare: a Comparative Study of Trade and Labour Market Policies in Sweden and New Zealand, 1880–1980* (Oxford: Clarendon Press, 1995); M.A. Capling and B. Galligan, *Beyond the Protective State: The Political Economy of Australia's Manufacturing Industry* (Cambridge: Cambridge University Press, 1992).

69. I. Duncan, R. Lattimore, and A. Bollard, 'Dismantling the Barriers: Tariff Policy in New Zealand', *NZIER Research Monograph No. 57* (Wellington, NZIER, 1992), pp. 10–11.

70. J. Stewart, 'Traditional Australian Industry Policy: What Went Wrong', *Prometheus*, 1991 9(2): 249–64; A. Amsden, *Asia's Next Giant: South Korea and Late Industrialisation* (New York: Oxford University Press, 1989); H. Hughes, 'Why Have East Asian Countries Led Economic Development?', *Economic Record*, 1995 71(212): 88–104; R. Wade, *Governing the Market: Economic Theory and the Role of Government in East Asian Industrialization* (Princeton: Princeton University Press, 1990).

71. A notable exception was the Tasman Pulp and Paper Company in New Zealand, discussed in Chapter 4 below.

72. K. Kojima, 'An Impression of the Oceanian Economy', *Economic Record*, 1964 40(1): 46–57.

73. Meredith and Dyster, *Australia in the Global Economy*, pp. 195–7; Mabbett, *Trade, Employment and Welfare*, pp. 137, 151.
74. C.B. Schedvin, 'Staples and Regions of the Pax Britannica', *Economic History Review*, 1990 43(4): 533–59.
75. D. Greasley and L. Oxley, 'A Tale of Two Dominions: Comparing the Macroeconomic Records of Australia and Canada Since 1870', *Economic History Review*, 1998 51(2): 294–318.
76. P.J. Pedersen, 'Postwar Growth in the Danish Economy', in Crafts and Toniolo, *Economic Growth*, p. 558.

Chapter 2: Australia, New Zealand, and International Reconstruction

1. G.L. Wood, 'International Economic Co-operation and the Australian Economy', *Economic Record*, 1947 23(2): 173.
2. In addition, Australia was anxious to proceed with economic development, while Britain was concerned with physical reconstruction and the revival of outward foreign investment.
3. Memorandum on Meeting of the Executive Committee on Economic Foreign Policy, Dec. 27, 1947. HSTL: Papers of John W. Snyder, Box 34, File: UK Trade 1946–8.
4. *FRUS*, 1947, I, p. 963.
5. Foreman–Peck, *History of the World Economy*, chs 10–11; B. Eichengreen, *Golden Fetters: The Gold Standard and the Great Depression 1919–1939* (New York: Oxford University Press, 1992).
6. A.P. Dobson, *The Politics of the Anglo-American Economic Special Relationship* (Brighton: Wheatsheaf, 1988), esp. chs 1–4; A.V. Dormael, *Bretton Woods* (London: Macmillan, 1978); R.N. Gardner, *Sterling–Dollar Diplomacy* (New York: McGraw-Hill, 1969); J.G. Ikenberry, 'A World Economy Restored: Expert Consensus and the Anglo-American Postwar Settlement', *International Organization*, 1992 46(1): 289–321; L.S. Pressnell, *External Economic Policy Since the War* (London: HMSO, 1986); R.B. Woods, *A Changing of the Guard: Anglo-American Relations, 1941–1946* (Chapel Hill: University of North Carolina Press, 1990); T.W. Zeiler, *Free Trade Free World: the Advent of GATT* (Chapel Hill: University of North Carolina Press, 1999).
7. Quoted in Pressnell, *External Economic Policy*, p. 372.
8. However, the Anglo-American Agreement was a bilateral affair that did not commit countries such as Australia and New Zealand to abolish dollar discrimination.
9. Labour is used in preference to Labor unless with specific reference to the Australian Labor Party.
10. Quoted in J.G. Crawford, *Australian Trade Policy 1942–1966: A Documentary History* (Canberra: ANU Press, 1968), p. 23. See also G. Whitwell, *The Treasury Line* (Sydney: Allen & Unwin, 1986), ch. 3; D.H. Merry and G.R. Bruns, 'Full Employment: the British, Canadian and Australian White Papers', *Economic Record*, 1945 21(2): 223–35; D.B. Copland and R.H. Barback (eds), *The Conflict of Expansion and Stability* (Melbourne: Cheshire, 1957), pp. 1–80.

11. Quoted in J.E. Martin, *Holding the Balance: A History of New Zealand's Department of Labour 1891–1995* (Christchurch: Canterbury University Press, 1996), p. 232.
12. C.G.F. Simkin, 'Insulationism and the Problem of Economic Stability', *Economic Record*, 1946 22(1): 50–65; D. Mabbett, *Trade, Employment, and Welfare*; M. Bassett, *The State in New Zealand 1840–1984* (Auckland: Auckland University Press, 1998), chs 7–10; Review of the Customs (Import Licensing) Regulations, June 1945. NAA: SP378.
13. M. Beresford and P. Kerr, 'A Turning Point for Australian Capitalism: 1945–52', in E.L. Wheelwright and K. Buckley (eds), *Essays in the Political Economy of Australian Capitalism* (Sydney: Australia & New Zealand Book Company, 1980), vol. 4, pp. 152–5.
14. *Documents on Australian Foreign Policy 1937–49*, VII, pp. 626–31; L.F. Crisp, 'The Australian Full Employment Pledge at San Francisco', *Australian Outlook*, 1965 19(1): 5–19; Gardner, *Sterling–Dollar Diplomacy*, p. 272.
15. Zeiler, *Free Trade Free World*, pp. 32–3; Pressnell, *External Economic Policy*, pp. 25, 106–9. PCP (43) 1st mtg, 15 June 1943. PRO: T 230/129.
16. Ibid., 2nd mtg, 16 June 1943.
17. Ibid., 4th mtg, 18 June 1943; 7th mtg, 23 June 1943.
18. Ibid., 2nd mtg, 16 June 1943; 6th mtg, 22 June 1943. Postwar Commercial Policy: Note on UK/Dominions Discussions, London, June 1943. NZA: PM 23, 1/4.
19. Pressnell, *External Economic Policy*, p. 135.
20. The UK imported sheepmeat duty free from all sources, but Commonwealth sheepmeat producers gained indirectly from the tariffs on other types of foreign meat. Memorandum on Imperial Preference, 16 April 1946. NZA: EA 1, 104/4/1, pt 5.
21. H. Belshaw, 'Post War Economic Reconstruction in New Zealand', *Pacific Affairs*, 1944 17(4): 434.
22. F. McKenzie, 'Renegotiating a Special Relationship: the Commonwealth and Anglo-American Economic Discussions, September–December 1945', *Journal of Imperial and Commonwealth History*, 1998 26(3): 71–93.
23. UK Senior Trade Commissioner in Australia to Department of Overseas Trade, 23 Oct. 1945. PRO: BT 60/86/6. H.C. Coombs, *Trial Balance* (South Melbourne: Macmillan, 1981), pp. 86–7.
24. Attlee to Fraser, 6 Dec. 1945. NZA: EA 1, 104/4/1, pt 4.
25. UK Senior Trade Commissioner in Australia to Department of Overseas Trade, 4 Jan. and 4 March 1946. PRO: BT 60/86/6.
26. Notes of interview with Melville, 24 Dec. 1945. NZA: EA 1, 104/4/1, pt 4.
27. UK Senior Trade Commissioner in Australia to Department of Overseas Trade, 4 Jan. and 29 Jan. 1946. PRO: BT 60/86/6.
28. Notes of Commercial Policy Discussions in Australia, 24 Dec. 1945. NZA: EA 1, 104/4/1, pt 4.
29. Preference to New Zealand Products in UK Market, 6 Feb. 1946. NZA: EA 1, 104/4/1, pt 5.
30. Cabinet Agendum 1019A, United States Trade and Employment Proposals, 11 Jan. 1946. NAA: A2700XM, vol. 22. UK Senior Trade Commissioner in Australia to Department of Overseas Trade, 11 Jan. 1946. PRO: BT 60/86/6.

31. Commercial Policy – ITO – Position of New Zealand, 14 Oct. 1946. NZA: EA 1, 104/4/1, pt 6.
32. Notes of Meetings on Commercial Policy, 6 Aug. 1946. NZA: EA 1, 104/4/1, pt 5.
33. Preparatory Committee on Trade and Development, British Commonwealth Talks, Summary of Results, 18 Oct. 1946. PRO: CAB 134/541.
34. Crawford, *Australian Trade Policy*, pp. 42–3.
35. Copland and Barback, *Expansion and Stability*, pp. 529–46.
36. Cabinet Agendum 1019E, Trade and Employment Conference, Progress Report, undated, 1947, Appendix, p. 1. NAA: A2700XM, vol. 22. A. Capling, 'The "Enfant Terrible": Australia and the Reconstruction of the Multilateral Trade System', *Australian Economic History Review*, 2000 40(1): 1–21.
37. Zeiler, *Free Trade Free World*, p. 154.
38. Cabinet Agendum 1019E, Appendix, pp. 2–4, 8–12. NAA: A2700XM, vol. 22.
39. External Affairs to NZ Trade Delegation, 9 June 1947. NZA: EA 1, 104/4/1, pt 7.
40. Ibid., NZ Trade Delegation to External Affairs, 27 June 1947.
41. Ibid., NZ Trade Delegation to External Affairs, 13 July 1947.
42. Ibid., Chifley to Nash, 26 June 1947.
43. K. Sinclair, *Walter Nash* (Auckland: Auckland University Press, 1976), p. 253; NZ Trade Delegation to External Affairs, 17 July 1947. NZA: EA 1, 104/4/1, pt 7. Notes on Discussions in Geneva, Articles 21, 23, and 24 Sept. 1947. NAA: A571, 44/1109 PX14.
44. *CAPD*, vol. 194, 11 Nov. 1947, p. 1885.
45. Ibid., p. 1887.
46. Coombs, *Trial Balance*, p. 93.
47. Crawford, *Australian Trade Policy*, pp. 83–4; Memorandum on Western Union, 21 Sept. 1948. Reserve Bank of Australia Archive, Sydney: C3931.
48. Sinclair, *Nash*, pp. 254–5.
49. *NZPD*, vol. 279, 12 Nov. 1947, p. 624.
50. M. McKinnon, 'The New World of the Dollar', in M. McKinnon (ed.), *The American Connection* (Wellington: Allen & Unwin, 1988), pp. 109–25.
51. T.W. Zeiler, 'GATT Fifty Years Ago: US Trade Policy and Imperial Tariff Preferences', *Business and Economic History*, 1997 26(2): 709–19.
52. Coombs to Chifley, 24 March 1947; Trade and Employment Conference, First Progress Report, 14 April 1947. NAA: A571, 44/1109 PX14. Preparatory Committee on Trade and Employment (Second Session), British Commonwealth Talks, Report by UK Delegation, 14 April 1947, p. 6. PRO: CAB 134/541. NZ Delegation Geneva to Customs Department, 31 Aug. 1947. NZA: EA 1, Acc. W1784, 58/9/4, pt 3.
53. Zeiler, *Free Trade Free World*, p. 100. Inward Telegram, Nash to External Affairs, 26 April 1947. NZA: EA 1, 104/4/8/1, pt 3.
54. Letter from G.C. Marshall to the President, July 30, 1947. HSTL: Papers of Harry S. Truman, White House Central Files, Confidential Files, Box 51, Folder: International Trade Agreements, 2 of 4.
55. Zeiler, *Free Trade Free World*, pp. 94–104; Copland and Barback, *Expansion and Stability*, pp. 509–29; Cabinet Agendum 1019E, Trade and Employment

Conference, Progress Report, undated, 1947, pp. 13–14. NAA: A2700XM, vol. 22.

56. Cabinet Agendum 1019F, GATT Progress Report, 24 Oct. 1947, pp. 3, 4. NAA: A571, 44/1109 PX14.

57. Ibid., p. 7.

58. General Agreement on Tariffs and Trade, 18 Nov. 1947. NZA: EA 1, 104/4/8/1, pt 5.

59. Gardner, *Sterling-Dollar Diplomacy*, p. 360; *Report on the Geneva Tariff Negotiations*, Cmd 7258 (London: HMSO, 1947).

60. Memorandum for the President from Winthrop G. Brown, Chairman, Committee of Trade Agreements. Subject: Action at Geneva with Respect to British Preferential System. Oct. 17, 1947. HSTL: Papers of Harry S. Truman, White House Central Files, Confidential Files, Box 51, Folder: International Trade Agreements, 2 of 4.

61. G. Curzon, *Multilateral Commercial Diplomacy* (London: Michael Joseph, 1965), p. 168.

62. *NZPD*, vol. 280, 29 June 1948, p. 115.

63. Quoted in Crawford, *Australian Trade Policy*, p. 84.

64. Comments on Proposed Treaty with the USA, by Fussell, 18 May 1948; Proposed Treaty between the USA and New Zealand, by Clinkard, 17 June 1948. NZA: EA 1, Acc. W1784, 58/9/27, pt 2. B. McFarlane, 'Australian Postwar Economic Policy, 1947–53', in A. Curthoys and J. Meritt (eds), *Australia's First Cold War 1945–1953* (Sydney: Allen & Unwin, 1984), vol. 1, pp. 33–7.

65. C.B. Schedvin, *In Reserve: Central Banking in Australia, 1945–75* (St. Leonards, NSW: Allen & Unwin, 1992), pp. 102–3; S.W. Black, *A Levite Among the Priests: Edward M. Bernstein and the Origins of the Bretton Woods System* (Boulder: Westview, 1991), pp. 37, 46–7; Dormael, *Bretton Woods*, pp. 66, 82–3.

66. International Conference on Post-War Monetary Organization, 29 May 1944. NAA: A2700XM, vol. 11.

67. Ibid., International Conference on Post-War Monetary Organization, Supplement by the Treasurer to Full Cabinet Agendum No. 669, 30 May 1944.

68. Ibid., Cabinet Agendum No. 669: International Conference. Proposed International Monetary Fund, 13 June 1944.

69. J. Singleton, 'Anglo-New Zealand Financial Relations, 1945–61', *Financial History Review*, 1998 5(2): 142–5.

70. Nash to External Affairs, 14 March 1947. NZA: PM 23, 3/1.

71. Postwar Financial Plans, January 1944, p. 9. NZA: PM 22, 7/8.

72. Sinclair, *Nash*, p. 242.

73. J.K. Horsefield, *The International Monetary Fund 1945–1965* (Washington, DC: IMF, 1969), vol. 1, p. 96.

74. S. Cornish, 'Sir Leslie Melville: an Interview', *Economic Record*, 1993 69(207): 448–9; Coombs, *Trial Balance*, pp. 46–7; Schedvin, *In Reserve*, p. 107; Sinclair, *Nash*, p. 243.

75. *NZPD*, vol. 265, 10 Aug. 1944, pp. 325–6.

76. *CAPD*, vol. 190, 20 March 1947, p. 938.

77. J. Bennett, 'Social Security, the "Money Power" and the Great Depression: the International Dimension to Australian and New Zealand Labour in

Office', *Australian Journal of Politics and History*, 1997 43(3): 312–30. On Social Credit theory see J.E. King, *Economic Exiles* (London: Macmillan, 1988), pp. 136–60.

78. Crawford, *Australian Trade Policy*, pp. 87–9; Schedvin, *In Reserve*, pp. 106–9; Sinclair, *Nash*, pp. 241–6.

79. Notes on Bretton Woods, 20 Dec. 1945. NZA: EA 1, 104/4/1, pt 4. Addison to External Affairs, 19 July 1947. EA 1, 104/4/1, pt 7. Subjects for Discussion with Nash, 22 May 1947. PRO: T 236/1300.

80. J.K. Horsefield and M.G. de Vries, *The International Monetary Fund 1945–1965* (Washington, DC: IMF, 1969), vol. 2, pp. 230, 238–40; *FRUS*, 1949, I, pp. 722–3. Position paper on Special Exchange Agreements, Sept. 1, 1953. DDEL: White House Central File, Box 767, Official File OF 149-B, File 1952–1953 (2).

81. Copland, 'Problems of the Sterling Area'.

82. Bell, *Sterling Area*, pp. 56–7.

83. Cabinet Agendum No. 869, Australia's External Trade Situation Following End of European War and Post-War, 19 June 1945. NAA: 2700XM, 83/410, vol. 11.

84. G. Krozewski, 'Sterling, the "Minor" Territories and the End of Formal Empire, 1939–1958', *Economic History Review*, 1993 46(2): 239–65.

85. BP (ON) (47) 115th mtg, 10 Oct 1947. PRO: BT 11/1677. Dollar Earnings, 21 Feb. 1949. NAA: A571, 48/1555. Notes of Meeting on Dollar and Sterling Position, 31 Oct. 1947. NZA: T1, 61/1/1. Export Policy in Relation to Potential Dollar Earners, 15 Oct. 1948. EA 1, 154/7/3, pt 1. Notes of Talks between UK and New Zealand Officials, 16 Feb. 1950. EA 1, Acc. W1784, 58/9/4, pt 4.

86. Crawford, *Australian Trade Policy*, pp. 221–5, 230–8; D. Hayward, *Golden Jubilee: the Story of the First Fifty Years of the New Zealand Meat Producers' Board* (Wellington: New Zealand Meat Producers Board, 1972), pp. 66–87; M.A. McKinnon, 'The Impact of War: a Diplomatic History of New Zealand's Economic Relations with Britain, 1939–1954', unpublished Ph.D. thesis, Victoria University of Wellington (1981), pp. 242–87, 313–57; A.H. Ward, *A Command of Cooperatives: the Development of Leadership, Marketing and Price Control in the Cooperative Dairy Industry of New Zealand* (Wellington: New Zealand Dairy Board, 1975), pp. 109–62.

87. Long Term Food Contracts, 23 Jan. 1952. PRO: T 230/245. E. McCarthy, *Wool Disposals, 1945–52* (Southampton: Hobbs, 1967).

88. Correspondence between Treasury, Department of Trade and Customs, and Ministry of Postwar Reconstruction on Doughnut Machines, Dec. 1946 to Jan 1947. NAA: A571, 47/452.

89. New Zealand Balance of Payments, 13 May 1948, p. 2. NZA: T1, 61/1, pt 1.

90. Schenk, *Britain and the Sterling Area*, p. 2.

91. P.L. Robertson, 'The Decline of Economic Complementarity? Australia and Britain 1945–1952', *Australian Economic History Review*, 1997 37(2): 96; 'The Dollar Situation, Statement by Chifley in the House of Representatives', 4 Dec. 1947, in *Parliamentary Papers: Finance, Session 1946–47–48*, vol. III.

92. Inward Telegram, Secretary of State to CRO, 2 Sept. 1947. PRO: T 236/1752. How the US Loan Was Spent, undated, 1947. NZA: EA 1, 153/24/1.

93. Lee, *Search for Security*.
94. This outcome had been foreseen by the Harvard economist J.H. Williams in his *Postwar Monetary Plans and Other Essays* (New York: Knopf, 1944).
95. Cabinet Agendum No. 1001, Washington Discussions on Finance, Lend-Lease, and Commercial Policy, 19 Nov. 1945. NAA: A2700XM, vol. 21.
96. Bretton Woods, the ITO and the Dollar Loan, 10 Dec. 1945. NZA: EA 1, 104/4/1, pt 4.
97. Bell, *The Sterling Area*, p. 22; Pollard, *Development of the British Economy*, p. 172; McKinnon, 'Equality of Sacrifice', pp. 54–76; S.J. Butlin, and C.B Schedvin, *War Economy 1942–1945* (Canberra: Australian War Memorial, 1977), vol. 2, pp. 598–603; J.M. Keynes, 'Overseas Financial Policy in Stage III', in *Collected Works*, vol. XXIV, p. 269.
98. Cabinet Agendum No. 1001, Washington Discussions on Finance, Lend-Lease, and Commercial Policy, 19 Nov. 1945. NAA: A2700XM, vol. 21.
99. Ibid., Cabinet Agendum 1001A, Washington Discussions on Finance, Lend-Lease, and Commercial Policy, 13 Dec. 1945, pp. 6, 9.
100. Scaling Down of New Zealand's Sterling Assets, 5 Dec. 1945. NZA: EA 1, 104/4/1, pt 4.
101. Note of Conversation between the Chancellor and the Prime Minister of New Zealand, 19 Feb. 1946. NZA: T 1, 61/1, pt 1.
102. J.S. Fforde, *The Bank of England and Public Policy, 1941–1958* (Cambridge: Cambridge University Press, 1992), pp. 101–3.
103. C.C.S. Newton, 'The Sterling Crisis of 1947 and the British Response to the Marshall Plan', *Economic History Review*, 1984 37(3): 398.
104. Lee, *Search for Security*, pp. 42–57; Robertson, 'Complementarity': 98–100; M.J. Hogan, *The Marshall Plan* (Cambridge: Cambridge University Press, 1987), pp. 170–3; H. Pelling, *Britain and the Marshall Plan* (Basingstoke: Macmillan, 1988), pp. 47–8. Webb to McIntosh, 6 Aug. 1948. NZA: EA 1, 154/7/2, pt 1.
105. Note of Conversation with Finletter on 16 July 1948. PRO: T 232/68.
106. Ibid., Franks to Makins, 20 July 1948; Message from ECA Washington to Finletter, undated, 1948.
107. Ibid., Sterling Area and ERP, undated, 1948.
108. Memorandum on the Dollar Problem of the Self-Governing Sterling Area Countries, undated 1948. HSTL: Papers of John W. Snyder, Box 11, File: ERP, 3.22–9.21.48. Noel Baker to External Affairs, 7 Oct. 1948. NZA: EA 1, 154/7/3, pt 1.
109. CRO to UK High Commissioner in Australia, 28 July 1948. PRO: T 232/71.
110. Ibid., Acting UK High Commissioner in Australia to CRO, 2 Aug. 1948; Australian Treasury to Wilson, 5 Aug. 1948; UK High Commissioner in New Zealand to CRO, 17 Aug. 1948 and 19 Aug. 1948; CRO to Acting UK High Commission in Australia, 28 Aug. and 31 Aug. 1948; Foreign Office to Washington, 3 Sept. 1948; Acting UK High Commissioner in Australia to CRO, 20 Dec. 1948; CRO to UK High Commissioner in Australia, 7 Sept. 1949.
111. Chifley, 'Dollar Situation', p. 6, para. 20 and 22. Determination of the Ceiling for 1949/50: Dollar Import Licensing Budget, 21 Mar. 1949, pp. 1–4. NAA: A571, 39/2485, pt 14. Statements by Chifley, reprinted in Copland and Barback, *Expansion and Stability*, pp. 412–15; Lee, *Search for*

Security, pp. 52–4; Robertson, 'Complementarity', p. 101; A.C. Cairncross, *The Years of Recovery: British Economic Policy 1945–51* (London: Methuen, 1985), ch. 7.

112. McKinnon, 'World of the Dollar', pp. 120–1. Snelling to Nash, 9 Aug. 1949. NZA: EA 1, 154/7/3, pt 2. Extract from Letter dated 2 Sept. [1949] from Nash to Berendson. T1, 61/1/5. Note on Visit of Walter Nash. HSTL: Papers of Dean Acheson, Box 64, File: Memorandum of Conversation, Aug.–Sept. 1949.

Chapter 3: Development Policy in Australia

1. Snelling to Percival, 21 May 1952. PRO: T 236/3027.
2. Robertson, 'Complementarity'; G. Zappalà, 'The Decline of Economic Complementarity: Australia and the Sterling Area', *Australian Economic History Review*, 1994 34(1): 5–21; T. Rooth, 'Imperial Self-insufficiency Rediscovered: Britain and Australia 1945–51', *Australian Economic History Review*, 1999 39(1): 29–51.
3. P. Robertson and K. Trace, 'Government Involvement in the Development of Australian Manufacturing since 1945', *Business and Economic History*, 1983 12: 109–123.
4. A.W. Martin, *Robert Menzies, A Life* (Melboune: Melbourne University Press, 1993), vol. 1, p. 230. As early as 1936, Menzies had openly supported increased immigration and support for secondary industry. Ibid., pp. 193–4.
5. S. Constantine, 'Waving Goodbye? Australia, Assisted Passages, and the Empire and Commonwealth Resettlement Acts, 1945–72', *Journal of Imperial and Commonwealth History*, 1998 26(2): 180; Butlin and Schedvin, *War Economy 1942–1945*, 2, pp. 701–6.
6. Cranborne to Bruce (draft), April 1945; United Kingdom Industrial Participation in Secondary Industries in India and the Dominions, undated, 1945. PRO: DO 35/1225.
7. Ibid., Liesching to Eady, 3 April 1945.
8. Manpower Allocation for Planning Essential Post-War Conversion and Expansion in Civilian Manufacturing Industries, 29 Dec. 1944. NAA: A2700XM, vol. 13.
9. Statement by the Prime Minister to Representatives of the Associated Chambers of Manufactures, 15 Feb. 1945. NAA: A571, 44/4395. Butlin and Schedvin, *War Economy*, 2, pp. 748–52.
10. Australia's External Trade Situation Following End of European War and Post-War, 19 June 1945. NAA: A2700XM, vol. 16.
11. Importation of Capital Plant for Industry in Australia: the Question of Administrative Machinery, 30 Oct. 1946. NAA: A571, 47/452.
12. Statement by the Prime Minister to Representatives of the Associated Chambers of Manufactures, 15 Feb. 1945. NAA: A571, 44/4395.
13. Decentralization of Secondary Industry, July 1945. NAA: A2700XM, vol. 17.
14. Manpower Allocation for Planning Essential Post-War Conversion and Expansion in Civilian Manufacturing Industries, 29 Dec. 1944. NAA: A2700XM, vol. 13.

15. Policy in Relation to the Dollar Problem, Attachment A, Australian Replacement Production, 18 Aug. 1948. NAA: A571, 48/1555.
16. Butlin and Schedvin, *War Economy*, 2, p. 501; R.K. Hefford, *Farm Policy in Australia* (St Lucia: University of Queensland Press, 1985), pp. 79–81; Crawford, *Australian Trade Policy*, pp. 28–9.
17. C. Clark, *The Economics of 1960* (London: Macmillan, 1942). Despatches from Dalton, 9 Dec. 1942 and 2 March 1943. PRO: DO 35/1215.
18. D.B. Copland, 'The Australian Post-War Economy: a Study in Economic Administration', *Canadian Journal of Economics and Political Science*, 1954 20(4): 422.
19. Lee, *Search for Security*, p. 31.
20. Copy of Cable from Bank of England, 21 Aug. 1947; Import Control – Licensing Treatment of Goods from Dollar Areas, 25 Aug. 1947. NAA: A571, 39/2485, pt 7.
21. Secretary of State to CRO, 1 Sept. 1947. PRO: T 236/1752.
22. Ibid., Secretary of State to CRO, 2 Sept. 1947.
23. Undated copy of letter from Chifley to Addison. NAA: A571, 39/2485, pt 7.
24. Implications of Message from Lord Addison, 3 Sept. 1947. NAA: A571, 39/2485, pt 7. UK Treasury Minute of mid-December 1947. PRO: T 236/1753.
25. Notes for Interdepartmental Conference on Import Licensing Policy in Relation to Capital Plant and Equipment and Raw Materials for Australian Industry, 3 Sept. 1947; Summary of Dollar Conservation Measures Approved by Cabinet on 2nd Sept. 1947, p. 2; Draft Revision of Existing 'Charter', 4 Sept. 1947. NAA: A571, 39/2485, pt 7.
26. Minutes of a Discussion between an Australian Delegation and Representatives of the British Treasury and Board of Trade, 22 Sept. 1947. PRO: T 236/1752.
27. D. Lee, 'Protecting the Sterling Area: the Chifley Government's Response to Multilateralism 1945–9', *Australian Journal of Political Science*, 1990 25: 184.
28. Report of the Inter-Departmental Committee. Review of Dollar Import Licensing, 14 Dec. 1947. NAA: A571, 39/2485, pt 9.
29. B. Dyster and D. Meredith, *Australia in the International Economy in the Twentieth Century* (Cambridge: Cambridge University Press, 1990), pp. 194–95, 209.
30. D.B. Copland, 'Balance of Production in the Australian Post-War Economy', *Economic Record*, 1949 25(2): 1–6.
31. P.L. Robertson, 'Official Policy on American Direct Investment in Australia, 1945–1952', *Australian Economic History Review*, 1986 26(2): 160–1.
32. Memorandum Prepared by Exchange Control, Sydney, on Dollar Borrowing and Exports, July 1949. NAA: A571, 49/2321, pt 1. Fadden to Scott, 15 Jan. 1951. A571, 45/2024A, pt 2. A.R. Conan, *The Sterling Area* (London: Macmillan, 1952), pp. 95–101.
33. Nette to the Secretary, Department of Commerce and Agriculture, 24 May 1948; Memorandum from Nette to Wheeler, 8 Feb. 1952. NAA: A571, 45/2024, pt 1. *Commonwealth Parliamentary Debates, Representatives*, 198, 10 Sept. 1948, pp. 391–2. Nette to the Treasurer, 3 March 1950. NAA: A571, 45/2024, pt 2. E. Penrose, 'Foreign Investment and the Growth of the Firm', *Economic Journal*, 1956 66: 220–35.

34. Memorandum by Coombs on Policy in Relation to the Dollar Problem, 7 May 1948, and Attachment A, Australian Replacement Production. See also The General Shortage, 15 June 1949, and letter from Turner to Coombs, 23 Aug. 1948. NAA: A571, 48/1555.
35. Coombs to the Secretary of the Treasury, 9 March 1950. NAA: A571, 45/2024, pt 1.
36. Robertson, 'Official Policy'; D. Lee, 'Australia, the British Commonwealth, and the United States 1950–53', *Journal of Imperial and Commonwealth History*, 1992 20(3): 445–69; *idem*, *Search for Security*; Zappalà, 'Decline'.
37. Quoted in Copland and Barback, *Expansion and Stability*, p. 408.
38. Ibid., pp. 408–12.
39. Australian Prime Minister's Visit: General Financial Questions, undated, 1950, p. 1. PRO: T 236/2451.
40. A Plan of Campaign, 28 June 1950. NAA: A571, 49/2777, pt 1.
41. Survey of Development Requirements, 19 Jan. 1950; Population Increases and Investment Requirements, 8 Feb. 1950. NAA: A4933XMI, vol. 17.
42. Cabinet Submission No. 69, Department of National Development, 16 March 1950. NAA: A4639XMI, vol. 3. Cabinet Agendum No. 200, Ministry of National Development, 10 Oct. 1950. A4639XMI, vol. 7.
43. Casey to Watt, 30 March 1950. NAA: A571, 45/2024, pt 2.
44. Cabinet Committee on Industry and Development and Committee on Oversea Commercial Relations, Minutes of Joint Meeting, 30th May 1950; Agendum for a Joint Meeting, 26 May 1950. NAA: A571, 50/613, pt 2.
45. Possible Sources of US dollars, 6 July 1949 (prepared by Commonwealth Bank); Dollar Loan Possibilities, 6 July 1949 (prepared by the Treasury). NAA: A571, 49/2777, pt 1.
46. Ibid., Coombs to Fadden, 3 Feb. 1950.
47. Ibid., A Plan of Campaign, 28 June 1950.
48. Note by Clarke on Discussions with Australian Ministers and Officials on Treasury Matters, May 1950. PRO: T 236/2450.
49. Australian Prime Minister's Visit: General Financial Questions, July 1950, p. 1. PRO: T 236/2451.
50. Ibid., pp. 5–6, 8 (underlining in original text). Cobbold, the Governor of the Bank of England, thought that the World 'Bank would be delighted to find a borrower of good standing with such encouraging prospects.' Cobbold to Wilson Smith, 7 July 1950. PRO: T 236/2450.
51. Dollar Borrowing by Australia: Summary of Discussions between Australian and United Kingdom Officials, 18 July 1950; Account of Meeting of 19 July 1950 between Cripps and Menzies. PRO: T 236/2450. Visit of Mr. Menzies, Australian Prime Minister (Note by Board of Trade): Economic Aspects of a Treaty of Friendship, Commerce and Navigation between Australia and USA, 11 July 1950. T 236/2451.
52. Meetings between Australian and British Representatives, 18 and 19 July 1950. PRO: T 236/2450.
53. Menzies to Fadden, 28 July 1950. NAA: A571/143, 50/2241.
54. *FRUS*, 1950, VI, pp. 189–97, 200–1, 203, 205–6.
55. Cablegrams from Menzies to Fadden, 3 Aug. 1950. NAA: A571/143, 50/2241, pt 1. Wheeler to Watt, 20 Aug. 1950. A1838/1, 706/1/5.

56. Schedvin, *In Reserve*, p. 171; Pollard, *Development of the British Economy*, p. 197.
57. Robertson, 'Complementarity': 103–4.
58. 24th Report of the Inter-Departmental Dollar Committee, 21 March 1951. NAA: 1967/391/1, Box 2/1.
59. Ibid., 26th Report of the Inter-Departmental Dollar Committee, 20 July 1951; Dollar Import Licensing Budget for September Quarter, 1951; Texts of Letters dated 2 Aug. 1951 from the Treasurer to the Prime Minister and to the Minister for Trade and Customs.
60. Meeting of Commonwealth Finance Ministers, Preliminary Meeting of Officials, Minutes of a Meeting Held on 8 Jan. 1952, pp. 126–9. PRO: CAB 133/123.
61. Finance Ministers' Conference: Opening Statement by Sir Arthur Fadden, 15 Jan. 1952. NAA: A4905XMI, vol. 9.
62. Ibid., Report on Commonwealth Finance Ministers' Conference, London, 15th to 21st Jan. 1952, undated, p. 4.
63. Mr. Menzies [*sic*] Visit: Economic Development in Australia (Note by the Board of Trade), undated, p. 1. PRO: T 236/3026.
64. Ibid., Mr. Menzies [*sic*] Visit: Brief by the Ministry of Food, 19 May 1952.
65. Snelling to Percival, 21 May 1952. PRO: T 236/3027.
66. Menzies to Butler, 8 April 1952; Draft Letter from Butler to Menzies, 1 May 1952; Note on Credit for Australia, by M.T. Flett, 6 May 1952; Policy Regarding Credits for Australia: Notes of a Meeting at Treasury on 8 May 1952; Note on Credits for Australia by D.M.B. Butt, 12 May 1952. PRO: T 236/3026.
67. IBRD Loan Department, Memorandum on Description of Australian Development Programs, July 3, 1952; Loan Agreement between the Commonwealth of Australia and the IBRD dated July 8, 1952. NAA: A571/2, 52/1068, pt 2.
68. Memorandum from Nette to Wheeler on Expansion of Dollar Investment, 8 Feb. 1952. NAA: A571, 45/2024, pt 1.
69. Robertson, 'Official Policy': 180.
70. Development in the Commonwealth, 1 Sept. 1952. PRO: CAB 133/131. Development in the Sterling Area, 31 Oct. 1952. PRO: CAB 129/56.
71. Development in Australia: Memorandum by the Australian Delegation, 1 Oct. 1952, p. 5. PRO: DO 35/5585.
72. Ibid., p. 3.
73. Lee, *Search for Security*, pp. 151–2.
74. CEC (DC) (52) 1st mtg, 1 Dec. 1952. PRO: DO 35/5582.
75. Schedvin, *In Reserve*, pp. 191–2; Hefford, *Farm Policy*, pp. 81–93.
76. CEC (O) (DP) (52) 6th mtg, 6 Oct. 1952. PRO: DO 35/5585.
77. FM (54) 6th mtg, 12 Jan. 1954. NZA: EA 1, Acc. W2619, 153/38/4.
78. The evolution of British policy on development between 1952 and 1958 can be traced in PRO: T 236/4993–5012.
79. J.K. Gifford et al., *Australian Banking* (St Lucia: University of Queensland Press, 1966), pp. 314–15; Conan, *Capital Imports*, pp. 6–7.
80. New Service Will Aid American Investment in Australia, March 21, 1955. NAA: A694/1, B15, pt 5.
81. The Place of Overseas Investment in the Australian Economy, Article for

Sydney Morning Herald Annual Survey of National Progress 'Australia Unlimited, 1959' by Rt. Hon. Harold Holt. NAA: M2607/1, Item 43.

82. R. Mathews, *Public Investment in Australia* (Melbourne: F.W. Cheshire, 1967), pp. 183–93, 350–60; J.B. Condliffe, *The Development of Australia* (Christchurch: Whitcombe and Tombs, 1964), pp. 98, 162.

83. D.T. Merrett, 'Capital Markets and Capital Formation in Australia, 1945–1990', *Australian Economic History Review*, 1998 38(2): 151.

84. Hefford, *Farm Policy*, pp. 89–93.

85. For a list of iron-ore export developments in the 1960s see Mathews, *Public Investment*, pp. 294–5. For a case study see G. Boyce, 'The Western Mining Corporation-Hanna/Homestake Joint Venture: Game Theory and Inter-Organizational Cooperation', *Australian Economic History Review*, 1997 37(3): 202–21.

86. P. Groenwegen and B. McFarlane, *A History of Australian Economic Thought* (London: Routledge, 1990), pp. 190–1.

87. C. Clark, 'Economic Growth', in J. Wilkes (ed.), *Economic Growth in Australia* (Sydney: Angus & Robertson, 1962), pp. 1–29.

88. Crawford, *Australian Trade Policy*, p. 599.

89. H.W. Arndt, 'Sir John Crawford', *Economic Record*, 1985 61(2): 507–15.

90. Commonwealth of Australia, *Report of the Committee of Economic Enquiry* (Canberra: Commonwealth of Australia, 1965), 2 vols.

91. Cabinet Submission 143, 15 March 1967, Attachment, p. 6 (emphasis in original). NAA: A5842/2, vol. 5.

92. Cabinet Submission No. 963, 9 Aug. 1965. NAA: A5827/1 vol. 27.

93. A.G. Kenwood, *Australian Economic Interests since Federation* (Melbourne: Oxford University Press, 1995), pp. 197–207; D.W. Edgington, 'Japanese Business Down-Under: Patterns of Japanese Investment in Australia, 1957–1984', Transnational Corporations Research Project, University of Sydney, 1988.

94. Whitwell, *Treasury Line*, pp. 156–75.

Chapter 4: Development Policy in New Zealand

1. PMM (48) 5th mtg, 13 Oct. 1948. NZA: EA 1, Acc. W2619, 153/26/4.

2. The New Zealand pound was at parity with sterling 1948–67. Net capital inflow of the public and private sectors was NZ£92.1 million between 1949–50 and 1957–8. W. Rosenberg, 'Capital Imports and Growth – The Case of New Zealand – Foreign Investment in New Zealand, 1840–1958', *Economic Journal*, 1961 71(1): 101; A.R. Conan, *Capital Imports into Sterling Countries* (London: Macmillan 1960), pp. 8–13.

3. Hawke, *Making of New Zealand*, p. 294; Schenk, *Britain and the Sterling Area*, p. 111.

4. J.D. Gould, *The Rake's Progress: the New Zealand Economy Since 1945* (Auckland: Hodder & Stoughton, 1982), p. 187.

5. Mabbett, *Trade, Employment and Welfare*, p. 131.

6. The eighteenth-century physiocrats held that all value derived from the produce of the land. C. Clark, 'Development Economics: the Early Years', in G.M. Meier and D. Seers (eds) *Pioneers in Development* (New York: Oxford

University Press, 1984), pp. 69–70; A.M. Endres, 'The Development of Economists' Policy Advice in New Zealand, 1930–34: With Particular Reference to Belshaw's Contribution', *Australian Economic History Review*, 1990 30(1): 64–78. Clark, *Economics of 1960*, pp. 70–1; Keynes, *Collected Works*, vol. XXVII, pp. 342–3.

7. A.G.B. Fisher, *The Clash of Progress and Security* (London: Macmillan, 1935); A.M. Endres, ' "Structural" Economic Thought in New Zealand: the Interwar Contribution of A.G.B. Fisher', *New Zealand Economic Papers*, 1988 22: 35–49; *idem*, 'The Political Economy of W.B. Sutch: Toward a critical Appreciation', *New Zealand Economic Papers*, 1986 20: 19–23; Hawke, *Making of New Zealand*, p. 164.

8. J.V.T. Baker, *The New Zealand People at War: War Economy* (Wellington: Department of Internal Affairs, 1965), pp. 147–80.

9. External Affairs to NZ Charge d'Affaires, Washington, 2 Feb. 1946. NZA: EA, 104/4/1, pt 5.

10. Ibid. The Future Role of the Manufacturing Industries in the New Zealand Economy, 1 May 1946, preface.

11. Ibid., pp. 7–8, 12–16.

12. J. Meade, *Collected Papers*, eds S. Howson and D. Moggridge (London: Unwin Hyman, 1990), vol. 4, p. 328.

13. Some Points Made by Mr Ashwin, 20 June 1944. BoEA: OV 59/20.

14. UK High Commission Wellington to Dominions Office, 18 Feb. 1947. PRO: BT 11/4046.

15. Note of Meeting Between the President of the Board of Trade and Mr Sullivan, New Zealand Minister of Supply and Munitions, 4 Jan. 1945. PRO: BT 11/2771.

16. J. Martin, 'Economic Policy-Making in the Early Post-War Years', in J. Whitwell and M.A. Thompson (eds), *Society and Culture: Economic Perspectives* (Wellington: New Zealand Association of Economists, 1991), vol. 1, pp. 256–72.

17. Notes Prepared by the Department of Agriculture on the Possible Consequences on New Zealand Farming of the US Proposals for International Trade and Employment, 24 April 1946. NZA: EA, 104/4/1, pt 5; J.B. Condliffe, 'The International Position as it Affects New Zealand', *Economic Record*, 1939 15 (New Zealand Centennial Supplement): 17–24; *idem*, 'New Zealand's Experiment in Economic Planning', *American Economic Review*, 1957 47(6): 930–45.

18. J. Singleton, 'Anglo-New Zealand Financial Relations', p. 142; Ministry of External Affairs to UK High Commission Wellington, 11 May 1948. NZA: T 1, 61/1, pt 1.

19. Martin, *Holding the Balance*, pp. 267–71.

20. Quoted in I. McGibbon (ed.), *Undiplomatic Dialogue: Letters Between Carl Berendsen and Alister McIntosh 1943–1952* (Auckland: Auckland University Press, 1993), p. 177.

21. New Zealand and the European Recovery Programme: Development of Resources, 27 Sept. 1948. NZA: EA 1, 153/26/5. Discussions on Long-term Economic Planning with Representatives of Commonwealth Governments, 21 Sept. 1948; SADWP (48) 10th mtg, 22 Sept. 1948; Official Talks with Australia and New Zealand on Long-term Planning and Development,

27 Oct. 1948. PRO: T 229/545. Fraser to Addison, 30 Sept. 1947. T 238/249. McKinnon, 'Impact of War', pp. 202–6.

22. Boulter to Board of Trade, 19 Jan. 1948. PRO: BT 11/4045.

23. Notes on Talks with Australian and New Zealand Representatives, 29 Sept. 1948. PRO: T 229/545.

24. M.W. Guest, 'The Murupara Project: the Tasman Pulp and Paper Company Ltd and Industrial Development in New Zealand 1945–1963', MA thesis, Victoria University of Wellington, 1997; M. Guest and J. Singleton, 'The Murupara Project and Industrial Development in New Zealand 1945–65', *Australian Economic History Review*, 1999 39(1): 52–71.

25. Guest and Singleton, 'Murupara': 54–5.

26. Underlined in original. The World Pulp and Paper Trade, undated, 1943. NZA: F, Acc. W3129, 80.002.

27. Murupara Pulp and Paper Scheme, 24 Aug. 1949. NZA: F, Acc. W3129, 80.002.

28. Works Programme and Inflation, 21 Dec. 1949; Capital Works Programme, 24 March 1950. NZA: T 1, 25/23.

29. Mabbett, *Trade, Employment, and Welfare*, pp. 115, 117, 129, 140. The phrase 'colonial socialism' derives from N.G. Butlin, 'Trends in Public/Private Relations, 1901–75', in B. Head (ed.), *State and Economy in Australia* (Melbourne: Oxford University Press, 1983).

30. On this firm see S. Parker, *Made in New Zealand: the Story of Jim Fletcher* (Wellington: Hodder & Stoughton, 1994).

31. Guest and Singleton, 'Murupara': 57–9.

32. Memorandum from Committee to Investigate the Tasman Proposal, 7 Dec. 1951. NZA: F, Acc. W3192, 80.002. Cobbold to Gilbert, 13 June 1952. BoEA: G 3/56. Snelling to Stevenson, 22 April 1952; Snelling to Morley, 22 April 1952. OV 59/4.

33. Notes of Conversation with Rowan, 18 June 1952. BoEA: G 3/16.

34. Prime Ministers' Conference: Note from Financial Adviser at the British High Commission, Wellington, 8 Nov. 1952. PRO: DO 35/6478. A. Cairn-cross (ed.), *The Robert Hall Diaries 1947–53* (London: Unwin Hyman, 1989), p. 248. Ashwin to Beevor, 9 Nov. 1954 and 22 Feb. 1955; Beevor to Ashwin, 29 Nov. 1954. NZA: T 1, 52/539/29.

35. Ashwin to Woodward, 9 Oct. 1952; Ashwin to Gaston, 12 Nov. 1952, Woodward to Ashwin, 18 Sept. 1953 and 2 Oct. 1953; NZ Ambassador Washington to External Affairs, 30 July 1953 and 11 Feb. 1954; Memo-randum from NZ Foreign Service, 23 Oct. 1953; Woodward to Ashwin, 27 Nov. 1953. NZA: T 1, 52/539/14. J. Hirsch, 'Export Credit Insurance and Investment Guaranties', in US Senate, Committee on Banking and Cur-rency, *Study of Export–Import Bank and World Bank* (Washington, DC, 1954), pt 2, p. 1243; B.I. Kaufman, *Trade and Aid: Eisenhower's Foreign Economic Policy, 1953–1961* (Baltimore: Johns Hopkins University Press, 1982), pp. 29–32.

36. Gould, *Rake's Progress*, p. 222; Guest and Singleton, 'Murupara': 64–5; M.A. Amsalem, *Technology Choice in Developing Countries: the Textile and Pulp and Paper Industries* (Cambridge, Mass.: MIT Press, 1983).

37. Brief for Commonwealth Economic Conference, Oct. 1952, pp. 165–6. NZA: T 1, 61/3/12, pt 5.

38. New Zealand Pulp and Paper Development, 29 Jan. 1952. BoEA: G 3/107. Confidential Annex to Proceedings of the Commonwealth Economic Conference, Dec. 1952, pp. 2–3. PRO: DO 35/6489. Fforde, *Bank of England*, pp. 423–5; Singleton, 'British Engineering'; Schenk, *Britain and the Sterling Area*, p. 38.

39. New Zealand Studies, Paper B, Factors in Increasing Farm Production, 8 Sept. 1952. PRO: T 236/4995. Development in New Zealand, 4 Dec. 1953. NZA: EA 1, Acc. W2619, 153/38/6.

40. New Zealand Development, Paper A, 22 Sept. 1952, p. 1. NZA: T 1, 61/3/12, pt 5.

41. Ibid., New Zealand Development, Paper B, 22 Sept. 1952, p. 14.

42. Development in New Zealand in 1953, 29 Oct. 1953, p. 2. PRO: T 236/5000.

43. Notes on New Zealand Studies, 29 Sept. 1952, pp. 2, 4. PRO: T 236/4996.

44. Development in the United Kingdom, 22 Sept. 1952, p. 28. NZA: T 1, 61/3/12, pt 5.

45. Commonwealth Economic Conference, Preparatory Meeting of Officials, Committee on Development Policy, Minutes of 2nd Meeting, 29 Sept. 1952, and 3rd Meeting, 30 Sept. 1952. NZA: T 1, 61/3/12, pt 4. R.S. Parker (ed.), *Economic Stability in New Zealand* (Wellington: New Zealand Institute of Public Administration, 1953), pp. 7, 46, 124.

46. Martin, *Holding the Balance*, pp. 271–5; N.S. Woods, 'Immigration and the Labour Force', *Industrial Development Conference Papers* (Wellington: Government Printer, 1960), p. 6. EP (53) 34, Immigration, 27 Nov. 1953. NZA: T 1, 61/1/8.

47. Singleton, 'Anglo-New Zealand Financial Relations': 139–57.

48. Price to Swinton, 19 Feb. 1953. PRO: DO 35/6479.

49. Ashwin to Rowan, 26 March 1954; Rowan to Ashwin, 15 April 1954. NZA: T 1, 61/1/5. First Progress Report on UK Investment in the Sterling Commonwealth, 10 Aug. 1953. PRO: T 236/5439. Second Progress Report on UK Investment, 27 Nov. 1953; Third Progress Report on UK Investment, 31 May 1954. T 236/5440. New Zealand: Application for a £10 million Loan from London, 28 May 1954. BoEA: OV 59/4.

50. Greensmith to Rowan, 2 Dec. 1955. BoEA: OV 59/5. Note of Meeting at the UK Treasury, 23 Sept. 1955. NZA: T 1, 61/1/5. Washington Meetings, Sept. 1956: State of the London Market, 13 Sept. 1956. PRO: T 236/5442.

51. This operation was later merged into the £20 million sterling loan of 1958. Singleton, 'Anglo-New Zealand Financial Relations': 150.

52. Jenkyns to Haslam, 10 Oct. 1956; New Zealand: London Market Borrowing, 17 Oct. 1956. BoEA: OV 59/5. Rowan to Greensmith, 29 Oct. 1956. NZA: T 1, 61/1/5.

53. Lee to Littler, 16 May 1957. PRO: BT 213/96.

54. Schenk, *Britain and the Sterling Area*, pp. 48, 92–3; Scrimgeour to Greensmith, 19 Sept. 1957. NZA: T 1, 61/1/5.

55. *Report of the Royal Commission on Monetary, Banking, and Credit Systems* (Wellington: Government Printer, 1956), pp. 179, 180–8; G.R. Hawke and B.A.D. Wijewardane, 'New Zealand and the International Monetary Fund', *Economic Record*, 1972 48(1): 93. IMF – New Zealand Capital Needs, 20 April 1956. NZA: T 1, 52/880/2/2.

56. New Zealand: London Market Borrowing, 17 Oct. 1956. BoEA: OV 59/5.

57. G.R. Hawke, *Between Governments and Banks: a History of the Reserve Bank of New Zealand* (Wellington: A.R. Shearer, 1973), p. 117. RBNZ Board Minutes, 14 Nov. 1957, 12 Dec. 1957, 19 Feb. 1958, 21 May 1958. NZA: ABTW 6986, Acc. W4656, vol. 5.

58. This sum included the £10 million sterling issue already authorized for 1957–8, but delayed at Britain's request. Discussion between the Prime Ministers of the UK and New Zealand on 24 Jan. 1958. PRO: DO 35/6522. Jenkyns to Bailey, 21 Feb. 1958. BoEA: OV 59/5. Hawke and Wijewardane, 'New Zealand and the IMF': 96.

59. Greensmith to Rowan, 30 April 1958. BoEA: OV 59/5.

60. Ibid., New Zealand: Note of Meeting at Treasury, 14 May 1958.

61. Report by the Sub-Committee on United Kingdom External Investments, 6 March 1959, paras 31, 32, 37. PRO: CAB 134/1905.

62. The RBNZ also arranged a credit of A£10 million with the Commonwealth Bank of Australia, and £4.1 million sterling was borrowed from Australian insurance companies operating in New Zealand. B.A.D. Wijewardane, 'Official Overseas Borrowing of New Zealand, 1950/51 to 1967/68, With Particular Reference to Drawings from the International Monetary Fund', MA thesis, Victoria University of Wellington, 1970, p. 19.

63. W.S. Goosman in *NZPD*, vol. 319, 22 July 1959, p. 345.

64. Fisher to Nash, 10 Nov. 1958. NZA: T 1, 52/880/2/2. Hawke and Wijewardane, 'New Zealand and the IMF': 95; C.G.F. Simkin, 'What Should Be Done About the Sterling Area: New Zealand', *Bulletin of the Oxford University Institute of Statistics*, 1959 21(4): 272.

65. MacGillivray to Symons, 4 April 1960, 15 June 1960. PRO: T 236/6490.

66. *International Monetary Fund and World Bank: Implications of New Zealand Membership* (Wellington: Government Printer, 1961); Singleton, 'Anglo-New Zealand Financial Relations': 154–5.

67. Wijewardane, 'Official Overseas Borrowing', pp. 21–30; Horsefield and Vries, *The IMF 1945–1965*, vol. 2, pp. 460–1; Gifford et al., *Australian Banking*, p. 315.

68. Exchange Allocation and Import Selection, 21 Jan. 1958, p. 14. NZA: IC 1, Acc. W1955, 72/1. W.B. Sutch, 'New Zealand's Manufacturing Development Since 1 January 1958' in *Industrial Development Conference Papers* (Wellington: Government Printer, 1960).

69. W.B. Sutch, *Colony or Nation? Economic Crises in New Zealand from the 1860s to the 1960s* (Sydney: Sydney University Press, 1966), pp. 91, 98–9.

70. Import Quotas for Protective Purposes, 25 May 1956, p. 6. NZA: T 1, 61/1/8, pt 2.

71. D. Copland, 'Economic Problems for New Zealand in an Expanding World'; W. Nash, 'Building the Future: Opening Address to the Conference'; W.B. Sutch, 'Programme for Growth'; *idem*, 'Education for Industry', all in *IDC Papers*; *Industrial Development Conference Report* (Wellington: Government Printer, 1960); Endres, 'Sutch': 26–30.

72. E (61) 1, Nelson Cotton Mill, 17 Jan. 1961; E (61) M4, CCEFP Minutes, 31 Jan. 1961. NZA: T, Acc. W2666, 61/1/8. J. Foreman-Peck, *Smith & Nephew in the Health Care Industry* (Aldershot: Edward Elgar, 1995), p.192; J. Marshall, *Memoirs* (Auckland: Collins, 1989), vol. 2, pp. 15–18; Hawke, *Making of New Zealand*, p. 263, A.P. O' Shea, 'The New Zealand Farming Industry Present and Future', in *IDC Papers*, pp. 6, 10–12.

73. Hawke, *Making of New Zealand*, p. 251.
74. *The World Bank Report on the New Zealand Economy 1968* (Wellington: Government Printer, 1968), pp. 31–48.
75. R.S. Deane, *Foreign Investment in New Zealand Manufacturing* (Wellington: Sweet & Maxwell, 1970), pp. 30, 357, 359.
76. J.H. Bamberg, *The History of the British Petroleum Company* (Cambridge: Cambridge University Press, 1984), vol. 2, p. 297. Record of an Interview with Mr Bromley, Chairman of the Industries Committee, 31 July 1945; Boulter to Board of Trade, 17 Dec. 1945. PRO: BT 11/4046.
77. Proposed Treaty Between the USA and New Zealand, 17 June 1948. NZA: EA 1, Acc. W1784, 58/9/27, pt 2.
78. Stanley to Berendson, 25 May 1951. NZA: EA 1, 35/22/1.
79. Ibid., Shanahan to New Zealand Embassy, Washington, 26 June 1950.
80. Schenk, *Britain and the Sterling Area*, p. 110; J.N. Behrman, 'Foreign Associates and their Financing', in R.F. Mikesell (ed.), *US Private and Government Investment Abroad* (Eugene: University of Oregon Press, 1962), p. 80. Note on US Investment in New Zealand, 14 April 1953; Memorandum from US Government to New Zealand Government, 27 April 1953; Dollar Investment, 16 Sept. 1953; CCEFP Minutes, 15 Dec. 1953. NZA: EA 1, 35/22/1.
81. Memo from Sutch for Minister of Industries and Commerce, 21 Sept. 1959. NZA: IC 1, 29/11/1, pt 5.
82. Nash, 'Building the Future', p. 14.
83. Wright to Superior Waxes, 3 April 1959. NZA: IC 1, 29/11/1, pt 4.
84. Victa to Datson, 21 Sept. 1959. NZA: IC 1, 29/11/1, pt 5.
85. W. Fisher, 'Ownership and Control of Industry in New Zealand Manufacturing', in *IDC Papers*, pp. 4–5.
86. Note on Japanese Investment in New Zealand, April 1959. NZA: IC 1, 29/11/1, pt 4. Memos from Sutch for Minister of Industries and Commerce, 21 Sept. 1959 and 22 Sept. 1959. E (59) M49, CCEFP Minutes, 30 Sept 1959; Lewin to NZ Commercial Secretary, Tokyo, 11 May 1960. IC 1, 29/11/1, pt 5.
87. W. Rosenberg, 'Financial and Monetary Policy and Capital Requirements for Industrial Development in New Zealand', in *IDC Papers*; *idem*, 'A Critical Perspective on Foreign Investment', in P. Enderwick (ed.), *Foreign Investment: the New Zealand Experience* (Palmerston North: Dunmore, 1998), pp. 199–214; Sutch, 'Colony or Nation', pp. 99–102.
88. Record of Discussion between Kono and Marshall, 1 March 1962. NZA: T 1, 61/6/20, pt 1.
89. B. Rosenberg, 'Foreign Investment in New Zealand: the Current Position', in Enderwick, *Foreign Investment*, p. 32.
90. Deane, *Foreign Investment*, pp. 5–7 M. Akoorie, 'The Historical Role of Foreign Investment in the New Zealand Economy', in Enderwick, *Foreign Investment*, pp. 67–91.

Chapter 5: Stresses in the Ottawa System

1. CM (56) 49th mtg, 12 July 1956. PRO: CAB 128/30.
2. PEC (52) 11, CEC, Memorandum by the Minister of Housing and Local Government, 5 Aug. 1952. PRO: T 236/3071.

3. EEP (54) 1st mtg, 9 July 1954. PRO: CAB 134/869.
4. Robertson, 'Complementarity': 106–9.
5. Dyster and Meredith, *Australia in the International Economy*, pp. 202–3.
6. Lee, *Search for Security*, p. 147.
7. 24th Report of the Inter-Departmental Dollar Committee, 21 March 1951; 26th Report, 20 July 1951; Dollar Import Licensing Budget for Sept. Quarter, 1951; Texts of Letters dated 2nd Aug. 1951 from the Treasurer to the Prime Minister and to the Minister for Trade and Customs. NAA: 1967/391/1, Box 2/1.
8. Hawke, *Government and Banks*, p. 115; Reserve Bank of New Zealand, *Overseas Trade and Finance with Particular Reference to New Zealand* (Wellington: RBNZ, 1966), pp. 208–9. Removal of Import Control and the Balance of Payments if Wool Prices Fall, 27 June 1951; Reduction of Protection by Import Control: Wool Receipts, 18 July 1951; The Balance of Payments and Import Policy, 13 Dec. 1951. NZA: T 1, 61/1. RBNZ Board Minutes, 19 Dec. 1951. ABTW 6986, Acc. W4656, vol. 4. UK High Commissioner in New Zealand to CRO, undated, 1951. PRO: T 236/3287.
9. Decision No. 254, Sterling Area Dollar Position and Recent UK Measures, 4 Dec. 1951. NAA: A4905XMI, vol. 7.
10. Meeting of Commonwealth Finance Ministers, Preliminary Meeting of Officials, Minutes of Meeting on 9 Jan. 1952, pp. 148–9. PRO: CAB 133/123.
11. Ibid., p. 149.
12. Record of Meeting of Commonwealth Finance Ministers, 15 Jan. 1952, pp. 27–9. PRO: CAB 133/123. The Long-Term Problem and Convertibility of Sterling, Jan. 1952. NAA: A4905XMI, vol. 9.
13. Fforde, *Bank of England*, pp. 423–5.
14. Record of Meeting of Commonwealth Finance Ministers, 17 and 18 Jan. 1952, pp. 8–9, 13, 27. PRO: CAB 133/123.
15. Crawford, *Australian Trade Policy*, pp. 508–10, 565.
16. Submission No. 262, Australia's Balance of Payments, 29 April 1952, Appendix 'B'. NAA: A4905XMI, vol. 10.
17. Crawford, *Australian Trade Policy*, p. 492.
18. See clipping in NAA: A571, 1950/614, pt 3.
19. Ibid. Import Licensing and Great Britain: Statement by the Prime Minister, 17 March 1952.
20. Importers could apply for additional overseas exchange, but such cases were referred to the Reserve Bank. RBNZ, *Overseas Trade*, pp. 240–2; Schenk, *Britain and the Sterling Area*, pp. 82–3. Minister of External Affairs to All New Zealand Posts Overseas, 11 March 1952; Aide Memoire from UK High Commissioner, 22 April 1952. NZA: T 1, 61/1.
21. Using a phrase that might have been more appropriately applied to the Australian end of the industry. Draft Message to Australian Prime Minister, 31 March 1952. PRO: T 236/3026.
22. Note of Meeting with Australian Delegation on Import Restrictions, 29 May 1952. PRO: T 236/3027.
23. UK High Commissioner in Australia to CRO, 31 March 1952; Menzies to Butler, 8 April 1952. PRO: T 236/3026. Notes of Meetings with Australian Delegation, 29 May and 9 June 1952. T 236/3027. Mr. Menzies' Visit:

Minutes of a Meeting of Ministers, 28 May 1952, pp. 3–6. NAA: A1209/23, 57/5919, pt 1.

24. Schenk, *Britain and the Sterling Area*, pp. 81–2; J.O.N. Perkins, *Britain and Australia* (Melbourne: Melbourne University Press, 1962), pp. 33–5, 40–2.

25. S. Onslow, *Backbench Debate Within the Conservative Party and its Influence on British Foreign Policy, 1948–57* (Basingstoke: Macmillan, 1997), pp. 20–1, 51, 85–7; A. Seldon, *Churchill's Indian Summer* (London: Hodder & Stoughton, 1981), pp. 178–86; W.A. Brusse, *Tariffs, Trade and European Integration, 1947–1957* (New York: St. Martin's Press, 1997), pp. 198–9.

26. Proposals for CEC; Meeting of Commonwealth Ministers, undated, apparently taken from the minutes of the UK Cabinet, including an account of Menzies' reasons for wanting such a meeting and the decision of Cabinet. NAA: A1209/23, 57/5919.

27. Fforde, *Bank of England*, pp. 417–92.

28. Brusse, *Tariffs, Trade*, p. 109. PEC (52) 5th mtg, 5 Sept. 1952, 7th mtg, 11 Sept. 1952; PEC (52) 33, Imperial Preference: Memorandum by the President of the Board of Trade, 9 Sept. 1952. PRO: T 236/3072.

29. PEC (52) 7th mtg, 11 Sept 1952; PEC (52) 32, Japan and the GATT, 9 Sept. 1952; Note on Japan and the GATT, 10 Sept. 1952. PRO: T 236/3072.

30. CEC (FT) (52) 5th mtg, 2 Dec. 1952. NAA: A1209/42, 57/5717.

31. Brief for CEC, undated, pp. 98, 99. NZA: T 1, 61/3/12, pt 5.

32. CEC (FT) (52) 3rd mtg, 1 Dec. 1952; 5th mtg, 2 Dec. 1952. NAA: A1209/42, 57/5717.

33. Economic Policy Conference: General Objective, 16 Sept. 1952. NAA: A1209/23, 57/5919, pt 2. Summary of Australia's Obligations on Trade Policy, 25 Aug. 1952. A1209/23, 57/5723, pt 2. Cabinet Minute, Decision No. 594, 11–12 Nov. 1952. A1209/23, 57/5723, pt 3.

34. CEC (FT) (A) 5th and 6th mtgs, 6 Dec. 1952; CEC (52) 7, Imperial Preference: Report by Officials, 7 Dec. 1952. NAA: A1209/42, 57/5717.

35. Quoted in Polk, *Sterling*, pp. 267–8; Schenk, 'Sterling Alternatives': 277.

36. Curzon. *Mulilateral Commercial Diplomacy*, p. 66; Seldon, *Indian Summer*, p. 181.

37. R.H. Snape, 'Australia's Relations with GATT', *Economic Record*, 1984 60(1): 18. Review of the GATT, 17 May 1955. NAA: A4906, vol. 14. Brief for GATT sessions, undated, 1954; CRG (54) 10th and 11th mtgs, 11 Oct. 1954; Commonwealth Meeting on the Review of GATT: Report of the New Zealand Delegation, 15 Oct. 1954. NZA: T 1, 52/904/2/4, pt 1. Commonwealth Discussions and Review of GATT; View of Industries and Commerce Department, undated, 1954; EFP (E) (55) 56, Review of GATT, 29 July 1955. T 1, 52/904/2/4, pt 2.

38. Pollard, *Development of the British Economy*, p. 166.

39. R.E. Rowthorn and J.R. Wells, *De-Industrialization and Foreign Trade* (Cambridge: Cambridge University Press, 1987), p. 106; J.K. Bowers, 'British Agricultural Policy Since the Second World War', *Agricultural History Review*, 1985 33: 66–76; M.J. Smith, *The Politics of Agricultural Support in Britain* (Aldershot: Dartmouth, 1990). Agricultural Policy, 5 June 1952. PRO: T 230/245.

40. UK High Commissioner in New Zealand to Dominions Office, 30 March 1943. PRO: BT 11/2276.

41. Crawford, *Australian Trade Policy*, p. 223; Hayward, *Golden Jubilee*, p. 83. EA (52) 21st mtg, 9 July 1952. PRO: CAB 134/842.
42. Seldon, *Indian Summer*, pp. 207–13, 217; M.F.W. Hemming, C.M. Miles, and G.F. Ray, 'A Statistical Summary of the Extent of Import Control in the UK since the War', *Review of Economic Studies*, 1959 26(2): 83, 105; F. Gordon-Ashworth, *International Commodity Control* (London: Croom Helm, 1984), pp. 141–6; I. Zweiniger-Bargielowska, *Austerity in Britain: Rationing, Controls, and Consumption 1939–1955* (Oxford: Oxford University Press, 2000), pp. 29–30, 34–6. Long-Term Food Contracts, 23 Jan. 1952. PRO: T 230/245.
43. Economist Intelligence Unit, *The Commonwealth and Europe* (London: EIU, 1960), p. 104. Forthcoming Negotiations on Agricultural Policy with the UK Government, undated, 1957. NZA: T 1, 61/3/21/2/57, pt 1. UK/New Zealand Trade Discussions, UK Desiderata, Annex A, 25 Feb. 1958. PRO: BT 11/5659.
44. UK High Commissioner in New Zealand to Lord Home, 20 May 1956. PRO: DO 35/5720.
45. Rooth, 'Imperial Self-insufficiency': 33–8.
46. CTEC, September 1958, Report of the New Zealand Delegation, pp. 5–6. NZA: T 1, 61/3/24, pt 3. Minutes of CTEC, Sept. 1958, pp. 107–20, 135–40. NZA: IC 22, Acc. W1837, Box 26, Item 63.
47. UKATA was dated 1957 but came into force in 1956. Crawford, *Australian Trade Policy*, p. 319.
48. Cabinet Submission No. 116, Ottawa Agreement, 16 April 1956, p. 1. NAA: A4926XMI, vol. 6.
49. Ibid., Cabinet Submission No. 138, Proposals Concerning the UK and Australia Trade Agreement, 7 May 1956. NAA: A4926XMI, vol. 6. Cabinet Submission No. 410, UK Trade Talks, undated, 1956. A4926XMI, vol. 17.
50. Crawford, *Australian Trade Policy*, p. 322. Cabinet Submission No. 138, Proposals Concerning the UK and Australia Trade Agreement, 7 May 1956, pp. 5–7. NAA: A4926XMI, vol. 6.
51. Crawford, *Australian Trade Policy*, p. 331.
52. Note for Menzies from Brown, 10 May 1956; Notes on Cabinet Submission No. 138, undated, 1956; Cabinet Minute, Decision No. 174, 10 May 1956. NAA: A4926XMI, vol. 6.
53. Trade Talks with Australian Ministers, Brief for Prime Minister, 6 June 1956. PRO: DO 35/5677.
54. J.R.V. Ellison, 'Perfidious Albion? Britain, Plan G and European Integration, 1955–1956', *Contemporary British History*, 1996 10(4): 13–14, 22–3. Notes of Ministerial Meeting on Trade Talks with Australia and the Question of a European Common Market, 22 June 1956; Our Preferences in Australia, by Officials Group, undated, 1956. PRO: DO 35/5678.
55. Note of Talk with Crawford, 30 June 1956. PRO: DO 35/5678.
56. Ibid., Rumbold to Home, 2 July and 6 July 1956; UK/Australian Trade Talks, Notes of Third Meeting, 5 July 1956. PRO: DO 35/5678. UK/Australia Trade Discussions, Notes of Eighth Meeting, 13 July 1956. DO 35/5679. Australian Import Restrictions, 3 Oct. 1956. DO 35/5680.
57. UK/Australian Trade Discussions, Note by Lee, 9 July 1956. PRO: DO 35/5678.
58. CM (56) 49th mtg, 12 July 1956. PRO: CAB 128/30.

59. UK/Australia Trade Discussions, Notes of Eighth Meeting, 13 July 1956. PRO: DO 35/5679.
60. Further Examination of Possible Concessions on Wheat, undated, 1956. PRO: DO 35/5678. Bowen to Curson, 14 Aug. 1956. DO 35/5679.
61. UK/Australia Trade Discussions, Notes of Thirteenth Meeting, 20 July 1956. PRO: DO 35/5679.
62. CM (56) 51st mtg, 20 July 1956. PRO: CAB 128/30.
63. Ibid., CM (56) 52nd mtg, 24 July 1956.
64. Ibid., CM (56) 66th mtg, 18 Sept. 1956.
65. Cabinet Submission No. 410, UK Trade Talks, undated, 1956; Cabinet Decision No. 481, 10 Oct. 1956. NAA: A4926/XMI, vol. 17.
66. CM (56) 75th mtg, 30 Oct. 1956. PRO: CAB 128/30.
67. Crawford, *Australian Trade Policy*, pp. 342–6. Cabinet Submission No. 410, UK Trade Talks, undated, 1956; Cabinet Decision No. 481, 10 Oct. 1956. NAA: A4926/XMI, vol. 17. CM (56) 75th mtg, 30 Oct. 1956. PRO: CAB 128/30.
68. *The Economist*, 17 Nov. 1956: 618–19.
69. Crawford, *Australian Trade Policy*, p. 324.
70. J. Singleton, 'New Zealand, Britain and the Survival of the Ottawa Agreement, 1945–77', *Australian Journal of Politics and History*, 1997 43(2): 168–82.
71. Proposed Review of New Zealand's Trade Policy, 30 Nov. 1956. NZA: T 1, 61/1/8. Record of Talk between Rumbold and McIntosh, 10 July 1956. PRO: DO 35/5720. Commonwealth Economic Committee, *Meat: a Review 1958* (London: HMSO, 1958), p. 25.
72. EP (56) 17th mtg, 19 Sept. 1956. PRO: CAB 134/1229.
73. Submission of the New Zealand Meat Producers' Board, Dec. 1956. NZA: T 1, 61/3/21, pt 2.
74. Ibid., Minutes of Meeting on Review of Trade Policy, 5 Dec. 1956. Endres, 'Sutch': 25.
75. Review of New Zealand's Trade Policy, 16 Jan. 1957. NZA: T 1, 61/3/21, pt 1.
76. Brief for UK/NZ Trade Discussions, undated, 1958. NZA: IC 1, Box 21, Item 45. Commonwealth Secretary to New Zealand Prime Minister, 12 Feb. 1957. T 1, 61/3/21, pt 1. Notes of Trade Discussions between New Zealand and the UK, 8 April to 29 May 1957, pp. 13–14. T 1, 61/3/25.
77. New Zealand, *Appendix to the Journals of the House of Representatives* (1957), vol. 1, A15: 4.
78. *Financial Times*, 30 May 1957.
79. Gould, *Rake's Progress*, pp. 83, 86.
80. Note of Discussion on Timing of Negotiation of UK/New Zealand Trade Agreement, 15 Oct. 1957. PRO: DO 35/8736.
81. Memorandum on the Revision of the Ottawa Agreement, 2 May 1958. NZA: T 1, 61/3/25,
82. P.G. Elkan, 'Industrial Protection in New Zealand 1952 to 1967', Technical Memorandum No. 15, New Zealand Institute of Economic Research (Wellington: NZIER, 1972), p. 41; Brief for UK/NZ Trade Discussions, undated, 1958. NZA: IC 1, Box 21, Item 45.
83. UK/NZ Trade Talks, Minutes of First Meeting between Delegations, 22 April

1958. NZA: T 1, 61/3/25. UK/NZ Trade Discussions, UK Desiderata, 25 Feb. 1958. PRO: BT 11/5659.

84. New Zealand cited collusion in various industries, including electric cables, linoleum, and cotton textiles. A call for tenders for the supply of railway axles and tyres elicited five identical proposals from UK firms. UK/NZ Trade Talks, Minutes of Second Meeting between Delegations, 23 April 1958. NZA: T 1, 61/3/25. Brief for UK/NZ Trade Discussions, undated, 1958. IC 1, Box 21, Item 45.

85. In June 1956 the export price of US steel sections was US$111.75 compared with US$145.60 for British sections. UK/NZ Trade Talks, Minutes of Third Meeting between Delegations, 23 April 1958; Minutes of Seventh Meeting, 13 May 1958. NZA: T 1, 61/3/25.

86. Import Quotas for Protective Purposes, 25 May 1956. NZA: T 1, 61/1/8. Mallaby to Laithwaite, 14 July 1958. PRO: DO 35/8470.

87. Johnsen to External Affairs, 17 May 1958. NZA: T 1, 61/3/25.

88. Ibid., Eccles to Skinner, 23 June 1958.

89. Memorandum on UK/NZ Trade Discussions, July 1958, p. 3. PRO: BT 11/5655.

90. An exception would be made if New Zealand formed a free trade area with Australia. New Zealand Trade Talks: Brief for Ministers' Meeting with Mr Nash, 26 Aug. 1958, p. 3. PRO: BT 11/5659.

91. Nash to Macmillan, 25 July 1958. NZA: T 1, 61/3/25.

92. Ibid., Nash to Macmillan, 18 Aug. 1958.

93. Ibid., Macmillan to Nash, 18 Aug. 1958.

94. Ibid., UK/NZ Trade Discussions 1958, Heads of Agreement, 30 Sept. 1958; Memorandum for Mr Nordmeyer on Trade Relations with UK, 16 Sept. 1958.

95. *United Nations Treaty Series* 354 (1960), pp. 162–93.

96. Memorandum for Mr Nordmeyer on Trade Relations with UK, 16 Sept. 1958. NZA: T 1, 61/3/25.

97. Ward, *Command of Cooperatives*, pp. 175–7; Stone to Treasury, 29 April 1958. NAA: A571/68, 55/2566, pt 4. Stone to Treasury, 28 May 1958. A571/68, 55/2566, pt 2. CC (58) 39th mtg, 8 May 1958. PRO: CAB 128/32.

98. Minutes of Officials' Meeting on New Zealand Trade Discussions, 11 Aug. 1958. PRO: BT 11/5660.

99. Sinclair, *Nash*, p. 317.

100. J.G. Diefenbaker, *One Canada* (Toronto: Macmillan, 1976), vol. 2, p. 92; *The Round Table*, 1958 193: 50–6.

Chapter 6: The Search for New Markets

1. EFP D-16, Working Group on Review of American Economic Foreign Policy, Special Problem of Japan, December 9, 1952, pp. 1, 11. DDEL: U.S. President's Commission on Foreign Economic Policy: Records, 1953–1954, Box 63, File: Studies – State Dept Documents (4).

2. *NZPD*, vol. 305, 24 March 1955, p. 26.

3. *CAPD*, vol. 194, 11 Nov. 1947, pp. 1885–7.

4. R. Ovendale, *The English-Speaking Alliance: Britain, the United States, the*

Dominions and the Cold War, 1945–1951 (London: George Allen & Unwin 1985), pp. 153, 161–5.

5. W.S Borden, *The Pacific Alliance: United States Foreign Economic Policy and Japanese Trade Recovery, 1947–1955* (Madison: University of Wisconsin Press, 1984).

6. B.I. Kaufman, 'Eisenhower's Foreign Economic Policy With Respect to Asia', in W.I. Cohen and A. Iriye (eds), *The Great Powers in East Asia: 1953–1960* (New York: Columbia University Press, 1990), p. 107.

7. K.E. Calder, *Crisis and Compensation: Public Policy and Political Stability in Japan, 1949–1986* (Princeton: Princeton University Press, 1988), pp. 36–7, 77–86; J. Welfield, *An Empire in Eclipse: Japan in the Postwar American Alliance System* (London: Athlone, 1988); pp. 37–41, 54–6; H. Kapur, *The Awakening Giant: China's Ascension in World Politics* (Alphen aan den Rijn: Sijthoff & Noordhoff, 1981), pp. 108–19; C.M. Wilbur, 'Japan and the Rise of Communist China', in H. Borton et al., *Japan Between East and West* (New York: Harper, 1957), pp. 199–239.

8. Minutes of Cabinet Meeting, Aug. 6, 1954; Briefing Paper for Cabinet, What Japan Must Do To Balance its Trade, Aug. 3, 1954. DDEL: Ann Whitman File, Cabinet Series, Box 3, File: Cabinet Meeting of Aug. 6, 1954.

9. Foreign Service Despatch from American Embassy, Tokyo. Subject: US Economic Policy for Japan. Signed Robert Murphy. Feb. 4, 1953, pp. 5–6. DDEL: White House Central Files, Confidential File, Subject Series, Box 67, File: Dept of State (thru Sept. 1953) (2).

10. NSC 5713/2 – Long-Range US Policy Interests in Australia and New Zealand, August 23, 1957. DDEL: White House Office, Office of the Special Assistant for National Security Affairs: Records, 1952–61, Policy Papers Subseries, Box 21, File: NSC 5713/2. NSC 6109 Long-range US Policy Interests in Australia and New Zealand, Jan. 16, 1961. White House Office, Office of the Special Assistant for National Security Affairs: Records, 1952–61, Papers Received since Jan. 10, 1961 Series, Box 1, File (6).

11. K. Tsokhas, *Markets, Money and Empire* (Carlton, Vic.: Melbourne University Press, 1990); C. Wurm, *Business, Politics, and International Relations* (Cambridge: Cambridge University Press, 1993).

12. G.C. Allen, *Japan's Economic Policy* (London: Macmillan, 1980), pp. 186–94; G. Daniels, 'Britain's View of Post-war Japan, 1945–9', in I. Nish (ed.), *Anglo-Japanese Alienation, 1919–1952* (Cambridge: Cambridge University Press, 1982); Rix, *Coming to Terms*, pp. 16–17, 29–61, 103, 119–22, 149–51; Pinkstone, *Global Connections*, p. 178.

13. L.P. Singh, *The Politics of Economic Cooperation in Asia* (Columbia: University of Missouri Press, 1966), pp. 169–82. Report on Trade Possibilities for New Zealand in south-east Asian Area, 28 June 1951, p. 2. NZA: EA 1, Acc. W2619, 40/16/1. Memorandum on the General Trend of Trade Between Japan and New Zealand, 30 Dec. 1952. T 1, 61/6/20/1.

14. Rix, *Coming to Terms*, pp. 87–90; J. Singleton, 'New Zealand's Economic Relations with Japan in the 1950s', *Australian Economic History Review*, 1997 37(1): 2–3.

15. Japan Cablegram No. 16 from Thomas, 16 Jan. 1951; Report of Cabinet Working Party on Long Term Economic Relations with Japan, 6 Feb. 1951. BoEA: OV 16/69.

16. Rix, *Coming to Terms*, p. 132. Report on Trade Relations with Japan, Annexes A and B, 26 Sept. 1952. NZA: IC 1, Acc. W2006, 114/1/1, pt 3. Japanese Competition, 23 Nov. 1951. PRO: BT 11/4909. Report on Japanese Competition from the Tokyo Embassy, 9 Nov. 1951. BT 11/4918.

17. V. Ferretti, 'Japan's Admission to GATT (1951–1955)', in P. Lowe, V. Ferretti, and I. Nish, *Japan in the 1950s*, STICERD Discussion Paper, IS/97/322, LSE, 1997; P. Korhonen, *Japan and the Pacific Free Trade Area* (London: Routledge, 1994), pp. 73–80; G. Patterson, *Discrimination in International Trade* (Princeton: Princeton University Press, 1965), pp. 272–86; T. Shiraishi, *Japan's Trade Policies 1945 to the Present Day* (London: Athlone, 1989), pp. 63–92; Kaufman, *Trade and Aid*, pp. 39–41.

18. PEC (52) 5th mtg, 5 Sept. 1952; Note on Japan and the GATT, 10 Sept. 1952. PRO: T 236/3072. EEP (54) 1st mtg, 9 July 1954. CAB 134/869. CC (55) 6th mtg, 24 Jan. 1955. CAB 128/28. *Manchester Guardian*, 3 Aug. 1954.

19. Scheduled Territories in the Import Licensing Schedule, 2 April 1954. NZA: T 1, 61/6/20/1.

20. Submission OT/1 to Cabinet Committee on Overseas Commercial Relations, 3 Sept. 1952, in Australia, Department of Foreign Affairs and Trade, *Documents on Australian Foreign Policy: the Australia–Japan Agreement on Commerce 1957* (Canberra: Commonwealth of Australia, 1997), p. 30.

21. Singleton, 'Economic Relations with Japan': 5–6.

22. Existing emergency controls under GATT Article XIX were non-discriminatory and slow. The arrangements suggested by the British were unrelated to the later commercial agreements. Japanese Membership of GATT: Note for Working Party on the Effect of Provisions of the General Agreement, 29 April 1954. NZA: T 1, 61/1/8, pt 2. Brief for Commonwealth Meeting on the Review of GATT, Sept. 1954, pp. 39–42. T 1, 52/904/2/4. New Zealand Delegation, GATT, to External Affairs, Wellington, 25 Jan. 1955. T 1, Acc. W2619, 104/4/8/37. Review of the GATT: First Meeting with Officials of the State Dept and US Treasury, Sept. 27 1954. PRO: T 236/3697.

23. Walker to External Affairs, 29 July 1955, in DFAT, *Australia–Japan Agreement*, p.179. GATT Tenth Session: Report of the New Zealand Delegation, pp. 41–3. NZA: EA 1, Acc. W2619, 104/4/8/27. US Embassy to External Affairs, Wellington, 14 July 1954; New Zealand Legation, Tokyo to External Affairs, Wellington, 11 Aug. 1955. EA 1, Acc. W2619, 104/4/8/37. Note of Meeting with Berger and Kling of the US Embassy, 19 May 1955. EA 1, Acc. W2619, 40/12/1. Summary of Action since Trade Arrangements Drafted, Nov. 1955. IC 22, Acc. W1837, Box 6, Record 14. Brief for New Zealand–Japan Trade Talks, 1958–9, Paper C, p. 1. Box 22, Item 47a.

24. Japan and the GATT, 7 Jan. 1955. PRO: CAB 134/855.

25. The agreement between Australia and Japan is discussed at length in Rix, *Coming to Terms*. Numerous official documents pertaining to this treaty are reprinted in DFAT, *Australia–Japan Agreement*. On the agreement between New Zealand and Japan, see Singleton, 'Economic Relations with Japan'; A. Trotter, 'From Suspicion to Growing Partnership: New Zealand and Japan', in M. McKinnon (ed.), *New Zealand in World Affairs* (Wellington: New Zealand Institute for International Affairs, 1991), vol. 2, pp. 195–226. Since the issues were similar for both countries we concentrate on New

Zealand, and commend Rix's work to readers who require a detailed account of negotiations between Australia and Japan.

26. Memorandum from H.C. Menzies to Department of Commerce & Agriculture, 8 May 1952, in DFAT, *Australia–Japan Agreement*, pp. 21–3.
27. Rix, *Coming to Terms*, p. 133.
28. Japanese Accession to GATT, 24 Aug. 1953. NZA: T 1, 61/1/8.
29. CCEFP minutes, 27 Aug. 1953. NZA: T 1, 61/1/8. CCEFP minutes, 26 March 1954; Trade and Tariff Arrangements – Japan/New Zealand, External Affairs' Views, April 1954. T 1, 61/6/20/1.
30. Agreed Minute of Discussions between Japanese and New Zealand Officials at Wellington, 29 March–1 April 1954. NZA: T 1, 61/6/20/1.
31. Ibid., Minutes of Second Meeting with the Japanese, 24 June 1954; Note on Negotiations with Japan, 29 June 1954.
32. Calder, *Crisis and Compensation*, pp. 231–73.
33. Trade Relations with Japan, 19 March 1954. NZA: T 1, 61/6/20/1.
34. Ibid., Minutes of Fifth Meeting with the Japanese, 25 June 1954.
35. Ibid.
36. New Zealand was Lancashire's fourth largest export market for cotton cloth. The Cotton Board's policy on Japanese penetration of Commonwealth markets was uncompromising: 'every endeavour should be made to limit the displacement of British export trade by Japanese trade'. Streat to Cohen, 11 Jan. 1954. PRO: BT175/7. J. Singleton, *Lancashire on the Scrapheap: the Cotton Industry, 1945–70* (Oxford: Oxford University Press, 1991).
37. Scheduled Territories in the Import Licensing Schedule, 2 April 1954; Notes of Sixth Meeting with the Japanese, 8 July 1954. NZA: T 1, 61/6/20/1.
38. Ibid., CCEFP minutes, 25 June 1954, 1 July 1954.
39. *NZPD*, vol. 304, 21 Sept. 1954, p. 1856; vol. 303, 5 Aug. 1954, p. 972.
40. Thomson to White, 13 July 1954. NZA: T 1, 61/6/20/1.
41. CCEFP minutes, 29 July 1954; Trade Agreement with Japan: Comptroller of Customs' Report and Recommendations for Approval: Industries and Commerce Department Reservations, 28 July 1954. NZA: T 1, 61/6/20/1.
42. C (55) 14, Japan and the GATT: Memorandum by the President of the Board of Trade, 19 Jan. 1955. PRO: CAB 129/73.
43. Summary of Action since Trade Arrangements Drafted, Nov. 1955. NZA: IC 22, Acc. W1837, Box 6, Record 14.
44. DFAT, *Australia–Japan Agreement*; Rix, *Coming to Terms*, pp. 198–209; J. Golding, *Black Jack McEwen* (Melbourne: Melbourne University Press, 1996), p. 197.
45. New Zealand Embassy, Tokyo to External Affairs, 4 Dec. 1957. NZA: T 1, 61/6/20/1.
46. *Otago Daily Times*, 31 July 1958.
47. CCEFP minutes, 22 May 1958. NZA: EA 1, Acc. W2619, 40/12/2, pt 1.
48. Brief for New Zealand–Japan Trade Talks, 1958–9, Paper C, p. 2. NZA: IC 22, Acc. W1837, Box 22, Item 47a.
49. Trotter, 'Suspicion', pp. 206–7.
50. Proposal for Trade and Payments Agreement with Japan, 15 May 1958. NZA: T 1, 61/6/20/1. British High Commissioner to Minister of Industries and Commerce, 24 Sept. 1957. EA 1, Acc. W2619, 40/12/1.

51. Trade Talks with Japan: Consultations with New Zealand Interests, 24 July 1958; Submission of New Zealand Manufacturers' Federation, 24 July 1958. NZA: EA 1, Acc. W2619, 40/12/2, pt 2.
52. Opening Statement by the Leader of the Japanese Delegation, 20 July 1958. NZA: IC 22, Acc. W1837, Box 22, Item 47b.
53. Brief for New Zealand–Japan Trade Talks, 1958–9, Paper C, p. 4; Item 47b, Score Sheet – New Zealand Requests to Japan, 1 Sept. 1958. NZA: IC 22, Acc. W1837, Box 22, Item 47a. Proposal for Trade and Payments Agreement with Japan, 19 May 1958. EA 1, Acc. W2619, 40/12/2, pt 1.
54. Officials' Committee on Financial and Economic Policy, 29 July 1958. NZA: EA 1, Acc. W2619, 40/12/2, pt 2.
55. Ibid., Note of Conversation with Akiyama, 29 July 1958.
56. Japan/New Zealand Trade Negotiations, 1 Sept. 1958, pp. 1–3. NZA: IC 22, Acc. W1837, Box 22, Item 47B.
57. *NZPD*, vol. 318, 9 Sept. 1958, p. 1615. The National leader agreed, as did the financial press. *NZPD*, vol. 318, p. 1616; *New Zealand Financial Times*, 10 Oct. 1958, p. 5.
58. Singleton, 'Economic Relations with Japan': 12–14; Rix, *Coming to Terms*, p. 209.
59. W.W. Cochrane and M.E. Ryan, *American Farm Policy, 1948–1973* (Minneapolis: University of Minnesota Press, 1976); T.H. Peterson, *Agricultural Exports, Farm Income, and the Eisenhower Administration* (Lincoln, Neb.: University of Nebraska Press, 1979); E.L. Schapsmeier and H.H. Schapsmeier, *Ezra Taft Benson and the Politics of Agriculture* (Danville, Ill.: Interstate, 1975).
60. *FRUS*, 1952–4, I, 1, pp. 74–5.
61. *FRUS*, 1951, I, pp. 1427–30. Report of NZ Delegation to Sixth Session of GATT, Feb. 1952, pp. 29–30; Report of NZ Delegation to Seventh Session of GATT, March 1953, Annexes E and F; Report of NZ Delegation to Eighth Session of GATT, 18 Dec. 1953. NZA: EA 1, 104/4/8/27. McKinnon, 'World of the Dollar', p. 123; Kaufman, *Trade and Aid*, pp. 26–9.
62. Australian Ambassador to Secretary of State, 30 March 1953; Ambassador of New Zealand to Secretary of State, 31 March 1953. DDEL: US President's Commission on Foreign Economic Policy: Records, 1953–1954, Box 64, File: Studies 8 – Psychological Impact Abroad of US Trade Policy.
63. Memorandum: Background on Wool Imports, Attached to note from Samuel C. Waugh to Dr Gabriel Hauge, June 18, 1953. DDEL: White House Central Files, Official File 149-B-2, Box 808, File: Wool (1). See also Memorandum for Dr Hauge from Department of State, Subject: Preliminary Comments on Department of Agriculture Draft Paper on Wool Policy, Nov. 5, 1953. DDEL: White House Central Files, Confidential File, 1953–61, Subject Series, Box 98, File: Trade Agreements and Tariff Matters – Wool (1).
64. Geneva to Secretary of State, Nov. 23, 1954. DDEL: White House Central Files, Official File 149-B-2, Box 768, File: July–Dec. 1954 (2).
65. Aide Memoire from New Zealand Government, 12 Jan. 1955. DDEL: US Council on Foreign Economic Policy: Records, 1954–61, Policy Papers Series, Box 3, File: CFEP 509 Recommendations Francis Committee.
66. Peterson, *Agricultural Exports*, pp. 19–27, 46–7, 55; Schapsmeier and

Schapsmeier, *Benson*, pp. 111–13. Department of State, Memorandum of Conversation with J.G. Crawford, March 15, 1954; Ambassador of New Zealand to Secretary of State, 11 May 1954; Philip C. Habib to Department of State, April 21, 1954. DDEL: Clarence Francis Papers, Box 4, File: Disposal of US Surpluses Abroad. Ambassador R.C. Hendrickson to Department of State, June 10, 1955. Clarence Francis Papers, Box 1, File: New Zealand. Geneva to Secretary of State, November 23, 1954. White House Central Files, Official File 149-B-2, Box 768, File: July–Dec. 1954 (2).

67. Oakley to Secretary of State, Sept. 19, 1953. DDEL: White House Central Files, Confidential File, Box 84, File: Trade Agreements and Tariff Matters (1953) (7).

68. EFP (E) (55) 56, Review of the GATT: Report of New Zealand Delegation, July 1955, p. 1. NZA: T 1, 61/1/8, pt 2.

69. Report by Treasury Representative on the New Zealand Delegation on Fourth Session of the Contracting Parties to the GATT, April 1950, p.11. NZA: EA 1, Acc. W2619, 104/4/8/27.

70. Ibid., Statement by the New Zealand Delegate to the Intersessional Committee of GATT on the Review of the Agreement, 26 Aug. 1954.

71. EP (52) 8, Memorandum by Comptroller of Customs on Seventh Session of Contracting Parties to GATT, 20 Aug. 1952, p. 7. NZA: T 1, 61/1/8, pt 2. Brief for CEC, undated, 1952, pp. 99–100. T 1, 61/3/12, pt 5.

72. Crawford, *Australian Trade Policy*, pp. 147–62.

73. Snape, 'Australia's Relations with GATT', p. 21; Curzon, *Multilateral Commercial Diplomacy*, pp. 170–1, 174–6. Cabinet Submission No. 355, GATT, 16 May 1955; Cabinet Submission No. 359, Review of the GATT: Report of the Australian Delegation, 17 May 1955; Cabinet Minute, Decision No. 440 (HOC), 18 May 1955. NAA: A4906, vol. 14.

74. GATT, *Trends in International Trade* (Geneva: GATT, 1958); Crawford, *Australian Trade Policy*, pp. 133–4; Curzon, *Multilateral Commercial Diplomacy*, pp. 179–86.

75. Memorandum From Christian Herter to John B. Hollister. Subject: Australian Protest Over US Surplus Disposal Programs. May 4, 1957. DDEL: Christian Herter Papers, Box 1, Chronological File, May 1957 (4). Commonwealth reactions to the operation of PL480 are reported in the minutes of the Pre-GATT Meeting of Commonwealth Officials on 14 Oct. 1957. NAA: CRS A571/73, 59/2383, pt 4.

76. Kaufman, *Trade and Aid*, p. 149. Department of State Memorandum, April 30, 1957. DDEL, Christian Herter Papers, Box 1, Chronological File, May 1957 (4).

77. CO (J) (TP) (58) 17th mtg, CTEC: Second Preparatory Meeting of Officials, Minutes of Committee on Trade Policy, 18 June 1958. PRO: T 236/4071.

78. Kaufman, *Trade and Aid*, pp. 38–9, 118–19. Eisenhower to Menzies, Sept. 29, 1958. DDEL: White House Office, Office of the Staff Secretary, Records of Paul T. Carroll, Andrew J. Goodpaster, L. Arthur Minnich, and Christopher H. Russell, 1952–61, International Series, Box 1, File: Australia [Sept. 1958–Dec. 1960].

79. Food for Peace Conference, Joint Communique, May 6, 1959. DDEL: US Council on Foreign Economic Policy: Records, 1954–61, Policy Papers Series, Box 15, File CFEP 583 Amendment of PL 480 (2). Remarks of the

Vice President of the United States, Minot, North Dakota, June 20, 1960. Don Paarlberg Papers, Box 9, File: Vice-President (2). Food-for-Peace: an Interim Report to the President by Don Paarlberg, Food-for-Peace Coordinator, July 15, 1960. Don Paarlberg Papers, Box 11, File: FFP Coordinator (2). E (59) 37, United States Food for Peace Initiative, 8 June 1959. NZA: T1, 61/1/8, pt 2.

80. Crawford to O'Donnell, 7 Feb. 1958. NAA: A571/71, 57/4065, pt 3.

81. W. Rosenberg, 'Financial and Monetary Policy and Capital Requirements', pp. 7–8. Review of New Zealand's External Economic Policy, 16 Jan. 1957, p. 4. NZA: T 1, 61/3/21, pt 1. Minutes of Meeting on Review of Trade Policy, 5 Dec. 1956. T 1, 61/3/21, pt 2.

82. Economic Relations Between New Zealand and the United States, 1 May 1953, p. 22. NZA: EA 1, Acc. W2619, 40/9/1, pt 1.

83. Hayward, *Golden Jubilee*, pp. 110–19. New Zealand Ambassador, Washington to Hunn, 13 March 1957. NZA: IC 1, Acc. W2267, 194/1/3, pt 1, Box 8. Meat Exports to the US, 24 June 1957; Woodward to Secretary of Industries and Commerce, 23 Jan. 1958. MINFAT: TRA 15/19.

84. T.W. Zeiler, *American Trade and Power in the 1960s* (New York: Columbia University Press, 1992), pp. 180–1. Brief Report on Pacific Trade Trip of Secretary of Agriculture Ezra Taft Benson, Nov. 10–Nov. 28, 1960. DDEL: Ann Whitman File, Administration Series, Box 7, File: Ezra Benson 1960–61 (1). Memorandum for President Eisenhower from Ezra Taft Benson, Oct. 19, 1960, File: Trade Agreements & Tariff Matters 1960 (16). White House Central Files, Confidential File, Subject Series, Box 89.

85. US/Australian Talks on Wool, First Meeting, 11 a.m., June 1, 1960, File: Trade Agreements & Tariff Matters – Wool (5). DDEL: White House Central Files, Confidential File (CF), 1953–61, Subject Series, Box 98.

86. Paarlberg to Dillon, March 29, 1960. DDEL: Don Paarlberg Papers, Box 8, File: State Dept (2), Box 8.

87. Hefford, *Farm Policy*, chs 7–8; N.V. Lough, 'New Zealand's External Economic Relations', in T.C. Larkin (ed.), *New Zealand's External Relations* (London: Oxford University Press, 1962), pp. 126–7; Curzon, *Multilateral Commercial Diplomacy*, p. 187. Report to the Secretary of State by the Chairman of the United States Delegation to the Eleventh Session of the Contracting Parties to the GATT, Oct. 11–Nov. 17, 1956, p. 18. DDEL: White House Central Files, Official File 149-B-2, Box 771, File: 1956 (2).

88. A.S. Milward, *The European Rescue of the Nation-State* (London: Routledge, 1992), ch. 5.

89. H. Johnson, 'Trade Challenges to Commonwealth Countries', in P. Streeten and H. Corbet (eds), *Commonwealth Policy in a Global Context* (Toronto: University of Toronto Press, 1971), p. 88. On the mechanics of the CAP and its subsequent application to Britain, see Moore, *Britain's Trade*, ch. 9; M. Tracy, *Agriculture in Western Europe* (London: Granada, 1982), chs 11–12.

90. Note of Action Taken by New Zealand to Protect its Trading Interest in Europe, 1 Aug. 1959. NZA: T 1, 61/5/2, pt 12.

91. Intersessional Committee of GATT, 19th–23rd Sept., 1957, Report of Australian Delegation, pp. 4–5. NAA: A571/73, 59/2383, pt 4.

92. Ibid., Minutes of the Pre-GATT Meeting of Commonwealth Officials, 10.30

a.m., 10 Oct. 1957, pp. 5–6; Report of the Australian Delegation to the Pre-GATT Meeting, pp. 2–3, 7.

93. Ibid., Minutes of the Pre-GATT Meeting of Commonwealth Officials, 3.0 p.m., 11 Oct. 1957 (revised), p. 5.

94. Extract from Brief for 15th Session [of GATT], Agenda Item No. 15, The Rome Treaty, undated, 1959. NAA: A571/73, 59/2383, pt 6.

95. Note from New Zealand Embassy, Paris to the French Ministry of Foreign Affairs, 8 July 1958. NAA: A571/2, 59/2382, pt 1.

96. Ibid., Draft Aide Memoire from Australian Government to Governments of the Six, 1 July 1958.

97. Note of Action Taken by New Zealand to Protect its Trading Interest in Europe, 1 Aug. 1959. NZA: T 1, 61/5/2, pt. 12.

98. At its own request, Argentina was added to the list at the last moment.

99. Inward Cablegram No. 170 from Australian High Commission, Ottawa, 23 March, 1960. NAA: A571/2, 59/2382, pt 2.

100. ES (CW) (60) 43, Brief for Commonwealth Finance Ministers' meeting, Note by Board of Trade, 7 Sept. 1960. PRO: CAB 134/1845.

101. NAA: A571/2, 59/2382, esp. pts 2–4.

102. Briefings on EEC Countries and their Trade with New Zealand, undated, 1962. NZA: T 1, 61/5/2, pt 12.

103. Memorandum on GATT Tariff Negotiations: Article XXIV: 6, undated, 1961. NZA: IC 1, Acc. W1842, 107/7/25, Box 1995.

104. New Zealand High Commission, Canberra to External Affairs, 1 May 1959; External Affairs to New Zealand High Commission, London, 8 May 1959. NZA: T 1, 61/5/2, pt 11.

105. The Impact of the Common Market on Australia: Speech by Sir John Crawford at the University of Sydney, 31 Aug. 1962. NAA: A1838/275, 727/4/2, pt 4.

Chapter 7: Britain, the Commonwealth, and Europe, 1945–60

1. Department of State, Office of Intelligence Research, Intelligence Report No. 7447, Imperial Preference, Feb. 19, 1957, p. ii. DDEL: White House Office, National Security Council Staff: Papers, 1953–61, CFEP Series, Box 7, File: CFEP 539 Regional Economic Integration (1).

2. W. Lipgens, *A History of European Integration* (Oxford: Clarendon Press, 1982), vol. 1, p. 164.

3. A.S. Milward, *The Reconstruction of Western Europe, 1945–1952* (London: Methuen, 1984); Hogan, *Marshall Plan*.

4. R.W.D. Boyce, 'Britain's First "No" to Europe: Britain and the Briand Plan, 1929–30', *European Studies Review*, 1980 10(1): 17–45.1, pp. 17–45; J. Kent, *British Imperial Strategy and the Origins of the Cold War 1944–49* (Leicester: Leicester University Press, 1993), pp. 119–25; Lipgens, *European Integration*, pp. 168–85; A.S. Milward, 'The Committee of European Economic Cooperation (CEEC) and the Advent of the Customs Union', in Lipgens, *European Integration*, pp. 542–3, 548–57; Hogan, *Marshall Plan*, pp. 46–9, 109–28, 179–87; Brusse, *Tariffs, Trade*, pp. 58–9.

5. E47/9/8, Cablegram D706, 21 Aug. 1947. NAA: A1068/1.
6. Ibid., E47/9/8, Cablegram D713, 25 Aug. 1947.
7. Ibid., E47/64, Cablegram 4064 from Hartnell in London to External Affairs, 12 Nov. 1947. British Commonwealth Talks on a Western European Customs Union, CU (H) (BC) (47) 1, 28 Nov. 1947. NAA: CP434/1/1, 9346/45.
8. Memorandum on New Zealand Balance of Payments, 13 May 1948; Notes on Australia's and New Zealand's Problems, June 1948, 2. NZA: T 1, 61/1, pt 1. Nash to External Affairs, 30 Jan. 1948; External Affairs to Secretary of State for Commonwealth Relations, 28 Aug. 1948. T 1, 61/5/2, pt 1. Milward, 'CEEC', p. 558.
9. Nash to Fraser, 17 March 1948. NZA: T 1, 61/5/2, pt 1.
10. Memorandum on European Recovery Programme, April 1948. NZA: T 1, 61/1, pt 1.
11. Kent, *British Imperial Strategy*, p. 141.
12. E47/9/8, Cablegram 10 from the Australian Delegation to the World Trade Conference to the Department of External Affairs, 29 Nov. 1947. NAA: A1068/1.
13. The UK was the only Sterling Area country with actual membership of the EPU. J.J. Kaplan and G. Schleiminger, *The European Payments Union* (Oxford: Clarendon Press, 1989); Fforde, *Bank of England*, pp. 193–219; Perkins, *Regional Payments Systems*, pp. 106–9.
14. R. Ranieri, 'Inside or Outside the Magic Circle? The Italian and British Steel Industries Face to Face with the Schuman Plan and the European Coal and Steel Community', in A.S. Milward et al., *The Frontier of National Sovereignty* (London: Routledge, 1994), pp. 117–54; C. Lord, *Absent at the Creation: Britain and the Formation of the European Community, 1950–2* (Aldershot: Dartmouth, 1996), pp. 65–76.
15. S. Burgess and G. Edwards, 'The Six Plus One: British Policy-Making and the Question of European Economic Integration, 1955', *International Affairs*, 1988 64: 393–413; Ellison, 'Perfidious Albion'; N.P. Ludlow, *Dealing with Britain: the Six and the First UK Application to Join the EEC* (Cambridge: Cambridge University Press, 1997), p. 26.
16. EP (55) 54, The Economic Implications of a European Common Market, 7 Nov. 1955. PRO: CAB 134/1228.
17. Rowan to Harcourt, 21 Oct. 1955. PRO: T 236/6018.
18. Ellison, 'Perfidious Albion': pp. 8, 13.
19. J.W. Young, 'British Officials and European Integration, 1944–60', in A. Deighton (ed.), *Building Postwar Europe* (Basingstoke: Macmillan, 1995), p. 97.
20. Cablegram No. 321, Winthrop G. Brown to Dept. of State, Aug. 2, 1956. DDEL: US Council on Foreign Economic Policy: Records, 1954–61, Policy Papers Series, Box 7, File: CFEP 539 Effect of Regional Economic Integration on US Trade and Other Economic Interests (5). M. Camps, *Britain and the European Community 1955–1963* (Princeton: Princeton University Press, 1964), ch. 4.
21. J. Tratt, *The Macmillan Government and Europe* (Basingstoke: Macmillan, 1996), pp. 13–14.
22. CM (56) 65th mtg, 14 Sept. 1956, p. 3. PRO: CAB 128/30.

23. Ibid., CM (56) 66th mtg, 18 Sept. 1956, p. 6.
24. Ibid., CM (56) 65th mtg, 14 Sept. 1956, p. 6.
25. EP (56) 16th mtg, 5 Sept 1956, pp. 5, 6. PRO: CAB 134/1229. CM (56) 66th mtg, 18 Sept. 1956, p. 6. CAB 128/30.
26. CM (56) 66th mtg, 18 Sept. 1956, p. 7. PRO: CAB 128/30.
27. Franco-British Union, Meeting of Ministers, 1 Oct. 1956. PRO: CAB 130/120. F.M.B Lynch, *France and the International Economy* (London: Routledge, 1997), pp. 178–90.
28. Personal message from the Chancellor of the Exchequer to the Minister of Finance, Wellington, 16 Sept. 1956. NZA: T 1, 61/5/2, pt 1.
29. Ibid., FM (W) (56) 2nd mtg, 29 Sept. 1956; Briefing for Finance Minister on European Common Market, Sept. 1956.
30. CM (56) 68th mtg, 3 Oct. 1956. PRO: CAB 128/30.
31. Draft Savingram on European Common Market and Free Trade Area, Dec. 1956. NAA: A571/73, 59/2383, pt 4.
32. Cabinet Submission No. 444, European Free Trade Area, 29 Oct. 1956, p. 8. NAA: A4926/XMI, vol. 18.
33. External Affairs to New Zealand High Commission, London, 17 Oct. 1956; Lord Home to New Zealand High Commission, London, 10 Jan. 1957. NZA: T 1, 61/5/2, pt 1.
34. Department of State, Office of Intelligence Research, Intelligence Report No. 7447, Imperial Preference, Feb. 19, 1957, pp. 16–17. DDEL: White House Office, National Security Council Staff: Papers, 1953–61, CFEP Series, Box 7, File: CFEP 539 Regional Economic Integration (1). CFEP 539, Regional Economic Integration, A Report by a Subcommittee of the Council on Foreign Economic Policy, Nov. 20, 1956, pp. 47, 49, 55. File: CFEP 539 Regional Economic Integration (4). P. Winand, *Eisenhower, Kennedy, and the United States of Europe* (New York: St. Martin's, 1993), pp. 111–20.
35. C.R. Schenk, 'Decolonization and European Economic Integration: the Free Trade Area Negotiations, 1956–58', *Journal of Imperial and Commonwealth History*, 1996 24(3): 444–63.
36. Cabinet Submission No. 444, European Free Trade Area, 29 Oct. 1956, p. 9. NAA: A4926/XMI, vol. 18.
37. Moroney to Secretary of Prime Minister's Department, 23 Jan. 1957. NAA: A1209/23, 57/4595, pt 1.
38. Minutes of Working Party on Economic Policy, 8 Jan. 1957; New Zealand and the Free Trade Area and Common Market, undated, 1957. NZA: T 1, 61/5/2, pt 2.
39. CC (57) 43rd mtg, 29 May 1957; CC (57) 62nd mtg, 27 Aug. 1957. PRO: CAB 128/31. CC (58) 5th Conclusions, 14 Jan. 1958, CC (58) 14th mtg, 4 Feb. 1958. CAB 128/32. Tratt, *Macmillan and Europe*, p. 17.
40. Cabinet Submission No. 862, European Economic Community and European Free Trade Area, 12 Sept. 1957, pp. 5, 8 and attachment, pt 2. NAA: A4926/XMI, vol. 34.
41. Ibid., Decision No. 1007, 17 Sept. 1957.
42. W.M. Corden, 'Australia and European Free Trade', *Economic Record*, 1958 31(2): 171. For similar recommendations, see R.I. Downing and J.O.N. Perkins, 'What Should Be Done About the Sterling Area? Australia', *Bulletin of the Oxford University Institute of Statistics*, 1959 21(4): 262.

43. New Zealand High Commission, London to External Affairs, 23 Jan. 1957. NZA: T 1, 61/5/2, pt 2.

44. New Zealand and Proposals for European Economic Integration, by C.H. Fowler, F.W. Holmes, H.G. Lang and D.P. Taylor, March 1957. NZA: T 1, 61/5/2, pt 3. On Dutch interest in the FTA proposals see R. Dingemans and A.J. Boekestijn, 'The Netherlands and the Enlargement Proposals 1957–1963', in A. Deighton and A.S. Milward (eds), *Widening, Deepening and Acceleration: the European Economic Community, 1957–1963* (Baden-Baden: Nomos, 1999), pp. 225–9.

45. Memorandum on Free Trade Area by Keith Holyoake, 28 May 1957. NZA: T 1, 61/5/2, pt 4.

46. Minutes of Meeting of Commonwealth Officials on the EEC and FTA, London, 9 July 1957, p. 7; New Zealand High Commission, London to Greensmith, 16 July 1957. NZA: T 1, 61/5/2, pt 5.

47. CC (57) 29th mtg, 3 April 1957. PRO: CAB 128/31.

48. New Zealand High Commission, London to External Affairs, 27 Aug. 1957. NZA: T 1, 61/5/2, pt 5.

49. Cabinet Submission No. 862, European Economic Community and European Free Trade Area, 12 Sept. 1957, attachment, pt 2, pp. 8–10. NAA: A4926/XMI, vol. 34.

50. Bunting to Crawford, 24 Dec. 1957. NAA: A1838/1, 727/4/2/1, pt 3. Australia's Policy Towards Europe, 6 Jan. 1958. A4901/1, C2186. Stone to McCarthy, 10 March 1958. A571/71, 58/1174, pt 2.

51. FM (C) 27, 2nd mtg, 28 Sept. 1957. NZA: IC 1, Acc. W1955, 74/1/6.

52. New Zealand High Commission, London to External Affairs, 13 Nov. 1957; New Zealand Delegation to GATT to External Affairs, 15 Nov. 1957. NZA: T 1, 61/5/2, pt 6.

53. Ibid., New Zealand Ambassador, Paris to External Affairs, 28 Oct. 1957.

54. Ibid., European Free Trade Area Negotiations, 8 Nov. 1957.

55. New Zealand Embassy, Paris to External Affairs, 6 March 1958. NZA: T 1, 61/5/2, pt 8.

56. CC (58) 27th mtg, 27 March 1958, p. 4. PRO: CAB 128/32.

57. Maudling to Nash, 2 April 1958. NZA: T 1, 61/5/2, pt 8.

58. New Zealand High Commission, London to External Affairs, 27 June 1958. NZA: T 1, 61/5/2, pt 9.

59. CTEC (58) 13th mtg, 23 Sept. 1958. NZA: IC 22, Acc. W1837, Box 26, Item 63.

60. Tratt, *Macmillan and Europe*, pp. 25–6; *Financial Times*, 12 Feb. 1959.

61. Memorandum on Trade with Europe, 8 April 1959; E (59) 14 mtg, 15 April 1959. NZA: T 1, 61/5/2, pt 11.

62. Memorandum from Thompson McCausland to Governor, 19 Aug. 1959. BoEA: ADM 14/51.

63. Stone to Treasury, 9 July, 24 July, 27 Aug. 1959. NAA: 571/71, 58/1174, pt 7. Memorandum on Trade with Europe, 8 April 1959; Note on New Zealand and European Economic Integration, 6 May 1959. NZA: T 1, 61/5/2, pt 11. Summary of and Comments on Interim Report of Commonwealth Liaison Committee Sub-committee on European Trade Relations, 24 Aug. 1959. T 1, 61/5/2, pt 12.

64. The New Zealanders were rattled by Eccles: 'The manner of his statement

...was somewhat superior and condescending.' Report on Common-wealth Economic Consultative Council Ministerial Meeting, London, 22–3 Sept. 1959, p. 4. NZA: IC 1, Acc. W1955, 74/1/6, pt 4.

65. Camps, *Britain and the EC*, ch. 7.

66. Cabinet Submission No. 219, 8 June 1959. NAA: A5818/2, vol. 5. Stone to Treasury, 9 July 1959. A571/71, 58/1174, pt 7.

67. E (59) M37 mtg, 16 July 1959. NZA: T 1, 61/5/2, pt 12. Tratt, *Macmillan and Europe*, pp. 32–3; E.F. Nash and E.A. Attwood, *The Agricultural Policies of Britain and Denmark* (London: Land, 1961), p. 48.

68. Tratt, *Macmillan and Europe*, p. 50.

Chapter 8: Britain's First EEC Application

1. *The Times*, 14 Oct. 1960, p. 9.

2. P. Robertson and J. Singleton, 'The Old Commonwealth and Britain's First Application to Join the EEC', *Australian Economic History Review*, 2000 40(2): 153–77; *idem*, 'Britain, the Dominions, and the EEC, 1961–1963', in Deighton and Milward, *Widening, Deepening and Acceleration*, pp. 107–22; Ludlow, *Dealing with Britain*; G. Wilkes (ed.), *Britain's Failure to Enter the European Economic Community, 1961–63* (London: Frank Cass, 1997). Cumming Bruce to Rumbold, 24 Feb. 1961. PRO: T 236/6549.

3. R. Lamb, *The Macmillan Years 1957–1963* (London: John Murray, 1995), p. 155; Tratt, *Macmillan and Europe*, pp. 76–7.

4. The Six and the Seven, 22 April 1960. PRO: PREM 11/3558. Lamb, *Macmillan Years*, pp. 136–8; Tratt, *Macmillan and Europe*, pp. 92–101; N. Rollings, 'British Industry and European Integration 1961–73: from First Application to Final Membership', *Business and Economic History*, 1998 27(2): 444–54.

5. Tratt, *Macmillan and Europe*, pp. 135–6.

6. Commonwealth Economic Consultative Council, Ministerial Meeting, London, 20–1 Sept. 1961, Report of New Zealand Delegation, pp. 3–4. NZA: IC 1, Acc. W1955, 74/1/6, pts 1–3.

7. Bowers, 'British Agricultural Policy': 67–71; W. Kaiser, 'To Join or Not to Join? The "Appeasement" Policy of Britain's First EEC Application', in B. Brivati and H. Jones (eds), *From Reconstruction to Integration* (Leicester: Leicester University Press, 1993), p. 148; W. Kaiser, 'From Laggard to Leader? The United Kingdom's 1961 Decision to Apply for EEC Membership', in Deighton and Milward, *Widening, Deepening and Acceleration*, pp. 260–1.

8. EQ (61) 4th mtg, 17 May, 1961, Confidential Annex, The Common Market and United Kingdom Food and Agriculture, pp. 1, 3. PRO: CAB 134/1821.

9. Lamb, *Macmillan Years*, pp. 140–1; G.W. Ball, *The Discipline of Power* (Boston: Little, Brown, 1968), pp. 78–9; Winand, *Eisenhower*, pp. 266–8; Kaiser, 'To Join or Not to Join', p. 153; Tratt, *Macmillan and Europe*, pp. 179–86.

10. *FRUS*, 1961–3, XIII, pp. 10–13.

11. *FRUS*, 1961–3, XIII, p. 25.

12. Line to be Taken in Consultations with the Commonwealth, 16 June 1961. PRO: CAB 134/1821. Lamb, *Macmillan Years*, pp. 145–52.

13. O. Bange, *The EEC Crisis of 1963* (Basingstoke: Macmillan, 2000), pp. 33, 57; Ludlow, *Dealing with Britain*, pp. 30–42.

14. Draft Paper on the UK's Attitude Towards European Economic Integration, and its Implications for New Zealand, 23 June 1960; New Zealand High Commission, London to External Affairs, 19 April 1960; New Zealand Delegation to GATT to External Affairs, 19 May 1961. NZA: T 1, 61/5/4, pt 1.

15. Ibid., Public Relations Aspects of the Consequences of the UK Joining the EEC, 19 May 1961.

16. Minutes of Meetings with New Zealand Ministers, 3–5 July 1961. PRO: FO 371/158325. Discussions on the Possible Entry of the United Kingdom into the EEC, 3–5 July 1961; Memorandum on Visit of Mr Sandys to Discuss the United Kingdom and Europe, 26 June 1961. NZA: T, Acc. W2666, 61/1/8. J.R. Marshall, *Memoirs, 1960–88* (Auckland: Collins, 1989), pp. 61–92; R. McLuskie, *The Great Debate: New Zealand, Britain, and the EEC* (Wellington: Victoria University of Wellington, 1986).

17. Meade, *Collected Papers*, 3, p. 257.

18. Cabinet Submission No. 996, The Possible Association of the United Kingdom with the European Economic Community, 9 Feb. 1961, p. 6. NAA: A4940/1, C3368, pt 1.

19. Brief for Visits of United Kingdom Ministers to Commonwealth Countries (June–July, 1961): Australia (Country Brief). PRO: FO 371/158315. Telegram No. 535 to CRO from Canberra, 10 June 1961; Telegram No. 571 to CRO from Canberra, 21 June 1961. FO 371/158316.

20. Cabinet Submission No. 1108, Possible Association of the United Kingdom with the European Economic Community, 9 May 1961, pp. 6–7. NAA: A1838/283, 727/4/2, pt 1. Cabinet Submission no. 1188, United Kingdom and the European Economic Community: Implications for Australia's Trade, 1 July 1961, pp. 1–2. A4940/1, C3368, pt. 1.

21. NAA: A4940/1, C3368, pt 1, pp. 8–13. One staffer in the Prime Minister's Department was far more optimistic about securing British aid. The British Queen is also, quite independently, the Queen of Australia, and 'A Queen of Australia is most unlikely to acquiesce in say an Indonesian attack on Australia.' The separate Australian status of the Queen was seen as an important insurance policy 'if the US failed us.' Ibid., Note on Cabinet Submission No. 1183, 30 June 1961, p. 6.

22. Ibid., Cabinet Submission No. 1183, The Political Implications for Australia of United Kingdom Entry into the European Economic Community, 26 June 1961, pp. 13, 16.

23. Commonwealth Consultations on Britain's Relations with the EEC: Documents Relating to Talks Between Duncan Sandys and Ministers of the Government of Australia on 8th–11th July 1961. PRO: FO 371/158326.

24. Cabinet Submission No. 1182, Implications of United Kingdom Entry into the European Economic Community – Financial Aspects, 27 June 1961. NAA: A4940/1, C3368, pt 1.

25. Financial Implications of United Kingdom Entry into the European Economic Community, Attachment to Cabinet Submission No. 1317, 14 Aug. 1961. NAA: A4940/1, C3368, pt 2.

26. Cabinet Submission No. 1366, Implications of United Kingdom Entry into

the European Economic Community – Financial Aspects, 4 Oct. 1961. NAA: A4940/1, C3368, pt 3.

27. Meade, *Collected Works*, Vol. 3, pp. 265–9; C.R. Schenk, 'The UK, the Sterling Area and the EEC, 1957–63', in Deighton and Milward, *Widening, Deepening and Acceleration*, pp. 123–38.

28. Europe: Talks with the New Zealand, Australian and Canadian Governments, 21 July 1961. PRO: CAB 129/106.

29. Common Market Negotiations: Canadian Tactics at Accra Meeting of Commonwealth Finance Ministers, September 1961. PRO: FO 371/158327.

30. H. Macmillan, *At the End of the Day 1961–1963* (London: Macmillan, 1973), p. 29.

31. Pomfret, *Regional Trading Arrangements*, pp. 2–12.

32. Statement by Edward Heath in Paris, 10 Oct. 1961. PRO: CAB 134/1520. G. Hendriks, 'The Creation of the Common Agricultural Policy', in Deighton and Milward, *Widening, Deepening and Acceleration*, pp. 139–50.

33. J. Campbell, *Edward Heath* (London: Jonathan Cape 1993), pp. 121–2; Lamb, *Macmillan Years*, pp. 159–61; Ludlow, *Dealing with Britain*, pp. 74–9.

34. Menzies to Macmillan, 30 Oct. 1961; Macmillan to Menzies, 3 Nov. 1961; Menzies to Harrison, 27 Nov. 1961. NAA: A1838/283, 727/4/2, pt 1.

35. Draft Cabinet Paper on the Commonwealth and Europe, 20 June 1961, p. 3. PRO: FO 371/158314.

36. UK and the Common Market: Note from Interdepartmental Committee, Annex B, Special Arrangements to Safeguard Australian Trade Interests, 24 Oct. 1961, p. 11. NAA: A4940/1, C3368, pt 3. UK/EEC Discussions: Comparable Outlets for Commonwealth Temperate Foodstuffs, March 1962. NZA: T, Acc. W2666, 61/5/4/2/2.

37. Westerman to External Affairs, 23 June 1961. NAA: A4940/1, C3368, pt 1.

38. Transcript of Discussion Among Australian Officials on Talks with the Americans, undated, 1962, p. 1. NAA: A1838/275, 727/4/1/4, pt 1.

39. Negotiating Brief for Milk and Milk Products, 12 Sept. 1961, pp. 12–13. PRO: FO 371/158360. Temperate Agricultural Produce Brief for Mr. Marshall's Visit, 17 May 1962, pp. 5–8. CAB 134/1534. J. Singleton and P.L. Robertson, 'Britain, Butter, and European Integration, 1957–1964', *Economic History Review*, 1997 50(2): 335–7; A.W. Tansey, 'British Import Controls and World Trade in Butter', *Journal of Agricultural Economics*, 1967 18(2): 257–69.

40. Draft Cabinet Paper on the Commonwealth and Europe, 20 June 1961, p. 3. PRO: FO 371/158314.

41. Industrial Products for Canada, Australia and New Zealand, 9 April 1962. PRO: CAB 134/1532.

42. Cabinet Decision No. 1620 (HOC), 4 Oct 1961. NAA: A4940/1, C3368, pt 3.

43. Menzies to Macmillan, 6 Oct. 1961; Macmillan to Menzies, 10 Oct. 1961. NAA: A1838/283, 727/4/2, pt 1.

44. Australia and the Common Market Negotiations, 27 April 1962. NAA: A4940/1, C3368, pt 3.

45. Golding, *McEwen*, p. 207.

46. E (61) M52, 28 Sept. 1961, Annex I, p. 2. NZA: T, Acc. W2666, 61/1/8.

47. Notes for Consultations with Producer Representatives, 13 Feb. 1962;

Memorandum from New Zealand Meat Producers' Board, 14 Feb. 1962. NZA: T, Acc. W2666, 61/5/4/1/1.

48. Camps, *Britain and the EC*, p. 384.
49. P.G. Elkan, 'New Zealand's Butter and Cheese in the European Economic Community', NZIER Research Paper No. 2 (Wellington: NZIER, 1962), p. 24; Record of Meeting of Australia/New Zealand Consultative Committee on Trade, 1 Sept. 1961. NZA: T 1, 61/3/30/61. Notes for Consultations with Producer Representatives, 13 Feb. 1962. T, Acc. W2666, 61/5/4/1/1. United Kingdom Observations on Milk and Butter, 2 May 1962, p. 3. PRO: CAB 134/1532. Australia and the Common Market Negotiations, 27 April 1962. NAA: A4940/1, C3368, pt 3. J. Molegraaf and R. Dingemans, 'The Netherlands and the Common Agricultural Policy', in Deighton and Milward, *Widening, Deepening and Acceleration*, pp. 151–66.
50. Curzon, *Multilateral Commercial Diplomacy*, pp. 195–202; F. Knox, *The Common Market and World Agriculture* (New York: Praeger, 1972), p. 92; Ludlow, *Dealing with Britain*, pp. 97–8.
51. E (61) M64, pt 2, 23 Nov. 1961. NAA: A571/73, 59/2383, pt 16. Visit of the Executive Secretary to the European Commission, Brussels, 16–18 May 1962. NZA: T, Acc. W2666, 61/1/8. E.H. Preeg, *Traders and Diplomats* (Washington, DC: Brookings Institution, 1970), p. 153; Gordon-Ashworth, *International Commodity Control*, p. 34.
52. Australia and the Common Market Negotiations, 27 April 1962. NAA: A4940/1, C3368, pt 3.
53. Transcript of Discussion Among Australian Officials on Talks with the Americans, undated, 1962, p. 1. NAA: A1838/275, 727/4/1/4, pt 1.
54. UK/EEC Discussions: Comparable Outlets, March 1962. E (62) M20, pt 2, 30 March 1962; NZ High Commission, London to External Affairs, 19 April 1962. NZA: T, Acc. W2666, 61/5/4/2/2.
55. Notes on Cabinet Submission No. 1327: UK and the EEC – Attitude in London Consultations, 29 Aug. 1961. NAA: A4940/1, C3368, pt 3.
56. *FRUS*, 1961–3, XIII, p. 35.
57. *FRUS*, 1961–3, XIII, pp. 41, 51. British High Commission, Wellington to CRO, 14 June 1961. PRO: T 236/6549.
58. *FRUS*, 1961–3, XIII, pp. 85, 87.
59. *FRUS*, 1961–3, XIII, p. 95.
60. Winand, *Eisenhower*, pp. 292–3. Comment by Mr McEwen on the statement by the US Secretary of State, 13 May 1962. NAA: A4940/1, pt 4.
61. The Commonwealth and the Common Market, 4 Sept. 1961. PRO: CAB 134/1846.
62. Brief for Visits by UK Ministers to Commonwealth Countries (June–July 1961): New Zealand. PRO: FO 371/158315. Mr. Marshall's Visit: Steering Brief, 17 May 1962, pp. 6–7. CAB 134/1534. E (61) M27, 22 May 1961, p. 4. NZA: T, Acc. W2666, 61/1/8. Memo from Nimmo for Bunting, 23 June 1961; pt 3, Cabinet Submission No. 1327, UK and the EEC: Attitude in London Consultations, Minister of State for Trade, 28 Aug. 1961, p. 46. NAA: A4940/1, 3368, pt 1. Lamb, *Macmillan Years*, p. 147; Winand, *Eisenhower*, pp. 292–3.
63. Notes on Cabinet Submission No. 1327: UK and the EEC – Attitude in London Consultations, 29 Aug. 1961. NAA: A4940/1, C3368, pt 3.

64. Camps, *Britain and the EC*, pp. 401–9.
65. United Kingdom–EEC Negotiations, Progress Report No. 3, 24 July 1962. NZA: T, Acc. W2666, 61/1/8.
66. Quoted in Bange, *The EEC Crisis*, p. 66.
67. Commonwealth Temperate Foodstuffs – A Revised Formula, 7 June 1962. PRO: CAB 134/1535.
68. UK–EEC Negotiations, Progress Report No. 3, 24 July 1962, p. 1. NZA: T, Acc. W2666, 61/1/8.
69. Ludlow, *Dealing with Britain*, p. 144.
70. UK–EEC Negotiations, Progress Report No. 3, 24 July 1962, pp. 4–5. NZA: T, Acc. W2666, 61/1/8.
71. Report from New Zealand Mission, Brussels, Annex A, 29 June 1962. NZA: T 1, 61/5/2, pt 2.
72. UK–EEC Negotiations: Agriculture, 2 March 1962, p. 10. NZA: T, Acc. W2666, 61/1/8.
73. Britain and the EEC, Situation Report, Aug. 1962. NAA: A1838/275, 727/4/2, pt 3. Macmillan to Menzies, 11 Aug. 1962. A1838/275, 727/4/1, pt 4.
74. Westerman to Warwick-Smith, 17 Aug. 1962. NAA: A1838/275, 727/4/1, pt 1.
75. Menzies to Sandys, 28 July 1962. NAA: A1838/275, 727/4/2, pt 3.
76. Transcript of Discussion Among Australian Officials on Talks with the Americans, undated, 1962; Record of Discussions at State Department, 23–4 July 1962. NAA: A1838/275, 727/4/1/4, pt 1. Westerman to External Affairs, 10 Aug. 1962. A1838/275, 727/4/2, pt 3.
77. Brussels Negotiations: American Intervention, 6 Sept. 1962. PRO: CAB 134/1539.
78. Transcript of Menzies' Press Conference, 30 Sept. 1962. NAA: A4940/1, C3368, pt 4.
79. Macmillan, *End of the Day*, p. 349.
80. Brief for Visits by UK Ministers to Commonwealth Countries (June–July 1961): New Zealand. PRO: FO 371/158315. Record of Conversation Between British and European Officials, 17 Nov. 1961. FO 371/158342. *FRUS*, 1961–3, XIII, p. 26.
81. Camps, *Britain and the EC*, p. 408. EEC–UK Negotiations: Special Treatment for New Zealand, 18 Aug. 1962. NZA: T, Acc. W2666, 61/5/4/2/5.
82. New Zealand Mission, Brussels to External Affairs, 5 July 1962. NZA: T 1, 61/5/2, pt 2. EEC–UK Negotiations: Special Treatment for New Zealand, 18 Aug. 1962. T, Acc. W2666, 61/5/4/2/5. New Zealand Protocol, 23 July 1962. PRO: CAB 134/1534.
83. Address by John Marshall to Council of Europe, 25 Sept. 1962. PRO: FO 371/164815.
84. E (62) M33, 29 June 1962. NZA: T, Acc. W2666, 61/1/8. Note of Discussions of Marshall and Shanahan in Europe, Sept.–Oct. 1962. T, Acc. W2666, 61/5/4/2/5.
85. E (62) M44, 24 Aug. 1962. NZA: T, Acc. W2666, 61/1/8.
86. Westerman to Warwick-Smith, 17 Aug. 1962. NAA: A1838/275, 727/4/1, pt 1.
87. External Affairs to Australian Embassy, Brussels, 8 Aug. 1962. NAA: A1838/275, 727/3/22, pt 1.

88. Macmillan, *End of the Day*, p. 131.
89. Statement by Menzies in the House of Representatives, 16 Oct. 1962. NAA: A1838/275, 727/4/2, pt 5.
90. A. Horne, *Macmillan 1957–1986* (London: Macmillan, 1989), pp. 355–7; Robertson and Singleton, 'Old Commonwealth': pp. 168–9.
91. Note of Discussions of Marshall and Shanahan in Europe, Sept.–Oct. 1962. NZA: T, Acc. W2666, 61/5/4/2/5.
92. International Arrangements for Dairy Products, 26 Oct. 1962. NZA: T, Acc. W2666, 61/5/4/2/2. UK/EEC Negotiations: Special Arrangements for New Zealand, Annex C, 18 Dec. 1962. T, Acc. W2666, 61/1/8. Note of Discussions of Marshall and Shanahan in Europe, Sept.–Oct. 1962. T, Acc. W2666, 61/5/4/2/5. A Special Solution for New Zealand, 17 Jan. 1963. PRO: CAB 134/1544.
93. UK/EEC Negotiations: French Policy and the Kojeve Plan, May 1962. NZA: T 1, 61/5/4/2/4. EEC: Commodity Agreements, 6 July 1962. T, Acc. W2666, 61/5/4/2/2.
94. Brief for Consultations with Producer Representatives, 13 Feb. 1962. NZA, T, Acc. W2666, 61/5/4/1/1. E (62) M29, 5 June 1962; UK–EEC Negotiations: Progress Report, 7 Dec. 1962. T, Acc. W2666, 61/1/8. The Implications of Signing the Treaty of Rome: Food and Agriculture, 17 May 1961. PRO: CAB 134/1821. CMN (O) (63) 7th mtg, 23 Jan. 1963. CAB 134/1544.
95. E (62) M57 pt. 2, 20 Dec. 1962. NZA: T, Acc. W2666, 61/5/4/2/5.
96. UK/EEC Negotiations: Special Arrangement for New Zealand, 19 Dec. 1962. NZA: T, Acc. W2666, 61/5/4/2/5. CMN (O) (63) 7th mtg, 23 Jan. 1963. PRO: CAB 134/1544.
97. Oliver to Menzies, 19 Dec. 1962; Smith to the Secretary, Prime Minister's Department, 27 Dec. 1962; Note for File by O'Donnell, 7 Jan. 1963. NAA: A571/95, 61/791, pt 49.
98. F.W. Holmes, 'Security and Competitiveness 1935–94: Reflections on New Zealand's External Economic Strategy', unpublished paper, New Zealand Association of Economists' Conference, Massey University, Palmerston North, 1994, p. 3.
99. Note on Temperate Agricultural Products, 13 Aug. 1962. NZA: T, Acc. W2666, 61/5/4/2/2. See also: The Collapse of the Brussels Negotiations with Special Reference to New Zealand, 11 Feb. 1963. T 1, 61/5/4, pt 2.
100. Horne, *Macmillan*, pp. 256–62.
101. J.L. Granatstein, *Canada 1957–1967* (Toronto: McClelland and Stewart, 1986), p. 350; J. Lacouture, *De Gaulle: the Ruler 1945–1970* (London: Harvill, 1992), p. 360.
102. Cabinet Decision No. 638, 5 Feb. 1963. NAA: A4940/1, C3368, pt 4.

Chapter 9: After the Veto: Trade Policy in the Mid-1960s

1. Transcript of Interview, 31 Jan. 1963. NAA: A4940/1, C3368, pt 4.
2. Britain's Dilemma Following the Breakdown of the Brussels Negotiations and Policy Implications for New Zealand, 8 Feb. 1963; E (63) M4, 28 Feb. 1963. NZA: T 1, 61/5/4, pt 2.
3. Cabinet Minute, Decision No. 638, European Common Market, 5 Feb.

1963; European Common Market: Statement by Menzies, 5 Feb. 1963. NAA: A4940/1, C3368, pt 4. Cabinet Minute, Decision No. 684 (HOC), 14 March 1963. A4940/1, C3756. Britain Outside the European Community, 5 Feb. 1963; Inward Cablegram No. 460 from Australian High Commission London, 29 Jan 1963; Possible Breakdown in UK Negotiations with EEC – Implications for Australia, 18 Jan. 1963. A1838/275, 727/4/1, pt 4. Whitelaw to Randall, 1 Feb. 1963; Minute for Treasurer from O'Donnell, 4 Feb. 1963; O'Donnell to Whitelaw, 25 Jan. 1963. A571/78, 63/320, pt 1. Some Observations on the International Trade Scene, undated, 1963. A571/78, 63/320, pt 2.

4. If the Brussels Negotiations Fail, 24 July 1962; Minute from Soames to Macmillan, 19 July 1962. PRO: DO 159/11.

5. CC (63) 9th mtg, 31 Jan. 1963. PRO: CAB 128/37.

6. Ibid.

7. CC (63) 28th mtg, 2 May 1963. PRO: CAB 128/37. Hayward, *Golden Jubilee*, pp. 73–4; F.O. Grogan, *International Trade in Temperate Zone Products* (Edinburgh: Oliver & Boyd, 1972), pp. 49–50.

8. The Possibility of Trade Negotiations with Commonwealth Countries, 13 March 1963. PRO: CAB 134/1775.

9. Carter to Shannon, 27 June 1963. PRO: BT 241/741.

10. Note by Hughes, 30 Jan. 1963; Note by Jardine, 30 Jan. 1963. PRO: BT 241/740.

11. Figures refer to actual rather than contractual margins of preference in the case of British exports. Green, 'Commonwealth Preference: Tariff Duties and Preferences on UK Exports'; *idem*, 'Commonwealth Preference: UK Customs Duties and Tariff Preferences'; Elkan, 'Industrial Protection', p. 41; H. Johnson, 'The Commonwealth Preferences: a System in Need of Analysis', *Round Table*, 1965–6 56: 363–78.

12. Menzies to Macmillan, 9 March 1963; The Anglo-Australian Trade Agreement: Discussions with McEwen on 6–7 May, April 1963. PRO: BT 241/740. Minutes of UK/Australia Trade Discussions, 6 May 1963; Trade with Australia, Note of a Meeting of British Officials, 7 June 1963. BT 241/741.

13. Cabinet Minute, Decision No. 852, British Trade Treaty, GATT Kennedy Round Discussions, and Other Trade Matters, Report by Minister of Trade, 5 June 1963. NAA: A4940, C3784.

14. Brief for GATT Ministerial Meeting, 24 April 1963. NZA: T, Acc. W2666, 61/1/8.

15. Singleton and Robertson, 'Butter': 340–5.

16. Mr Harold Wilson's Economic Programme for the Commonwealth, 7 June 1963; Mr Harold Wilson's Ten Point Programme for the Commonwealth, 27 Aug. 1963. PRO: CAB 134/1777. B. Pimlott, *Harold Wilson* (London: HarperCollins, 1993), pp. 303, 433–5; 'Labour's Commonwealth Policy', *The Round Table*, 1964 217: 6–13; H. Wilson, *The Labour Government 1964–1970* (London: Weidenfeld & Nicolson and Michael Joseph, 1971), pp. 10–11, 117; W.D. McIntyre, *The Commonwealth of Nations: Origins and Impact 1869–1971* (Minneapolis: University of Minnesota Press, 1977), pp. 448–9; T. Balogh, *Unequal Partners* (Oxford: Blackwell, 1963), vol. 2.

17. Brief for Commonwealth Prime Ministers' Meeting, Economic Affairs, Paper 2, 2 June 1965. NZA: IC1, 74/1/6, pt 4.

18. Minutes of Official Committee on External Economic Policy, 25 March 1965. PRO: CAB 134/1771.
19. Extension of Bilateral Trade Arrangements with Commonwealth Countries, April 1965. PRO: BT 241/742. Review of Commercial Policy: Paper by the Board of Trade, Jan. 1966; Note by Allott, 27 Jan. 1966; Note by Sanders, 25 Jan. 1966. BT 11/6745.
20. Extension of Bilateral Trade Arrangements with Commonwealth Countries, April 1965, p. 9. PRO: BT 241/742.
21. Outward Telegram from CRO, 6 Oct. 1965. PRO: BT 241/743. GATT Kennedy Round – New Zealand Industrial Offer List, 8 March 1965. NZA: AAFD 811, Acc. W3738, Box 1177, 132/5/3, pt 13. GATT: Kennedy Round: Progress Report, 30 July 1965. Box 1177, 132/5/3, pt 14.
22. Trade Relations with Australia and New Zealand, 24 Sept. 1965. PRO: BT 241/743.
23. Singleton, 'New Zealand and the Survival of Ottawa': 176–7. Anglo-New Zealand Trade Talks, 1–5 Nov. 1965, Brief No. 2, Steering Brief, Oct. 1965. PRO: BT 241/745. Anglo-New Zealand Trade Talks: Duration of the 1959 Trade Agreement, 21 June 1966. BT 241/746. NZ/UK Trade Negotiations, London 1966, Brief A, pp. 2–5. NZA: IC 23, Acc. W2458, 183, pt 1.
24. Under the NNP rule it was permissible to bind the BP margin at a rate above the contractual margin where there was an additional non-contractual preference. This would increase the contractual but not the actual margin.
25. Wright to Adams, 1 Sept. 1965. PRO: BT 241/743. NZ/UK Trade Negotiations, London 1966, Brief A, pp. 7, 35–68. NZA: IC 23, Acc. W2458, 183, pt 1. NZ/UK Trade Talks, Minutes of the Second Ministerial Meeting, 10 June 1966; Minutes of the Third Officials' Meeting, 20 May 1966. IC 23, Acc. W2458, 195. D. Rendel, *Civil Aviation in New Zealand* (Wellington: Reed, 1975), p. 46.
26. NZ/UK Trade Talks, Record of Understanding Agreed Between J.R. Marshall and Douglas Jay, 28 June 1966. NZA: IC 23, Acc. W2458, 195. Aide Memoire from the Australian High Commission, 8 July 1966. PRO: BT 241/747.
27. *NZOYB*, 1967, p. 677; *NZOYB*, 1969, pp. 662–7.
28. Inward Cablegrams from Australian High Commission London, 22 Sept. 1967, 26 Sept. 1967, 30 Sept. 1967, 3 Oct. 1967; UK/Australian Trade Discussions, 12 Oct. 1967; Notes on UK Trade Talks, 17 Oct. 1967; Notes of Meeting Between McEwen and Crosland, 27 Nov. 1967. NAA: A10206/1, EHEC03.
29. GATT Kennedy Round of Negotiations, 30 June 1967. NAA: A4940, C3784.
30. 'Economic Review, 1967, Presented by Hon. R.D. Muldoon', *Appendix to the Journals of the House of Representatives*, 1967, 1, B5: 28–9; *NZOYB*, 1968, p. 677; J.W. Evans, *The Kennedy Round in American Trade Policy* (Cambridge, Mass.: Harvard University Press, 1971), pp. 243, 254–6, 289.
31. Marshall, *Memoirs*, 2, p. 21.
32. Note on Proposed Australia/New Zealand Trade Area, 2–4 July 1963. NAA: A1209/112, 64/6412, pt 2. Australian/New Zealand Study on Free Trade, 21 June 1963. NZA: AAFD 811, Acc. W3738, Box 1155, 131/2/2, pt 2. Proposed

Free Trade Area with Australia – Forest Products, 31 July 1964. Box 1177, 132/5/3, pt 2.

33. Limited Free Trade Arrangement with New Zealand in Forest Products, 7 Aug. 1964. NZA: AAFD 811, Acc. W3738, Box 1155, 131/2/2, pt 2.

34. Harry to Westerman, 2 Aug. 1963. NAA: A1209/112, 64/6412, pt 2.

35. Ibid., Dispatches from Cameron, 23 Jan. 1964, 5 March 1964.

36. Australia/New Zealand Limited Free Trade Arrangement, 16 Aug. 1965. NZA: AAFD 811, Acc. W3738, Box 1156, 131/2/2.

37. For presentational reasons there would be maximum quotas on some New Zealand forest and agricultural products. But New Zealand accepted that this did not alter the substance of the Australian commitment.

38. Australia/New Zealand Joint Standing Committee, Report of Study of Scope for a Free Trade Area, April 1964; Proposed Limited Free Trade Arrangement with Australia, 2 Oct. 1964. NZA: AAFD 811, Acc. W3738, Box 1155, 131/2/2, pt 2. Australia/New Zealand Limited Free Trade Area, Brief for Officials, 9 July 1965; Australia/New Zealand Limited Free Trade Arrangement, 16 Aug 1965; New Zealand–Australia Free Trade Agreement, Ratification, 1 Nov. 1965. Box 1156, 131/2/2. Industrial Cooperation with Australia, 13 Nov. 1964. Box 1177, 132/5/3, pt 13. Australia/New Zealand Free Trade Proposal, Brief for Officials and Ministerial Meetings, July/August 1965. NAA: A1209/112, 64/6412, pt 1. Inward Cablegram from Australian High Commission Wellington, 4 Aug. 1965; Proposed New Zealand–Australia Free Trade Area, 4 Aug. 1965. A1209/112, 64/6412, pt 2.

39. British Aide Memoire on NAFTA, 28 Aug. 1965. NAA: A1209/112, 64/6412, pt 3.

40. Inward Cablegram to External Affairs, 8 Oct. 1965. NAA: A1209/112, 64/6412, pt 3. Trade Relations with Australia and New Zealand, Memorandum by Board of Trade, Sept. 1965; Trade Relations with Australia and New Zealand, Brief for the Chairman, 24 Sept. 1965, Outward Telegram from CRO, 6 Oct. 1965. PRO: BT 241/743. Anglo-New Zealand Trade Talks: Duration of the 1959 Trade Agreement, 21 June 1966. BT 241/746.

41. Crawford, *Australian Trade Policy*, pp. 419–27; S. Brownie and P. Dalziel, 'Shift-share Analyses of New Zealand Exports, 1970–1984', *New Zealand Economic Papers*, 1993 27(2): 243, 245; P.J. Lloyd, 'Australia–New Zealand Trade Relations: NAFTA to CER', in K. Sinclair (ed.), *Tasman Relations: Australia and New Zealand, 1788–1988* (Auckland: Auckland University Press, 1987), pp. 142–63.

42. Guest and Singleton, 'Murupara': 65–7; Meredith and Dyster, *Australia in the Global Economy*, p. 274.

43. Address by McEwen to AJBCC Luncheon, 21 April 1966. NAA: A1838/1, 759/1/32, pt 2.

44. Dispatch from British High Commissioner in New Zealand to Commonwealth Secretary Concerning Trade Relations with New Zealand 1957–63, 26 June 1963; Dick to Board of Trade, 3 Sept. 1963. PRO: FO 11/6088/7304. Carter to Shannon, 27 June 1963. BT 241/741.

45. New Zealand Embassy, Tokyo to External Affairs, 13 Jan. 1960. NZA: IC 1, Acc. W1842, Box 2005, 107/10/1.

46. Note by Dalrymple, 18 Aug. 1964. NAA: A1838/280, 3103/7/2/1, pt 2. T.

Terada, 'The Japanese Origins of PAFTAD: The Beginning of an Asian Pacific Economic Community', *ANU Australia–Japan Research Centre, Pacific Economic Paper No. 222* (Canberra, 1999).

47. AJBCC Joint Statement, 3 Sept. 1964. NAA: A1838/1, 759/1/32, pt 2. Address by Nagano to Japan Economic Research Center, 21 Sept. 1964. A1838/2, 759/1, pt 12. AJBCC, Second Joint Meeting, Formation of Pacific Basin Organization for Economic Cooperation and Development. A1838/280, 3103/7/2/1, pt 2. K. Kojima (ed.), *Pacific Trade and Development: Papers and Proceedings of a Conference* (Tokyo: Japan Economic Research Center, 1968), 2 vols; K. Kojima, *Japan and a Pacific Free Trade Area* (Berkeley: University of California Press, 1971); P. Korhonen, *Japan and the Pacific Free Trade Area* (London: Routledge, 1994); *idem, Japan and Asia Pacific Integration: Pacific Romances, 1968–1996* (London: Routledge, 1998).

48. Draft letter from McIntyre to Anderson, April 1966. NAA: A1838/1, 759/1/32, pt 2.

49. Ibid., Jamieson to External Affairs, 11 May 1965; Report by Crawfour on Third Meeting of AJBCC, undated, 1965.

50. Observations on the Prospects for Japanese-Australian Trade by H.W. Arndt, undated, 1965. NAA: A1838/1, 759/1, pt 12. Note on Pacific Area Free Trade Alliance, April 1966. A1838/1, 759/1/32, pt 2.

51. Address by McEwen to AJBCC Luncheon, 21 April 1966. NAA: A1838/1, 759/1/32, pt 2.

52. E (67) M8, 20 April 1967. NZA: AAFD 811, Box 1163, 132/5/3, pt 5. Memorandum on Trade with Japan, 12 Dec. 1967. AAFD 811, Box 1181, 132/5/3, pt 20. L.V. Castle, 'New Zealand Trade and Aid Policies in Relation to the Pacific and Asian Region', in Kojima, *Pacific Trade and Development*, 1, pp. 79–108.

53. Terada, 'Origins of PAFTAD', p. 14.

54. *Canberra Times*, 9 Oct. 1965.

55. Note by Steel, 4 Jan. 1966. PRO: BT 11/6745.

56. Jamieson to External Affairs, 11 May 1965. NAA: A1838/1, 759/1/32, pt 2. Visit of Japanese Iron Ore Survey Mission, 5 Aug. 1964. A1838/2, 759/1, pt 12. Record of Meeting Between Prime Minister of Japan and Australian Cabinet, 12 Oct. 1967. A4940/1, C4682. Double Taxation Agreement with Japan, 25 Jan. 1968. A571/97, 67/6657, pt 1.

57. Address by McEwen to AJBCC Luncheon, 21 April 1966. NAA: A1838/1, 759/1/32, pt 2. Australian Cars to be Promoted at Japanese Trade Fair, 4 Nov. 1964. A1838/2, 759/1, pt 12.

58. Japanese Economic Penetration of Australia, Dec. 1963; Comments by C.H. Clark on Japanese Economic Penetration, undated, 1965. NAA: A1838/1, 759/1, pt 13.

59. Deane, Nicholl, and Walsh, *External Economic Structure*, p. 183. Japanese Agriculture in Relation to Markets for Butter, 29 July 1963. NZA: T 1, 61/6/20, pt 1. D. Ridler, 'Far East Markets for New Zealand's Meat and Milk', *NZIER Research Paper No. 3* (Wellington, 1962); L.V. Castle and I. McDougall, 'Japan as a Market for New Zealand Exports of Meat and Dairy Products', *NZIER Research Paper No. 14* (Wellington, 1969).

60. New Zealand Ambassador, Tokyo to Prime Minister, Wellington, 4 June 1963. NZA: T 1, 61/6/20, pt 1.

61. Brief for Official Visit to Japan by M.J. Moriarty, Secretary of Industries and Commerce, June 1969. NZA: IC 23, Acc. W2458, 249a.
62. Ibid., Report of Official Visit to Japan, June 1969.
63. R.Garnaut, *Open Regionalism and Trade Liberalization* (Sydney: Allen & Unwin, 1996), ch. 8.
64. E (67) M8, 20 April 1967; E (67) M12, 22 May 1967. NZA: AAFD 811, Acc. W3737, Box 1163, 132/5/2, pt 5. Memorandum on Reassessment of New Zealand Strategy, 23 Jan. 1967. T, Acc. W2666, 72/12/NZ/1.
65. Notes of Visit of Mr Muldoon to London, 18 Sept. 1967. NZA: T, Acc. W2666, 72/12/NZ/1.
66. Ibid., Report of Discussions with Sir Arthur Snelling, 1 Nov. 1967.
67. Ibid., New Zealand Mission, Brussels to External Affairs, 8 Nov. 1967.
68. A. Cairncross, *The Wilson Years: A Treasury Diary, 1964–1969* (London: Historians' Press, 1997), p. 208.
69. CCEFP Minutes, 22 May 1967, 11 Sept. 1967. NZA: AAFD 811, Box 1163, 132/5/2, pt 5. UK/EEC, Policy Brief on Consultations with the British, pt 2, 7 April 1967. AAFD 811, Box 1180, 132/5/3, pt 18. UK/EEC, Policy Brief on Consultations with the British, pt 3, 11 April 1967; UK/EEC, Consultations with the British Government, 12 May 1967. Box 1180, 132/5/3, pt 19.
70. Britain and the EEC, 15 Nov. 1967. NAA: A10206/1, EHEC03. I. Smith, 'Prospects for Commonwealth Sugar', *The Round Table*, 1975 257: 51–8.
71. Marshall, *Memoirs*, 2, ch. 7. Annual Report on the EEC from the New Zealand Mission Brussels, 20 March 1969. NZA: T, Acc. W2335, 75/4, pt 1.
72. P. Einzig, *The Case Against Joining the Common Market* (London: Macmillan, 1971), p. vii.
73. New Zealand High Commission, London to External Affairs, 1 March 1970. NZA: T, Acc. W2666, 72/12/NZ/1.
74. Ibid., E (70) M1, 26 Jan. 1970.
75. Ibid., Record of Meeting between Barber and Marshall, 9 July 1970. U. Kitzinger, *Diplomacy and Persuasion: How Britain Joined the Common Market* (London: Thames & Hudson, 1973), pp. 101–2, 117, 128–36; G. Barclay, 'The Diplomacy of British Entry into Europe: an Australian Perspective', *The Round Table*, 1972 245: 101–12; F. Nicholson and R. East, *From the Six to the Twelve* (Harlow: Keesing, 1987), pp. 68–73; A. Benvenuti, 'Australia's Battle Against the Common Agricultural Policy: the Fraser Government's Trade Diplomacy and the European Community', *Australian Journal of Politics and History*, 1999 45(2): 181–96.
76. UK/EEC: Report on Discussions between British and New Zealand Officials, 14 June 1970; Minutes of Cabinet Committee on Overseas Trade Policy, 14 Oct. 1970. NZA: T, Acc. W2666, 72/12/NZ/1. Kitzinger, *Diplomacy and Persuasion*, p. 141; M. Robson, *Decision at Dawn: New Zealand and the EEC* (London: Baynard-Hillier, 1972).
77. Memorandum on Visit of the German Minister of Agriculture, Nov. 1971. NZA: T, Acc. W2591, 75/4, pt 3. J. Lodge, *The European Community and New Zealand* (London: Frances Pinter, 1982), pp. 222–4; J.A. McMahon, *New Zealand and the Common Agricultural Policy* (Wellington: Victoria University Press, 1990), pp. 20–5.

Bibliography

Abramovitz, M., 'Catching Up, Forging Ahead, and Falling Behind', *Journal of Economic History*, 1986 46(2): 385–406.

Akoorie, M., 'The Historical Role of Foreign Investment in the New Zealand Economy', in Enderwick (ed.), *Foreign Investment* (1998).

Alford, B.W.E., *Britain in the World Economy since 1880* (London: Longman, 1996).

Allen, G.C., *Japan's Economic Policy* (London: Macmillan, 1980).

Amsalem, M.A., *Technology Choice in Developing Countries: the Textile and Pulp and Paper Industries* (Cambridge, MA: MIT Press, 1983).

Amsden, A., *Asia's Next Giant: South Korea and Late Industrialisation* (New York: Oxford University Press, 1989).

Anderson, K. and Garnaut, R., *Australian Protectionism* (Sydney: Allen & Unwin, 1987).

Anderson, K. and Norheim, H., 'From Imperial to Regional Trade Preferences: Its Effect on Europe's Intra– and Extra–Regional Trade', *Weltwirtschaftliches Archiv*, 1993 129(1): 78–101.

Arndt, H.W., 'Sir John Crawford', *Economic Record*, 1985 61(2): 507–15.

Australia, Commonwealth of, *Report of the Committee of Economic Enquiry* (Canberra: Commonwealth of Australia, 1965), 2 vols.

Australia, Department of Foreign Affairs and Trade, *Documents on Australian Foreign Policy: The Australia–Japan Agreement on Commerce 1957* (Canberra: Commonwealth of Australia, 1997).

Baker, B.V.T., *The New Zealand People at War: War Economy* (Wellington: Department of Internal Affairs, 1965).

Ball, G.W., *The Discipline of Power* (Boston: Little, Brown, 1968).

Balogh, T., *Unequal Partners* (Oxford: Blackwell, 1963), vol. 2.

Bamberg, J.H., *The History of the British Petroleum Company* (Cambridge: Cambridge University Press, 1984), vol. 2.

Bange, O., *The EEC Crisis of 1963* (Basingstoke: Macmillan, 2000).

Barclay, G., 'The Diplomacy of British Entry into Europe: an Australian Perspective', *The Round Table*, 1972 245: 101–12.

Bassett, M., *The State in New Zealand 1840–1984* (Auckland: Auckland University Press, 1998).

Behrman, J.N., 'Foreign Associates and their Financing', in R.F. Mikesell (ed.), *US Private and Government Investment Abroad* (Eugene: University of Oregon Press, 1962).

Bell, P.W., *The Sterling Area in the Postwar World* (Oxford: Oxford University Press, 1956).

Bell, S., *Australian Manufacturing and the State* (Cambridge: Cambridge University Press, 1993).

Belshaw, H., 'Post War Economic Reconstruction in New Zealand', *Pacific Affairs*, 1944 17(4): 421–43

Bennett, J., 'Social Security, the "Money Power" and the Great Depression: the International Dimension to Australian and New Zealand Labour in Office', *Australian Journal of Politics and History*, 1997 43(3): 312–30.

Benvenuti, A., 'Australia's Battle Against the Common Agricultural Policy: the Fraser Government's Trade Diplomacy and the European Community', *Australian Journal of Politics and History*, 1999 45(2): 181–96.

Beresford, M. and Kerr, P., 'A Turning Point for Australian Capitalism: 1945–52', in E.L. Wheelwright and K. Buckley (eds), *Essays in the Political Economy of Australian Capitalism* (Sydney: Australia & New Zealand Book Company, 1980), vol. 4.

Bernstein, E.M., 'British Policy and a World Economy', *American Economic Review*, 1945 35(5): 891–908.

Black, S.W., *A Levite Among the Priests: Edward M. Bernstein and the Origins of the Bretton Woods System* (Boulder: Westview, 1991).

Bollard, A., Lattimore, R. and Silverstone, B., 'Introduction', in B. Silverstone, A. Bollard and R. Lattimore (eds), *A Study of Economic Reform: the Case of New Zealand* (Amsterdam: North Holland, 1996).

Borden, W.S., *The Pacific Alliance: United States Foreign Economic Policy and Japanese Trade Recovery, 1947–1955* (Madison: University of Wisconsin Press, 1984).

Bowers, J.K., 'British Agricultural Policy Since the Second World War', *Agricultural History Review*, 1985 33: 66–76.

Boyce, G., 'The Western Mining Corporation–Hanna/Homestake Joint Venture: Game Theory and Inter-Organizational Cooperation', *Australian Economic History Review*, 1997 37(3): 202–21.

Boyce, R.W.D., 'Britain's First "No" to Europe: Britain and the Briand Plan, 1929–30', *European Studies Review*, 1980 10(1): 17–45.

Broadberry, S.N., *The Productivity Race: British Manufacturing in International Perspective, 1850–1990* (Cambridge: Cambridge University Press, 1997).

Brownie, S., and Dalziel, P., 'Shift–Share Analyses of New Zealand Exports, 1970–1984', *New Zealand Economic Papers*, 1993 27(2): 233–49.

Brusse, W.A., *Tariffs, Trade and European Integration, 1947–1957* (New York; St Martin's Press, 1997).

Burgess, S. and Edwards, G., 'The Six Plus One: British Policy–Making and the Question of European Economic Integration, 1955', *International Affairs*, 1988 64: 393–413.

Butlin, N.G., 'Trends in Public/Private Relations, 1901–75', in B. Head (ed.), *State and Economy in Australia* (Melbourne: Oxford University Press, 1983).

Butlin, S.J., and Schedvin, C.B., *War Economy 1942–1945* (Canberra: Australian War Memorial, 1977), vol. 2.

Cain, P.J. and Hopkins, A.G., *British Imperialism: Innovation and Expansion, 1688–1914* (London: Longman, 1993).

Cain, P.J. and Hopkins, A.G., *British Imperialism: Crisis and Deconstruction, 1914–1990* (London: Longman, 1993).

Cain, P.J. and Hopkins, A.G., 'Afterword: The Theory and Practice of British Imperialism', in R.E. Dumett (ed.), *Gentlemanly Capitalism and British Imperialism* (London: Longman, 1999).

Cairncross, A.C., *The Years of Recovery: British Economic Policy 1945–51* (London: Methuen, 1985).

Cairncross, A.C. (ed.), *The Robert Hall Diaries 1947–53* (London: Unwin Hyman, 1989).

Cairncross, A.C., 'Economic Policy and Performance, 1945–1964', in R. Floud and D.N. McCloskey (eds), *The Economic History of Britain* (Cambridge: Cambridge University Press, 1994), vol. 3.

Cairncross, A.C., *The Wilson Years: a Treasury Diary, 1964–1969* (London: Historians' Press, 1997).

Calder, K.E., *Crisis and Compensation: Public Policy and Political Stability in Japan, 1949–1986* (Princeton: Princeton University Press, 1988).

Campbell, J., *Edward Heath* (London: Jonathan Cape 1993).

Camps, M., *Britain and the European Community 1955–1963* (Princeton: Princeton University Press, 1964).

Capling, A., 'The "Enfant Terrible": Australia and the Reconstruction of the Multilateral Trade System', *Australian Economic History Review*, 2000 40(1): 1–21.

Capling, M.A. and Galligan, B., *Beyond the Protective State: the Political Economy of Australia's Manufacturing Industry* (Cambridge: Cambridge University Press, 1992).

Carey, D.A. and Smith, A.A., 'The External Dependence of the New Zealand Economy', in Deane, Nicholl, and Walsh (eds), *External Economic Structure* (1981).

Carney, W.R., 'The Ottawa Agreement Now', *Economic Record*, 1956 32(1): 99–105.

Cashin, P.A., 'Real GDP in the Seven Colonies of Australasia: 1861–1991', *Review of Income and Wealth*, 1995 41(1): 19–39.

Casson, M., *Enterprise and Competitiveness* (Oxford: Clarendon Press, 1990).

Castle, L.V. and McDougall, I., 'Japan as a Market for New Zealand Exports of Meat and Dairy Products', *NZIER Research Paper No. 14* (Wellington, 1969).

Charmley, J., *Churchill's Grand Alliance* (London: Hodder & Stoughton, 1995).

Clark, C., *The Economics of 1960* (London: Macmillan, 1942).

Clark, C., 'Economic Growth', in J. Wilkes (ed.), *Economic Growth in Australia* (Sydney: Angus & Robertson, 1962).

Clark, C., 'Development Economics: The Early Years', in G.M. Meier and D. Seers (eds), *Pioneers in Development* (New York: Oxford University Press, 1984).

Cochrane, W.W. and Ryan, M.E., *American Farm Policy, 1948–1973* (Minneapolis: University of Minnesota Press, 1976).

Commonwealth Economic Committee, *Meat: A Review 1958* (London: HMSO, 1958).

Commonwealth Economic Committee, *Commonwealth Trade 1950 to 57* (London: HMSO, 1959).

Conan, A.R., *The Sterling Area* (London: Macmillan, 1952).

Conan, A.R., *Capital Imports into Sterling Countries* (London: Macmillan 1960).

Condliffe, J.B., 'The International Position as it Affects New Zealand', *Economic Record*, 1939 15 (New Zealand Centennial Supplement): 17–24.

Condliffe, J.B., 'New Zealand's Experiment in Economic Planning', *American Economic Review*, 1957 47(6): 930–45.

Condliffe, J.B., *The Development of Australia* (Christchurch: Whitcombe and Tombs, 1964).

Constantine, S., 'Waving Goodbye? Australia, Assisted Passages, and the Empire and Commonwealth Resettlement Acts, 1945–72', *Journal of Imperial and Commonwealth History*, 1998, 26(2): 176–95.

Coombs, H.C., *Trial Balance* (South Melbourne: Macmillan, 1981).

Copland, D.B., 'Balance of Production in the Australian Post-war Economy', *Economic Record*, 1949 25(2): 1–6.

Copland, D.B., 'Problems of the Sterling Area With Special Reference to Australia', *Essays in International Finance No. 17* (Princeton: Princeton University Press, 1953).

Copland, D.B., 'The Australian Post-war Economy: a Study in Economic Administration', *Canadian Journal of Economics and Political Science*, 1954 20(4): 421–38.

Copland, D.B., 'Economic Problems for New Zealand in an Expanding World', *Industrial Development Conference Papers* (Wellington: Government Printer, 1960).

Copland, D.B and Barback, R.H. (eds), *The Conflict of Expansion and Stability* (Melbourne: Cheshire, 1957).

Corden, W.M., 'Australia and European Free Trade', *Economic Record*, 1958 31(2): 160–71.

Cornish, S., 'Sir Leslie Melville: an Interview', *Economic Record*, 1993 69: 437–57.

Crafts, N., 'Economic Growth in the Twentieth Century', *Oxford Review of Economic Policy*, 1999 15(4): 18–34.

Crawford, J.G., *Australian Trade Policy 1942–1966: a Documentary History* (Canberra: ANU Press, 1968).

Crisp, L.F., 'The Australian Full Employment Pledge at San Francisco', *Australian Outlook*, 1965 19(1): 5–19.

Curzon, G., *Multilateral Commercial Diplomacy* (London: Michael Joseph, 1965).

Daniels, G., 'Britain's View of Post-war Japan, 1945–9', in I. Nish (ed.), *Anglo–Japanese Alienation, 1919–1952* (Cambridge: Cambridge University Press, 1982).

Deane, R.S., *Foreign Investment in New Zealand Manufacturing* (Wellington: Sweet & Maxwell, 1970).

Deane, R.S., Nicholl, P.W.E. and Walsh, M.J. (eds), *External Economic Structure and Policy: an Analysis of New Zealand's Balance of Payments* (Wellington: RBNZ, 1981).

Deighton, A., and Milward, A.S. (eds), *Widening, Deepening and Acceleration: the European Economic Community, 1957–1963* (Baden-Baden: Nomos, 1999).

Denison, E.F., *Why Growth Rate Differ* (Washington: Brookings Institution, 1967).

Diefenbaker, J.G., *One Canada* (Toronto: Macmillan, 1976), vol. 2.

Dingemans, R. and Boekestijn, A.J., 'The Netherlands and the Enlargement Proposals 1957–1963', in Deighton and Milward (eds), *Widening, Deepening and Acceleration* (1999).

Dobson, A.P., *The Politics of the Anglo–American Economic Special Relationship* (Brighton: Wheatsheaf, 1988).

Dormael, A.V., *Bretton Woods* (London: Macmillan, 1978).

Downing, R.I. and Perkins, J.O.N, 'What Should Be Done About the Sterling Area? Australia', *Bulletin of the Oxford University Institute of Statistics*, 1959 21(4): 253–66.

Drummond, I.M., *Imperial Economic Policy 1917–1939* (London: Allen & Unwin, 1974).

Drummond, I.M., *The Floating Pound and the Sterling Area* (Cambridge: Cambridge University Press, 1981).

Duncan, I., Lattimore, R., and Bollard, A., 'Dismantling the Barriers: Tariff Policy in New Zealand', *NZIER Research Monograph No. 57* (Wellington, NZIER, 1992).

Dyster, B. and Meredith, D., *Australia in the International Economy in the Twentieth Century* (Cambridge: Cambridge University Press, 1990).

Easton, B., *In Stormy Seas: the Post-war New Zealand Economy* (Dunedin: University of Otago Press, 1997).

Economist Intelligence Unit, *The Commonwealth and Europe* (London: EIU, 1960).

Edgington, D.W., 'Japanese Business Down-Under: Patterns of Japanese Investment in Australia, 1957–1984', Transnational Corporations Research Project, University of Sydney, 1988.

Eichengreen, B., *Golden Fetters: the Gold Standard and the Great Depression 1919–1939* (New York: Oxford University Press, 1992).

Eichengreen, B. and Irwin, D.I., 'Trade Blocs, Currency Blocs and the Reorientation of World Trade in the 1930s', *Journal of International Economics*, 1995 38: 1–24.

Einzig, P., *The Case Against Joining the Common Market* (London: Macmillan, 1971).

Elkan, P.G. 'New Zealand's Butter and Cheese in the European Economic Community', *NZIER Research Paper No. 2* (Wellington: NZIER, 1962).

Elkan, P.G., 'Industrial Protection in New Zealand 1952 to 1967', *Technical Memorandum No. 15*, New Zealand Institute of Economic Research (Wellington: NZIER, 1972).

Ellison, J.R.V., 'Perfidious Albion? Britain, Plan G and European integration, 1955–1956', *Contemporary British History*, 1996 10(4): 1–34.

Enderwick, P. (ed.), *Foreign Investment: the New Zealand Experience* (Palmerston North: Dunmore, 1998).

Endres, A.M., 'The Political Economy of W.B. Sutch: Toward a Critical Appreciation', *New Zealand Economic Papers*, 1986 20: 17–39.

Endres, A.M., '"Structural" Economic Thought in New Zealand: the Inter-war Contribution of A.G.B. Fisher', *New Zealand Economic Papers*, 1988 22: 35–49.

Endres, A.M., 'The Development of Economists' Policy Advice in New Zealand, 1930–34: With Particular Reference to Belshaw's Contribution', *Australian Economic History Review*, 1990 30(1): 64–78.

Evans, D., 'The Long Run Determinants of North–South Terms of Trade and Some Recent Empirical Evidence', *World Development*, 1987 15(5): 657–71.

Evans, J.W., *The Kennedy Round in American Trade Policy* (Cambridge, MA: Harvard University Press, 1971).

Ferretti, V., 'Japan's Admission to GATT (1951–1955)', in P. Lowe, V. Ferretti, and I. Nish, *Japan in the 1950s*, STICERD Discussion Paper, IS/97/322, LSE, 1997.

Fforde, J.S., *The Bank of England and Public Policy, 1941–1958* (Cambridge: Cambridge University Press, 1992).

Fieldhouse, D.K., 'The Metropolitan Economics of Empire', in J.M. Brown and W.R. Louis (eds), *Oxford History of the British Empire* (Oxford: Oxford University Press, 1999), vol. 4.

Fisher, A.G.B., *The Clash of Progress and Security* (London: Macmillan, 1935).

Fisher, W., 'Ownership and Control of Industry in New Zealand Manufacturing', *Industrial Development Conference Papers* (Wellington: Government Printer, 1960).

Foreman-Peck, J., *A History of the World Economy* (Hemel Hempstead: Harvester Wheatsheaf, 1995).

Foreman-Peck, J., *Smith & Nephew in the Health Care Industry* (Aldershot: Edward Elgar, 1995).

Gardner, R.N., *Sterling–Dollar Diplomacy* (New York: McGraw-Hill, 1969).

Garnaut, R., *Open Regionalism and Trade Liberalization* (Sydney: Allen & Unwin, 1996).

Gifford, J.K. et al., *Australian Banking* (St Lucia: University of Queensland Press, 1966).

Golding, J., *Black Jack McEwen* (Melbourne: Melbourne University Press, 1996).

Gordon–Ashworth, F., *International Commodity Control* (London: Croom Helm, 1984).

Gould, J.D., *The Rake's Progress: the New Zealand Economy Since 1945* (Auckland: Hodder & Stoughton, 1982).

Granatstein, J.L., *Canada 1957–1967* (Toronto: McClelland and Stewart, 1986).

Greasley, D. and Oxley, L., 'A Tale of Two Dominions: Comparing the Macroeconomic Records of Australia and Canada Since 1870', *Economic History Review*, 1998 51(2): 294–318

Greasley, D. and L. Oxley, L., 'Outside the Club: New Zealand's Economic Growth, 1870–1993', *International Review of Applied Economics*, 2000 14(2): 173–92.

Green, R.W., 'Commonwealth Preference: Tariff Duties and Preferences on United Kingdom Exports to the Preference Area', *Board of Trade Journal*, 11 June 1965, pp. iv–xix.

Green, R.W., 'Commonwealth Preference: United Kingdom Customs Duties and Tariff Preferences on Imports from the Preference Area', *Board of Trade Journal*, 31 Dec. 1965, pp. 1551–8.

Groenwegen, P. and McFarlane, B., *A History of Australian Economic Thought* (London: Routledge, 1990).

Grogan, F.O., *International Trade in Temperate Zone Products* (Edinburgh: Oliver & Boyd, 1972).

Gruen, F.H., 'How Bad is Australia's Economic Performance and Why?', *Economic Record*, 1986 62(2): 180–93.

Guest, M.W., 'The Murupara Project: The Tasman Pulp and Paper Company Ltd and Industrial Development in New Zealand 1945–1963', MA thesis, Victoria University of Wellington, 1997.

Guest, M.W. and Singleton, J., 'The Murupara Project and Industrial Development in New Zealand 1945–65', *Australian Economic History Review*, 1999 39(1): 52–71.

Hancock, W.K., *Survey of British Commonwealth Affairs* (London: Oxford University Press, 1940), vol. II, pt 1.

Havinden, M. and Meredith, D., *Colonialism and Development: Britain and its Tropical Colonies* (London: Routledge, 1993).

Hawke, G.R., *Between Governments and Banks: a History of the Reserve Bank of New Zealand* (Wellington: A.R. Shearer, 1973).

Hawke, G.R., *The Making of New Zealand* (Cambridge: Cambridge University Press, 1985).

Hawke, G.R. and Wijewardane, B.A.D, 'New Zealand and the International Monetary Fund', *Economic Record*, 1972 48(1): 92–102.

Hayward, D., *Golden Jubilee: the Story of the First Fifty Years of the New Zealand Meat Producers' Board* (Wellington: New Zealand Meat Producers Board, 1972).

Hefford, R.K., *Farm Policy in Australia* (St Lucia: University of Queensland Press, 1985).

Hemming, M.F.W., Miles, C.M., and Ray, G.F., 'A Statistical Summary of the Extent of Import Control in the UK since the War', *Review of Economic Studies*, 1959 26(2): 75–109.

Henderson, H.D., *The Inter-war Years and Other Papers*, ed. H. Clay (Oxford: Clarendon Press, 1955).

Hendriks, G., 'The Creation of the Common Agricultural Policy', in Deighton and Milward (eds), *Widening, Deepening and Acceleration* (1999).

Hirsch, J., 'Export Credit Insurance and Investment Guaranties', in US Senate, Committee on Banking and Currency, *Study of Export–Import Bank and World Bank* (Washington, DC, 1954), pt 2.

Hogan, M.J., *The Marshall Plan* (Cambridge: Cambridge University Press, 1987).

Holmes, F.W., 'Security and Competitiveness 1935–94: Reflections on New Zealand's External Economic Strategy', unpublished paper, New Zealand Association of Economists' Conference, Massey University, Palmerston North, 1994.

Hopkins, T., 'Macmillan's Audit of Empire, 1957', in P. Clarke and C. Trebilcock (eds), *Understanding Decline: Perceptions and Realities of British Economic Performance* (Cambridge: Cambridge University Press, 1997).

Horne, A., *Macmillan 1957–1986* (London: Macmillan, 1989).

Horsefield, J.K., *The International Monetary Fund 1945–1965* (Washington, DC: IMF, 1969), vol. 1.

Horsefield J.K. and de Vries, M.G., *The International Monetary Fund 1945–1965* (Washington, DC: IMF, 1969), vol. 2.

Hughes, H., 'Why Have east Asian Countries Led Economic Development?', *Economic Record*, 1995 71(212): 88–104.

Ikenberry, J.G., 'A World Economy Restored: Expert Consensus and the Anglo–American Postwar Settlement', *International Organization*, 1992 46(1): 289–321.

Johnson, H., 'The Commonwealth Preferences: A System in Need of Analysis', *Round Table*, 1965–66 56: 363–78.

Johnson, H., 'Trade Challenges to Commonwealth Countries', in P. Streeten and H. Corbet, (eds), *Commonwealth Policy in a Global Context* (Toronto: University of Toronto Press, 1971).

Jones, G and Wale, J., 'Merchants as Business Groups: British Trading Companies in Asia before 1945', *Business History Review*, 1998 72(3): 367–408.

Jones, G and Wale, J., 'Diversification Strategies of British Trading Companies: Harrisons & Crosfield, c.1900–c.1980', *Business History*, 1999 41(2): 69–101.

Jones, S.R.H., 'Government Policy and Industry Structure in New Zealand, 1900–1970', *Australian Economic History Review*, 1999 39(3): 199–212.

Kaiser, W., 'To Join or Not to Join? The "Appeasement" Policy of Britain's First EEC Application', in B. Brivati and H. Jones (eds), *From Reconstruction to Integration* (Leicester: Leicester University Press, 1993).

Kaiser, W., 'From Laggard to Leader? The United Kingdom's 1961 Decision to Apply for EEC Membership', in Deighton and Milward (eds), *Widening, Deepening and Acceleration* (1999).

Kaplan, J.J. and Schleiminger, G., *The European Payments Union* (Oxford: Clarendon Press, 1989).

Kapur, H., *The Awakening Giant: China's Ascension in World Politics* (Alphen aan den Rijn: Sijthoff & Noordhoff, 1981).

Kaufman, B.I., *Trade and Aid: Eisenhower's Foreign Economic Policy, 1953–1961* (Baltimore: Johns Hopkins University Press, 1982).

Kaufman, B.I., 'Eisenhower's Foreign Economic Policy With Respect to Asia', in W.I. Cohen and A. Iriye (eds), *The Great Powers in east Asia: 1953–1960* (New York: Columbia University Press, 1990).

Kent, J., *British Imperial Strategy and the Origins of the Cold War 1944–49* (Leicester: Leicester University Press, 1993).

Kenwood, A.G., *Australian Economic Interests since Federation* (Melbourne: Oxford University Press, 1995).

Kenwood, A.G., and Lougheed, A.L., *The Growth of the International Economy 1820–1990* (London: Routledge, 1992).

Keynes, J.M., *The Collected Writings of John Maynard Keynes*, ed, D. Moggridge (London: Macmillan, 1979), vols. XXIV and XXVII.

King, J.E., *Economic Exiles* (London: Macmillan, 1988).

Kitzinger, U., *Diplomacy and Persuasion: How Britain Joined the Common Market* (London: Thames & Hudson, 1973).

Knox, F., *The Common Market and World Agriculture* (New York: Praeger, 1972).

Kojima, K., 'An Impression of the Oceanian Economy', *Economic Record*, 1964 40(1): 46–57.

Kojima, K. (ed.), *Pacific Trade and Development: Papers and Proceedings of a Conference* (Tokyo: Japan Economic Research Center, 1968), 2 vols.

Kojima, K., *Japan and a Pacific Free Trade Area* (Berkeley: University of California Press, 1971).

Korhonen, P., *Japan and the Pacific Free Trade Area* (London: Routledge, 1994).

Korhonen, P., *Japan and Asia Pacific Integration: Pacific Romances, 1968–1996* (London: Routledge, 1998).

Krozewski, G. 'Sterling, the "Minor" Territories and the End of Formal Empire, 1939–1958', *Economic History Review*, 1993 46(2): 239–265.

Lacouture, J., *De Gaulle: the Ruler 1945–1970* (London: Harvill, 1992).

Lamb, R., *The Macmillan Years 1957–1963* (London: John Murray, 1995).

Lee, D., 'Protecting the Sterling Area: The Chifley Government's Response to Multilateralism 1945–9', *Australian Journal of Political Science*, 1990 25: 178–95.

Lee, D., 'Australia, the British Commonwealth, and the United States 1950–53', *Journal of Imperial and Commonwealth History*, 1992 20(3): 445–469.

Lee, D., *Search for Security: the Political Economy of Australia's Postwar Foreign and Defence Policy* (St Leonard's, NSW: Allen & Unwin, 1995).

Lim, J.Y., 'The Macroeconomics of the east Asian Crisis and the Implications of the Crisis for Macroeconomic Theory', *The Manchester School*, 1999 67(5): 428–59.

Lipgens, W., *A History of European Integration* (Oxford: Clarendon Press, 1982), vol. 1.

Lloyd, P.J., 'Australia–New Zealand Trade Relations: NAFTA to CER', in K. Sinclair (ed.), *Tasman Relations: Australia and New Zealand, 1788–1988* (Auckland: Auckland University Press, 1987).

Lodge, J., *The European Community and New Zealand* (London: Frances Pinter, 1982).

Lord, C., *Absent at the Creation: Britain and the Formation of the European Community, 1950–2* (Aldershot: Dartmouth, 1996).

Lough, N.V., 'New Zealand's External Economic Relations', in T.C. Larkin (ed.), *New Zealand's External Relations* (London: Oxford University Press, 1962).

Ludlow, N.P., *Dealing with Britain: the Six and the First UK Application to Join the EEC* (Cambridge: Cambridge University Press, 1997).

Lynch, F.M.B., *France and the International Economy* (London: Routledge, 1997).

Mabbett, D., *Trade, Employment and Welfare: a Comparative Study of Trade and Labour Market Policies in Sweden and New Zealand, 1880–1980* (Oxford: Clarendon Press, 1995).

MacDougall, D. and Hutt, R., 'Imperial Preference: a Quantitative Analysis', in D. MacDougall, *Essays in Political Economy* (London: Macmillan, 1970), vol. 1.

Macmillan, H., *At the End of the Day 1961–1963* (London: Macmillan, 1973).

Maddison, A., *Dynamic Forces in Capitalist Development* (Oxford: Oxford University Press, 1991).

Mansergh, N., 'The Commonwealth: a Retrospective Survey, 1955–64', in W.B. Hamilton, K. Robinson, and C.D.W. Goodwin, *A Decade of the Commonwealth, 1955–1964* (Durham, NC: Duke University Press, 1966).

Marshall, J.R., *Memoirs, 1960–88* (Auckland: Collins, 1989).

Martin, A.W., *Robert Menzies, a Life* (Melboune: Melbourne University Press, 1993), vol. 1.

Martin, J., 'Economic Policy–Making in the Early Post-war Years', in J. Whitwell and M.A. Thompson (eds), *Society and Culture: Economic Perspectives* (Wellington: New Zealand Association of Economists, 1991), vol. 1.

Martin, J.E., *Holding the Balance: a History of New Zealand's Department of Labour 1891–1995* (Christchurch: Canterbury University Press, 1996).

Mathews, R., *Public Investment in Australia* (Melbourne: F. W. Cheshire, 1967).

McCarthy, E., *Wool Disposals, 1945–52* (Southampton: Hobbs, 1967).

McFarlane, B. 'Australian Postwar Economic Policy, 1947–53', in A. Curthoys and J. Meritt (eds), *Australia's First Cold War 1945–1953* (Sydney: Allen & Unwin, 1984), vol. 1.

McGibbon, I. (ed.), *Undiplomatic Dialogue: Letters Between Carl Berendsen and Alister McIntosh 1943–1952* (Auckland: Auckland University Press, 1993).

McIntyre, W.D., *The Commonwealth of Nations: Origins and Impact 1869–1971* (Minneapolis: University of Minnesota Press, 1977).

McKenzie, F., 'Renegotiating a Special Relationship: the Commonwealth and Anglo–American Economic Discussions, September–December 1945', *Journal of Imperial and Commonwealth History*, 1998 26(3): 71–93.

McLuskie, R., *The Great Debate: New Zealand, Britain, and the EEC* (Wellington: Victoria University of Wellington, 1986).

McKinnon, M.A., 'The Impact of War: a Diplomatic History of New Zealand's Economic Relations with Britain, 1939–1954', unpublished PhD thesis, Victoria University of Wellington (1981),

McKinnon, M., 'Equality of Sacrifice: Anglo-New Zealand Relations and the War Economy, 1939–45', *Journal of Imperial and Commonwealth History*, 1984 12(3): 54–76.

McKinnon, M., 'The New World of the Dollar', in M. McKinnon (ed.), *The American Connection* (Wellington: Allen & Unwin, 1988).

McMahon, J.A., *New Zealand and the Common Agricultural Policy* (Wellington: Victoria University Press, 1990).

Meade, J., *Collected Papers*, eds S. Howson and D. Moggridge (London: Unwin Hyman, 1990), vol. 4.

Meredith, D. and Dyster, B., *Australia in the Global Economy* (Cambridge: Cambridge University Press, 1999).

Merrett, D.T., 'Capital Markets and Capital Formation in Australia, 1945–1990', *Australian Economic History Review*, 1998 38(2): 135–54.

Merry, D.H. and Bruns, G.R., 'Full Employment: the British, Canadian and Australian White Papers', *Economic Record*, 1945 21(2): 223–35.

Meyer, F.V., *Britain, the Sterling Area and Europe* (Cambridge: Bowes & Bowes, 1952).

Milward, A.S., 'The Committee of European Economic Cooperation (CEEC) and the Advent of the Customs Union', in Lipgens, *European Integration* (1982).

Milward, A.S., *The Reconstruction of western Europe, 1945–1952* (London: Methuen, 1984).

Milward, A.S., *The European Rescue of the Nation-State* (London: Routledge, 1992).

Molegraaf, J. and Dingemans, R., 'The Netherlands and the Common Agricultural Policy', in Deighton and Milward (eds), *Widening, Deepening and Acceleration* (1999).

Moore, L., *Britain's Trade and Economic Structure* (London: Routledge, 1999).

Myrdal, G., *An International Economy* (London: Routledge and Kegan Paul, 1956.

Nash, E.F. and Attwood, E.A., *The Agricultural Policies of Britain and Denmark* (London: Land, 1961).

Nash, W., 'Building the Future: Opening Address to the Conference', *Industrial Development Conference Papers* (Wellington: Government Printer, 1960).

Newton, C.C.S., 'The Sterling Crisis of 1947 and the British Response to the Marshall Plan', *Economic History Review*, 1984 37(3): 391–408.

New Zealand, Dominion of, *Report of the Royal Commission on Monetary, Banking, and Credit Systems* (Wellington: Government Printer, 1956).

New Zealand, Dominion of, *Industrial Development Conference Report* (Wellington: Government Printer, 1960).

New Zealand, Dominion of, *International Monetary Fund and World Bank: Implications of New Zealand Membership* (Wellington: Government Printer, 1961).

New Zealand, Dominion of, *The World Bank Report on the New Zealand Economy 1968* (Wellington: Government Printer, 1968).

Nicholson, F. and East, R., *From the Six to the Twelve* (Harlow: Keesing, 1987), pp. 68–73.

Olson, M, *The Rise and Decline of Nations* (New Haven: Yale University Press, 1982).

Olson, M., 'The Varieties of Eurosclerosis: the Rise and Decline of Nations since 1982', in N. Crafts and G. Toniolo (eds), *Economic Growth in Europe since 1945* (Cambridge: Cambridge University Press, 1996).

Onslow, S., *Backbench Debate Within the Conservative Party and its Influence on British Foreign Policy, 1948–57* (Basingstoke: Macmillan, 1997).

O' Shea, A.P., 'The New Zealand Farming Industry Present and Future', *Industrial Development Conference Papers* (Wellington: Government Printer, 1960).

Ovendale, R., *The English-Speaking Alliance: Britain, the United States, the Dominions and the Cold War, 1945–1951* (London: George Allen & Unwin 1985).

Parker, R.S. (ed.), *Economic Stability in New Zealand* (Wellington: New Zealand Institute of Public Administration, 1953).

Parker, S., *Made in New Zealand, the Story of Jim Fletcher* (Wellington: Hodder & Stoughton, 1994).

Patterson, G., *Discrimination in International Trade* (Princeton: Princeton University Press, 1965).

Pedersen, P.J., 'Postwar Growth in the Danish Economy', in N. Crafts and G. Toniolo (eds), *Economic Growth in Europe since 1945* (Cambridge: Cambridge University Press, 1996).

Pelling, H., *Britain and the Marshall Plan* (Basingstoke: Macmillan, 1988).

Penrose, E., 'Foreign Investment and the Growth of the Firm', *Economic Journal*, 1956 66: 220–35.

Perkins, J.O.N., *Sterling and Regional Payments Systems* (Melbourne: Melbourne University Press, 1956).

Perkins, J.O.N., *Britain and Australia* (Melbourne: Melbourne University Press, 1962).

Perkins, J.O.N., *The Sterling Area, the Commonwealth and World Economic Growth* (Cambridge: Cambridge University Press, 1967).

Peterson, T.H., *Agricultural Exports, Farm Income, and the Eisenhower Administration* (Lincoln, Nebraska: University of Nebraska Press, 1979).

Petri, P.A., 'The east Asian Trading Bloc: An Analytical History', in J.A. Frankel and M. Kahler (eds), *Regionalism and Rivalry: Japan and the United States in Pacific Asia* (Chicago: University of Chicago Press, 1993).

Pimlott, B., *Harold Wilson* (London: HarperCollins, 1993).

Pinkstone, B., *Global Connections: a History of Exports and the Australian Economy* (Canberra: AGPS, 1992).

Pinkstone, B., 'The Terms of Trade Debate: a Critical Realist Approach', paper read to the Australasian Economic and Maritime History Conference, Wellington, Nov. 1998.

Polk, J., *Sterling: Its Meaning in World Finance* (New York: Harper & Brothers, 1956).

Pollard, S., *The Development of the British Economy, 1914–1990* (London: Edward Arnold, 1992).

Pomfret, R., *The Economics of Regional Trading Arrangements* (Oxford: Clarendon Press, 1997).

Pomfret, R., 'Trade Policy in Canada and Australia in the Twentieth Century', *Australian Economic History Review*, 2000 40(2): 114–26.

Preeg, E.H., *Traders and Diplomats* (Washington, DC: Brookings Institution, 1970).

Pressnell, L.S., *External Economic Policy Since the War* (London: HMSO, 1986).

Ranieri, R., 'Inside or Outside the Magic Circle? the Italian and British Steel Industries Face to Face with the Schuman Plan and the European Coal and Steel Community', in A.S. Milward et al., *The Frontier of National Sovereignty* (London: Routledge, 1994).

Rayner, A.C. and Lattimore, R., 'New Zealand', in D. Papageorgiou, M. Michaely, and A.M. Choksi (eds), *Liberalizing Foreign Trade* (Oxford: Blackwell, 1991), vol. 6.

Rendel, D., *Civil Aviation in New Zealand* (Wellington: Reed, 1975).

Reserve Bank of New Zealand, *Overseas Trade and Finance with Particular Reference to New Zealand* (Wellington: RBNZ, 1966).

Ridler, D., 'Far east Markets for New Zealand's Meat and Milk', *NZIER Research Paper No. 3* (Wellington, 1962).

Rix, A., *Coming to Terms: the Politics of Australia's Trade with Japan 1945–1957* (Sydney: Allen and Unwin, 1986).

Robertson, P.L., 'Official Policy on American Direct Investment in Australia, 1945–1952', *Australian Economic History Review*, 1986 26(2): 159–81.

Robertson, P.L., 'The Decline of Economic Complementarity? Australia and Britain 1945–1952', *Australian Economic History Review*, 1997 37(2): 91–117.

Robertson, P.L. and Singleton, J., 'Britain, the Dominions, and the EEC, 1961–1963', in Deighton and Milward (eds), *Widening, Deepening and Acceleration* (1999).

Robertson, P.L. and Singleton, J., 'The Old Commonwealth and Britain's First Application to Join the EEC', *Australian Economic History Review*, 2000 40(2): 153–77.

Robertson, P.L. and Singleton, J., 'The Commonwealth as an Economic Network', *Australian Economic History Review*, 2001 41(3) 241–66.

Robertson, P.L. and Trace, K., 'Government Involvement in the Development of Australian Manufacturing since 1945', *Business and Economic History*, 1983 12: 109–123.

Robson, M., *Decision at Dawn: New Zealand and the EEC* (London: Baynard-Hillier, 1972).

Rollings, N., 'British Industry and European Integration 1961–73: From First Application to Final Membership', *Business and Economic History*, 1998 27(2): 444–54.

Rooth, T., *British Protectionism and the International Economy* (Cambridge: Cambridge University Press, 1993).

Rooth, T., 'Imperial Self-insufficiency Rediscovered: Britain and Australia 1945–51', *Australian Economic History Review*, 1999 39(1): 29–51.

Rosenberg, B. 'Foreign Investment in New Zealand: The Current Position', in Enderwick (ed.), *Foreign Investment* (1998).

Rosenberg, W., 'Financial and Monetary Policy and Capital Requirements for Industrial Development in New Zealand', *Industrial Development Conference Papers* (Wellington: Government Printer, 1960).

Rosenberg, W., 'Capital Imports and Growth – The Case of New Zealand – Foreign Investment in New Zealand, 1840–1958', *Economic Journal*, 1961 71(1): 93–113.

Rosenberg, W., 'A Critical Perspective on Foreign Investment', in Enderwick (ed.), *Foreign Investment* (1998).

Rowland, B.M., *Commercial Conflict and Foreign Policy: a Study in Anglo–American Relations 1932–1938* (New York: Garland, 1987).

Rowthorn, R.E. and Wells, J.R., *De-Industrialization and Foreign Trade* (Cambridge: Cambridge University Press, 1987).

Sachs, J.D., 'Twentieth-century Political Economy: a Brief History of Global Capitalism', *Oxford Review of Economic Policy*, 1999 15(4): 90–101.

Schapsmeier, E.L. and Schapsmeier, H.H., *Ezra Taft Benson and the Politics of Agriculture* (Danville, Illinois: Interstate, 1975).

Schedvin, C.B., 'Staples and Regions of the Pax Britannica', *Economic History Review*, 1990 43(4): 533–59.

Schedvin, C.B., *In Reserve: Central Banking in Australia, 1945–75* (St. Leonards, NSW: Allen & Unwin, 1992).

Schenk, C.R., 'The Sterling Area and British Policy Alternatives in the 1950s', *Contemporary Record*, 1992 6(2): 266–86.

Schenk, C.R., *Britain and the Sterling Area* (London: Routledge, 1994).

Schenk, C.R., 'Decolonization and European Economic Integration: the Free Trade Area Negotiations, 1956–58', *Journal of Imperial and Commonwealth History*, 1996 24(3): 444–63.

Schenk, C.R., 'The UK, the Sterling Area and the EEC, 1957–63', in Deighton and Milward (eds), *Widening, Deepening and Acceleration* (1999).

Seldon, A., *Churchill's Indian Summer* (London: Hodder & Stoughton, 1981).

Shiraishi, T., *Japan's Trade Policies 1945 to the Present Day* (London: Athlone, 1989).

Simkin, C.G.H., 'Insulationism and the Problem of Economic Stability', *Economic Record*, 1946 22(1): 50–65.

Simkin, C.G.F., 'What Should Be Done About the Sterling Area: New Zealand', *Bulletin of the Oxford University Institute of Statistics*, 1959 21(4): 267–78.

Sinclair, K., *Walter Nash* (Auckland: Auckland University Press, 1976).

Singh, L.P., *The Politics of Economic Cooperation in Asia* (Columbia: University of Missouri Press, 1966).

Singleton, J., *Lancashire on the Scrapheap: the Cotton Industry, 1945–70* (Oxford: Oxford University Press, 1991).

Singleton, J., 'New Zealand, Britain and the Survival of the Ottawa Agreement, 1945–77', *Australian Journal of Politics and History*, 1997 43(2): 168–82.

Singleton, J., 'New Zealand's Economic Relations with Japan in the 1950s', *Australian Economic History Review*, 1997 37(1): 1–16.

Singleton, J., 'Anglo–New Zealand Financial Relations, 1945–61', *Financial History Review*, 1998 5(2): 139–57.

Singleton, J., 'The British Engineering Industry and Commonwealth Development', *Journal of European Economic History*, forthcoming.

Singleton, J. and Robertson, P.L., 'Britain, Butter, and European Integration, 1957–1964', *Economic History Review*, 1997 50(2): 327–47.

Smith, I., 'Prospects for Commonwealth Sugar', *The Round Table*, 1975 257: 51–8.

Smith, M.J., *The Politics of Agricultural Support in Britain* (Aldershot: Dartmouth, 1990).

Snape, R.H., 'Australia's Relations with GATT', *Economic Record*, 1984 60(1): 16–27.

Stewart, J., 'Traditional Australian Industry Policy: What Went Wrong', *Prometheus*, 1991 9(2): 249–64.

Sutch, W.B., 'Education for Industry', *Industrial Development Conference Papers* (Wellington: Government Printer, 1960).

Sutch, W.B., 'Programme for Growth', *Industrial Development Conference Papers* (Wellington: Government Printer, 1960).

Sutch, W.B., *Colony or Nation? Economic Crises in New Zealand from the 1860s to the 1960s* (Sydney: Sydney University Press, 1966).

Tansey, A.W., 'British Import Controls and World Trade in Butter', *Journal of Agricultural Economics*, 1967 18(2): 257–69.

Terada, T., 'The Japanese Origins of PAFTAD: The Beginning of an Asian Pacific Economic Community', *ANU Australia-Japan Research Centre, Pacific Economic Paper No. 222* (Canberra, 1999).

Tomlinson, B.R., 'Imperialism and After: the Economy of the Empire on the Periphery', in *Oxford History of the British Empire*, vol. 4.

Tracy, M., *Agriculture in western Europe: Challenge and Response 1880–1980* (London: Granada, 1982).

Tratt, J., *The Macmillan Government and Europe* (Basingstoke: Macmillan, 1996).

Trotter, A., 'From Suspicion to Growing Partnership: New Zealand and Japan', in M. McKinnon (ed.), *New Zealand in World Affairs* (Wellington: New Zealand Institute for International Affairs, 1991), vol. 2.

Tsokhas, K., *Markets, Money and Empire* (Carlton, Vic.: Melbourne University Press, 1990).

Van der Wee, H., *Prosperity and Upheaval: the World Economy 1945–1980* (Berkeley: University of California Press, 1986).

Wade, R., *Governing the Market: Economic Theory and the Role of Government in east Asian Industrialization* (Princeton: Princeton University Press, 1990).

Ward, A.H., *A Command of Cooperatives: the Development of Leadership, Marketing and Price Control in the Cooperative Dairy Industry of New Zealand* (Wellington: New Zealand Dairy Board, 1975).

Welfield, J., *An Empire in Eclipse: Japan in the Postwar American Alliance System* (London: Athlone, 1988).

Whitwell, G., *The Treasury Line* (Sydney: Allen & Unwin, 1986).

Wijewardane, B.A.D., 'Official Overseas Borrowing of New Zealand, 1950/51 to 1967/68, With Particular Reference to Drawings from the International Monetary Fund', MA thesis, Victoria University of Wellington, 1970.

Wilbur, C.M., 'Japan and the Rise of Communist China', in H. Borton et al., *Japan Between East and West* (New York: Harper, 1957).

Wilkes, G. (ed.), *Britain's Failure to Enter the European Economic Community, 1961–63* (London: Frank Cass, 1997).

Williams, J.H., *Postwar Monetary Plans and Other Essays* (New York: Knopf, 1944).

Wilson, H., *The Labour Government 1964–1970* (London: Weidenfeld & Nicolson and Michael Joseph, 1971).

Winand, P., *Eisenhower, Kennedy, and the United States of Europe* (New York: St. Martin's, 1993).

Wood, G.L., 'International Economic Co–operation and the Australian Economy', *Economic Record*, 1947 23(2): 159–76.

Woods, N.S., 'Immigration and the Labour Force', *Industrial Development Conference Papers* (Wellington: Government Printer, 1960).

Woods, R.B., *A Changing of the Guard: Anglo–American Relations, 1941–1946* (Chapel Hill: University of North Carolina Press, 1990).

Wurm, C., *Business, Politics, and International Relations* (Cambridge: Cambridge University Press, 1993).

Young, J.W., 'British Officials and European Integration, 1944–60', in A. Deighton (ed.), *Building Postwar Europe* (Basingstoke: Macmillan, 1995).

Zappalà, G., 'The Decline of Economic Complementarity: Australia and the Sterling Area', *Australian Economic History Review*, 1994 34(1): 5–21.

Zeiler, T.W., *American Trade and Power in the 1960s* (New York: Columbia University Press, 1992).

Zeiler, T.W., 'GATT Fifty Years Ago: US Trade Policy and Imperial Tariff Preferences', *Business and Economic History*, 1997 26(2): 709–19.

Zeiler, T.W., *Free Trade Free World: the Advent of GATT* (Chapel Hill: University of North Carolina Press, 1999).

Zweiniger-Bargielowska, I., *Austerity in Britain: Rationing, Controls, and Consumption 1939–1955* (Oxford: Oxford University Press, 2000).

Index